Civil Rights Music

Civil Rights Music

The Soundtracks of the Civil Rights Movement

Reiland Rabaka

LEXINGTON BOOKS
Lanham • Boulder • New York • London

Published by Lexington Books
An imprint of The Rowman & Littlefield Publishing Group, Inc.
4501 Forbes Boulevard, Suite 200, Lanham, Maryland 20706
www.rowman.com

Unit A, Whitacre Mews, 26-34 Stannary Street, London SE11 4AB

British Library Cataloguing in Publication Information Available

Library of Congress Cataloging-in-Publication Data

Names: Rabaka, Reiland, 1972-
Title: Civil rights music : the soundtracks of the civil rights movement / Reiland Rabaka.
Description: Lanham : Lexington Books, 2016. | Includes bibliographical references and index.
Identifiers: LCCN 2016011898| ISBN 9781498531788 (cloth : alk. paper) | ISBN 9781498531801 (pbk. : alk. paper) | ISBN 9781498531795 (electronic)
Subjects: LCSH: Popular music--Political aspects--United States--History--20th century. | Civil rights movements--United States--History--20th century.
Classification: LCC ML3917.U6 R33 2016 | DDC 781.5/990973--dc23 LC record available at http://lccn.loc.gov/2016011898

For the unsung singing soldiers of the Civil Rights Movement and their many musical heirs.

Contents

Lift Every Voice and Sing!: Acknowledgments   ix

1   The Sociology of Civil Rights Music   1
2   The Musicology of the Civil Rights Movement   23
3   Gospel and the Civil Rights Movement   53
4   Rhythm & Blues and the Civil Rights Movement   103
5   Rock & Roll and the Civil Rights Movement   159

Bibliography   203
Index   249
About the Author   257

Lift Every Voice and Sing!: Acknowledgments

Lift every voice and sing—and march, and boycott, and protest, and sit-in, and freedom ride, and register to vote . . . a luta continua . . . ad infinitum. This book is humbly dedicated to the hundreds, perhaps the thousands, of *unsung singing soldiers of the Civil Rights Movement.* Their ideas and actions, their words and deeds, their passion and folk poetry inspired those within and without the movement and, truth be told, continues to do so up to the present moment. Although I am as enamored with the famous figures of the Civil Rights Movement as many others born in the aftermath of the movement, since I was a boy I have always held a quiet curiosity about the lives and struggles of the rank and filers and foot soldiers of the movement who solemnly marched, faced high-pressure fire hoses, the snarling fangs of police dogs, billy club beatings, jailings, shootings, lynchings, burning crosses, and the Ku Klux Klan all the while *implicitly singing what they could not explicitly say* as a consequence of American apartheid.

The singing marchers of the Civil Rights Movement did not merely inspire each other, but they also influenced and seemed to stir something deep within the more noted leaders of the movement. As this volume details, their voices, their songs, their powerful and poignant lyrics linger on and free-float through contemporary culture and society, but few today critically understand the origins and early evolution of *why* and *how* song (both sacred and secular) came to play such a pivotal role in the Civil Rights Movement. This book turns readers' attention away from the famous figures of the movement to the rank and filers, foot soldiers, and seemingly forgotten figures of the Civil Rights Movement by focusing on the ways in which they captured and conveyed their collective views and values, as well as their heartfelt aspirations and frustrations, through various forms of black popular music, and specifically gospel, freedom songs, rhythm & blues, and rock & roll.

This book would not, and quite simply could not have been researched and written without the critical support of family and friends, as well as colleagues and comrades. Every word, sentence, paragraph, and chapter to follow bears the imprint of the diverse—although often antagonistic—intellectual, cultural, and political arenas I draw from, and endeavor to establish deep discursive dialogue with. As a consequence, the list of academics, organic intellectuals, activists, archivists, institutions, and organizations to which I am deeply indebted is, indeed, enormous. Such being the case, I hope I may be forgiven for deciding that the most appropriate way in which to acknowledge my sincere appreciation is simply to list them below without the protracted praise each so solemnly deserves.

My deepest gratitude and most heartfelt *asante sana* (a thousand thanks) is offered, first and foremost, to my family: my mother, Marilyn Giles; my father, Robert Dean Smith; my grandmothers, Lizzie Mae Davis and Elva Rita Warren; my great aunt, Arcressia Charlene Connor; my older brother and his wife, Robert Dean Smith II and Karen Smith; my younger brother, Dwight Randle Wellington Clewis; my nieces and nephews, Journée Clewis, Dominique Clewis, Kalyn Smith, Robert Dean Smith III, Ryan Smith, and Remington Smith; and my innumerable aunts, uncles, and cousins throughout the Americas, the Caribbean, and Africa.

A book project as ambitious as *Civil Rights Music* would have been impossible without the assistance of colleagues and comrades, both far and wide. As I have said on several occasions, my work is a reflection of my family and friends, as well as the research and writings of academics and organic intellectual-activists alike, who have made their own distinct contributions to my lifework and broader conceptions of social transformation and human liberation. Early versions of chapters of this book have been presented as work-in-progress papers in lectures, seminars, workshops, conferences, and symposia at many colleges, universities, churches, mosques, synagogues, museums, community centers, and prisons over the past few years. I would be remiss if I did not openly acknowledge how much I have appreciated all of the responses, constructive critiques, and help that I have received in thinking through the innumerable issues involved in offering a simultaneous sociology and musicology/alternative history and critical theory of the Civil Rights Movement. I have benefited immeasurably from critical discussions, whether on large or small points. Therefore, I express my earnest appreciation to the following fine folk, who each in their own special way contributed to the composition and completion of this book: William E. Cross, Jr.; Lucius Outlaw; Fred Lee Hord (aka Mzee Lasana Okpara); William M. King; Rhonda Nicole Tankerson; Martell Teasley; Denise Lovett; Adam Clark; Elzie Billops; Patrick De Walt; Awon Atuire; La'Neice Littleton; De Reef Jamison; Lynn Johnson; Gesel Mason; James Conyers; Jeffrey Ogbar; Molefi Asante; Maulana Karenga; Christel Temple; Jaime Duggan; Daniel Black (aka Omotosho Jojomani); Danielle Hodge; the editorial board of the *Critical Africana Studies* book series (Martell Teasley, Christel Temple, and Deborah Whaley); the Association for the Study of African American Life and History (ASALH); the Association of Black Women Historians (ABWH); the Association for the Study of the Worldwide African Diaspora (ASWAD); the National Council for Black Studies (NCBS); the National Association for Ethnic Studies (NAES); the Critical Ethnic Studies Association; the Critical Race Studies in Education Association; the American Studies Association (ASA); the Association for the Advancement of Creative Musicians (AACM); the Black Artists' Group (BAG); the Society for American Music (SAM); and the International Association for the Study of Popular Music (IASPM).

Several libraries, research centers, special collections, archives, and museums hosted and helped me transform this book from an inchoate idea into its fully-realized form. I am indelibly indebted to the directors, curators, librarians, archivists, and staffs of: the Highlander Research and Education Center, New Market, Tennessee; the National Civil Rights Museum, Memphis, Tennessee; the National Museum of African American Music, Nashville, Tennessee; the National Voting Rights Museum, Selma, Alabama; the Civil Rights Project, University of California, Los Angeles, California; the King Library and Archives, the Martin Luther King Center for Nonviolent Social Change, Atlanta, Georgia; the Martin Luther King Research and Education Institute, Stanford University, Stanford, California; the A. Philip Randolph Institute, Washington, D.C.; the Ella Baker Center for Human Rights, Oakland, California; the Manuscript Division of the Library of Congress, Washington, D.C.; the National Museum of African American History and Culture (NMAAHC), the Smithsonian Institution, Washington, D.C.; the National Museum of American History, the Smithsonian Institution, Washington, D.C.; the Association of African American Museums (AAAM), Washington, D.C.; the Banneker-Douglass Museum, Annapolis, Maryland; the African American Museum in Philadelphia, Philadelphia, Pennsylvania; Black History Museum and Cultural Center of Virginia, Richmond, Virginia; L. E. Coleman African American Museum, Halifax County, Virginia; Legacy Museum of African American History, Lynchburg, Virginia; the International Civil Rights Center and Museum, Greensboro, North Carolina; Afro-American Historical and Cultural Society Museum, Jersey City, New Jersey; Birmingham Civil Rights Institute, Birmingham, Alabama; Alabama State Black Archives Research Center and Museum, Huntsville, Alabama; the National African American Archives and Museum, Mobile, Alabama; Mississippi Civil Rights Museum, Jackson, Mississippi; the Center for the Study of Southern Culture, University of Mississippi, University, Mississippi; Tubman African American Museum, Macon, Georgia; the National Center for Civil and Human Rights, Atlanta, Georgia; Baton Rouge African American Museum, Baton Rouge, Louisiana; Bontemps African American Museum, Alexandria, Louisiana; New Orleans African American Museum, New Orleans, Louisiana; Northeast Louisiana Delta African American Heritage Museum, Monroe, Louisiana; the African American Museum, Dallas, Texas; DuSable Museum of African American History, Chicago, Illinois; Charles H. Wright Museum of African American History, Detroit, Michigan; America's Black Holocaust

Museum, Milwaukee, Wisconsin; Carter G. Woodson African American History Museum, St. Petersburg, Florida; John G. Riley Center/Museum of African American History and Culture, Tallahassee, Florida; California African American Museum, Los Angeles, California; the W. E. B. Du Bois Institute for African & African American Research, Harvard University; Arthur A. Houghton, Jr., Library, Harvard University; Arturo A. Schomburg Center for Research in Black Culture, a division of the New York Public Library; Nicholas Murray Butler Library, Columbia University; Institute for African American Affairs, New York University; Elmer Holmes Bobst Library, New York University; John Henrik Clarke Africana Library, Africana Studies and Research Center, Cornell University; Charles L. Blockson African American Collection, Temple University; Center for African American History and Culture, Temple University; Center for Africana Studies, University of Pennsylvania; August Wilson Center for African American Culture, Pittsburgh, Pennsylvania; Center for American Music, University of Pittsburgh; Center for Popular Culture Studies, Bowling Green State University; Center for Black Music Research, Columbia College Chicago; Karla Scherer Center for the Study of American Culture, University of Chicago; Center for Popular Music, Middle Tennessee State University; Center for the History of Music Theory & Literature, Jacobs School of Music, Indiana University; African American Cultural Center, University of Illinois at Chicago; Bruce Nesbitt African American Cultural Center, University of Illinois at Urbana-Champaign; African American Cultural Center, North Carolina State University; H. Fred Simons African American Cultural Center, University of Connecticut at Storrs; Moorland-Spingarn Research Center, Howard University; John Hope Franklin Collection for African and African American Documentation, Rare Book, Manuscript, and Special Collections Library, Duke University; Carter G. Woodson Center for African American and African Studies, University of Virginia; Robert W. Woodruff Library, Atlanta University Center Archives; Manuscript Sources for African American History, Special Collections, Emory University; John L. Warfield Center for African and African American Studies, University of Texas at Austin; Center for African American Studies, University of Houston; African and African American Collection, University Library, University of California, Berkeley; the Institute for Advanced Feminist Research, University of California, Santa Cruz; Ralph J. Bunche Center for African American Studies, University of California, Los Angeles; Blair-Caldwell African American Research Library, Denver Public Library; Center for Media, Arts, and Performance, Alliance for Technology, Learning, and Society (ATLAS) Institute, University of Colorado at Boulder; American Music Research Center, College of Music, University of Colorado at Boulder; Howard B. Waltz Music Library, College of Music, University of Colorado at Boulder; Department of Musicology, College of Music, University of Colorado at Boulder; African American Materials,

Special Collections, George Norlin Library, University of Colorado at Boulder.

A number of researchers and writers' work in what has come to be called "civil rights studies," as well as what I am wont to call "civil rights musicology," has indelibly influenced the alternative history and critical theory of the soundtracks of the Civil Rights Movement to follow. Here I would like to pay special tribute to them for opening up unimagined archives, research methods, and modes of interpretation, many of which blur the lines between history and critical theory, sociology, and musicology, as well as politics and aesthetics. I am grateful beyond words, indeed, beyond the literal debts cited in each chapters' endnotes to: W. E. B. Du Bois; Carter G. Woodson; William Leo Hansberry; Rayford Logan; Charles Wesley; Benjamin Quarles; John Blassingame; Lorenzo Greene; Horace Mann Bond; John Hope Franklin; Mary Frances Berry; Nathan Huggins; Edgar Toppin; Vincent Harding; Manning Marable; Clayborne Carson; Darlene Clark Hine; Lerone Bennett; Aldon Morris; Gerald Horne; Paula Giddings; V. P. Franklin; Betty Collier-Thomas; Thomas Holt; Nell Irvin Painter; Robin D. G. Kelley; Barbara Ransby; Doug McAdams; Vicki L. Crawford; Raymond Arsenault; Diane McWhorter; Charles M. Payne; Lynne Olson; Harvard Sitkoff; Henry Hampton; Faith S. Holsaert; Davis W. Houck; Sara Bullard; Robert Weisbrot; Jeanne Theoharis; Peter J. Ling; Barbara Harris Combs; Glenda Elizabeth Gilmore; Thomas J. Sugrue; Patricia Sullivan; Lance Hill; Erik S. Gellman; Timothy B. Tyson; Leon Litwack; David Garrow; Taylor Branch; Adam Fairclough; Steven F. Lawson; Juan Williams; Eileen Southern; Bernice Johnson Reagon; Horace Clarence Boyer; Portia Maultsby; Mellonee V. Burnim; Jon Michael Spencer; Arnold Shaw; Nelson George; Samuel A. Floyd, Jr.; Earl L. Stewart; Peter Guralnick; Kerran Sanger; Lawrence Redd; Ron Eyerman; Andrew Jamison; Brian Ward; Mark Anthony Neal; Guthrie P. Ramsey, Jr.; Guido van Rijn; Dick Weissman; Rob Rosenthal; Dorian Lynskey; John Street; William G. Roy; Ian Peddie; Benjamin Filene; Ruth Feldstein; and Shana L. Redmond.

I would like to sincerely thank the very talented artist, Evan O'Neal Kirkman of the California College of the Arts, who graciously granted permission to use his work for the book cover. Evan, who also created the cover art for my books *Concepts of Cabralism* and *The Negritude Movement*, is an innovative artist who is incredibly adept at bringing a wide-range of history, theory, politics, and aesthetics into his creative productions. As fluent in avant-garde aesthetics as he is radical politics and critical social theory, Evan is a specialist in *the art of social transformation*. He has beautifully translated the core concepts of *Civil Rights Music* into a work of art that embodies the various voices and visions of the Civil Rights Movement and its respective soundtracks. Collaborating with him has been one of the real highpoints of researching and writing this book. Indeed, it is a better book because of his creativity and keen artistic eye.

In closing, I would like to acknowledge my editor, Brighid Stone, as well as the entire Lexington Books editorial board, who deserve very special thanks (*maalum sana shukrani*) for working with me during the many months it took me to revise the manuscript and prepare it for production. Finally, I should state outright to my most respected readers: If any inspiration or insights are gained from the chronicles and critiques of the origins and evolution of the soundtracks of the Civil Rights Movement to follow, I pray you will attribute them to each of the aforementioned. However, if (and when) you find foibles and intellectual idiosyncrasies, contradictions and conceptual controversies, I humbly hope you will neither associate them with any of the forenamed nor, most especially, the unsung singing soldiers of the Civil Rights Movement. I, and I alone, am responsible for the alternative history and critical theory to follow. As is my custom, I will end in much the same manner that I began, once again, softly saying, almost silently singing my earnest and eternal prayer: *Lift Every Voice and Sing!*

ONE

The Sociology of Civil Rights Music

THE CIVIL RIGHTS MOVEMENT AND SONIC SECOND-SIGHT:
ON THE EXTRA-MUSICAL ELEMENTS OF BLACK POPULAR MUSIC
CIRCA 1945 TO 1965

Mahalia Jackson, Brother Joe May, Dorothy Love Coates, The Soul Stirrers, The Staple Singers, Sam Cooke, Nina Simone, Smokey Robinson & The Miracles, The Supremes, The Temptations, Martha Reeves & The Vandellas, The Four Tops, Odetta, Richie Havens, Ruth Brown, Little Richard, LaVern Baker—these artists' respective music is part of an often-unacknowledged continuum that stretches back to the spirituals and the Abolitionist Movement and reaches forward to rap and the Hip Hop Movement. In many quarters of the country there has been a longstanding belief that, if nowhere else in American culture and society, African Americans can be most true to themselves and truly express their aspirations and frustrations to each other and the wider world in their ever-evolving music, and African American art more generally speaking. One of the recurring themes of this book will be the notion that for black America during the Civil Rights Movement *music was much more than merely music.* Here I am, of course, building on Ralph Ellison's classic contention in *Shadow and Act* (1964), where he eloquently argued that black popular music constitutes an indispensable element and cultural indicator of African Americans' life-worlds and life-struggles.[1]

Black popular music, then, is much more than the soundtrack to black popular culture. It is more akin to a musical map and cultural compass that provides us with a window into black folk's world, and also a window into the ways in which African Americans' "second-sight" (as W. E. B. Du Bois termed it in *The Souls of Black Folk*) shapes and shades their worldview. Ellison (1964) went so far to argue that instead of "social or

1

political freedom . . . the art—the blues, the spirituals, the jazz, the dance—was what we had in place of freedom" (247–248).[2] In other words, black folk have long had aesthetic freedom instead of social and political freedom, linguistic wealth instead of monetary wealth. Art has offered African Americans one of the few avenues available to express themselves. However, even African American cultural expression through the arts has had to be masked and muted as a consequence of the rules and regulations of American apartheid.

My previous musicology/sociology mash-ups, *Hip Hop's Inheritance*, *Hip Hop's Amnesia*, and *The Hip Hop Movement*, collectively explored the ways in which the Hip Hop Generation has inherited and carried on (even as they have radically remixed) many of the core concepts of *the African American movement music tradition*. While there have been a number of studies that have explored African American "movement culture" and African American "movement politics," rarely has the mixture of black music and black politics or, rather, *black music an as expression of black movement politics*, been explored across several genres of African American "movement music," and certainly not with a central focus on the major soundtracks of the Civil Rights Movement: gospel, freedom songs, rhythm & blues, and rock & roll. Here the mixture of music and politics emerging out of the Civil Rights Movement is critically examined as an incredibly important site and source of spiritual rejuvenation, social organization, political education, and cultural transformation, not simply for the non-violent civil rights soldiers of the 1950s and 1960s, but for *organic intellectual-artist-activists* deeply committed to continuing the core ideals and ethos of the Civil Rights Movement in the twenty-first century.

That being said, *Civil Rights Music: The Soundtracks of the Civil Rights Movement* is primarily preoccupied with that liminal, in-between, and often inexplicable place where black popular music and black popular movements meet and merge. Black popular movements are more than merely social and political affairs. Beyond social organization and political activism, black popular movements provide much-needed spaces for cultural development and artistic experimentation, including the mixing of musical and other aesthetic traditions. "Movement music" experimentation has historically led to musical innovation, and musical innovation in turn has led to new music that has myriad meanings and messages— some social, some political, some cultural, some spiritual and, indeed, some sexual. Just as black popular movements have a multiplicity of meanings, this book argues that the music that emerges out of black popular movements has a multiplicity of meanings as well.

Whether we turn to the first great African American movement, the Abolitionist Movement, or a more recent movement like the Hip Hop Movement, *each major black popular movement has produced a signature soundtrack*. As a matter of fact, *African American movements are as musical as they are political*. The articulation of the motto and mission of African

American movements is typically communicated through song as much as, if not even more often than, through political speeches, pamphlets, and protests. Although there is a tendency to take this phenomenon for granted in black America (if not in America more generally), I honestly believe that critically engaging the soundtracks of African American social, political, and cultural movements will open up a new interpretive archive and angle that will enable us to deepen and develop our understanding of, not merely the politics and culture of the movement in question, but also the leaders, rank and file, intellectuals, artists, and activists of the movement.

African American movements are most often multidimensional. Therefore, the art arising out of these movements frequently has multiple meanings and serves a multiplicity of purposes. However, because there is a longstanding tendency to dismiss and downgrade black popular movements, African American "movement art" is often decontextualized and divorced from its movement origins and early evolution. It could probably go without saying that most U.S. citizens know more about the music of the Civil Rights Movement, even if they do not acknowledge it as such (meaning, as "civil rights music"), than they do the remarkable movement the music grew out of. At a time when the Civil Rights Movement seems no more than a relic of an ancient, almost foreign time and place, at a time when many would much rather forget or, at the very least, minimize the fact that the movement was waged against American apartheid, both the sacred and secular music of the movement continues to free-float through American culture and society, reminding us that the Civil Rights Movement irrevocably altered not only our culture and society, but also our understandings of American democracy and American citizenship.

For many young folk at the dawn of the twenty-first century, the Civil Rights Movement seems simultaneously foreign and familiar. Partly because many of the views and values of the movement have been coopted by the established order and made to appear as though they emerged from the ether, and not the countless anonymous rank and file civil rights soldiers. However, no mistake should be made about it: It was the countless anonymous rank and file civil rights soldiers who inspired Martin Luther King and Ella Baker, as well Septima Clark and Medgar Evers, and Fannie Lou Hamer and A. Philip Randolph. And, it was these same anonymous rank and file civil rights soldiers who, literally, mobilized centuries of African American traditions in their efforts to secure civil rights for all U.S. citizens, especially blacks and other racially oppressed and economically exploited non-whites.

When we turn our attention away from the almost incessant, if not often obsessive, over-focus on the famous figures of the Civil Rights Movement then, and perhaps only then, can we come to see that during the Civil Rights Movement musical and other myriad kinds of cultural traditions were made and remade, mixed, and remixed. Even after the Civil Rights Movement came to an end of sorts in the middle of the 1960s, "civil rights music" remained and, truth be told, continues to reverberate up to the present moment, serving as a reminder of the movement and, I honestly believe, as a potential way to inspire a new twenty-first century Civil Rights Movement. Here at the outset, I would like to be open and honest with my readers and unambiguously state that this book is my very humble attempt to incite a new twenty-first century Civil Rights Movement. In light of the recent political uproar and moral outrage over the murders (mostly police homicides) of Oscar Grant, Aiyana Stanley-Jones, Trayvon Martin, Tanisha Anderson, Tarika Wilson, John Crawford III, Shereese Francis, Michael Brown, Natasha McKenna, Tamar Rice, Ezell Ford, Rekia Boyd, Eric Garner, Walter Scott, Yvette Smith, Freddie Gray, Sandra Bland, and Samuel DuBose, among many others, I believe that now, perhaps more than at any other period after the movement, we need to return to, and deeply reflect on the Civil Rights Movement.

As was the sad situation in the middle of the twentieth century during the Civil Rights Movement, the African American masses continue to cry out for adequate health care, housing, employment, education, and an end to police brutality and other forms of state-sanctioned violence at the turn of the twenty-first century, and the ideals and ethos of the Civil Rights Movement continue to illuminate and offer solutions to key social, political, and cultural problems. Therefore, *Civil Rights Music* is not, nor was it ever intended to be, a work of music criticism divorced from cultural criticism, or a work of musicology written as though history, religion, sociology, politics, and economics do not directly and often direly impact African American music and musicians, especially during the Civil Rights Movement era. In other words, *Civil Rights Music* seeks to recontextualize or *rehistoricize* and, consequently, *repoliticize* a key form of "movement art" emerging from the Civil Rights Movement that many of us today have long taken for granted: "civil rights music." But, really now, what is "civil rights music?"

WHAT IS "CIVIL RIGHTS MUSIC" AND WHY IS IT RELEVANT TODAY?

"Civil rights music" is essentially those forms of music arising out of the Civil Rights Movement that insinuated or alluded to many of the dire aspirations and frustrations that African Americans could not openly express as a consequence of racial segregation and economic exploitation between 1954 and 1965—that is to say, from the 1954 *Brown v. Board of Education* Supreme Court decision to the Voting Rights Act of 1965.[3] It is music laden with multiple meanings and cultural codes, making it mean one thing to those active in the movement or with intimate knowledge of the movement, and wholly another thing to those who had or continue to have no real relationship with the movement. During the civil rights era, where many folk may have simply heard a pretty song, movement members often heard a call to action, a musical history of an important event, or a mute tribute to a fallen brother or sister in the struggle. Indeed, this *music was much more than merely music* to active movement members. But, even though I was born close to a decade after the March on Washington, many of my earliest memories are of me attentively listening to, deeply feeling, and desperately trying to decipher and make sense of what my grandmother repeatedly referred to as "civil rights music." For Mama Rita, my beloved grandmother, "civil rights music" was certainly the gospel music of the civil rights era, but it also selectively included those secular songs that were sung in a gospel-style and, however subtly, resonated with the mission and messages of the Civil Rights Movement.

When I was a boy, Mama Rita played "civil rights music" seemingly every day, and was fond of saying, "ain't no real records been made since Michael Jackson left the Jackson 5 and went solo!" In the most ritualized manner imaginable, each morning she would rise, put on Mahalia Jackson, the Soul Stirrers or Sister Rosetta Tharpe, and read the Bible. Some days the music was so affecting she would be driven to tears. Needless to say, her tears moved me and stirred something deep within. I desperately wanted to know what it was about this music that made Mama Rita cry "happy tears," as she once softly said to me. After her daily devotion of classic gospel, around lunchtime she would put on classic rhythm & blues, mostly Motown, Stax, Atlantic, Chess, Vee-Jay and Specialty, and even crossover rhythm & blues-cum-rock & roll artists, such as LaVern Baker, Little Richard, Etta James, Fats Domino, Ruth Brown, Chuck Berry, Tina Turner, and Bo Diddley.

As a consequence of almost obsessively listening to both sacred and secular "civil rights music" during my most formative years, at an early age I developed what can only be described as an usual habit of listening to music to *hear* what was being communicated beyond the lyrics and the sounds emanating from the singer's voice and the musicians' instruments. My grandmother taught me that the lyrics and the music were only part of what was being conveyed through "civil rights music." Over time I learned to listen intently, not simply to the words that were being sung, but to the way they were being sung, and the passion or purposeful dispassion with which they were being sung. More and more Mama Rita's old adage that "it ain't what you say, but often how you say it," haunted me and helped me understand the power of black popular music, especially her beloved "civil rights music."

Obviously, my introduction to what I will be calling "civil rights music" throughout this book initially came by way of my grandmother's gospel music, and specifically iconic gospel artists such as Mahalia Jackson, Clara Ward, the Blind Boys of Mississippi, Sister Rosetta Tharpe,

Brother Joe May, the Blind Boys of Alabama, Dorothy Love Coates and, of course, the Soul Stirrers. There was something about this music, especially when my grandmother and mother hummed or sang along with it, that made it seem as though it was, indeed, *more than music*—meaning more than the dance ditties, love songs, or rap hits popular during my childhood. As a matter of fact, in my little adolescent mind there was something magical about this music because even during the toughest times—when our electricity, water, and gas were turned off, when there was little or no food, when we were evicted from the public housing projects—this music inexplicably seemed to make our burdens bearable. Somewhere along the way I realized that I was not the only one who had experienced abject poverty, who wanted to turn my "nothing" into "something," and who deeply desired to change themself and their world. Classic gospel music, in particular, seemed to communicate all of this to me, but then there was something more that it seemed to capture and convey.

Early into my teenage years I realized that there was a big difference between what my grandmother referred to as "Golden Age" gospel and contemporary gospel. It wasn't just the sound of the music that was different. Often it seemed as though a lot of the classic gospel artists sang as though their lives depended on them expressing something in the subtext, something akin to secret messages to their listeners. Admittedly, I was a peculiar teenage boy, more interested in books, music, and film than I was in basketball, football, and girls, and somehow or another I got it in my mind that I would decipher the "secret messages" buried beneath or in-between the lyrics and music of my favorite gospel songs. It was a crude kind of musicology but, truth be told, it helped to plant the seeds of this book. Free from drum machines, synthesizers, and over-production techniques, "Golden Age" gospel music had an organic, earthy, often rickety soulful sound that seemed to simultaneously soothe *and* incite. The day I discovered that "Golden Age" gospel music coincided with the Civil Rights Movement was the faithful day that I honestly, albeit naïvely, believed that I had solved the mystery of this music. But, in reality it only made me more curious about the Civil Rights Movement. I began to think to myself: "Well, Mama Rita didn't call this music 'civil rights music' for nothing?" I was intrigued in a way that I had not been in all of my young life.

Questions swirled around in my mind for what seemed to be an eternity: Was the music inspired by the Civil Rights Movement, or was the Civil Rights Movement inspired by the music? Furthermore, was it foolish of me to believe that music could actually inspire people to action, to risk life and limb for a great cause? And, what was it about gospel music that was so contagious that even the most respected and renowned leaders of the Civil Rights Movement, such as Martin Luther King, Ella Baker, Bayard Rustin, and Fannie Lou Hamer, all seemed to draw strength from the singing of these songs with other movement members? From the vantage point of more than twenty-five years, when I think back to what tied everything together for me and really helped me to connect the music to the movement, and vice versa, I suppose I would have to say, first and foremost, that it was the initial airing of the *Eyes on the Prize: America's Civil Rights Years, 1954–1965* television series. I could never forget it. I watched it with Mama Rita because we had no television at home. It was one of the most beautiful experiences of my boyhood. Mama Rita was a master teacher, a folk philosopher, an organic intellectual, *par excellence*.

In almost every episode of *Eyes on the Prize* there were these fascinating *singing leaders* and *singing marchers*. It completely blew my mind that leaders like Fannie Lou Hamer and Martin Luther King seemed to love and enjoy gospel just as much as I did. I felt close to them, as though we shared a special connection through our love for the music and the secret messages in these songs. Soon afterwards, as I began to systematically read about the Civil Rights Movement throughout junior high school and high school, I developed an equally deep love and appreciation for the politics and overarching culture of the movement. It was, to say the least, an incredibly life-altering experience, one that I now credit with helping me begin the transition from adolescence to adulthood.

After a while I realized that it was not just "Golden Age" gospel music that seemed to express the ethos of the Civil Rights Movement. Indeed, I quickly discovered that certain classic rhythm & blues and rock & roll songs also had multiple meanings and carried cultural codes transmitting the core views and values of the Civil Rights Movement much like Mama Rita had shared with me when I was a youngster. At this point, being a brash teenager, I thought it was the coolest and best kept secret on earth, and only Odetta and Richie Havens, Nina Simone and Sam Cooke, LaVern Baker and Little Richard and I was in on it, or "in the know," as it were. It got giddy. Finally, there was something that could not be repossessed or denied to me simply because I was black, poor, and lived in the public housing projects. But, then again, in order to really and truly understand my love affair with, and affinity for "civil rights music," my readers will need to understand my intellectual love affair with, and affinity for W. E. B. Du Bois, who is widely considered one of the key founders of the Civil Rights Movement. As I have solemnly stated on many occasions previously, in my father's virtual absence from my boyhood, Du Bois miraculously stepped in to spiritually, intellectually, and culturally rear and raise me. Du Bois taught me all the things I wished my father had have but could not because, as I painfully discovered when I got a little older, he never had a father actively involved in his life either.

W. E. B. DU BOIS: AN INTELLECTUAL LIFE-ALTERING ENCOUNTER WITH ONE OF THE ARCHITECTS OF THE CIVIL RIGHTS MOVEMENT

It was my first grade teacher, Mrs. Robinson, who initially exposed me to the man who would ultimately become my greatest intellectual ancestor and philosophical father figure. It was Black History Month 1978 or, perhaps, 1979, and she passed around these glossy oversized cards with famous African Americans on them. I can still remember it now as though it were yesterday. Everyone in the class received a card: one student got Zora Neale Hurston. Another was given Langston Hughes. Another Josephine Baker. One got Bessie Smith. And another received Louis Armstrong. Then Martin Luther King. Rosa Parks. Paul Robeson. James Baldwin. Someone even got Mahalia Jackson. And it really ruffled my feathers when someone other than myself received the Duke Ellington card. I was beside myself because I believed that I had been mistakenly given a card featuring a Frenchman. I mean, really, I thought to my six year-old self, "what kind of brother has a name like *Du Bois*?" From the picture on the front of the card he seemed a little "ethnically ambiguous," but that didn't bother me as much because I have plenty of family members who can pass for white or, at the least, something other than black.

As I was prone to at the time, and my mother—bless her heart—can testify to this, I became quite impatient and then outright upset, perhaps even a little livid. How dare Mrs. Robinson make me stand in front of everyone and speak on a Frenchman in the middle of *Black* History Month? My six year-old self would have none of it. This situation was all the more bewildering because I secretly had a schoolboy's crush on Mrs. Robinson, who had the biggest and baddest Afro hairdo I had ever seen other than my mother's ultra-hip and always happening Afro. I was really upset, and I needed to let Mrs. Robinson know. So, I raised my little trembling hand. She winked at me, as she customarily did, and then came right over to my desk. I let her know that there had been a mistake, that it was Black History Month, and that we were supposed to be learning about black folk not French folk. Gosh! She graciously allowed me to verbally punch myself out, and then she said: "Reiland, if you would spend as much time following directions as you do creating your own little lesson plans there is no telling what you might amount to someday." She went on to say, as only a real soul sister could at the end of the 1970s, "Ba-a-aby, *please read* the back of the card and then let me know if you still have a problem with Dr. Du Bois." She smiled smartly, and then sashayed away.

I don't know. Maybe it was the way she said "Dr. Du Bois" with such reverence, or the tender tone she took with me even as she scolded me—which, of course, made my little heart skip a beat and tears well up in my eyes. Whichever it was, needless to say, eventually I read the paragraph or two on Du Bois on the back of the card. I was astonished. It shook my ship. It really rattled my cage. It opened up something deep inside of me. I got up in front of everyone that day and proudly presented on "Dr. Du Bois," of course, butchering his name every other time I attempted to say it. But, Mrs. Robinson was right there with me. I felt like Muhammad Ali, and she was my Angelo Dundee. After class I apologized for putting up such resistance to learning about "Dr. Du Bois" (once again unintentionally slaughtering his name), and then I sincerely asked her if she thought if I got really good grades I could go and study with him when I grew up. Immediately I sensed something was wrong, and this wasn't just a situation of "kids say the darndest things." Then I saw tears well up in Mrs. Robinson's eyes, and the more she held back her tears the more I was unable to hold back mine. She hugged me and then sat me down and told me that "Dr. Du Bois" died in 1963. I stood there, stock-still for a moment. I was devastated. Completely destroyed. In one afternoon it seemed as though my whole world had been turned right-side up, and then upside down again.

After our tough talk about Du Bois's death and why he is buried in Africa, perhaps sensing my profound sadness, Mrs. Robinson walked me over to the school library, showed me the black history and culture section, and then and there I checked out grade school level books on Du Bois and the organization he helped to establish, the National Association for the Advancement of Colored People (NAACP). It was heady stuff. It was like coming home for a kid who never had a real home to speak of. I couldn't wait to learn more about Du Bois. I started reading immediately. That afternoon there was no time for cartoons or toys or playing with my friends. It was Du Bois and I for hours and hours. We quickly became buddies. I practically immediately asked him if he would be my best friend. I thought he was something akin to a superhero, and over time he sort of became a superhero to my younger self, to that fatherless little boy suffering in the public housing projects. In a sense, Du Bois became my dad.

I will never forget the day that Mrs. Robinson shared Du Bois with me, that evening at the dinner table I told my mother everything I learned about Du Bois. She could tell I was obviously excited. She noted my reading material and was determined to outdo Mrs. Robinson by taking me to the public library and exposing me to Du Bois, the NAACP, and eventually the Civil Rights Movement. Over the next couple of years, each Saturday morning I was more excited about going to the library than I was about watching cartoons or playing basketball. It is in this sense that I often say that it was Du Bois who initially led me to the library, to the world of literature, and to the life of the mind. It was like some sort of divine intervention. Divine, indeed, and *Du Bois eventually became the equivalent of my intellectual guardian angel and philosophical father figure*. Thanks, of course, to Mrs. Robinson and my mama.

By the time I reached junior high school I had become aware of the fact that Du Bois's most famous book was *The Souls of Black Folk*. It was there in junior high school that I first attempted to read the weighted words of W. E. B. Du Bois. I had been diligently building my vocabulary and reading skills, just as my mother told me I should, in order to be able to actually read Du Bois, and not merely read about Du Bois. It was like I was on a mission from first grade through to junior high school to be able to read Du Bois and discover what all the fuss was about. Perhaps my twelve or thirteen year-old soul sensed that it was a magical, life-changing moment. I believed that I was ready to read *The Souls of Black Folk*. It was a big deal. Family, friends, church folk, and school teachers all enthusiastically chimed in about how the book had impacted them, and each seemed to emphasize that it was a very adult book, about very adult issues. I was counseled to take it slowly and to feel free to come to them with questions. It was as if my village elders were handing me over to some great godfather, some supreme high priest who had been tasked with guiding me through my rites of passage from childhood to adulthood, from boyhood to manhood.

Then the moment arrived. It was time to read and loose myself in *The Souls of Black Folk*, literally and figuratively speaking. I will never, ever, forget it. It was the cover of the book that drew me to it, that soulfully summoned me in a special, almost alchemic way. I feel sort of embarrassed saying it, but *The Souls of Black Folk* is the first book with a black person on the cover that my twelve year-old eyes had ever seen. Sure, my mother read me fiction and poetry by black writers growing up, and she certainly encouraged me to read books by black authors, but their pictures weren't on the covers of their books. Something happened to me when I saw Du Bois and, as I felt back then and still feel now, he saw me. I stared at him and studied that determined look on his face and the fire in his eyes, and he stared back at me, I imagined, with wild wonder. We went on like this for what seemed a lifetime, and then at last I opened the book. Along with James Baldwin's *The Fire Next Time*, *The Autobiography of Malcolm X*, and *Angela Davis: An Autobiography*, all of which I read the summer before I began high school, *The Souls of Black Folk* is a touchstone in my life and has traveled with me from adolescence to adulthood.

Growing up in a poor and extremely poverty-stricken family scattered throughout the South (but mostly based in Texas, Louisiana, Mississippi, Alabama, and Georgia), and being the son of a Southern Baptist minister (i.e., a "country preacher"), I was immediately taken by the candid discussion of racism and black spirituality in *The Souls of Black Folk*. Du Bois, it seemed to me, was writing about my life as much as he was writing about his, and he did so in such an extremely eloquent and lyrical manner that I found myself in his words. I too lived behind "the Veil," and pondered the world beyond it. I was all too familiar with that omnipresent question, which liberal and well-meaning white folk always seem to ask more with their actions than their words: "How does it feel to be a problem?"

Certainly my life stands as a testament to the fact that African Americans at the dawn of the twenty-first century are still approached more as problems than as persons—that is to say, as human beings with rights to be respected and protected. When and where I read Du Bois's blistering criticisms of racial domination and discrimination in *The Souls of Black Folk*, I found myself thinking, even in junior high school, that finally I had found someone who not only lived through the horror and harrowing experience of what it means to be black in an utterly anti-black and white supremacist world, but who unequivocally advocated anti-racist resistance in thought and action. He articulated, what appeared to me at twelve or thirteen years of age, some special secret truth that only he and I were privy. I did not know it then, but what Du Bois shared with me in that initial encounter, in those tattered and repeatedly read pages of *The Souls of Black Folk*, would alter my intellectual and political life forever.

Coming of age in the Deep South in the 1980s and early 1990s I was baffled by the constant displays of racism, and particularly "white supremacy," as Du Bois dubbed it in classic essays, such as "The Souls of White Folk" (1910) and "Of the Culture of White Folk" (1917). Throughout high school and undergraduate the more I read Du Bois, the more special secret truths he shared with me, and only adolescent me, or so I possessively thought. Our special secret truths transcended and, I am tempted to say, transgressed the rubric(s) of race and the harsh realities of racism to quickly include Pan-Africanism, anti-colonialism, black Marxism, democratic socialism, male-feminism, and pacifism, among others. Increasingly I began to interpret him as more than merely a "race man" or "race leader." In the fertile ground of my young mind he blossomed into a revolutionary humanist intellectual and political activist who spoke in novel and much-needed ways to my burgeoning and deep-seated desire to simultaneously become a radical political activist, insurgent intellectual, and avant-garde artist.

However, it was not simply Du Bois the insurgent intellectual, political radical, and littérateur that intrigued me. There were also the intense, often-painfully autobiographical moments strewn throughout his corpus that endeared him to me and fostered a special, extra-intellectual kinship. For instance, the fact that he grew up poor, without a father, had a close and loving relationship with his mother, was fascinated with Africa and its diaspora from an early age, read voraciously, told vivid stories, and respected but was extremely critical of the black church and other forms of organized religion, endeared him to me and aided me in my quest to make sense of the world and the "problems," not only that he identified and to which he sought solutions, but also the new "problems" of contemporary culture and society. As an undergrad student, I was particu-

larly moved when I read the often-overlooked passage from his "Last
Message," which the then ailing octogenarian, nearly nonagenarian Du
Bois composed sensing his imminent death:

> I have loved my work, I have loved people and my play, but always I
> have been uplifted by the thought that what I have done well will live
> long and justify my life; that what I have done ill or never finished can
> now be handed on to others for endless days to be finished, perhaps
> better than I could have done. (Du Bois 1971, 736)

After reading this, I simply couldn't keep the secret truths Du Bois shared
with me to myself; I had to tell someone else. I wondered if there were
others who had found themselves in his words, who were mesmerized
by his magic message, who possessed the intellectual audacity to attempt
to finish in the twenty-first century what he initiated at the end of the
nineteenth century. Increasingly, I also wondered whether anyone had
noticed how much of his work, especially *The Souls of Black Folk*, was
grounded in and placed a special emphasis on the power of black popular music and its connections with black politics and black social movements. Like Martin Luther King, Ella Baker, Bayard Rustin, and Fannie
Lou Hamer, Du Bois seemed to be as enamored with African American
sacred songs-cum-African American protest songs as much as I was. He
seemed to be able to hear *the secrets in the subtexts of black songs*.

As will be discussed in the next chapter, Du Bois's *The Souls of Black
Folk* identifies African American music as one of the major contributions
that African Americans have made to American history, culture, and
society. Consequently, there is a sense in which *Civil Rights Music* can
also be read as an effort to bring both Du Bois's sociology *and* musicology
to bear on the soundtracks of the Civil Rights Movement by simultaneously exploring the musical *and* "extra-musical" elements of gospel, freedom songs, rhythm & blues, and rock & roll during the civil rights era.
There will be more detailed discussion of Du Bois's sociology and musicology in the subsequent chapter, but here it is important to emphasize
that almost every word in this book is underwritten or, rather, written in
the aftermath of the enormous influence of W. E. B. Du Bois, arguably the
first great African American musicologist.[4]

Building on Du Bois's assertion that African American music is one of
the key elements of African American culture, over the last couple of
years I have thought long and hard about what a simultaneous sociology
and musicology of the Civil Rights Movement might reveal to us in the
twenty-first century. By moving away from the famous figures of the
Civil Rights Movement approach to the movement and instead turning
our attention to the rank and filers and "movement artist-activists," specifically "movement musicians," *Civil Rights Music* explores the mobilization of the black popular music of the Civil Rights Movement. It investi-
gates both sacred and secular, highbrow and lowbrow, as well as com-

mercial, and non-commercial forms of "civil rights music" with an eye on the ways in which the music reveals important elements or events of the Civil Rights Movement that are otherwise virtually inaccessible more than fifty years after the end of the movement.

THE "SUBJUGATED KNOWLEDGES" OF THE SOUNDTRACKS OF THE CIVIL RIGHTS MOVEMENT

The chapters to follow offer *a simultaneous history, sociology, and musicology of the Civil Rights Movement* with a focus on "movement music" or, rather, "civil rights music." Moreover, the subsequent chapters reveal that black popular music and black popular culture have always been more than merely "popular music" and "popular culture" in the conventional sense and most often reflect a broader social, political, and cultural movement. For example, the spirituals registered African American protest against enslavement and was the central soundtrack of the Abolitionist Movement. The blues revealed African American desperation and resistance during the Reconstruction and post-Reconstruction years and was in many ways a mouthpiece for working-class and underclass African Americans during the Black Women's Club Movement and the early years of the New Negro Movement. Further, ragtime and jazz expressed the incredibly evolving "New Negro" ethos during the New Negro Movement and Harlem Renaissance era.

As the ensuing chapters will reveal, the soundtracks of the Civil Rights Movement often tell us as much about the movement as its most eloquent leaders and participants. And, for those who might balk at the assertion that music can illustrate as much about a movement as its leaders, participants, and other more conventional political and cultural artifacts should bear in mind Ron Eyerman and Andrew Jamison's contentions in "Social Movements and Cultural Transformation: Popular Music in the 1960s" (1995), where they stated, "In the 1960s songs contributed to a political movement, and were often performed at political demonstrations and collective festivals. Singers and songs were central to the cognitive praxis of these social movements, indeed, they may be central to all social movements in their formative stages" (451). Eyerman and Jamison continued, "During the early to mid-1960s the collective identity of what was then called The Movement was articulated not merely through organizations or even mass demonstrations, although there were plenty of both, but perhaps even more significantly through popular music. Movement ideas, images and feelings were disseminated in and through popular music and, at the same time, the movements of the times influenced developments, both in form and content, in popular music" (452). Beginning with the sacred soundtracks of the Civil Rights Movement, gospel and freedom songs, and then turning to the secular soundtracks of the

Civil Rights Movement, rhythm & blues and rock & roll, *Civil Rights Music* essentially historicizes and critically analyzes how "[m]ovement ideas, images and feelings were disseminated in and through popular music." However, it also explores how the movement "influenced developments, both in form and content, in [black] popular music" between 1954 and 1965.

Civil Rights Music remixes the history of the Civil Rights Movement, in part, by utilizing aspects of Eyerman and Jamison's socio-musicology methodology and examining the ways in which "movement music" contributed to the "cognitive praxis" or, rather, the ideas *and* actions of the Civil Rights Movement, which were expressed through music as much as through conventional politics and social organization efforts. A qualitatively different interpretation of the Civil Rights Movement emerges when the movement is critically engaged from the point of view of both its national and local, commercial and non-commercial artist-activists, especially the musicians of the movement (including the musicians secretly associated with the movement as a consequence of violent anti-black racist and economic reprisal). From my point of view, *civil rights studies* is a wide-ranging and wide-reaching field of critical inquiry where an iconic black popular movement and the black popular culture (including the black popular music) that emerged out of it are conceived of as "text" and (re)situated and (re)interpreted within the wider "context" of, first and foremost, African American history, culture, aesthetics, politics, and economics, and then ultimately broader national and international history, culture, aesthetics, politics, and economics. [5]

Hence, here the soundtracks of the Civil Rights Movement can be said to represent what Michel Foucault (1980, 81) called "an insurrection of subjugated knowledges," which he defined as ways of thinking and doing that have been eclipsed, devalued, or rendered invisible within the dominant institutions of power/knowledge, but which nonetheless counter, disrupt, and provide progressive alternatives to the dominant institutions of power/knowledge. It is important to emphasize, however, that Foucault's concept of "subjugated knowledges" actually has two distinct meanings:

> By subjugated knowledges I mean two things: on the one hand, I am referring to the historical contents that have been buried and disguised in a functionalist coherence or formal systemization. Concretely, it is not a semiology of the life of the asylum, it is not even a sociology of delinquency, that has made it possible to produce an effective criticism of the asylum and likewise of the prison, but rather the immediate emergence of historical contents. And this is simply because only the historical contents allow us to rediscover the ruptural effects of conflict and struggle that the order imposed by functionalist or systematizing thought is designed to mask. Subjugated knowledges are thus those blocs of historical knowledge which were present but disguised within

the body of functionalist and systematizing theory and which criticism—which obviously draws upon scholarship—has been able to reveal. (81-82)

Here I wish to transpose Foucault's concept of "subjugated knowledges" and apply it to civil rights music and civil rights popular culture in an effort to chronicle and clarify the Civil Rights Movement's history, politics, and social justice agenda. As a consequence, when Foucault contended that "only the historical contents allow us to rediscover the ruptural effects of conflict and struggle that the order imposed by functionalist or systematizing thought is designed to mask," there is a sense in which more nuanced and alternative histories of the Civil Rights Movement that "allow us to rediscover the ruptural effects of conflict and struggle" within the movement will enable us to move away from the "order imposed by functionalist [famous figure-centered] or systematizing thought is designed to mask." "Subjugated knowledges" within the world of civil rights studies are essentially "those blocs of historical knowledge" which historically have been and remain "present but disguised" and buried beneath the conventional histories of the Civil Rights Movement.

All of this is to say that Foucault's double-sided concept of "subjugated knowledges" is applicable to civil rights studies, especially civil rights music. And, in many senses, the concept allows civil rights scholars and students to paint a more detailed and discursively dense picture of the history, politics, economics, and aesthetics of the whole of the Civil Rights Movement because of its focus on forgotten, un-inherited, or outright erased aspects of marginalized civil rights communities' thoughts and practices. The quotation above, however, is only one-side of Foucault's double-sided concept of "subjugated knowledges." He importantly further explained:

> On the other hand, I believe that by subjugated knowledges one should understand something else, something which in a sense is altogether different, namely, a whole set of knowledges that have been disqualified as inadequate to their task or insufficiently elaborated: naïve knowledges, located low down on the hierarchy, beneath the required level of cognition or scientificity. I also believe that it is through the re-emergence of these low-ranking knowledges, these unqualified, even directly disqualified knowledges (such as that of the psychiatric patient, of the ill person, of the nurse, of the doctor—parallel and marginal as they are to the knowledge of medicine—that of the delinquent, etc.), and which involve what I would call a popular knowledge *(le savoir des gens)* though it is far from being a general commonsense knowledge, but is on the contrary a particular, local, regional knowledge, a differential knowledge incapable of unanimity and which owes its force only to the harshness with which it is opposed by everything surrounding it—that it is through the re-appearance of this knowledge,

of these local popular knowledges, these disqualified knowledges, that criticism performs its work. (82)

Civil Rights Music is a work of music criticism, indeed. But, it is also a work of historical, social, political, and cultural criticism. It seeks to highlight and historize "a whole set of knowledges that have been disqualified as inadequate to their task or insufficiently elaborated" within the world of civil rights studies and within the wider society. It seeks to chronicle and, at times, critique, the "naïve knowledges, located low down on the hierarchy, beneath the required level of cognition or scientificity" and to develop *an epistemology of African American musicology* specifically aimed at revealing the "subjugated knowledges" of the soundtracks of the Civil Rights Movement. The emphasis here, then, is on the "parallel and marginal" histories and knowledges that have been and remain at the heart of the history of the Civil Rights Movement and its soundtracks, but which have been hidden as a consequence of ahistorical, apolitical, Eurocentric, and bourgeois famous-figure interpretations of the Civil Rights Movement, or interpretations that otherwise privilege Civil Rights Movement politics over Civil Rights Movement aesthetics.

In other words, *Civil Rights Music* seeks to set afoot a new version of civil rights history and cultural criticism that is grounded in black popular music, black popular culture, and black popular movement-based "popular knowledges" that break through the borders and boundaries of ahistorical, apolitical, Eurocentric, and bourgeois famous-figure interpretations of the Civil Rights Movement. It aims to articulate a new, Civil Rights Movement-inspired "popular knowledge," a "particular, local, regional knowledge, a differential knowledge incapable of unanimity and which owes its force only to the harshness with which it is opposed by everything surrounding it." It is through the re-emergence of these new, Civil Rights Movement-inspired "popular knowledges," these "parallel and marginal," "local [social justice-based] popular knowledges, these disqualified knowledges," that *Civil Rights Music* ultimately advances an alternative history and critical theory of the Civil Rights Movement and its soundtracks.[6]

When black popular music and black popular culture are conceived of as "subjugated knowledge" and "cognitive praxis" (as Eyerman and Jamison emphasized above), then it is possible to perceive the ways that they historically have and currently continue to indelibly influence and inform race relations, gender identity, sexuality, spirituality, religiosity, class struggles, cultural conventions, social views, and broader political values. Revealingly, black popular music and black popular culture are often relegated to the realm of "low culture" (as opposed to "high culture"), which means they are frequently overlooked and, accordingly, under-scrutinized as "serious" sites of historical, cultural, social, and political study. This lame line of logic also overlooks the fact that black popular music and black popular culture, in their own sometimes warped and sometimes wicked ways, represent distinct sites of ideological and counter-ideological production, articulation, and contestation. Consequently, the chapters to follow aim to critically engage the ideological and counter-ideological currents and undercurrents deeply embedded in the Civil Rights Movement, its popular culture and, most especially, its popular music.

The next chapter, "The Musicology of the Civil Rights Movement," will provide a substantive analysis of the unique role of music in black popular movements. In essence, it will discursively develop *a musicology of the Civil Rights Movement*. In specific it will place the soundtracks of the Civil Rights Movement within *the African American movement music tradition*. If, indeed, "music is more than merely music" for many, if not most, African Americans (especially those actively involved in social, political, and cultural movements), when, where, how, and why did such a distinct aesthetic develop? How was it historically handed down to the non-violent singing soldiers of the Civil Rights Movement? Why was there so much singing during the Civil Rights Movement? What meaning did these songs have for movement members? Who were the musicians who created "movement music," and what special, "extra-musical" meaning did this music and the broader movement have for them? These questions, among others, will be addressed in this chapter.

Chapter 3, "Gospel and the Civil Rights Movement," posits that gospel and its freedom songs subgenre are the major sacred soundtracks of the Civil Rights Movement in much the manner that rhythm & blues and rock & roll represent the major secular soundtracks of the Civil Rights Movement. Instead of *sonically segregating* the most popular expressions of black sacred song from the most popular expressions of black secular song during the Civil Rights Movement, in this chapter I utilize the elastic gospel aesthetic of the "Golden Age" of gospel music (circa 1945 to 1965) to bring disparate elements together and discursively develop a fresh interpretation of golden age gospel that places its musical *and* extra-musical contributions on par with the other major musics encapsulating the ideals and ethos of the Civil Rights Movement, specifically rhythm & blues and rock & roll. Whether we turn to freedom songs, rhythm & blues, or rock & roll, during its golden age gospel served as a kind of musical midwife, helping to birth, and then rear and raise the secular soundtracks of the Civil Rights Movement.

The fourth chapter, "Rhythm & Blues and the Civil Rights Movement," will examine classic rhythm & blues in relationship to the overarching aesthetics and politics of the Civil Rights Movement. Strongly stressing the notion that black popular music in essence serves as a barometer with which to measure the political, social, and cultural climate in black America, in this chapter classic rhythm & blues will be critically engaged as one of the major black popular music mouthpieces of the

Civil Rights Movement. It will be argued that even though classic rhythm & blues obviously built on and borrowed much from classic gospel (and its freedom songs subgenre), at times it lyrically and musically expressed views and values that coincided with the gospel aesthetic and then, at other times, lyrically and musically it conveyed qualitatively different, if not new and novel, aspects of African American life-worlds and life-struggles during the Civil Rights Movement. Flying in the face of analyses that downplay and diminish the connections between black popular music and black popular movements, this chapter challenges those scholars and students of black popular music who speak and write about classic rhythm & blues as though it was not significantly grounded in and grew out of the politics, poetics, and aesthetics of the Civil Rights Movement.

The fifth and final chapter of the book will explore early rhythm & blues-based rock & roll as a major soundtrack of the Civil Rights Movement. In particular it will critically treat rhythm & blues-cum-rock & roll's—even if only implicit—emphasis on desegregation, integration, and youth activism. The chapter's emphasis will be on the ways in which rock & roll's relationship with the Civil Rights Movement, even if often unwittingly and often unacknowledged, built on, and in many ways went beyond gospel and rhythm & blues' relationship with the Civil Rights Movement in the sense that it was able to capture and convey the movement's *integrationist ethos* and *integrationist impulse* in ways that gospel and rhythm & blues quite simply did not. The book will end by strongly stressing the *sonic segregation, musical colonization,* and *economic exploitation* that eventually befell the soundtracks of the Civil Rights Movement, especially as they culminated in rock & roll and the movement came to a close.

NOTES

1. For further discussion of Ralph Ellison's contention that black popular music constitutes an indispensable element and cultural indicator of African Americans' life-worlds and life-struggles, and for the most noteworthy works that influenced my interpretation here, see P. A. Anderson (2005), Bell (2003), Ellison (1995a, 1995b, 2001), Ellison and Murray (2000), Maxwell (2004), Muyumba (2009), O'Meally (2001), Porter (2001), Posnock (2005), Radford (2003), and Spaulding (2004). Ellison's influence on the subsequent analysis cannot be stressed strongly enough.

2. It is interesting here to observe how Ellison's assessment of the instrumentality and functionality of African American music mirrors Du Bois's turn of the twentieth century music criticism in *The Souls of Black Folk* (1903b), where he declared: "Little of beauty has America given the world save the rude grandeur God himself stamped on her bosom; the human spirit in this new world has expressed itself in vigor and ingenuity rather than in beauty. And so by fateful chance the Negro folk-song—the rhythmic cry of the slave—stands to-day not simply as the sole American music, but as the most beautiful expression of human experience born this side the seas. It has been neglected, it has been, and is, half despised, and above all it has been persistently mistaken and misunderstood; but notwithstanding, it still remains as the singular

spiritual heritage of the nation and the greatest gift of the Negro people" (251). What is truly amazing here is that Du Bois's age-old words could conceivably be applied to the soundtracks of the Civil Rights Movement, essentially the "Negro folk-song[s]—the rhythmic cry of the slave[s]" of mid-twentieth century American apartheid. Certainly, gospel, freedom songs, rhythm & blues, and early African American rock & roll have been "neglected," they have been, and in many instances remain, "half despised," and above all they have been "persistently mistaken and misunderstood," but none of this negates the fact that in their own varied ways gospel, freedom songs, rhythm & blues, and early African American rock & roll expressed the rhetoric, politics and aesthetics of the Civil Rights Movement. Therefore, if it is conceded that for black America *music is much more than music*, then, the framework and major foci of *Civil Rights Music* can be said to have been dictated by the longstanding instrumentality and multifunctionality of African American music, as asserted above by Du Bois and Ellison, among many others to be discussed below.

3. With regard to my periodization of the Civil Rights Movement as essentially beginning with the 1954 *Brown vs. the Board of Education* Supreme Court decision and more or less ending with the Voting Rights Act of 1965, I have drawn on a number of noteworthy works in Civil Rights Movement studies, including Branch (1988, 1998), Bullard (1993), Carson, Garrow, Gill, Harding, and Hine (1997), J. E. Davis (2001), Dierenfield (2008), Lawson and Payne (2006), Klarman (2007), Levine (1993), Levy (1998), Ling and Monteith (2004), Morris (1984), M. Newman (2004b), Patterson (2002), Weisbrot (1990), J. Williams (1987), and Winters (2000).

4. I am not alone in acknowledging or emphasizing the deep musicological implications of W. E. B. Du Bois's discourse, or the fact that a serious case could be made for Du Bois as "arguably the first great African American musicologist." For further discussion of Du Bois's musicology and relationship to African American music, and for the most noteworthy works that influenced my interpretation here, see P. A. Anderson (2001), Bilbija (2011), Kerkering (2001), Lutz (1991), Radano (1995), Schenbeck (2012), and Spencer (1990, 1993, 1995, 1997).

5. With regard to "civil rights studies," a number of noteworthy works have factored into my interpretation, including Armstrong (2015), Carson, Garrow, Gill, Harding and Hine (1997), Crawford, Rouse and Woods (1990), Collier-Thomas and Franklin (2001), J. E. Davis (2001), Dierenfield (2008), Glasrud and Pitre (2013), Houck and Dixon (2009), Lawson and Payne (2006), Lee (1992), Luders (2010), Morris (1984), Olson (2001), Romano and Raiford (2006), and Sugrue (2008).

6. The alternative history and critical theory of the Civil Rights Movement elaborated in the chapters to follow not only builds on Foucault's conception of "subjugated knowledges" but, perhaps even more importantly, on his discursively distinct conceptions of "archaeology" and "genealogy." For instance, my critical theory of the soundtracks of the Civil Rights Movement critically follows Foucault's philosophical histories and/or historicist philosophies: from his critique of psychiatry in *The History of Madness in the Classical Age* (2009) to his critique of the evolution of the medical industry in *The Birth of the Clinic: An Archaeology of Medical Perception* (1994); from his critique of the evolution of the human sciences in *The Order of Things: An Archaeology of the Human Sciences* (1971) to his critique of the historical-situatedness of truth, meaning, and reason (i.e., the *episteme* of an epoch), and the very methodologies through which they are arrived at or comprehended in his extremely innovative *The Archaeology of Knowledge* (1974) (see also Foucault 1973). According to Foucault (1994, 195), archaeology is distinguished from "the confused, under-structured, and ill-structured domain of the history of ideas." He, therefore, rejected the history of ideas as an idealist and liberal humanist, purely academic or ivory tower mode of writing that traces an uninterrupted evolution of thought in terms of the conscious construction of a tradition or the conscious production of subjects and objects. Against the bourgeois liberalism of the history of ideas approach, Foucaultian archaeology endeavors to identify the states and stages for the creation and critique of ongoing and open-ended or, rather, more nuanced knowledge, as well as the hidden rules and regulations

(re)structuring and ultimately determining the form and focus of discursive rationality that are deeply embedded within and often obfuscatingly operate below the perceived borders and boundaries of disciplinary development, methodological maneuvers, or interpretive intention. For instance, at the outset of *The Order of Things* (1971), Foucault contended: "It is these rules of formation, which were never formulated in their own right, but are to be found only in widely differing theories, concepts, and objects of study, that I have tried to reveal, by isolating, as their specific locus, a level that I have called . . . archaeological" (xi).

Moreover, this critical theory of the soundtracks of the Civil Rights Movement also draws from Foucault's more mature materialist genealogies, such as *Discipline and Punish: The Birth of the Prison* (1979), *The History of Sexuality, Vol. 1: The Will to Knowledge* (1990a), *The History of Sexuality, Vol. 2: The Use of Pleasure* (1990b), and *The History of Sexuality, Vol. 3: The Care of the Self* (1990c), where he deepened and developed his articulation of archaeology and evolved it into a unique conception of genealogy, which signaled an intensification of his critical theorization of power relations, social institutions, and social practices (see also Foucault 1980, 1984, 1988, 1996). However, my critical theory of the soundtracks of the Civil Rights Movement does not understand Foucault's later focus on genealogy to be a break with his earlier archaeological studies as much as it is taken to represent a shift of discursive direction and, even more, an extension and expansion of his discursive domain. Similar to his archaeologies, Foucault characterized his later genealogical studies as a new method of investigation, a new means of interpretation, and a new mode of historical writing.

Truth be told, then, both of these Foucaultian methodologies endeavor to radically reinterpret the social world from a micrological standpoint that allows one to identify discursive discontinuity and discursive dispersion instead of what has been commonly understood to be continuity and uninterrupted identity evolution and, as a consequence, Foucault's methodologies enable us to grapple with and, in many instances, firmly grasp historical happenings, cultural crises, political power-plays, and social situations in their complete and concrete complexity. Furthermore, both Foucaultian methodologies also attempt to invalidate and offer more nuanced narratives to commonly held conceptions of master narratives and great chains of historical continuity and their teleological destinations, as well as to hyper-historicize what has been long-thought to be indelibly etched into the heart of human history. In other words, and more meta-methodologically speaking, in discursively deploying archaeology and/or genealogy Foucault sought to disrupt and eventually destroy hard and fast bourgeois humanist historical identities, power relations, and imperial institutions by critically complicating, by profoundly problematizing and pluralizing the entire arena of discursive formations and discursive practices—hence, freeing historical research and writing from its hidden bourgeois humanist social and political hierarchies, by disavowing and displacing the bourgeois humanist (and, therefore, "socially acceptable") subject, and critically theorizing modern reason and increasing rationalization through reinterpreting and rewriting the history of the human sciences.

Here, my intentions are admittedly less ambitious than those of Foucault, although, I honestly believe, they are just as relevant considering the seemingly ever-increasing amnesia surrounding the Civil Rights Movement and its soundtracks in the twenty-first century. In *Civil Rights Music*, therefore, I seek to reinterpret and rewrite the history of contemporary cultural criticism, radical politics, critical social theory, and socio-political movements in light of the increasing "amnesia" surrounding the Civil Rights Movement and its soundtracks, as well as the Civil Rights Movement and its soundtracks' potential contributions to present and future black popular music, black popular culture, and black popular movements. By identifying and critical analyzing the soundtracks of the Civil Rights Movement, *Civil Rights Music* reinterprets and rewrites the conventionally conceived histories of the movement and its music, ultimately revealing that black popular music, black popular culture, and black popular movements historically have been and currently continue to be inextricable—constantly overlapping, interlocking, and intersecting, intensely infusing and informing each other. Black popular music, black popular culture, and black popular movements are not now and never have been created in a vacuum, but within the historical, cultural, social, political, and economic context of the U.S. This means, then, that like the black popular music, black popular culture, and black popular movements that preceded them, the soundtracks of the Civil Rights Movement are emblematic not only of African America between 1954 and 1965, but also eerily indicative of the state of the "America dream" (or, for many U.S. citizens, the "American nightmare") during the 1950s and 1960s.

TWO

The Musicology of the
Civil Rights Movement

THE CIVIL RIGHTS MOVEMENT AND THE AFRICAN AMERICAN
MOVEMENT MUSIC TRADITION

Over the last half century or so since its end, there has been a great deal of discussion concerning the Civil Rights Movement and the ways in which it, literally, deconstructed and reconstructed American democracy, citizenship, and education.[1] There have been a number of scholarly studies of the movement's politics, as well as several books centered around the social justice agenda and economic impact of the movement.[2] Additionally, there have been studies that have examined the ways in which the movement helped to revitalize mid-twentieth century American culture, and other studies that have explored the regional and local cultures, politics, and tactics of the movement.[3] In spite of these very often innovative studies, most work within the world of civil rights studies seems to only superficially treat its soundtracks, and the wider historical, cultural, social, political, economic, and aesthetic contexts from which *civil rights music* emerged and evolved.

Even in light of all of its sonic and aesthetic innovations, it is important to point to civil rights music's extra-musical aspects. Too often African American music is treated as though it exists outside of African American musical and other artistic traditions. This is not only unfortunate, it is extremely disingenuous, as it makes it seem as though each new form of black popular music is some sort of free-floating, "postmodern" sonic signifier, and not, as is most often the case, deeply connected to and undeniably indicative of the origins and evolution of African American musical history and culture, as well as African American social history and culture. Therefore, in order to really and truly understand civil rights music much must be understood about the history, culture, and ongoing struggles of its primary producers: black ghetto youth in specific, and African Americans in general.

In often unrecognized ways, the origins and evolution of civil rights music have actually come to be treated or, rather, ill-treated much like African Americans—especially, black ghetto youth—in mainstream American history, culture, and society. To return to the theme of one of my previous volumes of African American musicology, *Hip Hop's Amnesia,* there seems to be a serious *amnesia* surrounding the origins and evolution of civil rights music and the broader Civil Rights Movement that the music reflected. Conceptually *amnesia,* which according to *Merriam-Webster's Dictionary* means "a partial or total loss of memory," offers us an interesting angle to revisit, re-evaluate, and ultimately "remix" the origins and evolution of civil rights music and the Civil Rights Movement.

At this point it can be said with little or no fanfare that most work in civil rights studies only anecdotally explores the origins and evolution of civil rights music, and civil rights popular culture more generally. Consequently, civil rights studies stands in need of serious scholarly works that transcend the anecdotal and critically engage not only civil rights music's musical history, but also its spiritual, intellectual, cultural, social, and political history. If, as most civil rights studies scholars would more than likely concede, civil rights music reflects more than merely the "young folk's foolishness" and *naïveté* of Civil Rights Movement black ghetto youth and, eventually with the crossing-over of rock & roll, white suburban youth, then a study that treats civil rights music as a reflection of post-war youth's politics and social justice agenda between 1945 and 1965 is sorely needed. *Civil Rights Music* was researched, written, *and* routinely "remixed" specifically with this dire need in mind.

It is generally accepted that black popular music and black popular culture frequently reflect the conservatism *and* radicalism, the moderatism *and* militantism of the major African American movement of the milieu in which they initially emerged. Bearing this in mind, *Civil Rights Music* critically explores how the soundtracks of the Civil Rights Movement were more or less *movement musics.* Which is to say, classic gospel, freedom songs, rhythm & blues, and rock & roll literally (albeit most often implicitly) mirrored and served as mouthpieces for the views and values, as well as the aspirations and frustrations, of the Civil Rights Movement.

There is, indeed, a serious need for more historically-rooted, culturally-relevant, and politically-radical research within the world of civil rights studies. Too often fans and critics listen to, speak of, and write about civil rights music and civil rights popular culture as though contemporary black popular music and contemporary black popular culture are not in any way connected to a historical and cultural continuum that can be easily traced back to the black popular music and black popular culture of the Civil Rights Movement and Black Power Movement. Building on the sociology of music and politics of music-centered epistemologies and methodologies developed by Bernice Johnson Reagon (1975), Jon Michael Spencer (1990, 1996), Ron Eyerman and Andrew Jamison (1991, 1995, 1998), Kerran Sanger (1995), Nathan Davis (1996), Mark Mattern (1998), Mellonee Burnim and Portia Maultsby (2006, 2015), Ian Peddie (2006), Courtney Brown (2008), William Banfield (2010), William Roy (2010) and Ruth Feldstein (2013), *Civil Rights Music* is a study about music *and* socio-political movements, aesthetics *and* politics, as well as the ways in which African Americans' unique history, culture, and struggles have consistently led them to create musics that have served as the soundtracks or, more or less, the *mouthpieces* for their socio-political aspirations and frustrations, their socio-political organizations and movements.

Obviously at this point many of my readers may be asking themselves a couple questions: "But, does classic gospel, freedom songs, rhythm & blues, and rock & roll really reflect the ideals of the Civil Rights Movement? If there is really and truly such a thing as 'civil rights music,' how come I haven't heard of it before? And, can music be popular, but yet politically progressive and convey a serious social justice message?"

It is these questions that lie at the heart of this book, and which have burned and bothered me longer than I care to remember. It should be stated openly and outright: These are very valid questions. Indeed, they are critical questions that I am sincerely seeking to ask *and* answer throughout the following pages of this book. In a nutshell, what I have come to call "civil rights music" actually does not rotely resemble any previous African American musicological concept. But, by the time my readers get to the fifth and final chapter of this book they will see that, yet and still, "civil rights music" historically has been and currently continues to be a musical and political reality. As will be revealed in the three chapters to follow, the origins and early evolution of black popular music, especially civil rights musics such as classic gospel, freedom songs, rhythm & blues, and rock & roll, are very varied. Rapid and radical changes in "mainstream" American history, culture, politics, economics, and society have made it such that there are great and often grave differences between the origins and early evolution of each form of black popular music, just as there are great and often grave differences between the origins of each black popular movement.[4]

Civil Rights Music argues that many of these "great and often grave differences" are easily observed in the history of black popular music and black popular culture, and that, even more, black popular music and black popular culture are often incomprehensible without some sort of serious working-knowledge of historic African American social and political movements. Taking this line of logic even further, *Civil Rights Mu-*

sic contends that neither Civil Rights Movement aesthetics nor Civil Rights Movement politics can be adequately comprehended without some sort of serious working-knowledge of historic African American social and political movements. Ultimately, then, this book is about "partial or total loss of memory" or, rather, *what has been forgotten but should be remembered* about the origins and early evolution of civil rights music in direct relationship with the Civil Rights Movement.

However, *Civil Rights Music* is not simply about the historical, cultural, and musical "amnesia" surrounding civil rights music and the Civil Rights Movement. It is also about the intense interconnections between black popular culture and black political culture, both before and after the Civil Rights Movement, and the ways in which the Civil Rights Movement in many senses symbolizes the culmination of centuries of African American politics creatively combined with, and ingeniously conveyed through African American music. Even the term "civil rights music" can be seen as a code word for *African American message music* between 1945 and 1965, and this even though most of the messages in the music seem to have been missed by many, if not most, people who were not actively involved in, or in some significant way associated with, the Civil Rights Movement.

The main aim of this chapter is to offer an analysis of the unique role of black popular music in black popular movements in order to ultimately discursively develop *a musicology of the Civil Rights Movement*. Prior to our protracted exploration of civil rights music, it will be important to place the soundtracks of the Civil Rights Movement within *the African American movement music tradition*. If, indeed, "music is more than merely music" for many, if not most, African Americans (especially those actively involved in social, political, and cultural movements), when, where, how, and why the unique relationship between black popular music and black popular movements developed is a key question? Beginning with a brief discussion of the broader historical, cultural, social and political contexts of the Civil Rights Movement, next the chapter gives way to a discussion of the often overlooked popular culture of the Civil Rights Movement—what I call "civil rights popular culture." The chapter will conclude with an examination of black popular music as a form of cultural expression *and* cultural action, in a sense setting up the subsequent chapters by providing the reader with an overview of *the African American movement music tradition* that civil rights music arose out of.

THE CIVIL RIGHTS MOVEMENT, COLLECTIVE IDENTITY, COLLECTIVE AGENCY, AND COGNITIVE PRAXIS

In *Social Movements, 1768–2004* (2004), noted political sociologist Charles Tilly essentially argued that social movements are most often made up of ordinary people, rather than members of the politically powerful and elite, and it is these "ordinary people," these "organic intellectuals"—*à la* Antonio Gramsci's provocative work in his *Prison Notebooks*—who collectively think, act, and speak in the best interest of, and in concert with every day average people—the so-called "masses." Gramsci (1971, 9) famously contended that "[a]ll men are intellectuals," but "not all men have in society the function of intellectuals." It is extremely important to emphasize this point because neither black youth nor the ghettos they have been callously quarantined to have been recognized for their intellectual activities and positive cultural contributions. In other words, black ghetto youth have contributed much more than merely vice, vulgarity and viciousness, and their contributions to black popular music and black popular movements during the Civil Rights Movement are especially significant.

Although "one can speak of intellectuals," Gramsci declared, "one cannot speak of non-intellectuals, because non-intellectuals do not exist." In point of fact, "[t]here is no human activity from which every form of intellectual participation can be excluded: *homo faber* cannot be separated from *homo sapiens*," which is to say, the "primitive man" (*homo faber*) cannot be completely divorced from the evolution of the much-vaunted "wise man" (*homo sapiens*). Intellectuals do not simply inhabit college campuses and highbrow cafés, then, they can also be found in each and every community in this country, including the slums, ghettoes, and barrios. Right along with "philosophers" and "men of taste," Gramsci included artists in his conception of "organic intellectuals," contending: "Each man, finally, outside his professional activity, carries on some form of intellectual activity, that is, he is a 'philosopher,' an artist, a man of taste, he participates in a particular conception of the world, has a conscious line of moral conduct, and therefore contributes to sustain a conception of the world or to modify it, that is, to bring into being new modes of thought" (9; see also 3–43).[5]

It is not only movement leaders, but rank and file movement members in general, whether they consider themselves moderates or militants, intellectuals or activists, who have a "conscious line of moral [and frequently political] conduct," and who, consequently, contribute "to sustain a conception of the world or to modify it, that is, to bring into being new modes of thought." Many of the "new modes of thought" and political practices that the Civil Rights Movement brought into being did not stem from civil rights issues exclusively, but frequently arose from myriad social, political, cultural, economic, and employment issues. This conception of social movements is in clear contrast to those who embrace what could be termed the "old" conception of social movements, which holds that social protest and social movements are almost exclusively motivated by class interests and carried out by members who share the same class status. Generally the goals of conventional social movements revolve around institutional changes that yield political and economic redistribution along class lines.[6]

The "new" social movement model offers several correctives for the limitations of the "old," essentially Eurocentric social movement model which, from critical race, feminist, postcolonialist, pacifist, and queer theorists and activists' points of view, did not adequately engage social issues and injustices stemming from racism, sexism, heterosexism, war, and religious intolerance, among other issues. According to Rhys Williams in "The Cultural Contexts of Collective Action: Constraints, Opportunities, and the Symbolic Life of Social Movements" (2004):

> As a whole, new social movements scholarship emerged as a response to and interpretation of contemporary European social movements, such as the Greens, that were focused on cultural, moral, and identity issues, rather than on economic distribution. Much post-war European sociology was more influenced by Marxist theory than was its American counterpart; as such, it had often assumed that collective action came out of material interests and that collective actors were economic classes. "The social movement," for many European scholars, was the labor-socialist movement. By contrast, NSMs [i.e., new social movements] were often thought to be more like "moral crusades," and as such appeared as a new phenomenon that needed to be theorized distinctly for the historical moment in which they occurred. Thus the cultural component of new social movement theory had to do with the *content* of movement ideology, the *concerns motivating activists*, and the *arena* in which collective action was focused—that is, cultural understandings, norms, and identities rather than material interests and economic distribution. New social movement theory was generally macro in orientation, and retained the traditional Marxian concern with articulating the ways in which societal infrastructures produced and are reflected by culture and action. New social movement theory garnered attention, support, and critique from scholars. Many North American critics, not surprisingly, questioned whether the social movements themselves, or the social conditions that helped to produce them, were in fact "new." (92, all emphasis in original)

It is important to emphasize that new social movements usually focus on "cultural understandings, norms, and identities" rather than solely on class struggles or material interests *à la* "old" social movements. Additionally, Williams's emphasis on the cultural aspects of new social movement theory, which revolve around the "*content* of movement ideology, the *concerns motivating activists*, and the *arena* in which collective action [is] focused," seems to directly speak to the Civil Rights Movement's qualifications as a new social movement. The Civil Rights Movement distinguished itself from previous African American (if not other American) popular movements in light of its unique utilization of radio, television, print media, grassroots political organizing, and more traditional forms of social activism in its efforts to establish and express its "movement ideology," encapsulate the "concerns" of its organic intellectual-activists, and engage the new social, political, and cultural "arena" in the immediate post-war period, especially between 1954–1965.[7]

Drawing from a wide range of new social movement scholarship, the defining characteristics of new social movements can be essentially summarized as: (1) identity, autonomy, and self-realization; (2) defense rather than offense; (3) politicization of everyday life; (4) working-class *and* underclass (as opposed to merely middle-class) mobilization; (5) self-exemplification (organizational forms and styles that reproduce and circulate the ideology of the movement); (6) unconventional means (as opposed to conventional means such as voting); and (7) partial and overlapping commitments (a web of intermeshing memberships rather than traditional party loyalty).[8] In many ways the Civil Rights Movement resembles a "new" social movement much more than it does an "old" social movement, and this, almost in and of itself, may go far to explain why so many "old school" historians, sociologists, political scientists, economists, and cultural critics have failed to acknowledge the ways movement leaders and rank and file movement members politicized and utilized music to capture and convey the politics, culture, and social justice agenda of the movement.

Here it is important to observe that both the new social movement scholars and Civil Rights Movement scholars emphasize *collective identity and agency* as being central to their respective fields of critical inquiry. In fact, it could be said that like social movements in general, the Civil Rights Movement enabled its participants to not only imagine themselves as part of a larger community, but to actually **create** *art, culture,* and *communities of struggle.* As a result, the movement produced a sense of collective identity, as well as collective agency. Obviously the Civil Rights Movement's "politicization of everyday life," its "unconventional means" of utilizing radio, television, and print media to educate, decolonize and politicize, its "partial and overlapping commitments" to the strategies, tactics, and goals of both "old" *and* "new" popular movements, its "working-class *and* underclass (as opposed to merely middle-class) mobilization," and, perhaps most importantly, its "self-exemplification" and emphasis on "self-realization" all speak volumes about its clear qualifications as a "new" social, political, and cultural movement and also the ways in which it brazenly promoted a new post-war African American collective identity and form of agency.

Collective identity, as Francesca Polletta and James Jasper asserted in "Collective Identity and Social Movements" (2001), is "an individual's cognitive, moral, and emotional connection with a broader community, category, practice, or institution. It is a perception of a shared status or relation, which may be imagined rather than experienced directly, and it is distinct from personal identities, although it may form part of a personal identity" (285). Collective identities, they importantly continued, "are expressed in cultural materials—names, narratives, symbols, verbal styles, rituals, clothing, and so on—but not all cultural materials express collective identities. Collective identity does not imply the rational calculus for evaluating choices that 'interest' does. And unlike ideology, collective identity carries with it positive feelings for other members of the group" (285).

Indeed, it is possible to have an individual identity that is not directly tied to that of the broader collective and, as a result, one may argue that simply defining oneself does not in and of itself constitute a politically significant act or serve as adequate evidence of a social movement. As a matter of fact, it should be emphasized that any attempt to discuss the politics of the popular music and popular culture of the Civil Rights Movement demands careful delineation because, truth be told, it was variously preoccupied with style, performance, opposition, leisure, consumption, representation, and, increasingly, liberation. However, as Scott Hunt and Robert Benford in "Collective Identity, Solidarity, and Commitment" (1994) asserted, "[b]y virtue of constructing and elaborating a sense of who they are, movement participants and adherents also construct a sense of who they are not" (443). Needless to say, this process of differentiation is an extremely important one, and obviously registers as a politically significant act when we recall the unconventional politics, counterculture, and defensive posture of, as well as the emphasis on both self-realization and self-exemplification in, new social movements discourse discussed above.

In *Social Movements: A Cognitive Approach* (1991), Ron Eyerman and Andrew Jamison famously conceived of social movements as "forms of cognitive praxis which are shaped by both external and internal political processes" (4; see also 45–65). They went on to elaborate:

> Social movements express shifts in the consciousness of actors as they are articulated in the interactions between activists and their opposition(s) in historically situated political and cultural contexts. The content of this consciousness, what we call the cognitive praxis of a movement, is thus socially conditioned: it depends upon the conceptualization of a problem which is bound by the concerns of historically situated actors and on the reactions of their opponents. In other words, social movements are the result of an interactional process which centers around the articulation of a collective identity and which occurs within the boundaries of a particular society. Our approach thus focuses upon the process of articulating a movement identity (cognitive praxis), on the actors taking part in this process (movement intellectuals), and on the contexts of articulation (political cultures and institutions). (4)

Throughout this study my focus will be on three key themes. First, there will be an intense focus on the emergence of a new, post-war black identity and on the process (or, at times, processes) through which *movement intellectual-artist-activists* articulated a *Civil Rights Movement identity*. Second, the next three chapters will center on the principle actors or, rather, the *Civil Rights Movement organic intellectual-artist-activists* — mostly musicians, but also other unsung movement members — who significantly, although often subtly, contributed to the origins and evolution of the Civil Rights Movement. Lastly, the chapters to follow will focus on the social, political, and cultural contexts that historically influenced the Civil Rights Movement and one of its central, even if often unacknowledged, mediums of spiritual reinvigoration, cultural expression, political articulation, and social transformation: *civil rights music.* No matter what one may think of my conception of "civil rights music" at this point, if indeed the subsequent chapters are objectively engaged it will be difficult to deny the manner in which music helped the Civil Rights Movement "express shifts in the consciousness of [movement] actors," leaders *and* rank and filers, and in myriad ways symbolized a key kind of "cognitive praxis" of the Civil Rights Movement. As a matter of fact, as Eyerman and Jamison continued their groundbreaking research on social movements they made a remarkable discovery concerning the relationship between music and social movements, especially those of the 1960s.

Eyerman and Jamison linked collective identity and agency to the interconnections between popular music and popular movements in their sequel to *Social Movements*, the acclaimed *Music and Social Movements: Mobilizing Traditions in the Twentieth Century* (1998). In *Music and Social Movements*, Eyerman and Jamison argued that music is essentially a cognitive phenomenon with enormous potential to influence the politics and culture of social movements in light of its "knowledge-bearing" and "identity-giving qualities" (23, see also 48–73). This means that Civil Rights Movement intellectual-artist-activists' emphasis on the ways in which music and other aspects of post-war black popular culture actually enlightened them, politicized them, socialized them, mobilized them, and provided them with a deeper understanding of themselves and their respective communities, as well as the wider world, is not out of the ordinary or merely reflections of "old" black folk's foolishness.

In this book the Civil Rights Movement is reinterpreted as a central moment in, and the culmination of, the reconstitution of African American culture between 1945 and 1965. Beginning with the end of World War II in 1945 and extending through to the Voting Rights Act of 1965, an unprecedented creative turmoil led not only to the genesis of what quickly became the Civil Rights Movement, but also inspired new modes of cultural expression, which in turn gave way to new kinds of African American collective identity and socio-political agency. However seemingly haphazardly initially, the new cultural consciousness, energy, and almost palpable optimism of the first decade immediately following the war (circa 1945 to 1955) enabled African Americans to critically call into question longstanding "American" views, underlying values, and habitual behavior, causing a great deal of debate and reflection. Even as the optimism eventually turned to social and political pessimism in many quarters of black America, some of the initial sentiment seeped into, and was synthesized with the social and political lifeblood of the inchoate Civil Rights Movement in often unintended and circuitous ways.

One of the core contentions of this book is that both the culture of everyday life—the views, values, mores, and habits that form the very basis of social behavior—and the "art worlds" or aesthetics of cultural expression were deeply affected by the groundbreaking activities and exemplary cultural actions that took place during the Civil Rights Movement. In this sense, the Civil Rights Movement was as significant for artists as it was for social and political activists. It was, perhaps, the great cultural generator, the gargantuan cultural game-changer of the middle years and later half of the twentieth century. Its impact was simultaneously social *and* cultural. It impacted black politics *and* black aesthetics, as well as American politics *and* American aesthetics more generally.

Simultaneously a political and cultural quest, the Civil Rights Movement combined culture and politics, which ultimately reconstituted both, and provided a broader historical, cultural, and political context for African American cultural expression between 1945 and 1965. The fusion of politics and culture during the Civil Rights Movement meant that artists were incessantly inspired by the movement and that these same artists, in turn, offered the enormous resources and repertoire of African American artistic culture—various aesthetic traditions and cultural expressions, including musical genres—to Civil Rights Movement thought and practices. Moreover, in the Civil Rights Movement African American cultural traditions were mobilized and, in the process, transformed in the interest of the particular political project at hand: achieving civil rights and social justice, as well as making American citizenship and democracy a reality for all U.S. citizens, not merely wealthy and middle-class white Americans. I contend that this deconstruction and reconstruction of black expressive culture through mobilization is central to any serious understanding of the Civil Rights Movement, and its influential legacy in the twenty-first century.

Truth be told, the transformation of black expressive culture via mobilization has been generally neglected in historical, sociological and political studies of the Civil Rights Movement, where responsibility for "real" change is typically attributed either to anonymous, universal forces, such as war, racism, capitalism or modernization, or to charismatic movement leaders and other politically powerful individuals. Flying in the face of the conventional interpretations that privilege politics over aesthetics, *Civil Rights Music* argues that the cultural expression—especially the musical expression—that took place during the Civil Rights Movement was a central catalyst and symbolic of more pervasive changes in African American views, values, ideas, and ways of life. Here, I intend to place "civil rights music" right alongside of "civil rights politics" and give artistic expression the recognition it deserves as a key component of, and contributor to, both cultural *and* social transformation between 1945 and 1965.

In the following chapters we will critically consider the ways in which the Civil Rights Movement impacted black popular music and, vice versa, the ways in which black popular music impacted the Civil Rights Movement between 1945 and 1965, although especially between 1954 through 1965. Black popular music was important in the formation of, and remains key to the remembrance of the ideals and ethos of the Civil Rights Movement, but sadly the musical components of the new postwar collective black identity and agency have seldom been seriously examined in civil rights studies, or broader studies of black popular movements. By training my attention on, and critically treating the interaction of classic black popular music and the Civil Rights Movement, here I would like to accent a central and, perhaps even more, a seminal element of the movement's dual emphasis on both social *and* cultural transformation. Additionally, I would like to offer an alternative history and critical theory of the Civil Rights Movement that places its politics and social justice agenda in deep dialogue with its popular music and popular culture.

I conceive of these relations between black popular culture and black politics, between black popular music and black popular movements, as a kind of *collective learning process*, a form of *communal political education*, in continuation of my previous emphasis on both the sociology *and* musicology of black popular movements. In my previous work I sought to identify the epistemologies, methodologies, and praxeologies of African American social, political, and cultural movements by focusing on the ways in which musical and other aesthetic traditions typically reflect the ethos of the major movement of their era of inception. My previous musicology also attempted to explore how the extra-musical aspects of black popular music historically affected and continue to factor into African Americans' intellectual, cultural, social, and political identities and agency. In *Civil Rights Music* my primary preoccupation is with the ways in which the Civil Rights Movement provided a context for both *the politicization of knowledge* and *the mobilization of black popular music*. Moreover, the main aim of this book is to challenge the conventional conception of black popular music that disassociates it from black popular movements by critically exploring how arguably the most renowned movement in African American history produced or, at the least, significantly influenced black popular music soundtracks that captured and conveyed both individual and collective aspirations and frustrations, as well as both individual and collective triumphs and tragedies.

Sadly, although I will say it anyway, the Civil Rights Movement has undeniably faded as a living political force in U.S. society. However, I argue throughout this book, its ideals and ethos remain alive in our collective memory and social imagination. The movement was more than merely a social and political movement. It was also a transformative cultural movement that inspired myriad innovative artistic traditions. Reducing the Civil Rights Movement purely to politics, as most scholars and students of social movements tend to do, ignores and often erases a large part of the distinctiveness of black popular movements and what they really represent, especially to erstwhile active movement members. In essence, it is to dilute and dismiss these movements and relegate them to the dustbin of history, to a nostalgic, erstwhile activism that at its best can actually serve to inspire new politics and social movements, but all too often evokes little or no serious academic or political interest. Allow me, if you will, to briefly explain.

On the one hand, scholarly efforts to revisit and revise the spirit of the Civil Rights Movement through empirical analysis of the history and biography of movement activists seems to have unfortunately fallen victim to academic faddism and the intellectual fatigue surrounding the movement by the turn of the twenty-first century. The truth is most U.S. citizens, including academics and even many independent scholars, believe that they know all that is worthwhile knowing about the Civil Rights Movement. As a result, a discursively dismissive attitude taints the reception and interpretation of civil rights studies in the twenty-first century.

On the other hand, there is another tainted tendency in civil rights studies, this one most often put into play by humanities and cultural studies scholars. Namely, the tendency to limit the scope and scholarly attention of their studies almost exclusively to literary or artistic movements and, consequently, discursively downplay the ways in which the politics or actual protest practices of the Civil Rights Movement directly impacted and influenced virtually *all* African American artists between 1945 and 1965, whether they were openly associated with the Civil Rights Movement or not. Please, beloved reader, think seriously about it for a moment. It is not as though American apartheid only targeted African Americans who were openly associated with the Civil Rights Movement. No, absolutely not. Such an interpretation is completely historically inaccurate and utterly intellectually disingenuous. American apartheid assaulted *all* African Americans, as well as their kith and kin from other countries, whether they were moderates, militants, or "silent members" of the movement or not. That is, quite simply and quite sadly, the way the irrationality and blanket-style anti-black racism of American apartheid worked between 1945 and 1965.[9]

In most humanities and cultural studies scholarship on the Civil Rights Movement when black cultural expression is placed within historical and cultural contexts, typically it is the historical and cultural contexts of "art worlds" or "avant-garde movements." However, the broader social, political, and economic connections necessary in order to really and truly comprehend *the art of, and the art created during, the Civil Rights Movement era* is, at best, either barely brought up or, at worst, never even broached. Breaking with both of the tendencies discussed above, *Civil Rights Music* acknowledges that sociologists and political scientists over the years have produced one kind of civil rights studies that most often ignores and ultimately erases the art of, and the art created during, the Civil Rights Movement era, where humanities and cultural studies scholars over the years have produced work that has, more or less, ignored and ultimately erased the politics and social justice agenda of the Civil Rights Movement.

A third tendency in civil rights studies revolves around scholarship that emphasizes the cultural work of the Civil Rights Movement, and its music and musicians to be more specific. Similar to the scholars who focus on the "art worlds" or "avant-garde movements" of the broader movement, in this third tendency the academic takes on the role of the descriptive categorizer and cultural organizer of the Civil Rights Movement, giving selected singers and songs social and political functions and, as a result, putting into practice a form of what C. Wright Mills (1959, 55–59) termed "abstracted empiricism." Needless to say, here the point is not to discursively dismiss any form of civil rights studies as much as it is to challenge scholarship that privileges the political over the cultural instead of understanding the political and the cultural to be inextricable in the black popular movement tradition, as they are in African American life-worlds and life-struggles more generally speaking.

There are countless scholars of the Civil Rights Movement who have offered enormous insight to my effort here, and I should openly emphasize that my work seeks to *build up* and not *tear down* civil rights studies. It is in this sense that I do not necessarily fault other Civil Rights Movement scholars for neglecting the cultural, and more specifically the musical, innovations and expressions that took place during the Civil Rights Movement. I am only interested in emphasizing that the musical and extra-musical elements of music during the Civil Rights Movement should not be discursively divorced from the broader political praxes and conceptions of social change during the movement and, indeed, discursively divorced from other aspects of African American social life. In other words, civil rights music—as with *civil rights art* more generally—should not be relegated to some musicological or sociological subfield, but should be included in the most wholistic and interdisciplinary manner imaginable in the overarching historical, cultural, sociological, political, legal, educational, economic, and religious studies of the Civil Rights Movement.

Civil Rights Music seeks to find a middle ground between history, theory, politics, economics, sociology and musicology. Rather than superimposing "abstracted empiricism" onto the Civil Rights Movement, here I would like to extract and critically explore the extra-musical aspects of the music of the Civil Rights Movement while grounding those extra-musical aspects in the history, culture, politics, and economics of the movement. In fact, instead of advancing a grand sociological theory of the Civil Rights Movement, here my main focus will be on the ways in which Civil Rights Movement history, culture, and overarching struggle are uniquely captured in, and conveyed through the major forms of black popular music between 1945 to 1965. By re-examining the music of the Civil Rights Movement as "cognitive praxis," as cultural action and, in turn, utilizing the said "praxis" and "action" as a point of departure to develop an alternative history and critical theory of the Civil Rights Movement, I aim to avoid "abstracted empiricism." Admittedly, the work here is "theory-laden," but it is also "history-laden," and specifical-ly "music history-laden," and primarily preoccupied with answering the overarching research questions: Did the art of, and the art created during, the Civil Rights Movement era capture and convey aspects and events of the movement unlike any other expression or artifact of the movement? And, more specifically, did the black popular music of, or, rather, the black popular music created during, the Civil Rights Movement capture and convey aspects and events of the movement unlike any other expres-sion or artifact of the movement? Can art and cultural expression, and music more specifically, truly be transformative with respect to politics and social change?

Above I argued that the Civil Rights Movement was an important source of knowledge production, and that it is, in large measure, through the creation and dissemination of *social movement-inspired knowledge* that major social, political, and cultural transformation takes place in African America, if not in America more generally. At the dawn of the twenty-first century, ethnic studies, cultural studies, critical race studies, women and gender studies, queer studies, and environmental studies, not to mention the myriad "traditional" disciplines, have all inherited, even if often unwittingly, a great deal from the epistemology, which is to say, from *the knowledge and praxis production*, of the Civil Rights Movement. Here, the black popular music of the movement is considered a key part of the knowledge production, political practice, and cultural action of the Civil Rights Movement. On the one hand, civil rights music, as a matter of fact, actually challenged dominant—most often incredibly Eurocentric and bourgeois—categories of "good music," and even "good *black* mu-sic," as will be seen in our discussion of the "rock & roll controversy" in chapter 5. From gospel through to rock & roll, black popular music be-tween 1945 and 1965 called into question lily-white, albeit thoroughly whitewashed, categories of artistic merit by highlighting and problema-tizing the taken-for-granted frameworks for aesthetic evaluation and judgment. Between 1945 and 1965, the black popular music of the Civil Rights Movement simultaneously did this on a discursive as well as per-formative level, especially by inventing and incessantly experimenting with new, post-war black aesthetic principles and creating new, post-war black communal rituals and styles.

On the other hand, although often overlooked, the Civil Rights Movement innovatively utilized the media of artistic expression to communicate with the wider world and, by doing so, frequently decolonized, repoliticized, and mobilized popular culture and entertainment. In terms of African American music, literature, and art, the Civil Rights Movement in many instances provided a significant source of renewal and rejuvenation by injecting new "movement meanings" into, and reconstituting established aesthetic forms and genres. In more general terms, through its impact on popular culture, mores, views and values, the Civil Rights Movement ultimately lead to a deconstruction and reconstruction of the processes of African American identity formation, African American cultural transformation and, perhaps most important considering the present discussion, African American popular movement emergence and sustenance.

THE CIVIL RIGHTS MOVEMENT: A CREATIVE COMBINATION OF BLACK POLITICAL CULTURE AND BLACK POPULAR CULTURE

Although there is much nostalgia surrounding the Civil Rights Movement today, we should note that not every aspect of it and its popular culture were progressive or even morally commendable. As a matter of fact, during the Civil Rights Movement longstanding African American traditions were mobilized by movement leaders, intellectuals, artists, and rank and filers in the interest of a wide range of social visions and political agendas, some of which were obviously sexist, heterosexist, Eurocentric, and very often bourgeois, even though the African American masses of the era were, as they remain up to the present moment, primarily working-class and underclass. When engaged objectively, we must concede that the Civil Rights Movement harbored evident regressive, if not outright reactionary, elements. It was not the often-squeaky clean and ethically irreproachable movement it is often portrayed as today.[10]

However, whether deemed progressive or regressive, it is virtually impossible to deny that the Civil Rights Movement actually reconstituted African American cultural resources in the immediate post-war period. This reconstitution of African American cultural resources during the movement ultimately translated into myriad creative works of artistic experimentation and critical, extraordinarily reflective works of evaluation. Through its songs, theater, literature and art, over fifty years after its end the Civil Rights Movement has retained a presence in our collective cultural memory and social imagination in the absence of many of the particular social and political conditions that initially brought it into being. With this in mind, it is easy to see why I argue that even if only through the memory of its political praxes, cultural contributions, and innovative evaluative criteria, the Civil Rights Movement has a living legacy in the twenty-first century. But, its legacy is often shrouded in mystery and misinterpretation because most of its cultural contributions were subsumed under more urgent social and political matters. [11]

The popular culture, including the popular music, of the Civil Rights Movement has rarely been examined in a serious and systematic way, either by academics, activists, or general observers. In fact, many movement members have great difficulty distinguishing the political from the cultural in the Civil Rights Movement. And, partly as a consequence of this dichotomy, the Civil Rights Movement is typically discussed and interpreted in purely political terms: organizations, issues, ideologies, campaigns, marches, demonstrations, strategies and tactics. The dominant interpretive and discursive frameworks usually paint a picture of the Civil Rights Movement's famous political figures, and how these extraordinary individuals channeled the human, material, and organizational resources of the era into the overarching political struggle. What is of greatest interest is the effectiveness with which the Civil Rights Movement was able to achieve many, if not most, of its political goals. However, where most civil rights scholars have long overlooked it, here I am most interested in the deeper and longer-lasting impact that the Civil Rights Movement had on cultural transformation, and specifically cultural expression through the black popular music of the movement. While "movement cultures" have been taken more seriously in recent years, yet and still there has been little or no real attempt to come to terms with the ways in which the black popular culture and black popular music of the Civil Rights Movement often arose out of, and often in turn influenced the internal culture and external cultural work of the movement. [12]

Here, much of my analysis will go against the grain of more or less poststructuralist and postmodernist interpretations of the Civil Rights Movement that read it almost exclusively in textual terms, whether via actual literary products or the dialogical practices that can be read into social and political interactions of the era. In this discursive framework, the U.S. society of the Civil Rights Movement era is treated, for the most part, as a web of discourses, and the main emphasis is placed on the construction of meaning and identity through various forms of written articulation. Most often decontextualized and disembodied, the text in this discursive framework, whether it be a book, or a "social text," or even a "cultural text," is typically comprehended as a thing in and of itself. Admittedly, this often makes for fascinating analyses of particular political practices and cultural expressions, and has actually led to the production of an entirely new epistemological and methodological arsenal for extracting the essence out of an exemplary document or artifact. However, all too often when this framework is applied to African American movements the deeper structures of distinctly black theories and black praxes of social, political, and cultural change are left in the lurch.

The poststructuralist and postmodernist textual interpretation of the Civil Rights Movement dilutes the central importance of history, and especially the role of collective action, political praxis, and social movements in reconstructing the contexts in which all texts are created and recreated. All of this is nonchalantly negated, and the ways in which history, culture, politics, and economics impact the interpretation of all texts is essentially bracketed out. In essence, in order to exclusively focus on the specificity of texts, the generality of contexts is discursively dismissed. Obviously, I do not want to revive the "structuralist" theories that the poststructuralists and postmodernists have challenged. However, I would assert that there are very serious limitations in attempts such as these to read society and social movements in textual terms.

While there are innumerable works by historians of art, music, and literature on the cultural activities and cultural expressions of political movements, for the most part sociologists and musicologists have curiously left the cultural activities and cultural expressions of political movements, especially African American political movements, woefully under-analyzed. Frequently, the historians of art, music, and literature produce accounts of the cultural activities and cultural expressions of political movements that fall squarely in the idioms of cultural or literary history, where almost invariably aesthetic work takes precedence over social and political work. Although there have been biographies and scholarship about selected artists of the Civil Rights Movement, for the most part, this work has not significantly contributed to our understanding of the overarching movement because of the understandably narrow, *autobiocentric* nature of the focus of most of these studies.

For my purposes here, when taken collectively these studies open up a rich field for critical interdisciplinary analysis. On the one hand, these studies point to the crucial importance of political commitment in black cultural expression and artistic production during the Civil Rights Movement. As is now well known, many of the leading artists, writers, and musicians of the Civil Rights Movement era were involved, at arguably the most formative phase of their lives, in the movement. Although I would be the first to admit that this does not mean that the monumental artistic achievements of, for example: Lena Horne, Harry Belafonte, Mahalia Jackson, Sam Cooke, Lorraine Hansberry, Sidney Poitier, Dorothy Love Coates, Sammy Davis, Jr., Gwendolyn Brooks, James Baldwin, LeRoi Jones, Nat King Cole, Odetta, Richie Havens, Ossie Davis, Ruby Dee, Dick Gregory, Nina Simone, and Ray Charles, among many others, can be reduced to their political commitments to the Civil Rights Movement. However, it does seem to suggest that without having taken an active role in the Civil Rights Movement they probably would have produced distinctly different work. Additionally, it is important to observe that in most instances movement involvement was a defining moment and, more or less, remained, however furtively, central to their artistry even after the Civil Rights Movement came to a close.

These artists' activism was objectified in their art and, as a consequence, the movement came to be embodied in them. When the Civil Rights Movement ended the ideals and ethos of the movement lived on in their iconic art. In many instances, their "movement art" helped to inspire post-Civil Rights Movement popular movements (albeit not merely *black* popular movements) by serving to keep the Civil Rights Movement and its distinct aesthetic alive in the American social imagination and collective cultural memory long after 1965.

On the other hand, studies focused on the relationship between civil rights aesthetics and civil rights politics provided me with ideal examples and sources of inspiration for my conception of *music as a form of, and force for cultural transformation during the Civil Rights Movement*. What I previously proclaimed as the distinctive soundtracks of African American social movements and "movement musicians" can now be comprehended, with the intellectual assistance of this scholarship, as a kind of cultural production and cultural praxis that harbors deep historical, political, sociological, legal, educational, economic, and religious implications for the critical study of the Civil Rights Movement. Here the Civil Rights Movement is seen as a breeding ground for qualitatively new kinds of politicized and ritualized thought and practices, as well as for artistic, literary and, most especially, musical innovation and experimentation.

Bearing all of this in mind, I openly acknowledge how profoundly my work here has been influenced by a number of important studies that have focused on how the artist-activists of the Civil Rights Movement politicized and mobilized the black popular music of the movement in the interest of the movement's social and political goals. I would be remiss if I did not make special mention of Bernice Johnson Reagon's "Songs of the Civil Rights Movement, 1955–1965" (1975), Jonathan Kamin's "Rhythm & Blues in White America: Rock and Roll as Acculturation and Perceptual Learning" (1975), Pete Seeger and Bob Reiser's *Everybody Says Freedom: A History of the Civil Rights Movement in Songs and Pictures* (1989), Kerran Sanger's *"When the Spirit Says Sing!": The Role of Freedom Songs in the Civil Rights Movement* (1995), Laura Helper's "Whole Lot of Shakin' Goin' On: An Ethnography of Race Relations and Crossover Audiences for Rhythm & Blues and Rock & Roll in 1950s Memphis" (1996), Anne McCanless's "Uniting Voices in Song: The Music of the Civil Rights Movement" (1997), Brian Ward's *Just My Soul Responding: Rhythm & Blues, Black Consciousness, and Race Relations* (1998), Brian Ward's *Radio and the Struggle for Civil Rights in the South* (2004), Ruth Feldstein's *How It Feels to Be Free: Black Women Entertainers and the Civil Rights Movement* (2013), Bob Darden's *Nothing but Love in God's Water: Black Sacred Music from the Civil War to the Civil Rights Movement* (2014), and Shana Redmond's *Anthem: Social Movements and the Sound of Solidarity in the African Diaspora* (2014). These studies, along with the myriad others to be discussed in the subsequent chapters, not only enriched my conception of music as a form of, and force for cultural transformation during the Civil Rights Movement, but they also deftly demonstrate that civil rights music had a significant impact on subsequent popular music and popular culture both nationally and internationally.

A number of cultural historians, as well as historians of art, music, and literature have begun to look more closely at the social and political contexts within which culture is created and disseminated. As a result, we now have a body of literature on specific cultural and artistic "movements" and "worlds," ranging from the "slave narratives" of the Abolitionist Movement to the radical writers of the Harlem Renaissance, and extending through to the evolution of classic jazz into "bebop" during the Bebop Movement. In the bulk of this work there is a concerted effort to socialize the subject, to contextualize the individual artist as not simply expressing their personal views and values, but instead to comprehend, for instance, Mahalia Jackson, Smokey Robinson, Nina Simone, Little Richard, and Ruth Brown, to name some of the musicians who will appear later in this book, as representative figures who captured and communicated the ideals and ethos of the Civil Rights Movement.[13]

As much as I intellectually admire and greatly appreciate this work, I must admit that it has had virtually little or no influence on the sociology of social movements—one of my chief areas of concern here. This is primarily due to a discursive difference in focus: for most social movement theorists and other sociologists, culture is something that forms or "frames" social movements and other distinctly "social" activities as a set of (external) conditioning factors, while for cultural theorists it is social movements and social ecology that provide the external contexts or conditions that shape the primary objects of analysis, art, literature, music and their creators. Where the social theorists highlight the social background that the artist and their artistry is embedded in, or has shaped and shaded the artist and their artistry, the cultural theorists emphasize "movement culture" or a cultural frame for movement campaigns and activities. One might surmise that the real difference has to do with what is influencing what and the discursive direction of the context and conditioning. Even more important, however, seems to be a fundamental difference in discursive devices, language, methods, and epistemological orientation. Indeed, sociologists and humanists are subjected to different processes of academic acculturation, and are very rarely given an opportunity to learn about, let alone really critically engage, each other's work.

My approach here seeks to synthesize history, sociology, politics, economics, and African American studies in an effort to develop an alternative history and critical theory of the Civil Rights Movement by exploring the texts and contexts of black popular music as a form of, and force for cultural transformation between 1945 and 1965. As Houston Baker observed in *Modernism and the Harlem Renaissance* (1987), African American life, culture, and struggle has distinct, signature "soundings" and "resoundings," and it is an "'alien' *sound*" that "gives birth to notions of the indigenous—say, Africans, or Afro-Americans—as *deformed*" (51, all emphasis in original). But, Baker boldly asserted, African Americans' "indigenous *sound* appears monstrous and deformed *only* to the intruder" and, I would add, to the enslaver, to the colonizer, and to the oppressor (52, all emphasis in original). African Americans' unique "soundings" and "resoundings," therefore, have been a core component of black popular movements going all the way back to the spirituals and the Abolitionist Movement. And, according to Baker, African American musical traditions are recreated and given new life as they either arise out of, or intensely interact with black popular movements. However, the inverse is also true, black popular movements often express their meaning and frequently gain coherence and sustenance through the medium of black popular music.

Arguably, nowhere has the role of black popular music in a black popular movement been more pronounced than in the Civil Rights Movement. From the Abolitionist Movement through to the Civil Rights Movement, black popular music helped to shape the mission, message, and cultural memory of African American social and political movements. As a matter of fact, a case could be made concerning the ways in which it has been chiefly through black popular music that most black popular movements, especially the Civil Rights Movement, have exerted their enormous influence and long-lasting legacy on American culture, as well as on the wider world.

By focusing on black popular music as a form of, and force for cultural transformation during the Civil Rights Movement I hope to reveal a significant but neglected element of the movement that was central to its success and certainly deserves just as much scholarly attention as the more renowned social and political strategies and tactics of the movement. Even though the Civil Rights Movement will serve as our primary point of departure throughout this book, it is hoped that its politicization and mobilization of various African American traditions—spiritual, intellectual, cultural, social, political, and musical—will inspire a new politicization and mobilization of various African American traditions in the present, where many of the issues the Civil Rights Movement sought to eradicate have sadly returned with a vengeance.

By selectively and very critically recreating civil rights cultural traditions and cultural expressions, we can reinvent a new Civil Rights Movement (or something of the sort) aimed at the most pressing problems of the twenty-first century. Moreover, as was the case during the Civil Rights Movement in the 1950s and 1960s, black popular music will more than likely provide us with one of the key mediums through which to capture and convey the emancipatory ideals and ethos of the much-needed new movement. As a result, the analysis in the chapters to follow should be interpreted as part alternative history and critical theory of the Civil Rights Movement of the twentieth century, and part intense invocation and sacred summoning of a new Civil Rights Movement in the twenty-first century. The struggle, as they say, continues. *A luta continua, vitória é certa.*

BLACK POPULAR MUSIC AS CULTURAL EXPRESSION AND CULTURAL ACTION

My interest in the relationship between black popular movements and black popular music here can be comprehended as an elaboration of the work I began in *Hip Hop's Inheritance, Hip Hop's Amnesia*, and *The Hip Hop Movement.* The emphasis on black popular music as a form of, and force for cultural transformation during the Civil Rights Movement is ultimately about exploring the production of ideas and culture that arise out of the social justice agendas and political praxes of black popular movements, and on the role of "movement intellectual-artist-activists," specifically "movement musicians," in articulating the ideals, culture, and collective identity of black popular movements. A cognitive approach to black popular movements understands them, and the distinct black popular culture that seems to always accompany them, to be primarily knowledge producers, and social forces that open up novel arenas for the production and practice of new forms of knowledge, culture, and politics. By focusing on the cognitive dimensions of the black popular culture and black popular music of black popular movements, my more general aim here is to make the content and substance—literally, the distinct *movement culture*—of black popular movements' politics *and* praxis, rather than their form or organization, the central focus of analysis.

The cognitive approach to black popular movements and their distinct black popular culture, which obviously includes black popular music, has three core concepts: *context, process,* and *knowledge production.* Black popular movements emerge in particular times and particular places. Indeed, they are the products of specific social and political conditions, as well as deeper and more longstanding historical and cultural traditions. However, even though they are shaped by these broader contextual conditions, black popular movements typically temporarily transcend the specific situations from which they arise. In fact, they create new contexts, new public spaces for identifying and addressing the most pressing problems of their respective epochs. From my point of view, there quite simply is no need to incessantly reduce them to the organizations or institutions that they eventually evolved into. I honestly believe that what is truly significant is their jazz-like transience, their momentariness, their fluidity. Black popular movements are processes in formation and works-in-progress. They do not miraculously spring to socio-political life fully-formed, which is one of the reasons I critically explore the origins and early evolution of the Civil Rights Movement as far back as World War II and its immediate aftermath (circa 1939 to 1954). On the contrary, black popular movements can be conceived of as contingent and emergent arenas that evoke and evolve previous and present African American life-worlds and life-struggles. They are, therefore, creative and incredibly experimental, and provide arenas for the production and practice of new forms of social, political, cultural, and cognitive expression and action.[14]

In the new spaces that black popular movements open up, the enunciation of a new collective *and* cognitive identity is, for me, a core process. Black popular movements are typically the conveyors of some sort of historical project and political praxis. These movements offer a new epistemology by producing *praxis-promoting knowledge and culture* or, rather, *new knowledge and culture with practical intent*, often integrating a new cosmology or worldview, as well as organizational innovations and new approaches to everything from science to religion. Once separate areas of knowledge production, whether cosmological, technical, political or organizational, are most often combined into an integrated praxis in the space formed and informed by the emergence of black popular movements. However, we need to be clear here, when the utopian vision of the aforementioned integrated praxis is coupled with specific practical activities and organizational forms, it provides a cognitive core to movement activity as the movement members form both their historical project and political praxis, as well as their collective identity. In black popular movements, the process of collective identity formation coincides with what Eyerman and Jamison termed "cognitive praxis" above. Beyond the leaders and other famous figures of black popular movements who embody the "cognitive praxis" of the movement, rank and filers, artists, and most especially musicians, are directly involved in the evolution and articulation of the "cognitive praxis" of the movement. Consequently, here I am drawing on Eyerman and Jamison's concept of "cognitive praxis" to call attention to the creative role of consciousness and cognition in the thought and practices of *all* black popular movement members, not merely the more noted folk, and especially movement artists and movement musicians.

By elucidating the relationship between the Civil Rights Movement and black popular music, I would like to extend the range and reach of Eyerman and Jamison's concept of "cognitive praxis" and apply it in much greater discursive detail than they did in *Music and Social Movements* to the Civil Rights Movement and its major soundtracks. The "cognitive praxis" approach to the Civil Rights Movement and its major soundtracks will also enable me to analyze frequently forgotten forms of movement habituation—the habits, customs, mores, and movement ritu-als—as well as the symbolic representations that the movement pro-duced—in particular, the sounds and songs of the Civil Rights Move-ment. It was not merely American politics and society that were pro-foundly affected by the Civil Rights Movement. With this work, I would like to illustrate some of the myriad ways that the aspirations and frustra-tions of the Civil Rights Movement were not only given coherence through the medium of black popular music, but also that black popular music was impacted by, and often took on new meanings and messages as a consequence of the movement. Additionally, I would like to focus on, not only movement leaders and other famous figures, but also on movement intellectual-artist-activists, especially musicians, and those other forgotten figures who created, organized, and articulated the cultu-ral expressions and cultural actions of the movement.

Epistemologically, the reconstituted conception of "cognitive praxis" that I will utilize throughout this book is also discursively derived from *the Africana tradition of critical theory* (or, rather, *Africana critical theory*) and is meant as an alternative to conventional interpretations of the Civil Rights Movement, where civil rights leaders and other famous figures seemingly ingeniously impose order on a chaotic world with little or no reference to the centuries of African American social, political, cultural, and intellectual traditions that these leaders and other famous figures, in point of fact, actually emerged out of. In essence, Africana critical theory is *theory critical of domination and discrimination in classical and contempo-rary, continental and diasporan African life-worlds and life-struggles.* It is a style of critical theorizing, inextricably linked to progressive political practice(s), that highlights and accents black radicals' answers to the key questions posed by the major forms and forces of domination and dis-crimination that have historically, and continue currently, to shape and mold our modern/postmodern and neocolonial/postcolonial world.[15]

Africana critical theory involves not only the critique of domination and discrimination, but also—à la the Civil Rights Movement—a deep commitment to human liberation and radical democratic social transfor-mation. Similar to other traditions of critical social theory, Africana criti-cal theory is concerned with thoroughly analyzing contemporary society "in light of its used and unused or abused capabilities for improving the human [and deteriorating environmental] condition" (Marcuse 1964, xlii; see also Wilkerson and Paris 2001). What distinguishes and helps to de-fine Africana critical theory is its emphasis on the often-overlooked conti-nental *and* diasporan African contributions to critical theory. It draws from critical thought and philosophical traditions rooted in the realities of continental and diasporan African history, culture, and struggle. Which is to say, Africana critical theory inherently employs a methodo-logical orientation and modes of interpretation that highlight and accent black militantism and black radicalism.[16] Moreover, if it need be said at this point, the black liberation struggle is simultaneously national and international and, therefore, requires multidimensional and multiperspectival theory in which to interpret and explain the various diverse phenomena, philosophical motifs, and socio-political movements characteristic of—to use Frantz Fanon's famous phrase—*l'expérience vécue du noir* ("the lived-experience of the black")—that is to say, the reality of constantly and simultaneously wrestling and wrangling with racism, sexism, capitalism and colonialism, among other forms of domination, oppression and exploitation. [17]

Conceptually complementing cognitive praxis and Africana critical theory, another key notion that I will be borrowing from Eyerman and Jamison is their incisive emphasis on "exemplary action." In discursively developing their conception of "exemplary action," Eyerman and Jamison (1998) contended that it can be conceived of as a "specification of the symbolic action" and the "cognitive praxis of social movements" (23). Moreover, the "exemplary action of cognitive praxis is symbolic in several senses," but it is also, they strongly stressed, "'more' than merely symbolic. As real cultural representations—art, literature, songs—it is artifactual and material, as well." Which is to say, the music and other artistic expressions of popular socio-political movements are more than merely ideational and traditional art. Indeed, they are art in every sense of the word "art," but they are also "knowledge-bearing" and "identity-giving" social, political, cultural, intellectual, and spiritual expressions that are simultaneously symbolic *and* factual, if not often literal representations and articulations of the life-worlds and life-struggles of popular movement participants and adherents. Eyerman and Jamison went further to explain:

> What we are attempting to capture with the term [i.e., exemplary action] is the exemplary use of music and art in social movements, the various ways in which songs and singers can serve a function akin to the exemplary works that Thomas Kuhn [in *The Structure of Scientific Revolutions* (1970)] characterized as being central to scientific revolutions: the paradigm-constituting entities that serve to realign scientific thinking and that represent ideal examples of fundamentally innovative scientific work. The difference between culture and science, however, is that the exemplary action of music and art is lived as well as thought: it is cognitive, but it also draws on more emotive aspects of human consciousness. As cultural expression, exemplary action is self-revealing and thus a symbolic representation of the individual and the collective which are the movement. It is symbolic in that it symbolizes all the movement stands for, what is seen as virtuous and what is seen as evil. In the age of symbols, an age of electronic media and the transmission of virtual images, the exemplary action of a movement can serve an educative function for many more than the participants and their immediate public. This exemplary action can also be recorded, in film, word, and music. . . . (23)

Again, Eyerman and Jamison help to highlight that Civil Rights Movement members are not alone in viewing their beloved music and art—which is to say, gospel, freedom songs, rhythm & blues, rock & roll, and other cultural expressions—as having more than merely aesthetic implications. As we will witness in each of the subsequent chapters, music and other art created in the context of, or inspired by social movements, political struggles, and cultural crises most often takes on multiple meanings—some aesthetic and cultural meanings, and other more social and political meanings. Civil rights music and other Civil Rights Movement-inspired art forms are not exceptions to these rules. Moreover, when Eyerman and Jamison contended above that "songs and singers can serve a function akin to the exemplary works that Thomas Kuhn characterized as being central to scientific revolutions: the paradigm-constituting entities that serve to realign scientific thinking and that represent ideal examples of fundamentally innovative scientific work," it is possible for us to transpose Kuhn's conception of scientific revolutions and apply it to the popular music and popular culture of the Civil Rights Movement.

Where Kuhn conceived of scientific "paradigm-constituting entities" and "scientific revolutions," it is possible for us to conceive of *black popular music and black popular culture-constituting entities* and *countercultural revolutions* that historically have and currently continue to "serve to realign [social, political, and cultural] thinking and that represent ideal examples of fundamentally innovative [social, political, and cultural] work"—*à la* George Lipsitz's collective contentions in his volumes *Time Passages: Collective Memory and American Popular Culture* (1990b), *Dangerous Crossroads: Popular Music, Postmodernism, and the Poetics of Place* (1994), *The Possessive Investment in Whiteness: How White People Profit from Identity Politics* (1998), *American Studies in a Moment of Danger* (2001), *Footsteps in the Dark: The Hidden Histories of Popular Culture* (2007), and *How Racism Takes Place* (2011). In applying Kuhn's conception of scientific revolutions to the relationship between black popular music and black popular movements in general, and gospel, freedom songs, rhythm & blues, rock & roll and the Civil Rights Movement in specific, it is relatively easy to see how black popular "songs and singers can serve a function akin to the exemplary works that Thomas Kuhn characterized as being central to scientific revolutions." However, within the context of black popular music and black popular movements the focus logically shifts from natural science to the human, cultural, and social sciences, from scientific revolutions to social, political, and cultural revolutions. In this sense it would be difficult for anyone knowledgeable of the history of black popular music to deny the ways in which its unique dialogical and pedagogical relationship with black popular movements has consistently helped to "realign" and reinvigorate social, political, and cultural thinking and "represent ideal examples of fundamentally innovative" social, political, and cultural work either inspired by or emerging from black popular movements.

Hence, when black popular music and black popular culture between 1954 and 1965 is viewed as part of the "symbolic action" and "cognitive praxis" of the Civil Rights Movement a qualitatively different, and more constructive conversation emerges. As both cultural expressions and "exemplary actions" of the Civil Rights Movement, gospel, freedom songs, rhythm & blues, and rock & roll can be perceived as simultaneously "knowledge-bearing," "identity-giving," and "self-revealing." As a result, civil rights music constitutes "symbolic representation[s]" of civil rights individuals and the civil rights collective which, taken together, expose us to many of the core concerns, political views, and social visions of the Civil Rights Movement. Furthermore, the representational nature of civil rights music in many senses "symbolizes all the movement stands for, what is seen as virtuous and what is seen as evil"—from the groundbreaking gospel of Mahalia Jackson and the polished "pop R&B" sound of Motown to the blistering genre-jumping iconic sonic social criticism of Nina Simone and raucous rock & roll of Little Richard.

As Eyerman and Jamison (1998) observed, "art and music—culture—are forms of both knowledge and action," they are "part of the frameworks of interpretation and representation produced within social movements and through which they influence the broader societal culture. As such, they are much more than functional devices for recruitment or resources to be mobilized" (23–24). In other words, even though it often appeared as though gospel, rhythm & blues, and rock & roll did not have a political agenda or viable social vision in the traditional social movement sense, because the Civil Rights Movement was actually the culmination of every black popular movement and every black popular culture that preceded it, many of its most significant cultural concerns, political views, and social visions were actually articulated through its cultural expressions and "exemplary actions," including its music, dance, theater, literature, art, film, fashion and forays into more mainstream cultural conversations, social movements, and political struggles between 1954 and 1965.[18]

However, even as we acknowledge the ways in which civil rights "art and music—[essentially, civil rights] culture—are forms of both knowledge and action" and "part of the frameworks of interpretation and representation produced within [the Civil Rights Movement] and through which [it] influence[d] the broader societal culture," it is important for us not to overlook the myriad instrumental uses of black popular music in both "old" and "new" African American social and political movements. Tempering their discussion of the extra-musical functions of music within the context of social movements, Eyerman and Jamison maintained, "[i]t is not our intention to deny that there are instrumental uses of music in social movements and elsewhere, but, to the extent that social movements are able to transcend these instrumental (and commercial) usages, music as exemplary action becomes possible" (24). When we make critical distinctions between commercial and communal civil rights music and the myriad other forms of civil rights music—especially gospel, freedom songs, rhythm & blues, and rock & roll—then the ways that civil rights music "transcend[s] . . . instrumental (and commercial) usages" and simultaneously serves instrumental, intellectual, spiritual, cultural, social, and political functions is even more evident.

Many aspects of civil rights culture—not merely civil rights music— remarkably reflects the political views and social visions of the Civil Rights Movement. But, along with Eyerman and Jamison, I believe that music is an especially powerful political and pedagogical tool in relationship to modern social movements in light of the fact that it is essentially inextricable from, and at the heart of what could be called "civil rights popular culture," and especially civil rights style, performance, opposition, leisure, consumption, representation, and, increasingly, liberation (both physical *and* psychological liberation). Continuing this line of logic, Eyerman and Jamison insightfully asserted:

> As cognitive praxis, music and other forms of cultural activity contribute to the ideas that movements offer and create in opposition to the existing social and cultural order. Perhaps more effectively than any other form of expression, music also recalls a meaning that lies outside and beyond the self. In that sense it can be utopian or pre-modern. In saying this we do not mean to imply that such truth-bearing is inherent in music, part of some transcendent and metaphysical fundament. Our argument is more modest in that we restrict our claim to music in relation to social movements. In social movements, even mass-produced popular music can take on a truth-bearing significance. (24)

As will be witnessed when we reinterpret gospel, freedom songs, rhythm & blues, and rock & roll as "cognitive praxes" and "exemplary actions" emerging from within the cultural context of the Civil Rights Movement, the myriad genres of civil rights music consistently conveyed the collective "ideas that [the Civil Rights Movement] offer[ed] and create[d] in opposition to the existing social and cultural order" which, sad to say, continues to ideologically enslave, racially colonize, and economically exploit African America close to two decades into the twenty-first century. If nothing else, then, *Civil Rights Music* will discursively demonstrate how "even mass-produced [and mass-consumed] [black] popular music can take on a truth-bearing significance" and serve instrumental, intellectual, spiritual, cultural, social, and political functions within the context of arguably the most-noted black popular movement of all-time: the Civil Rights Movement. Moreover, this study will also take great pains to point out the ways past black popular movements' relationships with past black popular musics were handed down to the Civil Rights Movement and essentially provided it with a paradigm with which to incessantly invent and evolve its relationship with not simply civil rights music, but also other forms of civil rights popular culture.

African American movements historically have been and unrepentantly remain much more complicated and complex than most historians, sociologists, political scientists, and economists of social movements have been willing to concede. All of this is to say that when I write of "civil rights music" in the pages to follow, I am invoking a key cultural and aesthetic aspect of a momentous and multidimensional movement that is much like the turn of the twentieth century African American movements (e.g., the Black Women's Club Movement, New Negro Movement, and Harlem Renaissance) which, whether acknowledged or not, provided the Civil Rights Movement with not merely its aesthetics, but with the firm foundations upon which it built its pioneering desegregationist and integrationist history, culture, politics, and social justice agenda. Moreover, here by summoning "civil rights music" I wish to move the conversation concerning the Civil Rights Movement forward, above and beyond critiques—constructive or otherwise—about movement moderatism, conservatism, bourgeoisism and integrationism. Quite the contrary, *Civil Rights Music* seeks to turn our attention anew toward the ways in which one-dimensional discussions that crudely collapse the whole of the Civil Rights Movement into desegregationist and integrationist, non-violent and civil disobedient politics, erase or, at the very least, render invisible not only the Civil Rights Movement's unique aesthetics, culture, and popular culture (e.g., music, visual art, dance, theater, literature, film, and fashion, etc.), but also the myriad ways in which it articulated its ideals and ethos via an incredibly creative combination of both politics *and* aesthetics.

Perhaps, nothing exemplifies the Civil Rights Movement's expression of its ideals and ethos via an incredibly creative combination of both politics *and* aesthetics, both social movement *and* popular music, better than the sacred soundtracks of the movement: gospel music and freedom songs. Let us, therefore, turn our attention to the sacred soundtracks of the Civil Rights Movement and explore two often-muted and much-misunderstood mouthpieces of the movement. In the spirit of W. E. B. Du Bois, let us look at, and attentively listen to the 1950s and 1960s "sorrow songs" —*songs of heavenly salvation and earthly liberation. Songs of sorrow. Songs of hope. Songs of freedom.* Indeed, *freedom songs.*

NOTES

1. For further discussion of the ways in which the Civil Rights Movement deconstructed and reconstructed American democracy, citizenship, and education, and for the most noteworthy works that influenced my interpretation here, see Burns (1990), Butler (2016), Crosby (2011), Dudziak (2011), Francis (2014), Hale (2016), Hogan (2007),

Mantler (2013), Polsgrove (2001), Salmond (1997), Sitkoff (2008), Sullivan (2009), Thuesen (2013), and Tsesis (2008).

2. For examples of noteworthy works on the Civil Rights Movement's politics, economics, and social justice agenda, see K. T. Andrews (2004), Ashmore (2008), Chong (1991), Clayson (2010), Ezra (2013), Hall (2005), Katagiri (2014), Lawson (2014), Le Blanc and Yates (2013), Luders (2010), Mann (2007), and G. Wright (2013).

3. For examples of noteworthy works that engage the ways in which the Civil Rights Movement helped to revitalize mid-twentieth century American culture in general, and regional and local cultures in particular, see K. T. Andrews (2004), Ashmore (2008), Boyett (2015), Brown-Nagin (2011), Chappell (1994), Clayson (2010), Crosby (2011), de Jong (2002), Dittmer (1994), Eskew (1997), Estes (2015), Fairclough (2008), Friedland (1998), Gonda (2015), Greene (2005), Hale (2016), Katagiri (2014), Lefever (2005), Levy (2003), Little (2009), Lovett (2005), Marshall (2013), Moore and Burton (2008), Norrell (1998), Pfaff (2011), Ralph (1993), Rogers (1993), C. F. Smith (2008), Sokol (2006), Thuesen (2013), and Wallenstein (2008).

4. For further discussion of the distinct histories and cultures of African American social and political movements, and for the most noteworthy works that informed my analysis here, see D. W. Aldridge (2011), V. P. Franklin (1984), Giddings (1984), Gore, Theoharis and Woodard (2009), V. Harding (1981), Hine and Thompson (1998), Kelley and Lewis (2000), Kendi (2012), Marable and Mullings (2000), Payne and Green (2003), C. J. Robinson (1997), Singh (2004), Theoharis and Woodard (2005), Walters (1993), and Y.R. Williams (2015).

5. For further discussion of Antonio Gramsci's life and legacy, especially his intriguing conception of the "organic intellectual," and for the works which influenced my interpretation here, see Adamson (1980), Boggs (1976), Fiori (1990), Germino (1990), Gramsci (1977, 1978, 1985, 1995, 2000), Hoare and Sperber (2015), Holub (1992), S. J. Jones (2006), McNally (2015), and Rosengarten (2014).

6. My interpretation of the new social movement model has been influenced by Goodwin and Jasper (2003), Laraña, Johnston and Gusfield (1994), S. S. Lee (2014), Mullings (2009), Morris and Mueller (1992), Porta and Diani (2006), A. Scott (1990), and Snow, Soule and Kriesi (2004).

7. For further discussion of the Civil Rights Movement's unique utilization of radio, television, print media, grassroots political organizing, and more traditional forms of social activism in its efforts to establish and express its "movement ideology," and for the works which influenced my interpretation here, see Bodroghkyozy (2013), Classen (2004), Cripps (1977, 1993), Davies (2001), Delmont (2012), Savage (1999), Sturkey and Hale (2015), Torres (2003), and B. Ward (2001, 2004).

8. For examples of the scholarship that influenced my interpretation of the defining characteristics of new social movements, see Dalton and Kuechler (1990), Goodwin and Jasper (2003), Haynes (1997), C. A. Kelly (2001), Laraña, Johnston and Gusfield (1994), S. H. Lee (2007), McAdams, McCarthy and Zald (1996), Meyer and Tarrow (1998), Petras (2003), Snow, Soule and Kriesi (2004), and Sutton (2000).

9. For further discussion of the ways in which American apartheid assaulted *all* African Americans, as well as their kith and kin from other countries, whether they were moderates, militants, or "silent members" of the Civil Rights Movement or not, see Bartley (1969), Berger (2010), Bloom (1987), Chappell (1994), Colley (2013), Egerton (1994), Eskew (1997), Holsaert, Noonan and Richardson (2010), Houck and Dixon (2009), Lavelle (2014), Lefever (2005), Leidholdt (1997), G. Lewis (2006), Lovett (2005), McMillen (1971), Moore and Burton (2008), Ownby (2008), Rogers (1993), C. F. Smith (2008), and Webb (2005).

10. For further discussion of the Civil Rights Movement's regressive, if not outright reactionary, elements, and for the works which influenced my interpretation here, see Boyd (2012), Draper (1994), Dupont (2013), Ellis (2013), Isserman and Kazin (2015), Lawson (2014), Ownby (2002), C. Taylor (2011), J. M. Ward (2011), and J. E. Williams (2003).

11. My emphasis on the Civil Rights Movement in the American social imagination and American cultural memory has been influenced by a number of noteworthy works, including Armstrong (2015), Dwyer and Alderman (2008), Eagles (1986), Fosl and K'Meyer (2009), Lavelle (2014), Lyon (1992), Mendel-Reyes (1995), Rogers (1993), Romano and Raiford (2006), and Valk and Brown (2010).

12. For further discussion of the "movement cultures" within the wider Civil Rights Movement, and for the works which influenced my interpretation here, see Countryman (2006), Crosby (2011), Dittmer (1994), Eskew (1997), Gellman (2012), S. Hall (2005), S. S. Lee (2014), Moore and Burton (2008), Morgan and Davies (2012), Pfaff (2011), Sokol (2006), Street (2007), and Theoharis and Woodard (2005).

13. With regard to the cultural histories of the Civil Rights Movement that I have in mind, and that have influenced my interpretation here, see Chappell (1994), J. E. Davis (2001), Dierenfield (2008), Dittmer (1994), Eagles (1986), Egerton (1994), L. E. Hill (2004), Levy (1992, 2015), Lucks (2014), Norrell (1998), Polsgrove (2001), Robnett (1997), Sullivan (2009), and Weisbrot (1990).

14. My critical exploration of the origins and early evolution of the Civil Rights Movement as far back as World War II and its immediate aftermath (circa 1939 to 1954) has been indelibly influenced by C. Anderson (2003), Berrey (2015), Brown-Nagin (2011), Cashman (1991), Estes (2005), Ferguson (2002), Griffin (2013), Hamlin (2012), Jones-Branch (2014), Kruse and Tuck (2012), Kryder (2000), Rosenberg (2006), Savage (1999), Scott and Womack (1998), C. Taylor (2011), Wall (2008), and R. P. Young (1970).

15. For more detailed discussion of the Africana tradition of critical theory or, rather, Africana critical theory, see Rabaka (2009, 2010a, 2010b, 2014, 2015).

16. Along with Africana studies and more general critical social scientific research methods, Africana critical theory has also been deeply influenced by the monumental meta-methodological studies by Bonilla-Silva and Zuberi (2008), Chilisa (2012), Denzin, Lincoln and Smith (2008), Gunaratnam (2003), Kovach (2009), Mertens, Cram and Chilisa (2013), Sandoval (2000), L. T. Smith (1999), and S. Wilson (2008), each of which seeks to decolonize research methods and emphasize their importance for the development of critical theories of white supremacist patriarchal colonial capitalist societies. The influence of these works on Africana critical theory's methodological orientation cannot be overstated.

17. For further discussion of Fanon's conception of *l'expérience vécue du noir* ("the lived-experience of the black"), see Fanon (2001, 2008) and my more detailed discussion in *Forms of Fanonism* (Rabaka 2010b, 49–95).

18. For further discussion of the political nature of popular art, popular music, and popular culture more generally, and for the most noteworthy works that informed my interpretation here, see Brundage (2011), G. Burns (2016), Combs (1984), Garoian and Gaudelius (2008), Gray (2005), Horsfall, Meij and Probstfield (2013), Jenkins, McPherson and Shattuc (2002), Peddie (2006), Randall (2005), Rosenthal and Flacks (2015), Savage and Nimmo (1990), Street (1986, 1997, 2012), Tasker and Negra (2007), Wagnleitner and May (2000), and J. A. Walker (2001).

THREE

Gospel and the Civil Rights Movement

SONGS OF HEAVENLY SALVATION AND EARTHLY LIBERATION:
INTRODUCTION TO GOSPEL MUSIC, FREEDOM SONGS, AND
THEIR ROLE IN THE CIVIL RIGHTS MOVEMENT

W.E.B. Du Bois climatically closed *The Souls of Black Folk* (1903), a work widely considered a classic treatise on the African American experience, with a chapter on black music and its extraordinary ability to capture and convey black life, black love, black labor, and the black liberation struggle. In the chapter entitled "The Sorrow Songs," Du Bois declared that African American religious music most often reflects the pulse of black people, their culture and quest for freedom, as well as their aspirations and frustrations. Simultaneously looking backward to the spirituals of the enslaved ancestors and seemingly looking forward to the gospel music of the Civil Rights Movement soldiers, Du Bois prophetically intoned: "They that walked in darkness sang songs in the olden days—Sorrow Songs—for they were weary at heart" (250). Although not typically thought of in political terms or as a movement leader, at the height of the Montgomery Bus Boycott Mahalia Jackson was asked by Martin Luther King if she would sing to help the fledgling Montgomery Improvement Association raise much-needed funds. Jackson enthusiastically agreed. When King queried about her honorarium she is reported to have solemnly said: "I don't charge the walking people" (cited in Goreau 1975, 219).

Fifty years after Du Bois wrote of the "Sorrow Songs" and "[t]hey that walked in darkness [who] sang [those] songs in the olden days," Mahalia Jackson, by the 1950s acknowledged as the "World's Greatest Gospel Singer" (a sobriquet bestowed on her by her Columbia Records production and marketing team), refused to charge "[t]hey that [continued to] walk[…] in darkness" and sing sacred black songs—*songs of heavenly salvation and earthly liberation*. Just as African American gospel music (hereafter referred to simply as gospel music or, even more plainly, gospel) is emblematic of the evolution of the "Sorrow Songs" (what we now call "the spirituals"), the mass meetings, prayer vigils, boycotts, marches, sit-ins, freedom rides, voter registration drives, and other protest activities of the Civil Rights Movement symbolize the evolution of the political strategies and tactics of "[t]hey that walked in darkness [and] sang songs in the olden days." Gospel adapted and updated Du Bois's "Sorrow Songs," *black sacred song*, and in many ways gave voice to, not simply the development of *the African American sacred song tradition*, but also mid-twentieth century issues of African American migration, urbanization, determined desegregation, and intense emphasis on integration.[1]

This chapter argues that gospel is the major sacred soundtrack of the Civil Rights Movement in much the same way that rhythm & blues and rock & roll represent the major secular soundtracks of the Civil Rights Movement. Instead of quarantining, or *sonically segregating* the most popular expression of black sacred song from the most popular expressions of black secular song during the Civil Rights Movement, in what follows I utilize the elastic gospel aesthetic of the golden age to bring disparate elements together and discursively develop a fresh interpretation of golden age gospel that places its musical *and* extra-musical contributions on equal footing with the other major musics encapsulating the ethos of the Civil Rights Movement, specifically rhythm & blues and rock & roll. Whether we turn to freedom songs, rhythm & blues, or rock & roll, during its golden age gospel served as a kind of musical midwife, helping to birth, and then rear and raise the secular soundtracks of the Civil Rights Movement.

Between 1945 and 1965, which is to say, from the prelude to the postlude of the Civil Rights Movement, sometimes implicitly, and at other times explicitly, African American gospel music invariably focused on *freedom*. Moreover, like the spirituals sung by the enslaved ancestors, gospel most often unequivocally commented on *heavenly salvation* and only very vaguely discussed *earthly liberation*. Nevertheless, it would be a grave mistake to interpret the gospel music of the Civil Rights Movement years as politically uninvolved, escapist, and insouciant. As Anthony Heilbut observed in *The Gospel Sound: Good News and Bad Times* (1997), the first book-length study of African American gospel, "[g]ospel reflects the conditions and consciousness of its audience, no more, no less" (298). It stands to reason, then, that during one of the most tumultuous periods in post-enslavement African American history, culture, and struggle, black sacred song reflected African American's incessant emphasis on, and synthesis of heavenly salvation *and* earthly liberation.[2]

In "Sit-In, Stand Up, and Sing Out!: Black Gospel Music and the Civil Rights Movement" (2013), Michael Castellini importantly shared that gospel music was one of *the key socio-political and religio-cultural tools* utilized by the leaders and foot soldiers of the Civil Rights Movement to "attract the masses," raise consciousness, enliven elder activism, incite youth activism, "invigorate meetings," promote prayer vigils, and "instill confidence" (1). As a matter of fact, the "freedom songs" so fondly adapted and sung by the young folk of the Civil Rights Movement were almost without exception "based on familiar spirituals and gospel songs," and almost unfailingly sung in the gospel idiom (1). For instance, in *Protest & Praise: The Sacred Music of Black Religion* (1990), reputed black sacred musicologist Jon Michael Spencer revealed that freedom songs can be "divide[d] into two categories":

> (1) *group participation songs*, often extemporaneously adapted from existing material by a group involved in civil rights activities, and (2) professionally composed *topical songs*, which comment on protest events from the sideline. Many freedom songs were adaptations from traditional spiritual and gospel songs. Typically these forms, especially gospel songs, were brought down to the mundane by textual modifications. For example, "If You Miss Me from Praying Down Here" was changed to "If You Miss Me from the Back of the Bus," "This Little Light of Mine" to "This Little Light of Freedom," "Woke Up This Morning with My Mind on Jesus" to "Woke Up This Morning with My Mind on Freedom," "When I'm in Trouble, Lord, Walk with Me" to "Down in the Jailhouse, Lord, Walk with Me," and "If You Want to Get to Heaven, Do What Jesus Says" to "If You Want to Get Your Freedom, Register and Vote." (83, all emphasis in original)[3]

Most often the singing of a particular song during a mass meeting, prayer vigil, boycott, march, sit-in, or freedom ride, as well as in paddy wagons and prisons, typically lasted for an extended period of time. This meant that weary movement members needed to compose new, more immediate, relevant and reinvigorating verses, but not necessarily for artistic variance. *Freedom singer-songwriters* practiced a kind of intensified lyrical adaptation in order to intimately and urgently express the complexity of African Americans' critiques of, and resistance to ongoing American apartheid and anti-black racist economic exploitation. In many instances, an individual *freedom singer-songwriter* composed the new "freedom-focused" verses. At other times the new verses spontaneously evolved out of a group experience or collective struggle, or were offered up impromptu at a mass meeting, march, or sit-in by a song leader inspired by a particularly affecting testimony or event.

Singing, whether gospel or freedom songs, was not simply a key source of faith and courage during the Civil Rights Movement, but also a means of critically responding to harrowing events and "talking back" to the established order of American apartheid. Additionally, singing—

again, whether gospel or freedom songs—can be interpreted as *an act of rebellious self-assertion and self-determination* because it was usually prohibited in city jails and prisons, and otherwise sufficiently called attention to boycotts, marches, or protests, which undoubtedly disrupted the lily-white lies and "business as usual" attitudes and local environments of the Southern segregationists and their Northern liberal racist, however covert, counterparts. For example, in *SNCC: The New Abolitionists* (1965), Howard Zinn reported that while in Parchman Penitentiary as a consequence of his non-violent civil disobedience, Stokely Carmichael poignantly shared that his mattress was violently taken from his prison cell because he was singing. Zinn famously cited Carmichael as saying:

> I'll never forget this Sheriff Tyson—he used to wear those big boots. He'd say, "You goddam smart nigger, why you always trying to be so uppity for? I'm going to see to it that you don't ever get out of this place." They decided to take our mattresses because we were singing....So they dragged Hank Thomas out and he hung on to his mattress and they took him and it and dropped him with a loud clunk on his back....And then they put wristbreakers on Freddy Leonard, which makes you twist around and around in a snake-like motion, and Tyson said, "Oh, you want to hit me, don't you?," and Freddy just looked up at him meekly and said, "No, I just want you to break my arm." And Sheriff Tyson was visibly shaken, and told the trusty, "Put him back." I hung on to the mattress and said, "I think we have a right to them and I think you're unjust," and he said, "I don't want to hear all that shit nigger," and started to put on the wristbreakers. I wouldn't move and I started to sing "I'm Gonna Tell God How You Treat Me," and everybody started to sing it and by this time Tyson was really to pieces. He called to the trusties, "Get him in there!" and he went out the door and slammed it, and left everybody else with their mattresses.... (57)[4]

It would seem that Carmichael intimately understood that African American music, in this instance gospel and freedom songs, was an indispensable survival tool for the non-violent soldiers of the Civil Rights Movement. It should also be noted that even in the face of anti-black racist police brutality it was the solemn singing of gospel and freedom songs that, at least in part, gave Carmichael the courage to confront his oppressors and, even if only momentarily, transcend an incredibly odious and traumatic situation. In essence, by somberly singing "I'm Gonna Tell God How You Treat Me" within earshot of Sheriff Tyson and the other jailers, Carmichael was boldly bearing witness before God and the other jailed civil rights soldiers and testifying about his mistreatment and the jailers' malfeasance.

Part of what makes singing so central to the Civil Rights Movement is the fact that it subtly politicizes and ingeniously expands the realm of possibilities of *the black church tradition of call-and-response* and places it in unjust secular settings. The freedom singer is *the caller*, and God and the

people within earshot—whether desegregationists or segregationists—
are *the responders*. For instance, observe in Carmichael's comments above,
both the desegregationists *and* the segregationists had visceral and palpable responses to Carmichael singing "I'm Gonna Tell God How You Treat
Me" while he was being brutalized: the desegregationists chimed in and
began to defiantly sing along with Carmichael (he said, "everybody
started to sing it"), and the segregationists, even if only temporarily,
stopped brutalizing the civil rights soldiers (in fact, Carmichael shared,
"by this time Tyson was really to pieces. He called to the trusties, 'Get
him in there!' and he went out the door and slammed it, and left everybody else with their mattresses...").

Music, something immaterial or incorporeal, in certain situations can
actually move or alter the material or, rather, the physical and, as a result,
offers oppressed groups an important medium through which they can
express their grievances and agonizing endurances. The episode that Carmichael shared above is but one example of hundreds arising out of the
Civil Rights Movement where song was utilized to critique and combat
unjust treatment, inhospitable conditions, and unethical individuals and
inspire courage, raise-consciousness, and keep committed to the cause of
freedom. Even though Carmichael would eventually come to disagree
with Martin Luther King on many matters concerning the black freedom
struggle, both leaders agreed that music was the "soul of the movement."
Long before Carmichael came onto the national civil rights scene, indeed,
beginning with the Montgomery Bus Boycott, King emphasized the centrality of black song, especially freedom songs, within the civil rights
struggle. Consequently, by the time he published his classic *Why We
Can't Wait* (1964), King enthusiastically concluded:

> An important part of the mass meetings was the freedom songs. In a
> sense the freedom songs are the soul of the movement. They are more
> than just incantations of clever phrases designed to invigorate a cam-
> paign; they are as old as the history of the Negro in America. They are
> adaptations of the songs the slaves sang—the sorrow songs, the shouts
> for joy, the battle hymns and the anthems of our movement. I have
> heard people talk of their beat and rhythm, but we in the movement
> are as inspired by their words. "Woke Up This Morning with My Mind
> Stayed on Freedom" is a sentence that needs no music to make its
> point. We sing freedom songs today for the same reason the slaves
> sang them, because we too are in bondage and the songs add hope to
> our determination that "We shall overcome, black and white together,
> We shall overcome someday."
>
> I have stood in a meeting with hundreds of youngsters and joined
> in while they sang "Ain't Gonna Let Nobody Turn Me 'Round." It is
> not just a song; it is a resolve. A few minutes later, I have seen those
> same youngsters refuse to turn around from the onrush of a police dog,
> refuse to turn around before a pugnacious Bull Connor in command of

men armed with power hoses. These songs bind us together, give us
courage together, help us to march together. (61)

Acknowledging that the freedom songs were an important part of the
musical lineage of the spirituals, King candidly observed that the civil
rights soldiers sang freedom songs "for the same reason the slaves sang"
the spirituals, because "we too are in bondage and the songs add hope to
our determination." King was keen to note how the freedom songs inspired hope and determination, and with that in mind I would like to
strongly stress that *the freedom songs were religious because they were unambiguously based on the music arising out of African American religion (and
spirituality), and the African American church in specific*. Of course, the freedom songs were not necessarily or directly about God or *heavenly salvation*, but almost invariably about social justice, political struggles, and
earthly liberation. Yet and still, even though the freedom songs were not
necessarily or directly about God or *heavenly salvation*, they were solemnly sung with the understanding that God is *omnipotent, omnipresent, omni-
scient* and, mostly significantly for the freedom singer-songwriters, *ever-
listening* and *ever-hearing*. Here we have come back to a point I emphasized above: The freedom singer is *the caller*, and God and the people
within earshot—whether desegregationists or segregationists—are *the responders*.

When freedom singer-songwriters peppered their songs with the cry
and crisis-interjection "Oh, Lord," they were essentially pausing to say,
"Do you hear me, Lord?" or "Are you listening, God?" In appealing to
the Lord to listen, the singers were imploring God to intervene in human
history in much the same manner as was previously done for African
Americans' enslaved ancestors who sang the spirituals. Typically in the
freedom songs there were more references to God than to Jesus Christ (in
fact, the two were rarely mentioned together), which would go far to
explain the universal (not always and everywhere Christian) character of
the freedom songs, as well as Joseph Washington's (1964) assertion that
the freedom songs of the Civil Rights Movement were more or less
"sources of spirited support" rather than simply "songs of faith" (207).
However, here it is important to observe that it is apparent that when
compared with those movement members who did not sing, those who
did sing had faith, hope, courage, and determination in the face of seemingly the most insurmountable obstacles.

Culturally validated via their miraculous preservation in, and dissemination through the African American oral tradition and African
American sacred song tradition, the freedom songs were the culmination
and, in a sense, the secularization of the evolution and ongoing synthesis
of the spirituals and gospel in the interest of social commentary, political
critique, cultural consciousness-raising, and spiritual enlightenment (e.g.,
illumination, kenosis, metanoia, revelation, and conversion). This means,

then, that freedom songs indeed did carry over some of the religiosity of the spirituals and gospel, but the spirituality and sacred subtext of the freedom songs was not necessarily Christian or *Christocentric*, but more *theocentric*—meaning, more or less, God-focused or God-centered. Hence, the freedom songs helped to provide the freedom singer-songwriters and the movement community as a whole—including the Buddhists, Muslims, Jews, Catholics, and religious others actively involved in the movement—with a system of core beliefs that verified and testified to the prudence and providence of God regardless of religious affiliation or denomination.

Therefore, freedom songs were a central source of affirming God, and the singing of freedom songs, not only *an act of rebellious self-assertion and self-determination*, but also *an act of radical religious faith*, which is one of the reasons that none other than Martin Luther King openly applauded and actively participated in the singing of freedom songs. Consequently, the resulting reciprocation of *song reinvigorating protest* and *protest reinvigorating song* generated a dynamic and deep reservoir of courage and an awesome energy and ethos that obviously enabled fatigued civil rights soldiers, young and old, Jew and Gentile, to continue fighting for freedom. Above all else, it should be observed that both Carmichael and King give us a sense of the centrality of freedom songs in the Civil Rights Movement, and both seem to suggest that these songs instilled faith, hope, courage, and determination in the singers of the songs.

Here, however, it is important to emphasize that not all spirituals or gospel songs necessitated lyrical adaptation in order for them to qualify as freedom songs and be meaningful within the context of the Civil Rights Movement. This, of course, demonstrates the ways in which the spirituals, the first major music of the African American sacred song tradition, continued to evolve and speak to the special issues and ills of black life long after the Emancipation Proclamation and Juneteenth. Spencer (1990) insightfully explained:

> Not all existing church songs required textual revisions to meet the protester's needs. For instance, the spiritual "Wade in the Water" was sometimes sung in wade-in demonstrations aimed at integrating public swimming pools and beaches. Spirituals like "Over My Head I See Freedom in the Air," "Free At Last," "Oh, Freedom," and "I Been 'Buked and I Been Scorned" were interpreted with obvious liberative meaning without modification. These songs, which had equipped black people with a system of "folk wisdom," were reaffirmed in the sermons at mass meetings....The original meaning of old spirituals was applicable in the new context. The ancestral messages of justice and liberation were related to the present pursuit of civil rights. (85)

Now that we have a deeper understanding that *the freedom songs were religious because they were unambiguously based on the music arising out of*

African American religion (and spirituality), and the African American church in specific, we can comprehend that, whether lyrically adapted or not, three key points should be emphasized about the freedom songs. First, as Martin Luther King never wearied of reminding both civil rights soldiers and staunch segregationists, non-violence, passive resistance, civil disobedience, and moral suasion are all essentially Christian ethics that were articulated and practiced by Jesus himself. In this sense, then, solemnly singing a freedom song instead of physically fighting back was emblematic of an ardent embrace of Christian ethics and the moral holiness and healing that Christ continued to inspire even as civil rights soldiers faced unimaginable hardships and heinous acts.

Second, it is important to bear in mind that most of the freedom songs that were not explicitly religious nevertheless were focused on freedom and discursively developed *the theme of freedom*, which is a longstanding sacred leitmotif in African American history, culture, and struggle. To state the obvious, the ultimate concern and goal of the Civil Rights Movement was "freedom," which is one of the reasons that freedom songs attracted both the religious *and* the irreligious, both the godly *and* the ungodly. The one thing that the religious and the irreligious involved in the Civil Rights Movement could agree on was the need for "freedom," on the need for the eradication of racial segregation and the inauguration of authentic black liberation (both physical *and* psychological liberation).

Lastly, one of the main reasons the Civil Rights Movement was so successful in enlisting the black masses to the blood-stained battlefields of Montgomery, Little Rock, Albany, Birmingham, St. Augustine, and Selma, among others sites of serious struggle, had much to do with the fact that it did not attempt to reinvent the wheel and, therefore, built itself upon the most influential institution in African American life, culture, and struggle: *the African American church*. In *"Somebody's Calling My Name": Black Sacred Music and Social Change* (1979), respected civil rights leader Wyatt Walker spoke directly to this point:

> The entire non-violent movement was religious in tone, and the music did much to reflect and reinforce the religious base on which it stood. In the course of its development, the movement drew into its wake many people who were non-religious, irreligious, and anti-religious, but singing freedom songs for them and for others of diverse persuasions was a means of comfortable participation. It was this development which contributed most to minimizing the distinction between the sacred and the secular within the black music tradition. The evolution of freedom songs and the impact of rhythm & blues prepared most of the ground [out of which] modern gospel grew. (181)

Continuing to drive home the key point that the African American church embodies both sacred and secular interests, that it is fundamentally preoccupied with—to reiterate—heavenly salvation *and* earth liberation, and that the "non-religious, irreligious, and anti-religious" were attracted to aspects of African American church culture, especially black church music, in ways that enabled civil rights leaders and civil rights soldiers to *mobilize via music*, Walker went on to insightfully conclude:

> All of this review only serves to illustrate again the relationship between music and crisis in the black community. Since the chief repository of authentic black religious music remains in the church, and the church collectively attracts the largest segment of the black community, it follows, then, that the music of the black religious tradition can be a vital instrument for a ministry of social change. The black church has the troops and the inspiring music. The music of the black religious tradition operates on two levels: first, psychologically and emotionally—it locates the people's sense of heritage, their roots, where they are and where they want to go; and secondly, it mobilizes and strengthens the resolve for struggle. A people's sense of destiny is rooted in their sense of history. Black sacred music is the primary reservoir of black people's historical context and an important factor in the process of social change. (181)

This means, then, that the freedom songs, much like the spirituals and gospel, captured and conveyed the liberative or, rather, emancipatory aspects of God and black theology. In essence, they embody and express *a revolutionary liturgy of black sacred song*, which opened the door for religion to almost seamlessly move out of the churches of the black Protestant orthodoxy onto the highways and byways, as well as the country roads and ghetto streets, of black history, culture, and struggle. Religiously, it is on the country roads of the rural South and trash-filled ghetto streets of the urban North that the *Afro-Christian ethics* at the heart of the freedom songs could inspire civil rights soldiers to critique and confront the pharisaic system of white supremacy, racial segregation, and economic exploitation. Musically, the freedom songs were the epitome of Civil Rights Movement militancy with their remarkable mix of the sacred and the secular, as well as their committed quest for both heavenly salvation *and* earthly liberation. With these unique partly sacred and partly secular songs, African Americans were not simply singing about freedom but, more importantly, these songs were symbolic of black folk systematically fighting (via non-violence, passive resistance, and civil disobedience) for freedom.

Although often overlooked by professional historians, freedom songs serve as historical documents that chronicle myriad movement events, including the various forms of protest and communal responses to injustice, as well as individual reflections and testimonials. As a result, freedom singer-songwriters were simultaneously history-makers *and* historians—indeed, they were *participant historians*: simultaneously historical actors *and* chroniclers at the heart of the great drama of mid-twentieth century American life, culture, politics, and society. For example, a song

such as Sam Block's "Freedom Is A Constant Dying" should not be merely interpreted as an expression or testimony of faith. It was so much
more. As a matter of fact, "Freedom Is A Constant Dying" clearly indi-
cates that it was composed by a freedom singer-songwriter who had:
marched under the sweltering heat of the Southern sun; firsthand faced
segregationist police brutality and the unforgiving fangs of their attack
dogs; fallen unconscious as a result of the toxins of tear gas and the
pungent spray of high-pressure fire hoses; felt the cringing crack of the
horse whip and the brutality of the billy club against flesh, skull, and
bone; and suffered utterly unjust and deliberately dehumanizing imprisonment.[5] Indeed, at their best, freedom songs double as testimony, as
well as the essence of *participant history* and *documentary history*. By studying these songs in relationship to golden age gospel songs, including the
religiosity (and spirituality) inherent in both, we can follow the chronolo-
gy of the emerging history and theology of the Civil Rights Movement,
and humbly bear witness to the simplicity and solitude, the breathtaking-
ly beautiful private moments of prayer, praise, and protest in the Civil
Rights Movement.

Needless to say, a serious study of the Civil Rights Movement is contingent upon devoting ample critical attention to its gospel and freedom
songs, much like a critical engagement of African American enslavement
is incomplete without an in-depth exploration of the myriad meanings of
the spirituals. Nevertheless, much like the spirituals were once dismissed
and diminished in the history of African American enslavement, gospel
and freedom songs have been routinely isolated and disassociated from
the main currents of Civil Rights Movement history, culture, and politics
when, in fact, they were central to, and at the core of Civil Rights Movement history, culture, and politics. I strongly believe that as twenty-first
century scholars revisit the spirituals for their insight into the African
American experience during the antebellum era, a similar practice needs
to be put into play with respect to the prescient gospel and freedom
songs that served as the soundtracks of the Civil Rights Movement.

When we intentionally transgress the boundaries between either an
exclusively historical or exclusively musicological interpretation of the
Civil Rights Movement and combine both perspectives in our analysis,
then we can come to comprehend that at the height of the movement
(circa 1960 through 1965 — roughly running from the inception of the sit-
ins through to the Selma to Montgomery marches) gospel and freedom
songs embodied one of the major modes of expression and means of
interpretation of the Civil Rights Movement, and that key historical moments and political events of the movement are documented in the music
emerging out of the movement in ways they quite simply are not elsewhere in any other Civil Rights Movement artifacts or memorabilia. Obviously, then, the music of the African American church served as a
sounding board and primary point of departure during the Civil Rights

Movement years, enabling movement elders and youth organizers to create a transgenerational dialogue devoted to self *and* social change. During the movement years, the young and the old, the rich and the poor, black folk in the North and in the South were collectively entrenched in African American church culture, and one of the most obvious indicators of the modernization and urbanization of the black church by the middle decades of the twentieth century was the new soundtrack of church life and culture: *gospel music*.

THE GOLDEN AGE OF GOSPEL MUSIC: A SONIC SYMBOL OF TRADITION, INNOVATION, AND THE STRENGTH TO CONTINUE THE STRUGGLE

It was not the music of the enslaved ancestors, and it was not the music of the turn of the twentieth century Fisk Jubilee Singers. African American gospel music brought the past into dialogue with the present. It was a mixture of the old and the new. It sonically symbolized both tradition *and* innovation, as well as the fact that black folk were someway, somehow, almost miraculously summoning *the strength to continue the struggle* begun by the enslaved ancestors—as Du Bois aptly observed above, "[t]hey that walked in darkness [who] sang songs in the olden days—Sorrow Songs—for they were weary at heart." In his classic *The Power of Black Music: Interpreting Its History from Africa to the United States* (1995), eminent African American musicologist Samuel Floyd observed that during the "Golden Age of Gospel" (circa 1945 to 1965), "gospel music was involved in cross-fertilizations that embraced the music of the core-culture church, the entertainment arena, and the fight for social and political equality" (200–201). By the end of the Golden Age of Gospel, the music was so popular that "[g]ospel choirs were organized in colleges and universities across the land, and longtime gospel stars began to receive wider exposure. The musical styles of these artists, while reflecting the affirmations of the new age," Floyd went further, "were also continuous with the tradition" (196).[6]

Similar to other genres of black popular music during their peak periods, the Golden Age of Gospel was predicated on innovation and experimentation. Seeming to mirror African American integration into mainstream America, by the 1960s gospel artists "began to perform in theaters, auditoriums, and stadiums, bringing new sounds from the core culture into the cultural arenas of mainstream America." If, indeed, the spirituals are considered the foundational black musical form from which all others sprang, not merely gospel, then, golden age gospel's incorporation of blues, jazz, rhythm & blues, and rock & roll elements is tantamount to musical offspring influencing their musical parent. In other words, this is a natural and logical part of the evolution of black popular music, or any ongoing art form for that matter. As Floyd nimbly noted:

> [B]oth the sounds and the venues of 1960s gospel were wide-ranging. The instruments of R&B had become part of gospel's accompanying ensembles; church and community gospel choirs and choruses had begun to perform with symphony orchestras (although only on "special occasions"); performers had begun to feel comfortable on the concert stage and with the mass media; the material and stylistic borrowings from jazz and R&B were even more common in gospel than they had been before; and the down-home, gut-bucket fervor of earlier gospel had been overlaid and even replaced by the slick veneer of Motown-like productions. But the characteristic vocal sound of the gospel voice remained the same: the gospel delivery, with its typical embellishments and subtle rhythmic treatments, was retained and even enhanced, as were its yea-saying and call-and-response patterns and phrasings. In other words, the more refined contemporary black gospel music retained the characteristics of its predecessors, and its performance still depended on a performer-audience call-and-response rapport unlike that of any other musical experience. In addition, the role of the gospel singer as a caller, as a "leader of a service, not only the participant," continued, even in the crossover forms of the genre—the "message" songs that bridge the gap between gospel and soul, such as "Oh Happy Day" (1969) by the Edwin Hawkins Singers and "Respect Yourself" (1972) by the Staple Singers. Such message songs were the nucleus of the repertoire of contemporary gospel in the 1960s. (196–197; see also Boyer 1979, 8)

Expertly encapsulating the interplay of tradition and innovation within the gospel world of the 1960s, Floyd wrote of new "stylistic borrowings from jazz and R&B," but carefully noted that no matter how much the musical backing may have changed over the years the "characteristic vocal sound of the gospel voice remained the same." Call-and-response continued to be at the core of *the gospel aesthetic,* and the gospel singer, the modern black sacred song singer, continued to double as both a song leader *and* socio-cultural leader singing gospel songs that often doubled as "freedom songs" or "message songs," as was the case with many of the sorrow song singers during enslavement. Bearing this in mind, gospel music historian Robert Darden, in *Nothing But Love in God's Water: Black Sacred Music from the Civil War to the Civil Rights Movement* (2014), reminds us that "directed singing with an eye toward social and political transformation was a longstanding, almost ubiquitous by-product of African American religious institutions in the South" (103). In other words, African Americans singing sacred songs—which, as discussed above, includes freedom songs—"with an eye toward social and political transformation" was not new, but merely emblematic of "the next evolution in the history of the protest spiritual." Gospel music, then, was simply "a new permutation of the basic musical form," the "protest spiritu-al," essentially "the spiritual with a blues beat" (88).

From Darden's point of view, classic and golden age gospel were more or less *sacred blues* or, rather, what has been termed "gospel blues." In much the same manner that the blues often subtly comments on both the triumphs and tragedies of the African American experience, gospel (especially via its "freedom songs" subgenre) can be said to offer insights for both heavenly salvation *and* earthly liberation. According to Darden, golden age gospel music "combined religious lyrics, the biblically based storytelling of the spirituals, the close harmonies of jubilee, the rough-edged testifying voices of African American preachers, and the beat and improvisational musical and lyrical characteristics of the blues" (90). Here it is important to note that often when the blues influence on gospel music is acknowledged the term "the blues" is meant to denote not mere-ly the blues in the narrow sense of the word, but is most often employed as an umbrella term suggesting all of the blues-derived black popular musics that have successively influenced the gospel sound and the over-all gospel aesthetic (e.g., ragtime, jazz, boogie-woogie, jump blues, rhythm & blues, doo-wop, rock & roll, girl groups, soul, funk, disco, techno, house, and rap, etc.).

Undeniably, Du Bois's beloved black folk changed a great deal from their period of enslavement through to the Civil Rights Movement. How-ever, when we seriously consider the Fugitive Slave Act of 1850, the *Dred Scott v. Sandford* case of 1857, or the 1896 *Plessy v. Ferguson* Supreme Court decision, the society in which African Americans found themselves in from the turn of the twentieth century through to the Civil Rights Movement continued to be one predicated on American apartheid, racial segregation, racial violence (including the anti-black racist ritual of lynch-ing), and outright *anti-black racist terrorism*.[7] Obviously, all of this taken together is enough to sufficiently give any group of people the blues and make them place a high premium on the production of blues-derived music to serve as soundtracks for their life-worlds and life-struggles. When we couple history, sociology, political economy, and religious studies with musicology it is easy to see that each form of black popular music, whether sacred or secular, classical or contemporary, was created to capture and convey the ethos of the African American experience at the moment of creation, peak period, or revival of the music under scruti-ny.

In the first half of the twentieth century there were a number of geo-graphical and musical changes afoot in African America. For instance, the first "Great Migration" of African Americans from the South to the North and Midwest took place between 1910 and 1930, and culminated with the Black Women's Club Movement, New Negro Movement, Harlem Renais-sance, and Chicago Renaissance, respectively, and new city-centered blues and jazz.[8] A second "Great Migration" took place between 1940 and 1970, with African Americans not only moving from the South to the North and Midwest, but also to the West, and specifically California.[9] The soundtracks of the second "Great Migration" of African Americans include developments in the blues and jazz genres (e.g., the creation of jump blues and be-bop), as well as wholly new forms of black popular music such as rhythm & blues, rock & roll, soul, and funk. Since its emergence at the turn of the twentieth century, much like jazz, gospel has openly incorporated elements of other black popular musics into its aesthetic. As Mellonee Burnim (2015) noted: "The use of musical instruments, most of which previously had been associated with secular musics and denied entry into the worship of the mainline Baptist and Methodist congregations, was a compelling marker of this new form of religious music expression" (192).

However, in spite of all of the innovations and experimentations of the gospel tradition, as Floyd emphasized above, the "characteristic vocal sound of the gospel voice remained the same." Often described as "pushing the vocal register to the extreme," "hoarse," "raspy," "gruff," "gravelly," or "throaty," during the Golden Age of Gospel the *soundscape* changed much like the *landscape* changed for many African Americans, but the "characteristic vocal sound of the gospel voice" went unchanged. The irony is apparent. The more polished and pedestrian (i.e., "pop-sounding") the gospel productions became, the more gospel artists sought to contrast the sound of their voices with the softness, if not ultimately the blandness, of the musical accompaniment.

Gospel is about more than merely lyrics and musical accompaniment. Although, truth be told, lyrics and musical accompaniment are both an integral part of the overarching gospel aesthetic. At its core, to put it plainly, gospel is also about delivery, embellishment, non-verbal communication, the creation of a signature vocal sound (distinct vocalizations), and, above all else, *soul*. What does it say about gospel, if not the African American experience more generally speaking, that in the period between the issuing of the Emancipation Proclamation and the passage of the Civil Rights Act—a period roughly covering a century (circa 1863 through 1964)—the black sacred song tradition carried over and continued most of, if not *all*, of the major themes of the "Sorrow Songs" of enslavement? How truly "free" were African Americans in the century immediately following the Emancipation Proclamation (not to mention Juneteenth) if, indeed, countless song after song continued to express black pain and pathos, black suffering and social misery during the post-enslavement period? What does gospel, and golden age gospel in particular, tell us about African Americans' ongoing struggle for freedom and human dignity, even after the Emancipation Proclamation? Is it a coincidence that even after "emancipation," even in "freedom," the black sacred song tradition continues to sound, as I mentioned above, "hoarse," "raspy," "gruff," "gravelly," or "throaty"? Is it possible that golden age gospel artists were *non-verbally* saying with their artistry what they could not verbally say in any other way for fear of the anti-black racist reprisals that ultimately ignited the Civil Rights Movement? And, lastly and corollarily, is it also possible that golden age gospel artists' non-verbal communication deeply inspired non-violent civil rights soldiers—as we witnessed with the freedom singer-songwriters above—and was one of the key sources that gave them *the strength to continue the struggle*?

As can be easily ascertained from gospel artist autobiographies and biographies, whether we turn to Mahalia Jackson's *Movin' On Up* (1966) or Michael Harris's *The Rise of Gospel Blues: The Music of Thomas Andrew Dorsey in the Urban Church* (1992), or Nick Salvatore's *Singing in a Strange Land: C.L. Franklin, the Black Church, and the Transformation of America* (2006) or Greg Kot's *I'll Take You There: Mavis Staples, the Staple Singers, and the Music That Shaped the Civil Rights Era* (2014), golden age gospel artists faced a great deal of anti-black racism traveling along the "gospel highway." The same extra-musical, inconducive post-war social conditions that gave rise to new developments in blues and jazz, gave rise to new developments in gospel. In other words, it was not simply by historical happenstance that jump blues, be-bop, and "a music that began to challenge the Negro spiritual as the favored sacred music in the African American community"—that is to say, *gospel music*—simultaneously emerged.

As the acclaimed gospel musicologist Horace Clarence Boyer asserted in his classic *How Sweet the Sound: The Golden Age of Gospel* (1995), "[t]his new gospel music spoke in more immediate tones, both musically and textually, to the difficult life of being both black and Christian in the United States" during, between, and immediately after World War I and II (47). The black colloquialisms the "blues life," the "jazz life," and the "gospel life" all denote the great difficulty African American musicians faced traveling and performing along the segregated highways and byways in the first half of the twentieth century. Living the "gospel life" in the golden age meant not simply singing of *heavenly salvation*, but incessantly experiencing firsthand why the ongoing struggle for *earthly liberation* was of paramount importance. Just like blues and jazz artists in the 1940s, 1950s, and 1960s, gospel artists were quarantined to the "colored" section. American apartheid—whether we would like to call it "Jim Crow laws," "Black Codes," or simply "racial segregation"—impacted gospel artists in much the same manner as it did African Americans more generally from the turn of the twentieth century through to the 1960s. Hence, in his eye-opening discussion of the "gospel life" along the "gospel highway" during the golden age, Boyer revealed, "most singers preferred automobile travel." He importantly continued:

> Riding buses or trains meant having to travel in the "colored" section. On trains only one porter (or none at all) was assigned to two or three

cars. Seats in these cars were seldom in good repair, and luggage sat on passenger seats for lack of storage room above. Few food services were offered, and bathrooms were seldom cleaned. Many of the bus stops had no provisions for African Americans, requiring them to stand out-side a side window of a restaurant for food service....Except on visits to cities such as New York or Chicago, most singers had to stay in the one hotel or rooming house that would accommodate African Americans. If no rooms were available, friends or even strangers met on the street could direct singers to homes that took "overnight" boarders. Rather than endure this travail, singers would use their church network or family and friends to arrange accommodation. In many towns where singers were performing for two or more days, dinner invitations from church members or concerts attendees were eagerly accepted. Some-times the sponsor of multiple concerts would arrange to have the sing-ers dine at a different home each night. (55)

From the foregoing we can deduce that in many respects, touring gospel artists were exposed to higher levels and even more heinous forms of anti-black racism when compared with those African Americans who, for whatever reason, rarely left their respective cities or regions. During the golden age, then, it can be said that gospel artists wrestled against "flesh and blood" *and* "against principalities, against powers, against the rulers of the darkness of this world," as well as "against spiritual wickedness in high places" (This is obviously my admittedly very crude paraphrase of one of my favorite passages from *The Holy Bible*, Ephesians 6:12–13, which reads: "For we wrestle not against flesh and blood, but against principalities, against powers, against the rulers of the darkness of this world, against spiritual wickedness in high places. Wherefore take unto you the whole armour of God, that ye may be able to withstand in the evil day, and having done all, to stand.").

It would seem that the physical, psychological, and emotional toll that living the "gospel life" and traveling along the "gospel highway" had on golden age gospel artists may have registered, not so much in their song lyrics or the evolving musical accompaniment, but in the manner in which they sang their sacred songs. By continuing to "push[...] the vocal register to the extreme," and by not altering the characteristic "hoarse," "raspy," "gruff," "gravelly," or "throaty" sound that had been handed down from the enslaved inventors of the "Sorrow Songs," from their beloved genres genesis gospel artists made a distinctly emotional and expressive performance style a key, if not *the* key, defining aspect of anything that would pass itself off as authentic gospel. Far from being *ahistorical*, gospel—even prior to the golden age—was, as it remains, a *counter-historical*, sometimes surreptitiously insurgent art form where singers' wrestling "against principalities, against powers, against the rul-ers of the darkness of this world," as well as "against spiritual wicked-ness in high places" manifested itself vocally—literally, in the much-revered "hoarse," "raspy," "gruff," "gravelly," or "throaty" sounds that the masters of this music seem capable of conjuring up anywhere, and at any time.

Undoubtedly, golden age gospel artists, much like Civil Rights Movement leaders and civil rights soldiers in general, were preoccupied with both tradition *and* innovation: *tradition,* in the sense that they consciously adapted and updated the African American sacred song tradition, which went back to the "Sorrow Songs" that arose out of enslavement; and, *innovation,* in the sense that they consciously sought to modernize and urbanize the African American sacred song tradition, which ultimately meant opening it up and bring in into dialogue with subsequent genres of black popular music, such as blues and jazz, and later rhythm & blues and rock & roll. In essence, this chapter asserts that between 1945 and 1965 gospel simultaneously served as both a sonic symbol of the evolution of the African American sacred song tradition and one of the major forms of popular music that captured and conveyed the views and values, as well as the aspirations and frustrations, of the Civil Rights Movement.

During the Civil Rights Movement years, gospel (especially via its freedom songs subgenre) gave voice to African American culture, consciousness, and bleak social conditions. Simultaneously expressing a boundless faith in God and black Christians, and a sometimes subtle lack of faith in American democracy and white Christianity, golden age gospel reflected the culture, consciousness, and conditions from which the majority of gospel artists emerged: black working-class and black working-poor culture. It is in this sense that most golden age gospel artists can be said to have represented the black masses, who were between 1945 and 1965, as they remain at the dawn of the twenty-first century and surging into its second decade, disproportionately poor and working-class. Golden age gospel artists' intimacy with the life-worlds and life-struggles of the black poor and downtrodden, not to mention their first-hand harrowing experiences of anti-black racism at seemingly every twist and turn, made them almost ideal mouthpieces for the aspirations and frustrations, if not the overarching ethos, of the Civil Rights Movement.

At its core golden age gospel communicated emerging, simultaneously more modern and more urban African American socio-political views and cultural values. It was one of the major cultural tools African Americans used to deconstruct *"Negro" identity* (often nothing more than a figment of segregationist white folks' anti-black racist imaginations) and reconstruct the inchoate *"black" identity* that blossomed into the major motif of the Black Power Movement. Those unfamiliar with the inner-workings of African American culture are probably woefully unaware of the fact that gospel directly contributed to the culture of socio-political consciousness-raising during the Civil Rights Movement that, by the mid-1960s, mutated and translated itself into the "black aesthetic" or "soul aesthetic" that unambiguously advocated "black pride" during the Black Power Movement. In *The Gospel Sound* (1997), Heilbut drove this point home:

> Black pride and black power are easily assimilated in gospel, a music exclusively by and for blacks, to begin with....[B]lack pride in gospel is as old as the hymn "I'm a Child of the King." Reverend [W. Herbert] Brewster exhibited black gospel pride back in the thirties when he named Q.C. Anderson after Queen Candice of Ethiopia. In the forties, quartets sang "No Segregation in Heaven" and eulogized Roosevelt, "the poor man's friend," for helping black people....That may seem like naïve social consciousness, but it complements the soul protest songs like "Say It Loud, I'm Black and I'm Proud," "We're a Winner," "War, What Is It Good For?," "Ball of Confusion," or "Message From A Black Man." (298)

Golden age gospel was part of a musical cultural continuum that extended from the spirituals to the blues, gospel blues to rhythm & blues, and freedom songs to soul. Indeed, as Heilbut emphasized above, "black gospel pride," which predated the Black Power Movement's preoccupation with "black pride," has been one of the, however hidden, hallmarks of gospel since its inception, and *gospel protest songs* (once again, especially via the freedom songs subgenre) are undoubtedly a precursor to the more noted and much-revered "soul protest songs" of the Black Power Movement. However, if most academics and non-academics alike continue to conceive of gospel as an ahistorical, apolitical, other-worldly, and escapist musical art form more concerned with heavenly salvation than with earthly liberation, then the wide-range of extra-musical elements that gospel draws from, and contributes to African American history, culture, and struggle will be, at best, ignored or, at worst, erased altogether.

Long before the Civil Rights Movement African Americans turned to black church culture, and especially black church music, to express sadness, happiness, joy, "sacred blues," faith, hope, courage, and determination, among many other emotions. They utilized the black sacred song as a means of communicating with other congregants not only in the church, but also in myriad socio-political movements outside of the context of the church when words were simply not enough or just couldn't capture black life-struggles and lived-experiences. Hence, considering the centrality of the African American church in African American social and political movements, especially the Civil Rights Movement, the black sacred song tradition, as the central soundtrack of African American church culture, historically has been used to *speak the unspeakable* and *explain the inexplicable* both within and without the walls of the church. All that being said, in order for us to really and truly comprehend the origins and evolution of golden age gospel, we need to understand the origins and evolution of the African American church and the pivotal role music historically has played in African American religious culture and practices.

IMPLICITLY SINGING WHAT THEY CANNOT EXPLICITLY SAY: THE MULTI-FUNCTIONALITY OF THE BLACK CHURCH AND BLACK CHURCH MUSIC

The African American church has always served as a major site of, and source for African American music. All of the most distinctive features of black popular music—from *the characteristic call-and-response, cry, scream, and shout sound* that seems to be at the sonic center of the spirituals, classic blues, and jazz, to the amplified and electrified moans, groans, growls and howls that pulsate and permeate throughout rhythm & blues, rock & roll, soul, funk, and even rap and neo-soul—can be traced back to the black church and "[t]hey that walked in darkness [and] sang [sorrow] songs in the olden days." A pioneer in the study of African American religion, Du Bois's sociological treatment of black religion fundamentally centered on *syncretism*—that is to say, on how enslaved Africans, as Albert Raboteau observed in *Slave Religion: The "Invisible Institution" in the Antebellum South* (1978), fused their traditional religious thought and practices with the Christian theology of their white enslavers:

> In the New World slave control was based on the eradication of all forms of African culture because of their power to unify the slaves and thus enable them to resist or rebel. Nevertheless, African beliefs and customs persisted and were transmitted by slaves to their descendants. Shaped and modified by a new environment, elements of African folklore, music, language, and religion were transplanted in the New World by the African diaspora. Influenced by colonial European and indigenous Native American cultures, aspects of the African heritage have contributed, in greater or lesser degree, to the formation of various Afro-American cultures in the New World. One of the most durable and adaptable constituents of the slave's culture, linking the African past with the American present, was his religion. It is important to realize, however, that in the Americas the religions of Africa have not been merely preserved as static "Africanisms" or as archaic "retentions." The fact is that they have continued to develop as living traditions putting down new roots in new soil, bearing new fruit as unique hybrids of American origin. African styles of worship, forms of ritual, systems of belief, and fundamental perspectives have remained vital on this side of the Atlantic, not because they were preserved in a "pure" orthodoxy but because they were transformed. Adaptability, based upon respect for spiritual power wherever it originated, accounted for the openness of African religions to syncretism with other

religious traditions and for the continuity of a distinctively African
religious consciousness. At least in some areas of the Americas, the
gods of Africa continued to live—in exile. (4–5)

The gospel aesthetic, especially during the golden age, not only emphasized "[a]daptability" and a deep respect for "spiritual power" in keeping
with the core values of the African American church but, above all else,
its innovations and experimentations were emblematic of organic, "living
traditions putting down new roots in new soil," and "bearing new fruit
as unique hybrids of American origin." In other words, gospel, certainly
by the golden age, registered as a kind of *sonic syncretism* that served as
the soundtrack for the ongoing *religious and cultural syncretism* that
African Americans experienced during the first century after enslavement. At the turn of the twentieth century, it was Du Bois's African
American religious studies and African American church studies that set
the tone and timbre for virtually all subsequent African American religious studies, including Raboteau's research (ix, 209, 266). Considering the
emphasis that Du Bois placed on the black church, as well as his groundbreaking research that revealed *the multi-functionality of the black church*
for recently emancipated black folk in a severely Jim Crow segregated
society, our discussion here will greatly benefit from an engagement with
Du Bois's work, as it offers us insight into the African American church
during the fertile period in which gospel emerged.

It was in his chronicling and critiquing of *African American syncretism*
that Du Bois distinguished himself not simply as a sociologist of religion,
but also an historian of religion and political theologian. Without a doubt,
argued Du Bois, there were white and black Christians, but they were
bound together not by religion as much as by theology. Which is to say, I
am hinting here at what womanist theologian Jacquelyn Grant eloquently
argued in *White Women's Christ and Black Women's Jesus* (1989), and that is
that blacks and whites may be employing similar religious language and
drawing from the same sacred text (i.e., *The Holy Bible*), but their lived-
experiences and lived-endurances, their histories, cultural contexts, political persuasions, and social situations inspire them to draw comparably
different conclusions as to the nature and power of God. As the first great
historian and sociologist of the African American church, Du Bois's work
deftly demonstrates that racial colonization and enslavement changed
black folk's theology, but it did not in every instance, and certainly it did
not completely, destroy what Raboteau termed above, their "distinctively
African religious consciousness," which is to say, their religious thought
and practices. This is an insight Du Bois culled from his lived-experiences, sociological observations, and copious data collection at Fisk University, in Philadelphia's black community (under the auspices of the
University of Pennsylvania), and at Atlanta University, among other
sites, where black Christians practiced, literally, *lived* a wide variety of

Africanized versions of Christianity and where, in their daily lives, conscious and unconscious African retentions reigned.[10]

As an historian of religion with strong sociological leanings, Du Bois chronicled: 1) the radical thought and rebellious lives of early African American religious leaders; 2) intra-African American class divisions and how secular distinctions such as these played themselves out in the realm of religion; 3) the dual sacred and secular nature of African American religion and the black church; 4) the conflicts within several white Christian denominations over the issue of whether enslaved Africans could or should be baptized; and, 5) why the white Baptists and Methodists were more successful in sowing the seeds of Christianity in the hearts and minds of the enslaved.[11] Along with these issues, among others, Du Bois strongly stressed that African American religion, particularly as embodied in, and flowing out of the black church, was not only "the first distinctively Negro American social institution" but, and most importantly, "the sole surviving social institution of the African fatherland." Religion, he wrote in *The Negro Church*, was the lone social sphere in which enslaved Africans had any modicum of agency, and even in this realm they were severely regulated. Du Bois (1903a), writing with a sense of unmitigated awe and critical discovery, declared:

> At first sight it would seem that slavery completely destroyed every vestige of spontaneous social movement among Negroes; the home had deteriorated; political authority and economic initiative was in the hands of the masters, property, as a social institution, did not exist on the plantation, and, indeed, it is usually assumed by historians and sociologists that every vestige of internal development disappeared, leaving the slaves no means of expression for their common life, thought, and striving. This is not strictly true; the vast power of the priest in the African state has already been noted; his realm alone—the province of religion and medicine—remained largely unaffected by the plantation system in many important particulars. The Negro priest, therefore, early became an important figure on the plantation and found his function as the interpreter of the supernatural, the comforter of the sorrowing, and as the one who expressed, rudely, but picturesquely, the longing and disappointment and resentment of a stolen people. From such beginnings arose and spread with marvelous rapidity the Negro Church, the first distinctively Negro American social institution. It was not at first by any means a Christian Church, but a mere adaptation of those heathen rites which we roughly designate by the term Obe Worship, or "Voodoism." Association and missionary effort soon gave these rites a veneer of Christianity, and gradually, after two centuries, the Church became Christian, with a simple Calvinistic creed, but with many of the old customs still clinging to the services. It is this historic fact that the Negro Church of today bases itself upon the sole surviving social institution of the African fatherland, that accounts for its extraordinary growth and vitality....This institution, therefore,

> naturally assumed many functions which the other harshly suppressed
> social organs had to surrender; the Church become the center of
> amusements, of what little spontaneous economic activity remained, of
> education, and of all social intercourse. (5)

African American religion was forged in the fires of abolitionist struggle, and the quest for freedom was not quenched by the bellowing, but weak-willed words of the Emancipation Proclamation. Therefore, Du Bois studied the impact of African American religion, basically the black church, on post-enslavement African American social development and cultural survival. African American religious thought and practices, Du Bois had a hunch, changed during the decades after enslavement because, although they had *de jure* freedom, blacks were still in a white supremacist, hyper-racially-ruled social world and did not have *de facto* freedom. Hence, American apartheid lingered on, leaving its stench and stain on everyone and everything it came into contact with, even religion and, as will be witnessed below, just as religion was racialized, so too was religious music. Whether we turn to the spirituals, gospel, or freedom songs, post-enslavement African American religious music encapsulates and articulates *how it feels* and *what it means* to be granted *de jure* freedom but, after nearly 350 years of enslavement, have to continue to struggle for *de facto* freedom. Consequently, it is not a coincidence that black popular music in general, and the black sacred song tradition in particular, can be characterized by the distinct *call-and-response, cry, scream, and shout sound* that seems to be at its ever-evolving sonic center.

In *The Philadelphia Negro* (1899), Du Bois analyzed a wide-range of African American religious practices that illustrated the dramatic (sacred *and* secular) changes in black church life in the first three and a half decades after the issuing of the Emancipation Proclamation. Beginning with the history of the black church, Du Bois then turned his attention to its organizational structures and social functions, and was undoubtedly the first to systematically study and document its political positions, educational initiatives, amusement/entertainment activities, missionary efforts, charitable organizations, insurance societies, and homes for the aged and the infirmed. He scrupulously examined congregational economic life, what Robert Wortham (2009) has recently referred to as "religious economy": from debts and membership contributions, to the value of church properties and pastors' salaries. Further, Du Bois critically observed how black class divisions within the churches and various denominations played themselves out, causing continuous stratification and discontinuous congregational affiliation. He painstakingly detailed an intricate interrelation of church and/or religion-related social and political programs, and the lingering leitmotif of African retentions, which I have come to think is one of the hallmarks of his work, is ubiquitous. In words that read more like a sorrow-filled sinner testifying in a black church at Sunday morning service, Du Bois (1899) wrote:

> We often forget that the rise of a church organization among Negroes was a curious phenomenon. The church really represented all that was left of African tribal life, and was the sole expression of the organized efforts of the slaves. It was natural that any movement among freedmen should center about their religious life, the sole remaining element of their former tribal system....The Negro is, to be sure, a religious creature—most primitive folk are—but his rapid and even extraordinary founding of churches is not due to this fact alone, but is rather a measure of his development, an indication of the increasing intricacy of his social life and the consequent multiplication of the organ which is the function of his group life—the church....The Negro church is the peculiar and characteristic product of the transplanted African, and deserves especial study. As a social group the Negro church may be said to have antedated the Negro family on American soil; as such it has preserved, on the one hand, many functions of tribal organization, and on the other hand, many of the family functions. Its tribal functions are shown in its religious activity, its social authority and general guiding and coordinating work; its family functions are shown by the fact that the church is a center of social life and intercourse; acts as newspaper and intelligence bureau, is the center of amusements—indeed, is the world in which the Negro moves and acts. So far-reaching are these functions of the church that its organization is almost political. (197, 201)

His inexcusable politically incorrect language aside ("The Negro is, to be sure, a religious creature—most primitive folk are")—which demonstrates that one of the major architects of African American studies was not immune to internalized anti-black racism and *the diabolical dialectic of white superiority and black inferiority!*—Du Bois accentuated both the social and political functions of the black church. In his estimate, it is "the most remarkable product of American Negro civilization" because "[i]t is a democratic church; a church where the governing power is largely in the hands of the mass of membership" (Du Bois 1985a, 84). The democratic nature of the black church is a recurring theme in Du Bois's writings on religion, especially when he compared it with the white church, because in spite of what he was wont to term its "primitivisms" and "nativisms," yet and still, he stated: "The Negro church is at least democratic. It welcomes everybody. It draws no color-line" (Du Bois 2000, 141). He asserted that the African American church is further distinguished because it serves as *a multipurpose site for moral instruction, political education, social development, and racial/cultural awareness.* Obviously, the African American church also serves as a space where black folk can participate in *artistic creation*—not merely musical, but a broadly conceived conception of *artistic creation* elastic enough to encompass a wide-range of

African American artistry. Needless to say, if, as Du Bois asserted, "the church is a center of social life and intercourse," and if so wide-ranging and "far-reaching" is its cultural influence and functions that its "organization is almost political," then gospel music, being a key component of black church culture by the time of the emergence of the Civil Rights Movement, is also "almost political," if not in many instances, especially considering gospel music's freedom songs subgenre, outright and unambiguously political.[12]

African American women's special role in creating and sustaining the black church was not lost on Du Bois, and they received unprecedented praise from his pen. Radical religious convictions were not simply the cornerstone of individual black women's struggles against various forms of oppression, but it was also at the heart of their collective efforts to organize African Americans in the interest of social uplift. In *Darkwater*, Du Bois put forward the often noted names of Harriet Tubman and Sojourner Truth, fervently recalling, not merely their profound religiosity, but also how their religious beliefs inspired and, perhaps even, invoked their legendary "feminist-abolitionism" (Du Bois 1920, 175–177). The organizations that ultimately came to be collectively called the "Black Women's Club Movement" all emerged from the religious cultural context of the African American church and, it should be emphasized, the National Association of Colored Women (NACW)—i.e., the national association of black women's clubs—was "the first truly black national organization that functioned with strength and unity" (Hine and Thompson 1998, 180).[13]

So powerful and pervasive was the influence of the Black Women's Club Movement on him, when Du Bois turned to social organization and radical political activism, he used the Black Women's Club Movement as a model, going so far as to name the social organization he helped to found (along with two of the major leaders of the Black Women's Club Movement, Ida B. Wells and Mary Church Terrell), the National Association for the Advancement of Colored People (NAACP).[14] In *The Gift of Black Folk*, Du Bois candidly conceded:

> We have noted then the Negro woman in America as a worker tending to emancipate all women workers; as a mother nursing the white race and uniting the black and white races; as a conspirator urging forward emancipation in various sorts of ways; and we have finally only to remember that today the women of America who are doing humble but on the whole the most effective work in the social uplift of the lowly, not so much by money as by personal contact, are the colored women. Little is said or known about it but in thousands of churches and social clubs, in missionary societies and fraternal organizations, in unions like the National Association of Colored Women, these workers are founding and sustaining orphanages and old folk homes; distributing personal charity and relief; visiting prisoners; helping hospitals;

teaching children; and ministering to all sorts of needs. Their work, as it comes now and then in special cases to the attention of individuals of the white world, forms a splendid bond of encouragement and sympathy, and helps more than most realize in minimizing racial difficulties and encouraging human sympathy. (Du Bois 1970a, 149)

Without a doubt, Du Bois (1920) declared in *Darkwater*, "[i]t was...strong women that laid the foundations of the great Negro church of today, with its five million members and ninety millions of dollars in property" (174). He acknowledged the role of "early church mothers," such as Mary Still, in the establishment of the African Methodist Episcopal Church (174). Moreover, he suggested that "such [was the] spiritual ancestry" that spurred Harriet Tubman's legendary efforts to liberate the enslaved, sympathize with John Brown's revolutionary abolitionism, and enlist in the Union Army (174).

In an audacious turn of phrase, Du Bois further accentuated black women's special "spiritual ancestry" by placing the religious and resistance activities of black women on par with those of black men. He went so far as to recall Sojourner Truth's classic query to Frederick Douglass, "Frederick, *is God dead?*," when the black male-feminist abolitionist, in a moment of desperation, declared that African Americans would have to fight for their freedom by force of arms. Du Bois also acknowledged the work of Kate Ferguson, a nineteen year-old African American widow, who "took the children of the streets of New York, white and black, into her empty arms, taught them, found them homes" and, most pertinent to the present discussion, she "established the first modern Sunday School in Manhattan" (177–178).

In his writings on religion Du Bois also spoke highly of African American clergy, and often exhibited a great deal of sympathy for their peculiar simultaneous positions as "spiritual guides" and social leaders of their people. For instance, above he asserted: "The Negro priest, therefore, early became an important figure on the plantation and found his function as the interpreter of the supernatural, the comforter of the sorrowing, and as the one who expressed, rudely, but picturesquely, the longing and disappointment and resentment of a stolen people." In his chapter on Alexander Crummell and in "Of the Faith of the Fathers," both in *The Souls of Black Folk*, Du Bois heartily advanced: "The Preacher is the most unique personality developed by the Negro on American soil. A leader, a politician, an orator, a 'boss,' an idealist—all these he is, and ever, too, the center of a group of men" (Du Bois 1903c, 190; see also Du Bois, 1899, 205–207, 1982b, 328–329, 2000a, 21–22). African American ministers were often misunderstood, he argued, and very few were qualified to criticize them, as there were no serious studies (antedating Du Bois's) of their dual religious *and* socio-political roles. In perhaps his earliest essay on religion, "The Problem of Amusement" (originally published in 1897), Du Bois (1978) contended:

> The minister who directs this peculiar and anomalous institution must not be criticized without full knowledge of his difficult role. He is in reality the mayor, the chief magistrate of a community, ruling to be sure, but ruling according to the dictates of a not over-intelligent town council, according to time honored custom and law; and above all, hampered by the necessities of his budget; he may be a spiritual guide, he must be a social organizer, a leader of actual men; he may desire to enrich and reform the spiritual life of his flock, but above all he must have church members; he may desire to revolutionize church methods, to elevate the ideals of the people, to tell the hard, honest truth to a people who need a little more truth and a little less flattery—but how can he do this when the people of this social organism demand that he shall take from the purely spiritual activities of his flock, time to minister to their amusements, diversion, and physical comfort; when he sees the picnic masquerading as a camp-meeting, the revival becoming the social event of the season, the day of worship turned into a day of general reception and dining out, the rival church organizations plunging into debt to furnish their houses of worship with an elegance that far outruns the financial ability of a poverty-stricken people; when the church door becomes the trysting place for all the lovers and Lotharios of the community; when a ceaseless round of entertainments, socials, and necktie parties chase the week through—what minister can be more that most ministers are coming to be, the business managers of a picnic ground? (229)

Finally, with regard to Du Bois's reverence for African American religion, it must be said that he held black church music in especial high esteem. He frequently wrote beamingly and bemusingly of African American religious music, calling it "the most original and beautiful expression of human life and longing yet born on American soil" (Du Bois 1903c, 191). He adeptly described how black religious music had emanated from the "African forests" to be "adapted, changed, and intensified by the tragic soul-life of the slave, until, under the stress of law and whip, it became the one true expression of a people's sorrow, despair, and hope" (191; see also Castellini 2013, 4).

Where Du Bois emphasized the centrality of the black church in African American history, culture, and struggle, he placed an almost equal emphasis on the centrality of the black sacred song tradition, effusively proclaiming that it has become "the one true expression of a people's sorrow, despair, and hope." Because of the centrality of the church and its culture, Du Bois strongly stressed, "the study of Negro religion is not only a vital part of the history of the Negro in America, but no uninteresting part of American history." As a matter of fact, "[t]he Negro church of today is the social center of Negro life in the United States," he contended, and "the most characteristic expression of African character" (193; see also Castellini 2013, 4).

However, because of African American's "African character" and, what Raboteau called above, "African religious consciousness," Du Bois deduced that African Americans' *"Africanité"* —the distinctly African aspects of their *humanity, historicity,* and *identity*—had caused them to be crudely collapsed into their problems and seen as *a problem people,* as opposed to *a people with peculiar problems* (as with most other human groups). The incessant experience of racial reductionism and constant collapsing of black folk into their problems produced an acute condition where many, if not most, black folk came to internalize negative views of themselves and their "African fatherland." Du Bois dubbed this psycho-socio-cultural condition "double-consciousness." Elaborating on African Americans' *divided-selves* and *double-lives,* Du Bois wrote, "[f]rom the double-life every American Negro must live, as a Negro and as an American...must arise a painful self-consciousness, an almost morbid sense of personality and a moral hesitancy which is fatal to self-confidence" (202). Prophetically seeming to paint a picture of the kinds of politics and aesthetics that would predominate during the Civil Rights Movement, Du Bois outlined core strategies and tactics of African American survival utilized, not only by black preachers and black socio-political leaders, but also by black artists, including golden age gospel artists:

> The worlds within and without the Veil of Color are changing, and changing rapidly, but not at the same rate, not in the same way; and this must produce a peculiar wrenching of the soul, a peculiar sense of doubt and bewilderment. Such a double-life, with double-thoughts, double-duties, and double-social classes, must give rise to double-words and double-ideals, and tempt the mind to pretense or to revolt, to hypocrisy or to radicalism. (202)

Who can deny that during the Civil Rights Movement years, many African American artists—especially gospel, rhythm & blues, and rock & roll artists—felt the need to reconcile moral outrage and, sometimes, outright vengeful anger, with a veneer of deference and the appearance of a preference for heavenly salvation over earthly liberation? Indeed, the "double-life, with double-thoughts, double-duties, and double-social classes," which "give[s] rise to double-words and double-ideals," was incessantly and adroitly articulated in the gospel and freedom songs of the Civil Rights Movement, so much so that most folk, whether black or white, with little or no critical knowledge or real connection to the movement regularly miss the often masked multiple-meaning key symbols, signs, and sounds of the Civil Rights Movement—what could be otherwise termed *the semiotics of the Civil Rights Movement*? "Deception is the natural defense of the weak against the strong," Du Bois declared, and "the South used it for many years against its [Northern] conquerors." But, in the aftermath of the aftermath of Reconstruction, that same deceptive segregationist white South "must be prepared to see its black proletariat," which is the socio-economic class from which most gospel artists emerged, "turn that same two-edged weapon against itself" (204). Demonstrating that double-consciousness can be simultaneously self-negating *and* self-liberating, conceptually incarcerating *and* mentally emancipating, Du Bois described the seemingly schizophrenic moderatism *and* militantism of the young black folk who wield the double-edged sword of double-consciousness against their anti-black racist and well-intentioned white oppressors:

> Today the young Negro of the South who would succeed cannot be frank and outspoken, honest and self-assertive, but rather he is daily tempted to be silent and wary, politic and sly; he must flatter and be pleasant, endure petty insults with a smile, shut his eyes to wrong; in too many cases he sees positive personal advantage in deception and lying. His real thoughts, his real aspirations, must be guarded in whispers; he must not criticize, he must not complain. Patience, humility, and adroitness must, in these growing black youth, replace impulse, manliness, and courage. With this sacrifice there is an economic opening, and perhaps peace and some prosperity. Without this there is riot, migration, or crime. Nor is this situation peculiar to the Southern United States,—is it not rather the only method by which undeveloped races have gained the right to share modern culture? The price of culture is a Lie. (204–205)

Similar to most other African Americans living under the shadow of American apartheid during the Civil Rights Movement years, gospel artists, no matter how "radical" or "progressive" they may have actually been with respect to racial, social, and economic justice, were forced to feign apathy and religious escapism. As Du Bois observed, they simply could not be "frank and outspoken, honest and self-assertive," the evil socio-political etiquette of American apartheid demanded that they be "silent and wary, politic and sly," that they "flatter and be pleasant," that they "endure petty insults with a smile," and "shut [their tear-filled] eyes to wrong." Like most Civil Rights Movement leaders, gospel artists understood that in order to make a real and meaningful contribution to the movement, their "real thoughts," their "real aspirations, must be guarded in whispers," and that they "must not criticize," they "must not complain" but, in keeping with the majority of the core strategies and tactics of the movement, they must mask their protest and produce a culturally coded art that meant one thing to church folk and civil rights soldiers, and wholly another thing to folk who were not members of the wider black church world or active members of the Civil Rights Movement.

According to Du Bois, the masked, multiple meanings almost inherent in the African American sacred song tradition are not only why black church music has been so "persistently mistaken and misunderstood," but also what makes black sacred songs so brilliant and breathtaking. Few scholars of African American religious music, or black popular music in general, can resist commenting on that hauntingly famous passage from *The Souls of Black Folk* where Du Bois solemnly wrote:

> Little of beauty has America given the world save the rude grandeur God himself stamped on her bosom; the human spirit in this new world has expressed itself in vigor and ingenuity rather than in beauty. And so by fateful chance the Negro folk-song—the rhythmic cry of the slave—stands today not simply as the sole American music, but as the most beautiful expression of human experience born this side the seas. It has been neglected, it has been, and is, half despised, and above all it has been persistently mistaken and misunderstood; but notwithstanding, it still remains as the singular spiritual heritage of the nation and the greatest gift of the Negro people. (251)

From Du Bois's perspective, the black church was the cornerstone of African American culture, and in his studies he traced its connections to the spiritual and broader cultural traditions of Africa, while simultaneously demonstrating the process (i.e., syncretism) by which various disparate groups of enslaved Africans miraculously became a multicultural and transethnic diasporan community, a many-sided single people—in other words, *African Americans*. In *Slave Culture* (1987), Sterling Stuckey pointed out that even before enslaved Africans reached the shores of North America, they began to create a new culture, one where traditional "tribalisms" were nothing more than "a lingering memory in the minds of American slaves" (3). People from as far north as Senegal were piled onto people from Namibia and Angola in the south, people from Kenya in the east were sandwiched between Ghanaians and Nigerians from the west, and in their long and horror-filled voyage to the Americas they initiated the protracted and arduous process of creating a new culture. This new culture was primarily one of resistance, but it must be borne in mind that the bulk of this defiance was grounded in, and grew out of the enslaved Africans' hark back to the religions and social justice traditions of their ancestors, which, for all of the reasons observed above, are historically embodied in the African American church.

If the black church is a core component of African American culture, especially black social and political culture, then, the music that is so central to the African American church experience must in some manner reflect both the conservatism *and* radicalism of the church's core congregants. Admittedly, it is easier to detect expressions of conservatism in the African American sacred song tradition and arguably much more difficult to discern and decipher often intentionally ambiguous expressions of radicalism and resistance. Hence, Du Bois rhetorically queried, "What are these songs, and what do they mean?" Obviously, as our guide and goad through African American history, culture, and struggle, Du Bois was hinting at the fact that black sacred songs historically have been, and continue to be, more than merely sacred songs—which is to say, they are more than merely religious music. Going back to my above emphasis on *the multi-functionality of the black church,* here I would like to also strongly stress *the multi-functionality of black church music,* that is to say, *the multi-functionality of African American sacred songs*—obviously, a distinct characteristic that has been handed down to each and every form of black popular music that has been derived from the African American sacred song tradition (i.e., blues, ragtime, jazz, jump blues, doo-wop, rhythm & blues, rock & roll, girl groups, soul, funk, disco, techno, house, rap, neo-soul, etc.).

In response to his incredibly important rhetorical question, "What are these songs, and what do they mean?," Du Bois sternly stated, "I know little of music and can say nothing in technical phrase," but tellingly he went further, "I know something of men," of black folk, and "knowing them, I know that these songs are the articulate message of the slave to the world," which "tell in word and music of trouble and exile, of strife and hiding"—they are the "voice of exile" (253, 255, 257). African American sacred songs, whether we turn to the spirituals or gospel or freedom songs, "are the music of an unhappy people, of the children of disappointment," and these songs "tell of death and suffering and un-voiced longing toward a truer world, of misty wanderings and hidden ways" (253). However, even in the midst of such seeming despondency, Du Bois argued, "there breathes a hope—a faith in the ultimate justice of things."

Similar to *The Holy Bible* on which so much of it is based, the African American sacred song tradition contains elements of both pessimism *and* optimism, of the Old Testament "God of War" *and* the New Testament "Prince of Peace," and is undoubtedly more complex and complicated than most folk outside of the black church and the black church music tradition fully fathom. Black church music cannot and should not be reduced to pathos and pain, to apathy and escapism, and Du Bois challenged both its connoisseurs and critics to acknowledge that the "minor cadences of despair" in black church music often transforms and trans-lates themselves into "triumph and calm confidence." He continued, "[s]ometimes it is faith in life, sometimes a faith in death, sometimes assurance of boundless justice in some fair world beyond. But whichever it is," Du Bois waxed, "the meaning is always clear: that sometime, some-where, men will judge men by their souls and not by their skins. Is such a hope justified? Do the Sorrow Songs sing true?" (261–262).

In innumerable ways, gospel seems to be a response to Du Bois's queries, "Is such a hope justified?" And, most especially, "Do the Sorrow

Songs sing true?" By the very fact that gospel evolved out of the spirituals undoubtedly demonstrates that "the Sorrow Songs sing true," that the hope that is at the heart of even the most downhearted and dirge-like spiritual inspired subsequent generations of African Americans to "keep hope alive," to "keep the faith," and to—as Philippians 3:14 reads— "press toward the mark for the prize of the high calling of God in Christ Jesus."

Obviously, the message that "sometime, somewhere, men will judge men by their souls and not by their skins" is most often muted in gospel, as it was in the spirituals. According to Du Bois, it is "naturally veiled and half-articulate" in black church music, but buried beneath the surface of "conventional theology and unmeaning rhapsody," the spirituals— and the same could be said of gospel during the Civil Rights Movement—"conveyed the restless, plaintive 'soul-hunger'" of black folk in ways that were "revealing for what they *did not* say at least as much as for what they *did* say (257–258; Castellini 2013, 4–5). Once again Du Bois waxed, "[o]ver the inner-thoughts of the slaves and their relations with one another the shadow of fear ever hung, so that we get but glimpses here and there, and also with them, eloquent omissions and silences." An African American musicologist, a musicologist of African American music, whatever term adopted to describe one who seriously studies black popular music must, almost by default, develop a deep preoccupation with the "eloquent omissions and silences" of African American music, and especially black sacred songs.

Du Bois understood that black folk could not outright physically resist their white enslavers during enslavement and their white segregators during the Jim Crow era. However, African Americans could, however surreptitiously and ironically, *implicitly sing* what could not be *explicitly said* in light of the anti-black racist protocols and practices of American apartheid. It is in this sense, then, that Du Bois, however subtly, acknowledged the "subaltern status," the subaltern life-worlds and life-struggles insidiously and "violently imposed" on his beloved black folk (Castellini 2013, 5). Continuing the "black folk can implicitly sing what they cannot explicitly say" line of logic, Tricia Rose, in *Black Noise* (1994), asserted that since oppressed people cannot openly express their opposition, resistance is most often manifested in shrouded "oppositional transcripts"—which is to say, the vernacular or "folk" cultural discourse that diverts direct pugnacity and militancy into folktales, humor, fantasy, play, ritual, music and other cultural forms (99).

The spirituals were exemplary of the oppositional transcripts of the enslavement and Reconstruction periods, where classic blues and gospel sonically symbolized the oppositional transcripts of the epoch spanning from post-Reconstruction through to the Civil Rights Movement. For instance, as Castellini (2013, 5) pointed out, the major recurring characters of the spirituals were the oppressive Pharaoh and God's "chosen" children of Israel suffering in bondage and unceasingly praying for freedom. Other repeatedly referenced biblical heroes and episodes such as Joshua the warrior, the perseverance of Job, David's courage in the battle against Goliath, Daniel down in the lion's den, and the faithfulness of Shadrach, Meshach, and Abednego, are important oppositional paradigms and points of departure ubiquitous throughout the spirituals that were handed down to gospel artists and adapted and updated to surreptitiously comment on the incredibly *unchristian* (if not categorically *anti-Christian*) laws of American apartheid. Rose offers insight:

> Slave dances, blues lyrics, Mardi Gras parades, Jamaican patios, toasts, and signifying all carry the pleasure and ingenuity of disguised criticism of the powerful. Poor people learn from experience when and how explicitly they can express their discontent. Under social conditions in which sustained frontal attacks on powerful groups are strategically unwise or successfully contained, oppressed people use language, dance, and music to mock those in power, express rage, and produce fantasies of subversion. These cultural forms are especially rich and pleasurable places where oppositional transcripts, or the "unofficial truths" are developed, refined, and rehearsed. These cultural responses to oppression are not safety valves that protect and sustain the machines of oppression. Quite the contrary, these dances, languages, and musics produce communal bases of knowledge about social conditions, communal interpretations of them, and quite often serve as the cultural glue that fosters communal resistance. (99–100)

Classic and golden age gospel are part of the arsenal of cultural weapons that African Americans have utilized to combat American apartheid and evolve the tradition of "disguised criticism of the powerful." Just as *musical protest* was constantly operationalized and utilized for generations during and immediately after African American enslavement, more modern forms of musical protest were put into play to speak to the special issues of the Civil Rights Movement. Not only did the partially prophetic, and partially mystic allure of the spiritual tradition—truth be told, the core foundation of the gospel tradition—last long after the issuing of the Emancipation Proclamation, but cultural imperialism, economic exploitation, social segregation, political repression and, above all else, anti-black racism were still widespread enough by the middle of the twentieth century to justify new forms of "sustained subterfuge" (Castellini 2013, 5).

In an effort to avoid segregationist and violent anti-black racist backlash, and to surreptitiously evade the objections and heavy-handed restrictions of leery record companies and radio stations, gospel artists were "compelled to continue couching their protest in what might sound like" nothing more than "religious doggerel to both enemies and outsiders" (5). According to Heilbut (1997), this may go far to explain "why lyrics that to white listeners seem abstract" and quite "corny" are very often "charged with specific, resonant meaning"—which is to say, *black cultural meaning* (262). He continued, "[i]f the gospel world is dreadful," then it is important to bear in mind that "it merely reflects the inescapable conditions of black life."

Here Heilbut makes a key point about gospel music and helps us to see its pivotal place within the black sacred song tradition: "like the spirituals," which similarly encapsulated and enunciated the "existential sufferings" and social misery of African Americans, golden age gospel "was charged with meanings"—*movement meanings*—that "escaped" most whites, but "resonated" in a multiplicity of ways with blacks, especially blacks actively involved in the Civil Rights Movement. Consequently, for "strategic," aesthetic, and "poetic" reasons, *gospel protest* was "mostly masked in sacred symbolism" and the outward appearance of escapism (Castellini 2013, 5). But, in its own surreptitious and unique way, it was as critical—if not *even more critical*—of cultural imperialism, economic exploitation, social segregation, political repression, and anti-black racism as either rhythm & blues or rock & roll during the Civil Rights Movement.[15]

ON THE UNSUNG SINGING SOLDIERS OF THE CIVIL RIGHTS MOVEMENT: GOSPEL MUSIC AS "A GENRE WHICH REPRESENTS A UNIQUELY BLACK PERSPECTIVE" AND PROTEST PRAXIS

If we are willing to concede that culture is a key resource for combatting oppression, whatever form oppression may manifest itself in, then, it must also be conceded that the sermons, prayers, and songs of African American church culture were indispensable elements of the Civil Rights Movement. Between 1945 and 1965, gospel was one of the "oppositional transcripts" or "unofficial truths" that was "developed, refined, and rehearsed" to covertly convey what African Americans could not overtly do or say. In this sense, golden age gospel music had a multitude of political implications, a multiplicity of complex meanings—again, *movement meanings*—for African Americans, especially African Americans actively involved in the Civil Rights Movement, and a remarkable ability to mask black radicalism while it surreptitiously inspired and enabled consciousness-raising and unforeseen forms of activism (e.g., non-violence, civil disobedience, passive resistance, moral suasion, litigation, economic boycott, grassroots organizing, solicitation of corporate sponsors, and oppositional use of the media, especially television and radio, etc.).

The origins and evolution of gospel music are deeply intertwined with African American history, culture, and struggle—before, and certainly after, African American enslavement. Similar to its classic blues, ragtime, and jazz siblings, gospel was conceived and codified during the "bleak years between Reconstruction and World War I," what has been repeatedly referred to as the "nadir of American race relations" (Castellini 2013, 11).[16] Its development was emblematic of the enormous social, political, and cultural transformations of the era, as groundbreaking gospel composers and performers blended the "old spirituals and hymns" of enslavement and its aftermath with the "new rhythms" and harmonic advances of classic blues, ragtime, and jazz, and then coupled them with their own heartfelt sacred song lyrics to create a new style of black church music that spoke to the African American community's need for hope, faith, and encouragement (11). Even though the term "gospel" has been used to label many forms of African American sacred music since the nineteenth century, the "modern genre dates to the 1920s." By the late-1920s the "first 'gospel blues' compositions had appeared," and by the early-1930s the "gospel chorus was becoming a mainstay of the black church." Inchoate gospel culture was taking shape during the Great Depression years, and "by 1940 it was thoroughly entrenched in the African American community and found in all but the [most] elitist and conservative" African American churches (11).

It is not regularly realized in the twenty-first century how incredibly—in fact, one might say, "extraordinarily"—varied gospel music became during its formative phase. Certainly the "jubilee singers" and quartets of the turn of the twentieth century factored into gospel's formative phase but, from the 1920s onward, right alongside the popular quartets flourished manifold male and female groups, choirs, and soloists, some with, and some without musical accompaniment. At this early period in gospel history and culture, musical accompaniment varied from banjos, pianos, and tambourines to the frenzy-filled distortions of electrified and amplified blue note-blurring, guitar-shredding, and organ-grinding preachers, deacons, and elders. No matter what the situation, however, classic gospel—especially by the time of the golden age—was primarily "a singer's art," and an authentic gospel singer had to have *the characteristic call-and-response, cry, scream, and shout sound* coupled with *an angelic affinity for Holy Ghost-filled improvisation, a righteous and at times riotous sense of rhythm* (emphasis on the "gospel beat"), and *a proclivity for vocal acrobatics and praise-laden pyrotechnics* (12). Perhaps, Heilbut drove this point home best when he asserted:

> [T]he supreme architects of the gospel moment are the great gospel singers. With them, spirit and community are welded by art. Their phrasing distills the best in folk expression, while adding unparalleled style and talent. All by themselves, the best singers can invoke as much spirit as a cathedral of saints. (xviii)

Here Heilbut makes an important observation: it is in its fusing of "spirit and community," of religion and culture that gospel offered a remarkably relevant *spiritual weapon* and *cultural tool* for aiding and abetting a mass movement grounded in African American religion and growing out of the black church. Obviously, this aspect of the sacred songs and overarching ethos of the Civil Rights Movement was deeply grounded in biblical wisdom, such as 2 Corinthians 10:3–5, which reads: "For though we walk in the flesh, we do not war according to the flesh. For the weapons of our warfare are not carnal but mighty in God for pulling down strongholds, casting down arguments and every high thing that exalts itself against the knowledge of God, bringing every thought into captivity to the obedience of Christ." It is not a coincidence, then, that gospel artists, gospel records, gospel radio, and the gospel touring circuit, commonly called the "gospel highway," all reached the peak of their popularity during the same epoch in which we witness the highest level of African American activism since the abolitionist era (Castellini 2013, 12–13).

Indeed, during its pinnacle period, gospel's influence actually went well beyond the black church and the Civil Rights Movement. As the much-esteemed African American musicologist Portia Maultsby (1992) has importantly pointed out, during its golden age "gospel music slowly penetrated every artery of American life, linking the sacred and secular domains of the African American community, breathing life into new secular forms, and bringing flair and distinction to the American stage of entertainment" (21). However, Maultsby maintained, it should be strongly stressed that no matter how much it was commercialized and "crossed-over" during its golden age, gospel was "a complex form that embodie[d] the religious, cultural, historical, and social dimensions of black life in America." She continued, "[t]he current misinterpretation about the religious and cultural significance of this tradition emanates from the exploitation of gospel music as an economic commodity" (20).

If, as Maultsby noted above, gospel "penetrated every artery of American life," why then is it difficult for so many to accept the thesis that gospel was a major mouthpiece for, and soundtrack of the Civil Rights Movement, right alongside the more famous freedom songs, rhythm & blues, and rock & roll? Renowned African American religious music specialist Mellonee Burnim (1988) emphasized that for African Americans, "the essence of power in gospel music rests in the complex of cultural functions which it serves"—which brings us back to what I termed above, *the multi-functionality of black church music* or, rather, *the multi-functionality of the African American sacred song tradition* (112). All of this is to say, for black folk *music is more than merely music*, and any comprehensive engagement of African American history, culture, and struggle must take into serious consideration *the extra-musical aspects of African American music* and, most importantly, the ways in which black popular music has consistently enabled African Americans to implicitly sing what they are unable to explicitly say. Burnim broached the subject further, stating: "[g]ospel is not just a musical exercise; it is a process of esoteric sharing and affirmation. It is more than the beat; it is more than the movement; it even embodies much more than text, harmonies, or instrumental accompaniment." In other words, gospel is "greater than the sum of its parts," and all of its parts, incessantly intertwining with myriad other elements of African American culture, "produce a genre which represents a uniquely black perspective." As a matter of fact, gospel encapsulates and enunciates a "uniquely black perspective" that "manifests itself in a cogent, dynamic cultural philosophy or worldview" (112). After systematically surveying the genre, Burnim came to the conclusion that gospel has "four primary functions":

> (1) Gospel music reflects and transmits a sense of the historical past for black Americans, while simultaneously addressing immediate concerns and projecting future solutions. (2) Gospel music is an affirmation of life and the meaning of living. (3) Gospel music is a vehicle for individual expression within the context of a shared system of meaning. (4) Gospel music is simultaneously an agent for spiritual sustenance and an agent for reinforcement of cultural identity. (112)

Burnim's research strongly stresses that no matter how repetitively and passionately gospel music critics may dismiss (and sometimes even disavow) *the politics of gospel music*, gospel composers and performers, especially during the music's golden age, "readily identify the historical, social, cultural, and spiritual dimensions of this musical form." Hence, once again, my contention concerning *the multi-functionality of the African American sacred song tradition* comes into play. Gospel critics routinely overlook the *gospel localism* and *gospel regionalism* at the heart of the music. That is to say, most gospel scholarship frames the music as a black folk-derived, albeit "highly urbanized, professionalized, and commercialized phenomenon" that includes recordings, radio airplay, concerts, and conventions (Castellini 2013, 13). However, it is important to call attention to the wider world of *grassroots gospel*, which, Burt Feintuch (1980) asserted, "thrives in a number of less visible settings, where it is practiced by non-professional, non-commercially motivated performers." Feintuch importantly explained further:

> What we know of black gospel music is almost entirely centered on commercial performers and composers. As a consequence, any examination of the scholarship of this vital and unique musical genre results in a skewed conception of the music and its performers....This may well be the reason why the music is customarily described as an art form performed by commercially-motivated professionals and disseminated through the means of mass culture: concert appearances, record sales, and radio airplay....[But,] such a conception of black gospel music...is erroneous or, at best, half true. Gospel music also thrives in a number of less visible settings, where it is practiced by non-professional, non-commercially-motivated performers. I maintain that although the existence of such performers is virtually uninvestigated, non-commercial groups are one of the keystones of the expressive culture of many black churches. I also believe that the non-commercial

domain differs substantially from that of the professional, although the two are related, and that it is possible to speak of non-commercial performers who perceive and practice a "gospel life." (37)

Observe the emphasis that Feintuch places on the little discussed fact that the commercial and non-commercial arenas are "separate but codependent" and, as he ultimately concludes, actually "exist in a kind of symbiotic tension," incessantly "exchanging material, styles, and personnel" (41; Castellini 2013, 13–14). As a result, any serious analysis of gospel music must take into critical consideration the ways in which commercial gospel is frequently driven by, and routinely reflects the traditions and new trends in non-commercial, grassroots gospel. Bearing in mind Feintuch's contention concerning non-commercial gospel artists being "one of the keystones of the expressive culture of many black churches," it is important for us to consider how grassroots gospel may very well be even more reflective of the aspirations and frustrations of African Americans during the tumultuous years of the Civil Rights Movement.

On the local level, grassroots gospel singers—free from many of the trappings that come along with recording for a major record label—could lyrically and musically move in a more traditional *or* unconventional, regional *or*, most importantly, unrepentantly radical political direction (*à la* freedom singer-songwriters), if they chose to do so, when compared with their incredibly constrained commercial counterparts. Which is to say, instead of masking and muting the overarching ethos of the Civil Rights Movement, in most instances grassroots gospel artists—many of whom, as discussed above, doubled as freedom singer-songwriters— were able to put into play *the "explicit" or "overt," "tell it like it is," "let's call a spade a spade" truth-telling that lies at the heart of African American culture, especially African American religious culture*. This means, then, that there were actually benefits that came along with being a grassroots, non-professional, non-commercially-motivated gospel artist during the music's golden age: these virtually *unsung* (pun intended) *singing civil rights soldiers* could unapologetically and unambiguously minister to, and express—via the healing power of the African American sacred song tradition—what was in the hearts and on the minds of the beleaguered rank and file civil rights soldiers in the most unequivocally *African American* manner imaginable without fear of anti-black racist reprisal or economic indemnification because, as Martin Luther King once exclaimed: "Unfortunately, most of the major denominations still practice segregation in local churches, hospitals, schools, and other church institutions. It is appalling that the most segregated hour of Christian America is eleven o'clock on a Sunday morning," he critically continued, "the same hour when many are standing to sing, 'In Christ there is no East nor West'." King, characteristically went even further, "[e]qually appalling is the fact that the most segregated school of the week is Sunday School." He then climatically concluded, "[h]ow often the church has had a high blood count of creeds and an anemia of deeds!" (M.L. King 1958, 207–208).

Because even religion, in this instance Christianity, was thoroughly racially segregated leading up to, and during the Civil Rights Movement years, the black church was not under the purview of white America. As a consequence, those aspects of black church culture that could—and, indeed, demonstrably *did—incite social change, promote political activism*, or *raise African American cultural consciousness* were virtually unknown to white America and, therefore, could not be either coopted or quickly countered by the legion of white opponents of the black freedom struggle. The irony here is that there is a sense in which African American ingenuity increasingly used American apartheid against itself. Racial segregation forced African Americans to live and work with each other, to rely on each other, to unconditionally love each other's humble humanity in ways that white folk simply did not have to because they were not enduring the innumerable and ubiquitous evils of anti-black racism, including anti-black racist terrorism.

Instead of a continuation of the "divide and conquer" strategies that European imperialism insidiously perfected during African colonization and African American enslavement, by the middle of the twentieth century black folk ultimately turned American apartheid upside down and developed *a coded counter-ideology* (predicated on non-violence, civil disobedience, and passive resistance, etc.) to *socialize, politicize* and, most importantly, *mobilize*. An important, even if often overlooked, part of the *coded counter-ideology* of the Civil Rights Movement was the music emerging out of the movement, and gospel music, because it never "crossed-over" in the ways in which rhythm & blues or rock & roll did, could be said to capture and convey the ambitions, inner-workings, and overarching ethos of the movement in ways that neither rhythm & blues nor rock & roll did. This is, in part, because white consumption of black popular music has had a tendency to focus more on black secular music than black sacred music. Since major white record labels have never lavished the kind of attention on black sacred music as they have on black secular music, gospel music has been, and remains, demonstrably one of the most unambiguously "African American" or, rather, the "blackest" (to put it poorly) major forms of black popular music. It is in this sense, then, that gospel music can serve as a paradigm and key point of departure for critically exploring the *coded counter-ideology* of the major soundtracks of the Civil Rights Movement.

Most golden age gospel acts were products of greatly dispersed *gospel localism* and *gospel regionalism* and, as a result, did not have fanbases reaching much beyond their home towns or regions—or, in many instances, even beyond their own church communities (Castellini 2013, 14). "Therein lies the difference between gospel and virtually every other form of music," observed Alan Young in *Woke Me Up This Morning: Black*

Gospel Singers and the Gospel Life (1997). He continued, "[g]ospel still belongs to the community. It has national stars, big recording companies, and television and radio shows, but its foundation is still in thousands of churches throughout the United States, especially in the South." Young then noted that church "is a social as well as a religious occasion, and the church membership makes up a close-knit group within the larger community." Truth be told, "[e]very church has a choir, and most have members who sing in groups." Indeed, church folk "like to see the big name groups, such as the Pilgrim Jubilees or the Mighty Clouds of Joy," but, he emphasized, "they also like to see their own [local] singers" (xxxv).

The "many highly skilled," even "if little known," grassroots gospel performers "have always replenished gospel's deep reservoir" and guaranteed its ongoing evolution and innovations (Castellini 2013, 14). Obviously, the gospel produced during the golden age demonstrated the genre's predilection for *tradition, innovation,* and *experimentation.* But, Young importantly emphasized that even in light of its core characteristics of innovation and experimentation, it is the ways in which gospel gives the "gospel community" *a sense of tradition* that may be the most meaningful for the genre's fans. No matter how much the musical accompaniment changes, *the gospel sound, the characteristic call-and-response, cry, scream, and shout sound* of both classic and contemporary gospel are emblematic of the "old-time religion" of the enslaved ancestors being conceptually carried over and—this should be unambiguously accented—acknowledged and honored. Stylistic advances and musical innovations in gospel often create a greater demand for the older styles of the gospel tradition, and this is especially the case on the local or regional gospel scene. As Young's research revealed:

> Gospel in the community is not always the same as gospel on the big shows or on nationally selling records. While the fashion in radio listening or record buying may be for choirs or contemporary performers, all styles of gospel coexist within the community. Unlike pop music, where a new fashion will banish the previous vogue, gospel's successive new developments find their own place in the structure alongside the older ones. The sheer number of grassroots performers, many highly skilled despite their anonymity, means that gospel always has a substantial pool of potential new stars. And they do not sing in vast arenas to an anonymous mass. Their venues are churches, schools, and small community centers, where they perform to the people they will meet in church on Sunday. It is a world far away from the taste manipulators and trendsetters who infest other forms of music. Gospel music continues to develop because it is not only still in touch with its community, but still belongs to it. (xxxv–xxxvi)

Much like the Civil Rights Movement contained moderate and militant, conservative and radical elements, golden age gospel music eventually consisted of both traditional and experimental or, rather, "sweet" (or "soft") and "hard" elements. For instance, between 1955 and 1965 the Golden Gate Quartet, CBS Trumpeteers, Dixie Hummingbirds, Harmonizing Four, Pilgrim Travelers, and Swan Silvertones were the dominant "sweet" gospel quartets. The major "hard" gospel quartets included iconic artists such as the Blind Boys of Mississippi, Blind Boys of Alabama, Sensational Nightingales, Mighty Clouds of Joy, Spirit of Memphis, and Swanee Quintet. A number of quartets developed styles that blurred the imaginary line between the "soft" and "hard" gospel sounds, such as the Soul Stirrers, Fairfield Four, Pilgrim Jubilee Singers, Chosen Gospel Singers, Zion Travelers, Clefs of Calvary, and Bright Light Quartet.

Even when we seriously consider Young's two-tier, local/national model for exploring gospel music we must bear in mind that beyond internal, more or less cultural and aesthetic dynamics, a number of external social and political factors shape and shade the composition, production, distribution, and consumption of gospel music. Which is also to say, *even though gospel is an art form preoccupied with heaven, it has never been able to completely transcend the inhospitable earthly context of its origins and evolution.* As discussed above, the composition, production, distribution, and consumption of gospel music has been directly impacted by African Americans' collective incessant experience and endurance of cultural imperialism, economic exploitation, social segregation, political repression, and anti-black racism. Consequently, the story of this music's composition, production, distribution, and consumption, as gospel and blues scholar Guido van Rijn (2001) contended, actually "confirms how the racial situation provided a crucial context within which the artistry and commerce of African American popular music took place." However, it also illustrates "how much the story of the creation, distribution, and consumption of that music has much to tell historians about the African American community during years of great social upheaval and change" (140).

Arguably, one of the most interesting things golden age gospel reveals to us is that gospel artists did, indeed, create civil rights-themed gospel songs, and that these songs seemed to be the special providence of the B-sides or, rather, "flip sides" of records by incredibly obscure artists on equally incredibly obscure and poorly distributed local labels (Castellini 2013, 16). Bearing in mind the "underrepresentation of African American label owners in the recording industry" during the Civil Rights Movement, van Rijn maintained,

> a disproportionate number of these civil rights songs also appear to have been cut for black-owned labels. Maybe African American owners, as those within the industry with the greatest personal stake in the movement's success, were sometimes more willing to go out on a limb to record potentially controversial material. Yet, in truth, there was hardly a stampede to cut such songs from anyone, black or white. And there was no guarantee of a public airing for those songs that were

recorded: fears of possible reprisals, doubts about their commercial appeal, and the certain knowledge that even if they avoided formal ban, they would not get airplay on the radio, combined to ensure that many civil rights blues and gospel songs remained unissued. (139–140)

Nevertheless, no words should be minced about the fact that even in the context of civil rights-themed gospel songs, grassroots gospel artists were not alone. It is simply important to bear in mind that arguably the vast majority of civil rights-themed gospel songs, especially those either composed or performed by professional gospel singers, more than likely were not recorded or, if they did find their way onto wax, as van Rijn observed, "remained unissued." Here, then, the emphasis is on both unrecognized and unrecorded protest songs arising out of *the grassroots gospel community, gospel localism,* and *gospel regionalism* that feasibly indelibly influenced the intentionally understated protest praxis of national, commercial, and professional gospel music during the Civil Rights Movement.

Echoes of the angst of the African American experience during the Civil Rights Movement years reverberated in both the North and South, and at both the local and national levels. Obviously, even more subtly than grassroots gospel artists, elite gospel artists put into play *the "we can implicitly sing what we cannot explicitly say" aesthetic of the broader black popular music tradition* and, therefore, "explicit," "tell it like it is," "let's call a spade a spade" outright Civil Rights Movement songs were never more than a minor, local or, at best, regional phenomenon. Here, we have obviously returned to my above emphasis on the importance of acknowledging and critically engaging *gospel localism* and *gospel regionalism.* Yet and still, my conscience compels me to admit that it is, in some senses, completely understandable that many gospel music scholars and critics have been either nearly or completely silent concerning civil rights-themed gospel songs because of what Burnim identified above as gospel's processes and practices of "esoteric sharing and affirmation." If, indeed, a good number of gospel's inner-workings and folkways are "esoteric," which is to say, intended for, or likely to be understood by only a small number of people with specialized knowledge or insatiable interests in gospel music—then gospel music scholars and critics may be forgiven for overlooking what most folk seem wholly unaware of in the first place.

In other words, I am saying that when the situation became critical, and the time for unapologetic protest could no longer be evaded, when the African American church "assumed its leadership of the black freedom struggle" in the middle years of the twentieth century, it seems logical to expect to hear myriad civil rights-themed gospel songs. But, truth be told, for the most part, this was quite simply "*not* the case" (Castellini 2013, 17, emphasis added). Without a doubt, this does not mean that gospel artists were not actively involved and contributing in other important ways to the Civil Rights Movement, such as performing civil rights-themed gospel songs at mass meetings, "volunteering for movement work," or simply making (most often anonymous) monetary contributions. When one really and critically studies historical and bio-graphical (not merely musicological) work on golden age gospel artists, one walks away with the distinct impression that many of the greatest figures in gospel music were, in fact, *unsung singing civil rights soldiers*— that is to say, subtle, tight-tongued but undoubtedly politically active civil rights soldiers.

But, truth be told, for most members of the gospel community "open resistance," even open "passive resistance," whether participating in mass meetings, boycotts, marches, sit-ins or freedom rides, was most often shied away from, especially considering the frequent blowback movement members faced (Castellini 2013, 17). As van Rijn expertly ob-served, during the Civil Rights Movement era, African American artists, whether gospel, blues, jazz, rhythm & blues or rock & roll artists, "their managers, and their labels, not to mention distributors, theaters booking agencies, and radio station managers, were permanently concerned about the adverse effects overtly political songs might have on both their finan-cial and physical well-being" (126). This is precisely where a purely musicological interpretation of gospel music fails to fully appreciate the historical, cultural, social, political, and economic contexts surrounding the composition, production, distribution, and consumption of gospel during its golden age. Building on this point, van Rijn reminds us,

> regardless of any specific lyrical focus on civil rights issues, black pop-ular music has always been deeply implicated in constructing the African American sense of self, community, heritage and destiny. Al-though there was something of a post-war flight away from blues and, to a lesser extent, gospel toward their rhythm & blues and soul proge-ny, these older styles continued to be enjoyed by many in the black community. Moreover, by the mid-1960s, heightened racial conscious-ness meant that these two protean musical forms were again widely appreciated as cornerstones, not just of black—and much white—pop-ular music, but also of the entire African American experience. (123)

Obviously, van Rijn critically comprehends that *black popular music is more than merely music* when he asserted that it "has always been deeply impli-cated in constructing the African American sense of self, community, heritage and destiny." Similar to other genres of black popular music, gospel has deep extra-musical dimensions—especially during the Civil Rights Movement era—that should not be overlooked in favor of analy-ses that *a priori* argue that it is apathetic, escapist, and apolitical without taking into critical consideration the ways in which *gospel protest*, in most instances, looks, sounds, and feels very different when compared with either *rhythm & blues protest* or *rock & roll protest*. The significance and real distinctiveness of civil rights-themed songs, whether gospel, rhythm & blues or rock & roll, in the 1950s and 1960s African American community "depended as much on their musical stylings, performance practices, and historic place within black culture as on their lyrical content," van Rijn noted. Even if the corpus of explicit civil rights-themed gospel songs is relatively small compared with, for instance, civil rights-themed rhythm & blues songs, van Rijn importantly accented the fact that "at least one song was devoted to most of the major landmarks of the civil rights struggle." He concluded, "[a]s such they present a modest but impressive musical response to the struggle for African American freedom, a response that is undoubtedly representative of a much larger body of unrecorded protest songs in these styles" (123).

CONCLUSION: GOSPEL MUSIC AS A REFLECTION OF THE "CALM, COOL, AND COLLECTED" MAXIM OF THE CIVIL RIGHTS MOVEMENT

In the aftermath of World War II gospel artists were becoming increasingly professionalized and commercialized entertainers preoccupied with, among other things, making a decent living. Golden age gospel music fans, scholars, and critics need to understand that as with "professional performers of all (or [even] no) political persuasions," gospel singers "had to earn money" to support themselves and their families (Castellini 2013, 17). Here, we have stumbled upon what could be termed *the political economy of the composition, production, distribution, and consumption of gospel music during its golden age*. I am completely sensitive to the fact that within the African American church community, whether we are speaking of the local, regional or national African American church community, associating black church music with moneymaking, entertainment, or commercialism is, in some senses, sacrilegious. But, gospel artists need the bare necessities much like the rest of us, and no amount sanctimoniousness and high-sounding hyperbole will feed, clothe, and shelter them and their families. Point-blank: Musicology must be coupled with history, sociology, and political economy, at the very least, in order to critically comprehend my contention throughout this book that *when and where we come to black popular music the extra-musical is just as pertinent, if not in many instances even more significant, than the musical—for black folk music serves multiple functions that go far beyond music composition, music theory, and staid music criticism.*

A purely religious or musicological analysis of the professionalization of gospel artists simply fails to take into consideration the fact that professional gospel artists' careers would have been placed in peril if they even hinted at Civil Rights Movement support, whether moderate or

militant. Their recording contracts, radio airplay, and concert appear-
ances would all be jeopardized if they did not, as it were, "play it calm,
cool, and collected." Even semi-professional or amateur gospel artists
struggling to make ends meet while working on soul-sundering and
dream-destroying jobs in the South could easily engender the anger of
local segregationists and regional racists aplenty. Indeed, being "calm,
cool, and collected" was a dire, "life-or-death matter." Consequently,
golden age gospel songs, not surprisingly, reveal very "little evidence of
plainspoken 'protest,'" of the "double-conscious" inner-thoughts and in-
ner-feelings of the gospel artists themselves (Castellini 2013, 17–18).
Again, much had to be masked or, rather, "veiled," as Du Bois metaphorically put it in *The Souls of Black Folk* (Du Bois [1903, 2–3] famously wrote:
"[I]t dawned upon me with a certain suddenness that I was different
from the others; or like, mayhap, in heart and life and longing, but shut
out from their world by a vast veil….[T]he Negro is a sort of seventh son,
born with a veil, and gifted with second-sight in this American world").
To reiterate, disguising "gospel protest" was, literally, a matter of life-or-
death during the Civil Rights Movement.

   Not only had gospel spread throughout the African American community by the 1950s, but it had also gained an increasingly effusive white
audience as well. Bearing this in mind, according to Castellini (2013, 18),
it is not surprising to learn that most gospel artists steered clear of songs
that could jeopardize their livelihoods, if not, literally, "their very lives."
Taking into consideration the real possibility of economic retaliation or
worse, most gospel singers understandably shunned outright support for
the Civil Rights Movement, irrespective of their personal socio-political
inclinations. There was also considerable pressure from managers, record
companies, and radio stations for gospel singers to eschew any sem-
blance of civil rights support. Even a brief survey of the Civil Rights
Movement will reveal that for all of its emphasis on non-violence, civil
disobedience, and passive resistance, anti-black racist physical and economic violence awaited any African American who broke with the "calm,
cool, and collected" maxim of the movement and audaciously put into
play the "explicit," "tell it like it is," "let's call a spade a spade" truth-
telling that lies at the heart of African American culture, especially
African American religious culture. With this in mind, we should solemnly ask ourselves: Is it any wonder, then, that "gospel protest" during
the Civil Rights Movement was not explicit, and it did not unequivocally
voice the core views and values of the movement?

   Well-founded fears of physical and economic retaliatory violence kept
most African Americans, whether moderate or militant, from becoming
openly and actively involved in the movement. It should be recalled that
in many parts of the South white supremacist and anti-black racist terror-
ist organizations and associations such as the Ku Klux Klan, White Citizens' Council, and American Independent Party were in most instances

"indistinguishable from local, county, and even state government author-ities" (18). Keeping in mind that only a fraction of African Americans were actually members of civil rights organizations or actively participat-ed in the rallies, boycotts, marches, sit-ins, and freedom rides that became the signatures of the movement, once again, one has to wonder whether it is fair, realistic, or even reasonable to expect artists and entertainers to commit "career suicide" and "social suicide" while most other African Americans embraced more subtle forms of support, most often made clandestine contributions to the movement, and painfully swallowed their pride and did what they had to do to put food on their tables, clothes on their backs, and keep roofs over their heads?

As a matter of fact, artists and entertainers' higher public profile and greater reliance on "public approval arguably made them more reticent to instigate" or become openly and actively involved in anything that might elicit "negative public reaction" (18). However, and this should be strongly stressed, the exact same statement (minus the reference to artists and entertainers' higher public profile and greater reliance on public ap-proval) could be made about most members of the African American community during the Civil Rights Movement. If gospel artists wanted to have successful careers and really ply their crafts (e.g., make commercial recordings, have their work regularly featured on radio playlists, and get lucrative concert engagements), they simply could not "tell it like it is," or "call a spade a spade," or certainly not openly embrace and put into practice the special tradition of truth-telling that lies at the heart of African American culture (once again, I remind my readers that Du Bois declared at the dawn of the twentieth century, "the Negro is a sort of seventh son, born with a veil, and gifted with second-sight in this American world," and that what I am referring to here as "the special tradition of truth-telling that lies at the heart of African American cul-ture," is essentially black folks' ongoing articulation of their distinct "sec-ond-sight"). In other words, gospel artists quite simply could not utilize "protest language" or any sort of radical-sounding rhetoric in their songs (18). Once again, "gospel protest," as with much of African American musical protest more broadly speaking, is predicated on *the "we can impli-citly sing what we cannot explicitly say" aesthetic.*

To put it plainly, white supremacist watchdogs eagerly surveilled and policed the music emerging out of black America during the Civil Rights Movement. As a result, radio station owners and managers considered the tragic (and awfully ironic) reality that inhospitable ears were among the thousands and thousands of radio listeners, and that even the anti-black racists and hardcore segregationists understood that black popular music, in this instance gospel music, was *more than merely music* and that it indeed does have *extra-musical implications*. Needless to say, the anti-black racists and hardcore segregationists stayed on high-alert and were primed and ever-ready to react and attack at even the "slightest hint" of civil rights sympathy or criticism of racial segregation, not to mention the broader national policies, programs, and practices of American apartheid. As a matter of fact, "radio transmitters were sabotaged, [radio] lines were cut" or otherwise vandalized, and blazing "crosses were burned" to humiliate and intimidate black-oriented radio stations perceived to be supportive of, or in any way aligned with the Civil Rights Movement (19). Therefore, right along with White Citizens' Councils, the Ku Klux Klan, and other organizations of such disagreeable ilk, anxious advertisers and high-strung bureaucrats had to be appeased and assured in light of *the political economy of the composition, production, distribution, and consumption of black popular music.* In short, civil rights sympathy or unequivocal and unapologetic civil rights militancy was not simply bad for the artists health and well-being, but also "bad for business, big or small," white or black, Northern, Southern, Midwestern, or Western (19).

It seems more likely that non-professional and, therefore, non-commercial gospel singers, established in their local or regional racially segregated enclaves, were able to take more artistic liberties and poetic license than more famous professional and high-profile gospel artists were in either composing or singing others' civil rights-themed gospel (and freedom) songs. Also, it could almost go without saying that these mostly self-pressed and self-distributed gospel records were not subject to the same sort of severe censorship as those put out on the higher-stakes and higher-profile professional and commercial gospel scene. Logically, without the restrictions enforced on elite gospel artists with wider exposure, it seems to make perfect sense that it would have been these local, amateur and, therefore, incredibly obscure gospel singers with no major record label affiliation who recorded more or less explicit "protest" or "message" civil rights-themed gospel songs (19).

We should be clear here, so that there is no misunderstanding surrounding the point that I am making: I am not in anyway arguing that little-known local gospel singers were "somehow more militant" when compared with gospel's professional and commercial glitterati. On the contrary, considering that the personal, cultural, and artistic barriers between the major gospel artists and grassroots gospel communities have always intensely overlapped, and considering the incessant disinclination on the part of record labels, radio stations, and sponsors to touch the politically and economically "toxic" race issue, it can be safely assumed that more overt civil rights-themed gospel songs would have been recorded if elite gospel artists had have been provided with the "relative autonomy" of local or regional self-production, self-pressing, and self-distribution (19). Concentrating exclusively, if not often obsessively, on explicit or overt protest (conceived of in the most conventional sense), it cannot be overemphasized at this point, simply does not enable objective interpreters of "gospel protest" to critically comprehend how golden age gospel music, in fact, subtly served as a mouthpiece for the core views and values of the Civil Rights Movement. Along with gospel, and in some senses sonically representing the secularization of the spirituals and gospel's characteristic *call-and-response, cry, scream, and shout sound*, classic rhythm & blues also subtly served as a mouthpiece for the core views and values of the Civil Rights Movement. Consequently, let us now look at *the new rhythms* and *the new blues* black folk invented between 1945 and 1965 to encapsulate the ideals and ethos of the Civil Rights Movement.

NOTES

1. For further discussion of *black sacred song* and, more broadly speaking, *the African American sacred song tradition*, and for the most noteworthy works which influenced my interpretation here, see Abbington (2001a, 2001b, 2009, 2014), Baszak (2003), T. Brooks (1984), Costen (2004), Cruz (1999), Darden (2004, 2014), Dargan (2006), David (2007), Epstein (2003), T.F. Jones (1973), Keck and Martin (1988), Lovell (1972), R. Newman (1998), Peters (1993), Reagon (2001), Rublowsky (1971), Schenbeck (2012), T. Smith (2004), Spencer (1988, 1989, 1990, 1994), Stone (2010), W.T. Walker (1979), and A. Young (1997).

2. For further discussion of the heavenly salvation and earthly liberation leitmotif in "Golden Age" gospel music, and for the most noteworthy works that informed my interpretation here, see T.L.F. Brown (2003), Burnim (1980, 1985a, 1985b, 1988), Castellini (2013), Darden (2004, 2014), Edwards (2009), Frederick (2009), Gallien (2011), Goff (2002), Harvey (1986), Hinson (2000), Maultsby (1981), McGregory (2010), Reagon (2000), Ricks (1977), J. Ryan (2008), Salvatore (2006), W.T. Walker (1979), and D. Webster (2011).

3. For further discussion of freedom songs, and for the most noteworthy works that informed my interpretation here, see Baumann (2011), Bimmler (2008), Carawan and Carawan (1963, 1968, 2007), Castellini (2013), Dunaway (2008), Dunson (1965), Frederick (2009), Hampton and Fayer (2011), Kot (2014), Lincoln and Mamiya (1990), Lovell (1972), McCanless (1997), McGregory (2010), Payne (2011), Raines (1977), Reagon (1975, 1993), Sanger (1995), Seeger and Reiser (1989), W.T. Walker (1979), Watters (1971), Weber (2010), and J.E. Williams (2002).

4. For further discussion of Stokely Carmichael's early activism in the Civil Rights Movement, and for the most noteworthy works that informed my interpretation here, see Branch (2006), Carmichael (2003), Hullet and Carmichael (1966), Hunter (2006), and Joseph (2006b, 2014).

5. My interpretation of Sam Block's "Freedom Is A Constant Dying" has been indelibly influenced by Carawan and Carawan (1963, 1968, 2007), Lincoln and Mamiya (1990), Reagon (1975, 1993), Sanger (1995), and Seeger and Reiser (1989).

6. For further discussion of African American gospel music, and for the most noteworthy works that informed my interpretation here, see Anderson and North (1979), Boyer (1979, 1985, 1995, 2000, 2001), Broughton (1985, 1996), Burnim (1980a, 1980b, 1985a, 1985b, 1988), Costen (2004), Darden (2004, 2014), Dixon and Rye (1997), De Lerma (1973), Feintuch (1980), Frederick (2009), Gilmour (2005), Goff (2002), M.W. Harris (1992), Harvey (1986), Heilbut (1982, 1997), Hillsman (1983, 1990), Hinson (2000), J.A. Jackson (2004), Kemp (2011), Lornell (1995), Marovich (2015), Mason (2004), Maultsby (1981), McGregory (2010), Pollard (2008), Reagon (1992, 2001), T.L. Reed (2003), Ricks (1977), Seroff (1985), Spencer (1990), S. Turner (2010), W.T. Walker (1979), Williams-Jones (1975), A. Young (1997), and Zolten (2003).

7. For discussions of African American's experience and endurance of American apartheid, racial segregation, racial violence (including the anti-black racist ritual of lynching), and outright *anti-black racist terrorism* from the turn of the twentieth century through to the Civil Rights Movement, and for the most noteworthy works that in-

formed my interpretation here, see first and foremost W.E.B. Du Bois's *Black Recon-struction* (1935), as well as Ackerman (2014), Apel (2004), Apel and Smith (2007), B.E. Baker (2008), Berrey (2015), Blackmon (2008), Brown-Nagin (2011), Brundage (1993, 1997), Carle (2013), Carson (1981), Francis (2014), Garrow (1989), Harper (2010), Jeffries (2009), L.E. Hill (2004), G. Lewis (2006), Markovitz (2004), C.C. Miller (2012), Nevels, (2007), Payne (2011), Romano (2014), Shapiro (1988), Umoja (2013), Waldrep (2006, 2009), Williamson (1984, 1986), Wolcott (2012), and Wood (2009).

8. For further discussion of African American migration during the early-to-mid twentieth century that significantly impacted the emergence of the Civil Rights Move-ment and its sacred *and* secular soundtracks, and for the most noteworthy works that informed my interpretation here, see Adero (1993), Arnesen (2002), Athearn (1978), D.L. Baldwin (2007), Berlin (2010), T.D. Black (2003), Blocker (2008), Dodson and Diouf (2004), Fligstein (1982), Garb (2014), Gottlieb (1987), J.N. Gregory (2005), Groh (1972), Grossman (1991), Hahn (2003), A. Harrison (1991), Henri (1975), Johnson and Camp-bell (1981), Lehman (1991), Marks (1989), Painter (1976), Pleck (1979), Pruitt (2013), C.R. Reed (2014), Reich (2014), Sernett (1997), Tolnay and Beck (1992), Trotter (1991), Wilkerson (2010), and Woodson (1969).

9. For further discussion of the second migration of African Americans between 1940 and 1970 that significantly impacted the emergence of the Civil Rights Movement and its sacred *and* secular soundtracks, and for the most noteworthy works that in-formed my interpretation here, see L. Adams (2010), Askin (1970), Berlin (2010), T.D. Black (2008), Boehm (2009), Dodson and Diouf (2004), DuBose-Simons (2013), Flam-ming (2005), Fligstein (1982), Gill (1975), J.N. Gregory (2005), L.L. Harris (2012), A. Harrison (1991), Holley (2000), Lemke-Santangelo (1996), and Stack (1996).

10. For further discussion of African retentions in African American religious thought and practices, and for the most noteworthy works that informed my interpre-tation here, see L.E. Barrett (1974), Bascom (1980), Bastide (1971, 1978), Gomez (1998), J.E. Holloway (1991), S.A. Johnson (2015), J.M. Murphy (1994), Pitts (1993), Sernett, (1999), G.E. Simpson (1978), Trost (2007), and C.S. Wilder (2001).

11. For further discussion of Du Bois's distinct history of religion and sociology of religion, and for the most noteworthy works that informed my interpretation here, see Blum (2007), Blum and Young (2009), Dorrien (2015), Du Bois (1980, 2000), C. Evans (2007), Forney (2002), Hufford (1997), B.L. Johnson (2008), T.L. Johnson (2012), Kahn (2009), Levinson (2006), Savage (2000), Sinitiere (2012), S.J. Shaw (2013), C.L. Stewart (2008, 2010), Wilmore (1998), R.A. Wortham (2005a, 2005b, 2009), and Zuckerman (2002, 2009).

12. For further discussion of the politics of the African American church, especially during the Civil Rights Movement, and for the most noteworthy works that informed my interpretation here, see L.V. Baldwin (2010), Billingsley (1999), Dillard (2007), Findlay (1993), Friedland (1998), Glaude (2000), F.C. Harris (1999), Higginbotham (1993), Houck and Dixon (2006, 2014), London (2009), Manis (1999), McDaniel (2008), Murray (2004), M. Newman (2004a), O'Foran (2006), Owens (2007), Paris (1991), Sav-age (2012), R.D. Smith (2003, 2004, 2013), Smith and Harris (2005), C. Taylor (2002), White and Manis (2000), J.E. Williams (2003), and Wilmore (1998).

13. For further discussion of the Black Women's Club Movement, its origins and evolution, and for the most noteworthy works that informed my analysis here, see Bracks and Smith (2014), L. Brown (2008), Cash (1986, 2001), E.L. Davis (1996), Dickson (1982), Dublin, Arias, and Carreras (2003), Giddings (1984), Gilkes (2000), Guy-Sheftall (1990), Hendricks (1998), Higginbotham (1993), Hine (1997), Jenkins (1984), J.M. John-son (2004), Logan (1995, 1999), Maffly-Kipp and Lofton (2010), McCluskey (2014), Royster (2000), S.J. Shaw (1991), S.L. Smith (1986), Terborg-Penn (1998), Waters and Conway (2007), and Wesley (1984).

14. Nellie McKay, Gary Lemons, and Hazel Carby each bemoan the fact that there is a strong tendency in Du Bois studies to read him primarily as a "race man" and to discursively downplay his "feminist" and/or "womanist" discourse. In her essay, "The Souls of Black Women Folk in the Writings of W.E.B. Du Bois," McKay (1990) claims

that Du Bois was one of very few black men who wrote "feminist autobiography": "More than any other black man in our history, his three autobiographies [*Darkwater*, *Dusk of Dawn*, and *The Autobiography of W.E.B. Du Bois*] demonstrate that black women have been central to the development of his intellectual thought" (229, 231). McKay, who is a literary theorist and critic, argues that one of the reasons that so many Du Bois scholars read him almost exclusively as a "race man" is because they often overlook his "more creative, less sociological works, where most of his thoughts on women and his own fundamental spirituality are expressed" (230). "Few people, even those who have spent years reading and studying Du Bois," quips McKay, "know that he wrote five novels and published a volume of poetry" (231). In "'When and Where [We] Enter': In Search of a Feminist Forefather—Reclaiming the Womanist Legacy of W.E.B. Du Bois," Lemons (2001) laments: Du Bois's "womanist activism remains to be fully claimed by contemporary black men, as he continues to be viewed primarily as a 'race man'" (72). What perplexes Lemons is the fact that the critics who elide and erase Du Bois's women's decolonization and women's liberation work do not simply do Du Bois a disservice, but rob contemporary men, and men of African descent in particular, of an Africana male *anti-sexist* role model. According to Lemons, "not only" was Du Bois's "conception of anti-racist resistance feminist-inspired, his worldview was profoundly influenced by black women" (73). Finally, in the first chapter of her book, *Race Men*, "The Souls of Black Men," Hazel Carby (1998) offers contemporary academics and political activists a deconstruction of Du Bois as "race man" that acknowledges that he "advocated equality for women and consistently supported feminist causes" (12). Carby, who asserts that it is not her intention to claim that Du Bois was "a sexist male individual," is not, however, as concerned with Du Bois's "male-feminist" thought – although she certainly gives it a highly critical treatment – as with many black male intellectuals' erasure and omission of his black feminist thought from their discourse on Du Bois and their obsessive concerns with "the reproduction of Race Men" (12, 25). She states: "If, as intellectuals and as activists, we are committed, like Du Bois, to struggles for liberation and democratic egalitarianism, then surely it is not contradictory also to struggle to be critically aware of the ways in which *ideologies of gender* have undermined our egalitarian visions in the past and continue to do so in the present" (12, my emphasis). Carby's caveat, like the cautions of McKay and Lemons, essentially asks that we be cognizant of not only the "ideologies of gender" in the present, but also the "ideologies of gender" of the past, and how this specific species of ideology may have and/or, more than likely, indeed did influence the ways our intellectual ancestors theorized about this or that issue. In other words, we must make ourselves and others critically conscious of sexist sentiment in both classical and contemporary Africana decolonization and liberation theory and praxis. My work here, then, registers as an effort to simultaneously deepen and develop the anti-sexist aspects of Africana critical theory, and an attempt to move beyond one-dimensional interpretations of Du Bois which downplay the multidimensionality of his thought and texts. It is important here to note that because of the richness and wide range and reach of Du Bois's thought, within Du Bois studies there are various research areas and agendas—for example, history, philosophy, anthropology, sociology, politics, economics, aesthetics, literature, religion, education, and so forth. Depending on one's intellectual orientation and academic training and discipline, his thought and texts may serve a multiplicity of purposes and may be approached from a wide array of discursive directions. Needless to say, my interpretations of Du Bois have been deeply influenced by my training in and trek through African, African American, and Caribbean studies (i.e., *Africana studies*), and specifically my specialization in African, African American, and Caribbean history, philosophy, political economy, and critical social theory. For further discussion of Du Bois's contributions to black feminism, womanism, women's rights, women's suffrage, women's decolonization, and women's liberation, and for the most noteworthy works that informed my interpretation here, see Alston (2011), B. Aptheker (1975), Balfour (2005, 2011), Browne (2000), Dickerson (2008), Diggs (1974), Gilkes (1996), Gillman and Weinbaum (2007), Griffin (2000),

Hancock (2005), Hattery and Smith (2005), J.A. James (1996, 1997), Lemons (2001, 2009), Lucal (1996), McKay (1985, 1990), Pauley (2000), Rabaka (2007, 2008, 2010a, 2010c), Staton (2001), Weinbaum (2001, 2013), and Yellin (1973).

15. For further discussion of the, however subtle, politics of gospel music, especially during the Civil Rights Movement era, and for the most noteworthy works that informed my interpretation here, see Burnim (1980a, 1985a, 1985b, 2006, 2015), Darden (2004, 2014), Frederick (2009), Goff (2002), Heilbut (1997), J.A. Jackson (2004), Kot (2014), Marovich (2015), McGregory (2010), Reagon (1975, 1992, 2000, 2001), Seroff (1985), Spencer (1990), van Rijn (1997, 2001, 2004, 2007, 2009, 2011, 2012), W.T. Walker (1979), and Williams-Jones (1975).

16. In *The Negro in American Life and Thought: The Nadir, 1877-1901* (1954), noted African American historian Rayford Logan (1954) famously referred to the decade closing the nineteenth century as the "nadir" of African American history, and his work, along with the work of several other scholars, has brought to light more than 3,000 documented lynchings and other forms of anti-black racist terrorism during this unfortunate era. For further discussion, and for the most noteworthy works that informed my interpretation here, see J. Allen (2005), Apel (2004), Apel and Smith (2007), Brundage (1993, 1997), Carrigan (2004, 2008), Carrigan and Webb (2013), Carr (2006), Chadbourn (1933), Finkelmen (1992), Goldsby (2006), Gonzales-Day (2006), T. Harris (1984), Ifill (2007), Leonard (2002), Markovitz (2004), Nevels (2007), Pfeifer (2004), Pickens (1921), Raper (1969), Waldrep (2006), and Zangrando (1980).

FOUR

Rhythm & Blues and the Civil Rights Movement

INTRODUCTION: THE RHYTHMS & THE BLUES
OF THE CIVIL RIGHTS MOVEMENT

While mainstream American history, culture, politics, and economics have undoubtedly impacted the African American popular music tradition, black ghetto youth historically have been, and remain, its primary producers and practitioners. Their songs served as mouthpieces for the Civil Rights Movement, just as their songs remain central to the soundtracks of the Hip Hop Movement. As we shift our focus from *the African American sacred song tradition* to *the African American secular song tradition*, from black church music to black popular music during the Civil Rights Movement, it is important to bear in mind that the primary producers and practitioners of the gospel-derived freedom songs discussed in the previous chapter were working-class and underclass black youth. Moreover, at its inception many of the pioneers and popularizers of gospel were, relatively speaking, young, working-poor church folk. For instance, the widely acclaimed "father of gospel music," Thomas Dorsey, began his career performing and recording as a scuffling blues musician named "Georgia Tom" (he also performed and recorded as "Barrelhouse Tom" and "Texas Tommy"), but by the mid-1920s was recording early gospel along with his blues songs. Born in Villa Rica, Georgia, in 1899, in the mid-1920s Dorsey was a young, working but poor musician whose gospel music was long-reviled before it was eventually revered during the Civil Rights Movement. As Michael Harris observed in *The Rise of Gospel Blues: The Music of Thomas Andrew Dorsey in the Urban Church* (1992), it was Dorsey's "earlier experience with the revitalization of downhome blues that provided him with the assurance that that style was an appropriate form of music for [black] churches" (127).[1]

Much like its musical offspring, rhythm & blues and rock & roll, gospel creatively combined elements of both the African American sacred song tradition and the African American secular song tradition, both black church music and black popular music, and it is this sonic synthesis that was incredibly controversial at the emergence of gospel music in the 1920s. Most "old-time religion" or "old school" church folk in the 1920s and 1930s thought that gospel—what Dorsey called "gospel blues"—was nothing more than misguided young folks' foolishness. But, Harris contended:

> Dorsey could well remember that the strength of the resurgence of the older style of blues was a surprise to almost everyone in the business. Recordings by Bessie Smith and Ma Rainey exceeded all sales expectations. Because of the success of their records, Smith and Rainey now performed in the theaters and clubs that had been the exclusive domains of vaudeville blues artists who were considered the higher-class singers. Dorsey knew, therefore, that downhome secular blues was a powerful medium even outside the rent parties, wine rooms, and honky-tonks in which it was usually performed. To Dorsey these traditional contexts for the older blues were comparable to the storefront for the older style religion. As he had worked his way out of them and ultimately had been able to carry the music with him, he could now expect to remain in old-time churches and convince them of the virtues of the older music—no matter how formidable the challenge. (127)

Part of Dorsey's genius lies in his extraordinary ability to perceive that black popular music, in this instance "downhome secular blues," was in fact, "a powerful medium even outside the rent parties, wine rooms, and honky-tonks in which it was usually performed." If the spirituals could be sung in secular settings, as they were during and immediately after African American enslavement, Dorsey fervently believed that certain elements of the blues and jazz could be blended with the spirituals and adapted to create a new, more modern, twentieth century version of the spirituals that could be sung in the modern black church. Mixing black sacred song with black secular song, Dorsey blurred the lines between the sacred and the secular in ways that obviously resonated with the large majority of African Americans when we consider that gospel music is currently universally regarded as the central soundtrack of black church life and culture, and the fact that every major form of black popular music that has risen after the introduction of gospel has in some way been influenced by it—including rhythm & blues and rock & roll during the Civil Rights Movement, and soul and funk during the Black Power Movement. It would be virtually impossible to overlook the working-class and underclass roots of the blues. It stands to reason, then, if early gospel directly and unambiguously mixed the spirituals and the blues, both musics with undeniable working-class and underclass roots, then gospel, especially during its formative phase through to its peak period (circa 1925 to 1965), can be interpreted as an expression of working-class and underclass black folks' preoccupation with heavenly salvation and earthly liberation.

Where gospel could be said to be an expression of primarily working-class and underclass black folk, rhythm & blues (as with rock & roll at its inception), can be said to be an expression of primarily working-class and underclass *young* black folk. Again, it should be emphasized that a young Thomas Dorsey pioneered gospel music, and he selected a young, working-poor Mahalia Jackson to popularize his songs and the gospel sound. In 1927, at the age of sixteen, Jackson moved from New Orleans to Chicago, and in 1928 met Dorsey. Although Dorsey, according to Horace Boyer (1995), "was legitimately concerned with what she would do to his songs," as the teenage Jackson "was not always inclined to follow the Baptist style of singing, especially when she was caught up in the spirit," by the 1930s "the two became a team for fourteen years" (87). Just as ragtime was pioneered and popularized by a young Scott Joplin, and jazz by a young Louis Armstrong and a young Duke Ellington, gospel music was pioneered by a young Thomas Dorsey and popularized by a young Mahalia Jackson. As emphasized in the previous chapter, the extra-musical aspects of African American music are often just as important as, if not even more important than, the purely musical elements.

Whether we turn to the Abolitionist Movement or the New Negro Movement, the Civil Rights Movement or the Black Power Movement, the black popular music emerging out of the movement under consideration most often provides a mouthpiece for, and map of the movement. Musical texts often double as historical, cultural, social, and political texts that chronicle and, however codedly, critique many of the most pressing problems of the movement and its epoch. Which is to say, as discussed in the previous chapter, there is more than merely a casual relationship between black popular music and black politics, black aesthetics, and black ethics. At the heart of the connection between black popular music and black politics lies working-class and underclass black youth, who pioneered and popularized every form of post-enslavement black popular music, from the blues and ragtime to jazz and gospel. Consequently, the history, culture, and struggles of working-class and underclass black folk, especially black ghetto youth, should be at the heart of any serious analysis of black popular music and black popular movements. As a matter of fact, much of what historically has been, and currently continues to be called "black popular culture" is nothing more than *black ghetto youth culture* or, at the least, some derivation of it.[2]

Ironically, along with being the primary producers and practitioners of black popular culture, black ghetto youth have consistently served as the foot soldiers and very often the shock troops for the mostly middle-aged and middle-class leadership of post-enslavement black social and political movements: from the Black Women's Club Movement and the New Negro Movement through to the Harlem Renaissance and the Civil Rights Movement. For instance, with regard to the Civil Rights Movement, who can deny the pivotal role black ghetto youth played in the Montgomery Bus Boycott, the Voter Registration Movement, the Sit-In Movement, the Freedom Riders Movement, the Albany Movement, the March on Washington, or the Selma to Montgomery Marches? The point that I am making here has to do with the fact that black ghetto youth are often rendered *invisible* when and where we come to African American political thought and social movements. But, these same youths are usually rendered *hyper-visible* when and where we come to black popular culture, especially what is perceived to be the vices and vulgarities of black popular music.[3]

Needless to say, black popular music conveys more than vices and vulgarities. If one listens to it from a perspective that is sensitive to the lives and struggles of black ghetto youth, then—and, perhaps, only then—a whole new world, a whole new archive ripe for critical analysis is opened up. Often black ghetto youths' music, aesthetics, and politics are engaged, validated or invalidated utilizing either Eurocentric or black bourgeois criteria. This tendency reeks of the kind of dubious double-standard that working-class and poor black folk have long resented when and where their music, aesthetics, and politics have been examined by bourgeois and petit bourgeois scholars and critics. By grounding my analysis in the lives and struggles of working-class and poor African American youth; by sincerely and sensitively attempting to understand the ways in which they have historically used music as a prime medium through which to express their views and values (*à la* "implicitly singing what they cannot explicitly say"); and by (re)situating their sonic reflections and expressions within the wider contexts of African American political thought and popular social movements, and African American history, culture, and struggle more generally, here I will explore classic rhythm & blues as one of the major black popular music conduits for black ghetto youths' contributions to, and critiques of the Civil Rights Movement.

Ultimately I am undertaking this analysis to discover how the young unsung singing soldiers of the Civil Rights Movement put the "we can implicitly sing what we cannot explicitly say" aesthetic into play in secular song, specifically rhythm & blues. Therefore, this chapter is not in any way offered as a definitive or even a comprehensive history of classic rhythm & blues in relationship to the Civil Rights Movement, nor was it ever intended to serve such a purpose. Let me be real clear here at the outset: the main thrust or thesis of this chapter, and indeed this book, is that unsung singing members of the Civil Rights Movement utilized politics *and* music, rhetoric *and* aesthetics to combat racial segregation and ultimately topple mid-twentieth century American apartheid. The Civil Rights Movement was inspired and led by more than middle-aged and middle-class black church folk, and I hope that this book will go far to demonstrate that although their leadership and contributions may not mirror each and every contribution that emerged from middle-aged and middle-class, church-going black America, more than fifty years after the movement we can finally acknowledge and honor the unique leadership and contributions of the rank and file unsung singing foot soldiers of the Civil Rights Movement.

We have all inherited much from previous generations of African American youths—especially black ghetto youths' musics, aesthetics, and politics—than readily admitted or otherwise understood. Part of the reluctance to acknowledge connections between past and present black ghetto youth (including rap music and the Hip Hop Movement) has more to do with either the ignorance or amnesia surrounding working-class and poor African American youths' contributions to African American and mainstream American history, culture, and politics, especially the Civil Rights Movement. Racially oppressed and economically exploited groups have very few avenues open to them to dissent and express their opposition, even in a democratic society such as that of the United States. The situation is even more bleak when and where we come to black ghetto youth, whether we are considering their life-worlds and life-struggles in the twentieth or twenty-first century.

After all, the ghetto is supposedly a place where violence, vulgarity, poverty, illiteracy, promiscuity, and larceny reign supreme. In other words, to take this lame line of logic to its extreme, nothing of value can be found in or come out of the ghetto. Therefore, the contributions to African American and mainstream American history, culture, and politics that actually originated in, and emerged from the ghetto are either attributed to the black bourgeoisie or treated as free-floating postmodern signifiers whose architects and origins are unknown. As I discussed in critical detail in *The Hip Hop Movement*, this simultaneous *invisibility* and *anonymity* with respect to black ghetto youths' contributions to African American and mainstream American history, culture, and politics has been sadly handed down to the Hip Hop Generation.[4]

Working-class and poor African American youths' lives are situated at the intersections of both black popular music and black popular movements because, on the one hand, they are the primary producers of black popular music and, on the other hand, they are frequently the primary preoccupation of black popular movements. On this last point, it might be helpful to, however briefly, consider the fact that each and every major post-enslavement African American social and political movement has been, more or less, *black youth-centered*—if not *black ghetto youth-centered*. Think about the Black Women's Club Movement's work with working-class and poor under-age and unwed mothers, as well as their preschools and kindergartens for impoverished children. Think about the New Negro Movement's emphasis on employment and higher education opportunities for underprivileged African American youth, especially the black youth of the South, at the turn of the twentieth century. Think about how the 1954 *Brown v. Board of Education* Supreme Court decision, which desegregated public schools in the United States, and how the long and arduous battle to implement that decision helped to spark the Civil Rights Movement. Although often uncommented on, a major motif that runs throughout each of these movements and their political activities decidedly revolves around the lives and struggles of African American youth, especially working-class and poor African American youth.

Indeed, the lives and struggles of African American youth have been consistently at the center of black popular movements. Furthermore, their contributions to black popular movements have always been multidimensional—meaning, more than merely musical, artistic, or juvenile, but also political, cultural, intellectual, and spiritual. Yet and still, *the black popular music produced during the peak years of any post-enslavement black popular movement invariably seems to capture and convey the good and bad, the aspirations and frustrations, the thought and behavior of the black ghetto youth of the historical moment under consideration in ways that few other forms, aesthetic or otherwise, can.*

In short, working-class and poor African American youth's music, aesthetics, *and* politics at any given moment in African American history seems to serve as a crude kind of social, political, and cultural barometer, allowing us to measure the atmospheric pressure in black America. However, the foregoing should not be taken as a fast and firm uncritical embrace of subaltern theory as much as it should be understood to be a historical and cultural reality. Let's face it: there are more working-class and poor people in African America than any other class or group of people. Hence, my assertion that black politics and black popular culture are most often predicated on working-class and poor black folk's lives and struggles should not shock anyone.[5]

However, what may shock and awe many of my readers is the contention that black ghetto youth in particular have consistently contributed, not only to black popular culture, but also to black political culture and black social movements. As I argued in *Hip Hop's Amnesia* and *The Hip Hop Movement*, black ghetto youths' politics may not look like or sound like the Black Women's Club Movement, New Negro Movement, Civil Rights Movement, or Black Power Movement's politics but, no mistake should be made about it, working-class and poverty-stricken African Americans have consistently contributed to African American political thought and social movements. Again, one of the best gauges of the distinct worldview, politics, and culture of black ghetto youth historically has been, and remains, black popular culture, especially black popular music.

In fact, black popular music has consistently served as the bridge between black political culture and black popular culture: black political culture being traditionally thought of as the domain of the black bourgeoisie, and black popular culture being traditionally thought of as the domain of working-class and underclass black folk. From my point of view, gospel, rhythm & blues, and rock & roll during the Civil Rights Movement years, however unheralded, built on and carried over a pre-existing relationship between black popular culture and black political culture, which may go far to explain why each of the aforementioned incorporated elements of the spirituals, blues, ragtime, and jazz into their distinct expressions of the "we can implicitly sing what we cannot explicitly say" aesthetic. To put it another way, almost inexplicably the music of black ghetto youth and many of the mores of the black bourgeoisie have traveled along parallel paths, seeming to cyclically coalesce in every major post-enslavement black popular movement, from the Black Women's Club Movement through to the Black Power Movement.[6]

In many ways the major forms of *civil rights music*—that is to say, gospel, rhythm & blues, and rock & roll—resemble the various antecedent genres of black popular music that, from the Civil War through to the period immediately preceding the Civil Rights Movement, served as sonic expressions of the politics and aesthetics, the frustrations and aspirations of African America. For example, who can deny the ways in which Motown Records, undoubtedly the most successful rhythm & blues record company of the Civil Rights Movement, paradoxically appealed to working-class *and* middle-class black America, as well as black *and* white America in general, during one of the most turbulent, class-divided, and racially-charged eras in U.S. history? Similar to contemporary black popular music—obviously, the most popular expressions being rap and neo-soul—classical black popular music was given entry into spaces and places that black people, especially black ghetto youth, were unambiguously denied entry. This, too, is a part of the legacy left behind by the Civil Rights Movement, and black ghetto youth in particular continue to create music that is consumed and sometimes even seriously appreciated by middle-class black *and* suburban white America, even as middle-class black and suburban white America deny or, at the very least, vocally despise black ghetto youths' ever-increasing impact on mainstream American culture, politics, and society.

Consisting of several hybrid styles of pre-World War II, World War II, and post-World War II black popular music, early rhythm & blues derived its essential elements from the spirituals, gospel, blues, ragtime, jazz, and jump blues. Initially called "race music," rhythm & blues began as an umbrella term for all styles of African American music produced and performed by African American musicians exclusively for African American enjoyment and entertainment. Which is to say, as Paul Oliver pointed out in *Broadcasting the Blues: Black Blues in the Segregation Era*

(2006), Karl Miller observed in *Segregating Sound: Inventing Folk and Pop Music in the Age of Jim Crow* (2010), and Diane Pecknold and her colleagues emphasized in *Hidden in the Mix: The African American Presence in Country Music* (2013), just as pre-Civil Rights Movement American society was strictly segregated, so too was the pre-Civil Rights Movement American music industry. As will be discussed below, this *sonic segregation* created the very conditions under which African Americans were able to evolve the African American musical aesthetic virtually free from the "crossover" and "pop" pretensions of later forms of rhythm & blues (and rhythm & blues-derived) music (e.g., rock & roll, soul, funk, disco, techno, house, rap and neo-soul).

Evolving out of both the Northern bebop jazz and jump blues styles and the Southern boogie-woogie and Southern-inspired "electric" or "urban" blues styles, what came to be called "rhythm & blues" in the late 1940s was a sonic synthesis of arguably each and every major form of African American music from enslavement through to the post-World War II period. Similar to rap and other forms of hip hop music, classic rhythm & blues between 1945 and 1965 mixed or, rather, *remixed* African American musical history and culture, especially the "we can implicitly sing what we cannot explicitly say" aesthetic. Like contemporary hip hop DJs and producers, early rhythm & blues musicians drew from disparate aspects of previous African American music, culture and politics, in this instance pre-rhythm & blues music, culture and politics, to create music and messages that reflected a rising racial, cultural, social and political consciousness that reached back to the Black Women's Club Movement, New Negro Movement, and Harlem Renaissance, among other classical black popular movements.[7]

More than any previous form of black popular music, at its emergence rhythm & blues represented the wide range and wide reach of contemporary African American thought and culture. Borrowing the frenzy feeling and aural otherworldliness from the spirituals, the driving beat and droning sound from work songs, the blue notes (or "worried notes") and tragicomic narrative tradition from the blues, the "exotic" and erotic sounds of the red light district from ragtime, and the jive talk and updated juke joint sounds from bebop and jump blues, *early rhythm & blues symbolized the sound of African Americans in transition in mid-twentieth century America*. In other words, early rhythm & blues was *a music of motion*, the sound of a people on the move—figuratively, physically, socially, and politically speaking.[8]

Retaining the up-tempo and energetic drive of jump blues, early rhythm & blues' instrumentation was stripped-down and the overall emphasis was on the passionate performance of song lyrics, not improvisation (*à la* jump blues and slightly later bebop). In essence, it contained coded comedic or romantic lyrics sung over blues chord changes featuring an insistent backbeat. Distinguished from jump blues and bebop, early rhythm & blues openly embraced new technology, including the amplification and electrification of instruments. In fact, early rhythm & blues introduced and popularized the use of the electric bass in black popular music, in time evolving into a propulsive, dance beat-based music with unrelenting rhythms that seemed to perfectly mirror the migration, mores, and socio-political movements of mid-twentieth century black America. It is important here at the outset to emphasize that throughout this chapter, and indeed throughout this book, the term "rhythm & blues" has two meanings, one musical and the other decidedly extra-musical.[9]

Consequently, this chapter will examine classic rhythm & blues in relationship to the overarching aesthetics and politics of the Civil Rights Movement. Going back to the notion that black popular music in essence serves as a barometer with which to measure the political, social, and cultural climate in black America, here classic rhythm & blues represents one of the major black popular music mouthpieces of the Civil Rights Movement. Frequently the connections between black popular music and black popular movements are downplayed and diminished in favor of ahistorical and apolitical analyses that whitewash black popular music and black popular movements.

By (re)contextualizing classic rhythm & blues and (re)placing it within the social, political, cultural, and musical world of its origins and early evolution we are provided with new musical *and* extra-musical—we might go so far to say, historical musicological, cultural musicological, and socio-political musicological—tools that could (and, indeed, should) aid us in our efforts to revive, re-historicize, and re-politicize classic rhythm & blues in relation to the Civil Rights Movement. Whether my readers concede that there are many extra-musical elements in black popular music or not, is all beside the point. What most of us can agree on is the fact that some aspects of at least some of the black popular music produced and performed during the Civil Rights Movement years, indeed, did build on and carry over the "we can implicitly sing what we cannot explicitly say" aesthetic that has been unambiguously traced back to the spirituals and the blues, as well as jazz and, as we witnessed in the prior chapter, gospel.

Classic rhythm & blues was more than merely young black folk's foolishness in the face of American apartheid, which is not to say that it was not sometimes used as an escape or to express youthful energy and aspirations. However, if one really *listens* and *hears* classic rhythm & blues and carefully considers the racially segregated and economically exploitative conditions under which it emerged, it is almost impossible to miss its multiple meanings, double entendres, and cultural codes, as well as the fact that it was incredibly political by appearing to be apolitical and utterly unconnected to the Civil Rights Movement. Ingeniously, the pioneers and popularizers of rhythm & blues created a new and novel way to sing the blues and get the post-war world to listen and dance to both *the new rhythms* and *the new blues* of black America.

JUMPIN', HONKIN', AND SHOUTIN' THE BLUES: FROM JUMP BLUES TO THE EMERGENCE OF RHYTHM & BLUES

The emergence of rhythm & blues coincided with the World War II migration of African Americans from the South to the Northeast, Mid-West, and West to escape racial oppression and dehumanizing Jim Crow laws. African Americans also migrated from the South during this period in search of better economic, employment, and educational opportunities. Leaving their dream-destroying jobs as sharecroppers, general laborers, tenant farmers, washerwomen, and domestics, an estimated 5 million African Americans moved out of the South between 1940 and 1970.

However, these migrants quickly found out that the Northeast, Mid-West, and West were not the "promised land." Although they did, for the most part, find higher-paying jobs, especially in the wartime industries, life in the new cities was generally just as racially segregated and devoid of civil rights as it was in the South. Anti-black racist redlining quarantined African Americans to segregated and impoverished communities (i.e., ghettos), effectively turning their dreams into seemingly never-ending nightmares as more and more black folk sought refuge from the new and unfamiliar forms of Northern racism in alcohol, drugs, promiscuity, gambling, and other illicit activities.[10]

By the end of the migration period between 1940 and 1970 African Americans had become a city-centered and urbanized population. In fact, as African Americans entered into the Black Power Movement years (circa 1965 to 1975), more than 80 percent lived in cities. 53 percent remained in the South. Furthermore, 40 percent lived in the North, and 7 percent in the West. It could probably go without saying that all of this would ultimately impact the origins and evolution of rap music, hip hop culture, and the Hip Hop Movement in the late 1970s and early 1980s.[11]

From rhythm & blues forward, virtually each and every major form of black popular music has been city-centered. But, astute African American musicologists might also emphasize jazz's city-centered roots, and that is whether we discuss its Southern city origins, New Orleans, or the Mid-Western city, Chicago, or Northeastern city, New York, of its early evolution. Unlike the spirituals and the blues, which captured and conveyed the sights, sounds, and sorrows of African American life during the enslavement, Reconstruction, and post-Reconstruction years, respectively, jazz, ragtime, and rhythm & blues reflected African Americans' simultaneous post-enslavement segregation, industrialization, and urbanization. No longer predominantly widespread throughout the rural regions of the South, black popular music in the twentieth century symbolizes African

Americans' transition into urban environments, whether North, South, East, Mid-West, or West. However, even as they moved from rural regions to urban environments anti-black racism fiendishly followed them and reared its ugly head (and horns) at seemingly every twist and turn.[12]

Socially alienated, culturally isolated, and economically impoverished, segregated African American communities in the first half of the twentieth century created effervescent artistic practices and entertainment districts in virtually every major city in the United States. In the context of their new cities, the more than 5 million black migrants transformed old rural traditions into new urban forms of African American expression and entertainment, specifically with regard to the present discussion, inventing innovative musical styles predicated on a new city-centered set of criteria, cadences, and customs. The new city-centered aesthetic had a profound impact on African American music, as black musicians increasingly sought to incorporate the sights, sounds, sorrows, and celebrations of the city into their work. Hence, first urban blues, then jazz, and later rhythm & blues sonically signified city life, with its emphasis on regional customs, social conventions, local cuisine, communal rhythms, street noises, factory sounds and, of course, new technologies—especially, the amplification and electrification of instruments. It was this synthesis of African American folk music and folk culture with the then emerging African American urban music and urban culture that led black musicians to the intense period of experimentation that initially yielded bebop, jump blues, and ultimately birthed rhythm & blues (and rock & roll soon afterwards).

Classic rhythm & blues has a hallowed place in the history of modern African American music because it is fundamentally the musical foundation, the bedrock on which all modern black popular music has built its house or, rather, its houses—or maybe even its mansions. In other words, every major form of modern African American (or African American-derived) music, from rock & roll and soul to funk and disco, has utilized the innovations of early rhythm & blues as sonic paradigms and points of departure.[13] By critically exploring the origins and evolution of early rhythm & blues we are provided with a musical Rosetta Stone that will enable us to decipher the deep double entrendres and coded cultural messages buried beneath the basic structure of modern black popular music, many of which were, however unwittingly, inherited by early rock & roll. In fact, I am convinced that we will have a greater appreciation of, and be able to offer more contributions to, as well as more constructive criticisms of, post-Civil Rights Movement musics such as soul, funk, disco, rap, and neo-soul once we have a serious—as opposed to a superficial—sense of the history, culture, and struggles that coalesced to create the conditions under which rhythm & blues was pioneered and popularized. Needless to say, it is virtually impossible to fully understand early rhythm & blues without comprehending the ways in which it served as a harbinger and sonic symbol of the emergence, politics, and aesthetics of the Civil Rights Movement.

Where classic rhythm & blues represented the *sonic landscape* of African America between 1945 and 1965, the Civil Rights Movement represented the *socio-political landscape* of African America between 1945 and 1965. As argued in the foregoing chapter, African American music is more than merely music. It is also the spiritual, sexual, cultural, social, and political expression of an alienated and oppressed group who has historically had few other areas in which to fully express itself on its own terms. It is with this understanding that classic rhythm & blues may be interpreted or, rather, reinterpreted, as musical *and* spiritual, sexual, cultural, social, and political expression.

Moreover, when this line of logic is calmly conceded then it may also be openly acknowledged that classic rhythm & blues, along with its myriad extra-musical implications, has long served as a musical paradigm *and* a political point of departure for contemporary hip hop music: from neosoul, commercial rap, conscious rap, and reggaeton to glitch hop, trip hop, krunk, snap music, and wonky music. Just as each of these musics express elements of the politics, poetics, and aesthetics of the diverse hip hop communities they were created in, likewise classic rhythm & blues conveys the politics, poetics, and aesthetics of the conditions under which, and the various communities in which it was created. In fact, where classic rhythm & blues may be understood to be musical *and* spiritual, sexual, cultural, social, and political expression, the Civil Rights Movement can be interpreted as a decade-long synthesis and translation of classic rhythm & blues' extra-musical ethos into action, into collective struggle and radical political praxis via the mass meetings, prayer vigils, boycotts, marches, sit-ins, freedom rides, voter registration drives, and other protest activities that came to be the signatures of the Civil Rights Movement. And, indeed, as the hands of history have revealed, black folk sitting-in, registering to vote, marching, demonstrating, and protesting within the world of 1950s and 1960s America was nothing else if not "radical."[14]

It may not be going too far afield to observe that even though most classic rhythm & blues scholars locate its origins in the rambunctious early rhythm & blues of Louis Jordan & the Tympany Five, who began performing and recording in 1938, it is equally important to acknowledge early rhythm & blues' roots in the African American protest music tradition. Undoubtedly one of the finest protest songs ever produced was Billie Holiday's "Strange Fruit," recorded in 1939, the same year that saw the senseless violence of World War II begin (although the U.S. would not enter into the war until 1941). By observing rhythm & blues' relationship with broader struggles for justice and social transformation in mid-twentieth century America we will be able to more easily comprehend the ways in which black popular music represents more than music to the communities, musicians, and audiences who invented and continue to evolve it. Hence, both Jordan and Holiday's work hints at the hallmarks of not only early rhythm & blues, but of black popular music for the remainder of the twentieth century. With the work of Leslie Gourse (1997), Angela Davis (1998), David Margolick (2000, 2001), Farah Jasmine Griffin (2001, 2013), Stacy Jones (2007) and Evelyn Simien (2011), it is easy to understand how Holiday's "Strange Fruit" unambiguously contributes to the black protest music tradition. However, a closer look at Jordan's work demonstrates that he was much more than a jump blues "jive clown."[15]

Over the years there has been a lot of ink spilled concerning the comedic nature of Jordan's colorful narratives and performances. Without in anyway downplaying the freewheeling and outright fun-filled elements of his work, it is important not to lose sight of the undeniable fact that Louis Jordan was a serious musical and lyrical innovator. His songs were loaded with wry social commentary and coded cultural references. Interestingly, one of the most striking features of his slang-laden lyrics—as on his hit songs such as "I'm Gonna Leave You on the Outskirts of Town," "G. I. Jive," "Caldonia," "Buzz Me," "Choo Choo Ch' Boogie," "Ain't That Just Like A Woman," "Ain't Nobody Here But Us Chickens," "Boogie-Woogie Blue Plate," "Beans and Cornbread," "Saturday Night Fish Fry," "Blue Light Boogie," and "Weak-Minded Blues"—was the fact that he did not sing in the traditional sense but instead rendered his stories in an unusual rapid-fire, semi-sung, semi-spoken vocal style. Jordan's rhyming semi-sung, semi-spoken narration de-emphasized the lyrical melody while privileging highly syncopated phrasing and the percussive effects of alliteration and assonance. In other words, Louis Jordan arguably offered one of the earliest examples in American popular music of the slang-filled vocal stylings that eventually evolved into what we currently call rap music.

All of this means that rap music's roots, at least partially, can be traced back to the music that Louis Jordan helped to popularize and eventually helped to evolve into early rhythm & blues: *jump blues*. Jump blues was essentially the late 1930s and early 1940s synthesis of blues and jazz. Many interpreted the term "jump blues" to mean "bluesy jazz" or, rather, "jazzy blues" because by the late 1930s and early 1940s blues and jazz were simply two sides of the same coin, and most black musicians blurred the lines between these genres by being adept at playing both styles. Other than its emphasis on an updated and heavier rhythmic conception of big band-based swing, jump blues was characterized by its boisterous vocalists, flamboyant performances, and frequently light-hearted songs about partying, dancing, drinking, and jiving. The emphasis on partying, dancing, drinking, and jiving in jump blues can be easily explained by seriously considering the conditions under which it was created, and black migrants' cravings for an updated, city-centered juke joint experience. Which is also to say, jump blues emerged in racially oppressed and economically impoverished environments and, therefore, served as a kind of *bridge music* linking black life in the North and the South during a period of widespread musical *and* spiritual, sexual, cultural, social, and political transformation and transition in African America. Needless to say, ultimately what began as jump blues evolved into rhythm & blues in the mid-1940s.[16]

Just as the emergence of ragtime and jazz can be linked to larger patterns of urbanization, industrialization, and automation in the first quarter of the twentieth century, jump blues' development can be traced to a series of transformations taking place in mid-twentieth century American music, culture, politics, economics, and society. As a consequence of the Great Depression (1929–1939) and the beginning of World War II in 1939, by the early 1940s the large big bands of the 1930s had to be downsized to small combos. African Americans in the 1940s, like most other Americans in the 1940s, continued to storm dance halls and watering holes on week nights and especially on weekends, and they expected the small combos to keep the music just as "hot" and "jumpin'" as the big bands of the previous decade. In short, they wanted their music lively, loud, and danceable. This caused many of the combos to place greater emphasis on honking saxophonists and fiery, flamboyant, and seemingly frenzy-filled vocalists who could be heard over the rambunctious rhythms and hollering horn riffs (e.g., Big Maybelle, Big Joe Turner, Big Mama Thornton, Esquerita, Ruth Brown, Little Richard, LaVern Baker, Roy Brown, Varetta Dillard and, of course, Wynonie Harris). As a consequence of the honking saxophonists and shouting singers, early rhythm & blues musicians have been aptly characterized as "honkers and shouters."

In his brilliant book, *Honkers and Shouters: The Golden Years of Rhythm & Blues* (1978), Arnold Shaw explained that "[a]n expressiveness as extreme as the honking-falling down syndrome" popular among early rhythm & blues saxophonists was "unquestionably a social as well as a musical phenomenon" (171). In essence, he understood it to be an "expression of a threefold separation: from the sound of Western music; from white popular song; and from the Negro middle-class to whom R&B was anathema." Ultimately, Shaw concluded, "the syndrome was a conscious or unconscious projection of the post-war segregation of black people, an abysmal expression of the separateness of the black ghettos." In fact, he went further, the "post-war world was one that Negroes viewed with a mixture of disgust and frustration. Not only were they isolated from the mainstream of society, they not infrequently suffered white violence" (171).[17]

The violence that African Americans endured during and after World War II was both physical and psychological, and early rhythm & blues reflected the torture and daily turmoil they experienced. Jump blues and its rhythm & blues offspring represented that bubbling stream of African American music during the inter-war years that had been hailed as "city blues" and viewed as another step in the evolution of the urbanization of African American music. Jump blues and its early rhythm & blues off-spring also, however uncomfortably, captured and conveyed a great deal about the mid-twentieth century America it emerged in and, more tell-ingly, the African Americans who invented it, performed it, and lovingly listened to and identified with it. Although most African American histo-rians have generally agreed that the Civil Rights Movement essentially began with the 1954 *Brown v. Board of Education* Supreme Court decision, it is extremely important to understand the 15 year period between 1939 and 1954—which is to say, from the beginning of World War II to the *Brown* decision—that undeniably laid the social, political, cultural, and musical foundation for what can be considered the peak years of the Civil Rights Movement between 1954 and 1965.

The Great Depression and World War II fundamentally changed the racial, cultural, social, and political consciousness of African Americans, just as they had irrevocably altered American society as a whole. A decade of economic depression further devastated an already impover-ished and socially segregated people, coupled with the trials and tribula-tions of valiantly serving in a racially segregated military that was willing to fight for freedom abroad but not for freedom in the interests of African Americans at home, created a unique and perplexing historical moment. With America's preparation to join World War II, between 1939 and 1940 the U.S. economy was finally lifted out of the depths of the Depression.

However, according to Darlene Clark Hine, William Hine, and Stan-ley Harrold in *The African American Odyssey* (2010), when the United States went back to business it rebuilt its military just as it was prior to the Great Depression (542). Which is to say, the U.S. military continued its longstanding policy of segregation and other Jim Crow practices of racial "discrimination and exclusion." Teams of "unemployed white workers streamed into aircraft factories, shipyards, and other centers of war production," while the throngs of destitute and jobless African Americans were left standing at factory entrances day after dismal day (542). When African Americans were finally hired, no matter which jobs their education or hard-won skills qualified them for, they were usually quarantined to the most demeaning custodial positions.[18]

For the most part, African Americans did not fare any better when they sought employment in government jobs and government-funded training programs. For instance, black applicants were regularly rejected for government-funded training programs because training them was thought to be pointless in light of their low prospects for finding skilled work. It was a callous catch-22 that eventually saw the United States Employment Service (USES) fill "whites-only" requests for defense in-dustry workers. The U.S. military accepted African American men "in their proportion to the population, about 11 percent at the time," but placed them in segregated units and assigned them to degrading service duties. More specifically, the Navy limited African American servicemen to menial positions, while the Marine Corps and the Army Air Corps outright "refused to accept them altogether" (542).

In light of post-Great Depression segregation, in the larger society and in the military, the *Pittsburgh Courier* called for a "Double V" campaign. Eventually adopted as a battle cry among African Americans in the early 1940s, "Double V" stood for *victory over fascism abroad and victory over racism at home*. Embracing the "Double V" mentality, during World War II African Americans' simultaneous efforts to fight fascism *and* racism "transformed the worldview" of black "soldiers and civilians" alike, and led to the "further development" of African American civil rights efforts and organizations (542). A groundswell of protests removed the muzzle that had been on their mouths, and in the 1940s African Americans found the voices they had seemingly lost during the Depression years.[19]

A major catalyst for the change in African Americans' collective consciousness, A. Philip Randolph's 1941 March on Washington Movement called on African Americans to organize their protests and "direct them at the national government" (542). Indicating that he had ten thousand African Americans prepared to march on the nation's capital, Randolph defiantly declared the movement's motto: "We loyal Negro American citizens demand the right to work and fight for our country." Throughout the spring and summer months of 1941, Randolph's March on Washington Movement blossomed into the largest mass movement of African Americans since Marcus Garvey's Universal Negro Improvement Association during its New Negro Movement and Harlem Renaissance heyday in the 1920s.[20]

The 1940s March on Washington Movement demanded that President Roosevelt issue an order forbidding companies with government contracts from practicing racial discrimination. Randolph pushed for the complete elimination of race-based exclusion from defense training programs and also insisted that the USES provide work without regard to race. In short, Randolph wanted the president to "abolish segregation in the armed forces" (543).

The 1940s March on Washington Movement was a wide-ranging and wide-reaching movement, and its powerful appeal garnered the support of many African Americans who had never participated in social organization and political activism. Increasing the pressure on the president, Randolph let be known that as many as 50,000 African Americans had committed to march on Washington. Roosevelt, deeply concerned that the March on Washington would seriously undermine America's efforts to appear democratic before the world and give fodder to the Nazi fascists the U.S. claimed to be the opposite of, initially offered a set of "superficial changes" to appease African Americans (543). The March on

Washington Movement would have none of it and firmly stood its ground. Consequently, they raised the stakes by enlisting more than 100,000 African Americans to march on Washington. By the close of June in 1941, Roosevelt raised the white flag, offered an olive branch, and had his aides draft Executive Order 8802, effectively "prompting Randolph to call off the march" (543).

Even if only on a superficial or symbolic level, Roosevelt's order signaled an important change in African Americans' relationship with the government and, likewise, the government's relationship with African Americans. Perhaps the most meaningful lines of Executive Order 8802 read in part:

> WHEREAS there is evidence that available and needed workers have been barred from employment in industries engaged in defense production solely because of considerations of race, creed, color, or national origin, to the detriment of workers' morale and of national unity:
> NOW, THEREFORE, by virtue of the authority vested in me by the Constitution and the statutes, and as a prerequisite to the successful conduct of our national defense production effort, I do hereby reaffirm the policy of the United States that there shall be no discrimination in the employment of workers in defense industries or government because of race, creed, color, or national origin, and I do hereby declare that it is the duty of employers and of labor organizations, in furtherance of said policy and of this order, to provide for the full and equitable participation of all workers in defense industries, without discrimination because of race, creed, color, or national origin. (1)[21]

Although it was the first major blow to racial discrimination since Reconstruction, Executive Order 8802 was not the twentieth century's Emancipation Proclamation. Consequently, African American excitement over the order quickly faded when many industries, particularly those in the South, evaded the order's clear intent and almost exclusively engaged in "token hirings" (543). As they would repeatedly witness throughout the turbulent decades to come, in the 1940s African Americans learned a hard lesson that seems to have been passed down to the members of the Civil Rights Movement and Black Power Movement: the U.S. government's high-sounding and hyperbole-filled articulations of anti-discrimination principles and the establishment of civil rights commissions and committees did not necessarily lead to the eradication of racial inequalities. Hence, words without deeds are as useless as fish without water.

Taken on its own terms or, better yet, placed within the context of African American history, culture, and struggle, black popular music— from the spirituals and the blues through to rap and neo-soul—can be seen as a form of *sonic protest* that is inextricable from the more conventional *socio-political protest* of black popular movements. As Shaw contended above, early rhythm & blues was "unquestionably a social as well as a musical phenomenon." Therefore, it is important not to negate the interconnections between black popular music and black popular movements.

Without in any way downplaying the ways in which gospel, blues, folk, and jazz served as soundtracks for the Civil Rights Movement, it is important to comprehend how early rhythm & blues was undeniably the most popular and socially salient soundtrack of the Civil Rights Movement, even though most people have a tendency to deprecate and diminish its connections to, and significance for the movement. Part of the backlash against early rhythm & blues had to do with, not only its "heavy" rhythms and "hard-driving" backbeats, but also its raw expressiveness and "hard life" lyrical content that, in the most unprecedented manner imaginable, dealt openly with love, lust, loss, poverty, delinquency, partying, drinking, city life, and fast cars. Similar to the rock & roll, soul, and funk that built on the sonic breakthroughs and aural innovations of classic rhythm & blues, it is important to observe that long before rhythm & blues *rocked* and *rolled* onto the scene classic blues and classic jazz offered countless songs that brashly, and frequently with brutal honesty, dealt with love, lust, loss, poverty, delinquency, partying, drinking, city life, and fast cars. This should be held in mind as we continue to critically explore the relationship between early rhythm & blues and the Civil Rights Movement.

African American music, from the spirituals and the blues through to rap and neo-soul, seems to revolve around spirituality and sexuality, folk philosophy and new technology. To reiterate, black popular music often serves as a metaphor and medium of expression for black life, culture, and struggle. Consequently, the major issues and ills at any given moment in African America most often find their way into black popular music in particular, and black popular culture in general. At its core, black popular culture has always been a battlefield where a tug-of-war between black conservatives and black radicals, between black traditionalists and black modernists have consistently vied to have their respective views and values accepted as the dominant expression of the African American experience.

In many ways, the emergence of rhythm & blues in mid-twentieth century America is the musical and cultural culmination of African Americans' experiences from enslavement through to the 1941 March on Washington Movement, and it is important to note that the March on Washington Movement actually continued to rally and call for nonviolent civil disobedience long after World War II ended in 1945. Emphasizing the dialectic of *tradition* and *innovation* that is at the heart of early rhythm & blues—and, truth be told, all major forms of black popular music—in his classic *Blues People: The Negro Experience in White America and the Music that Developed From It* (1963), Amiri Baraka insightfully asserted:

There was a kind of frenzy and extra-local vulgarity to rhythm & blues that had never been present in older blues forms. Suddenly it was as if a great deal of the Euro-American humanist façade Afro-American music had taken on had been washed away by the war. Rhythm & blues singers literally had to shout to be heard above the clanging and strumming of the various electrified instruments and the churning rhythm sections. And somehow the louder the instrumental accompaniment and the more harshly screamed the singing, the more expressive the music was. Blues had always been a vocal music, and it must be said that the instrumental accompaniment for rhythm & blues singers was still very much in the vocal tradition, but now the human voice itself had to struggle, to scream, to be heard. (171–172)

Taking the music as a metaphor for the Civil Rights Movement and African Americans' position in U.S. society between 1945 and 1965, it is difficult not to conclude that early rhythm & blues mirrored the movement and expressed African Americans' thoughts and feelings about post-World War II segregation, racial discrimination, and ongoing economic exploitation. One of the reasons early rhythm & blues expressed "a kind of frenzy and extra-local vulgarity . . . that had never been present in older blues forms" is probably because at the beginning of the post-war period African Americans honestly believed that by helping to topple German fascism they would also be contributing to the eradication of American racism. Nothing could have been further from the truth, and U.S. history during this period reveals America's reluctance and outright refusal to come to terms with the fact that it had been practicing its own form of fascism against African Americans for several centuries. What else is "fascism" if it is not in part, according to *Merriam-Webster's Dictionary*, the "belief in the supremacy of one national or ethnic group," and "a contempt for democracy" or, at the least, a contempt for extending democracy to all citizens without regard to race, gender, class, sexual orientation, or religious affiliation? To put it another way, there is a sense in which early rhythm & blues can be seen as sonic protest against American apartheid and America's "whites-only" democracy, which basically reduced the citizenry to *white haves* and *non-white have-nots*.

Listening to early rhythm & blues, "it was as if a great deal of the Euro-American humanist façade Afro-American music had taken on had been washed away by the war," and the music increasingly reflected African Americans' heightened cultural consciousness and new radical spirit (*à la* the 1940s March on Washington Movement). Almost as if directly responding to the whitewashing of jazz in the 1930s and early 1940s, especially under the guises of big band and "sweet" swing jazz, early rhythm & blues unrepentantly returned to its roots in the blues and advanced *a new, amplified and electrified form of the blues*. Seeming to perfectly mirror the industrialization and urbanization taking place in the larger society, mid-twentieth century blues—which is to say, first, jump blues and later rhythm & blues—emerged within a segregated world that was frequently lawless, loud, harsh, and often either erased or silenced authentic representations and interpretations of African American life and culture. Hence, Baraka observed, early rhythm & blues singers "literally had to shout to be heard above the clanging and strumming of the various electrified instruments and the churning rhythm sections. And somehow the louder the instrumental accompaniment and the more harshly screamed the singing, the more expressive the music was."

Early rhythm & blues was the music or, rather, the searing sounds of a people in search of their human, civil, and voting rights in the concrete jungles of segregated U.S. cities. The "clanging and strumming of the various electrified instruments and the churning rhythm sections" could be said to metaphorically represent the impact of industrialization and the automation of factory work on African American life and culture. Moreover, the "screamed . . . singing" can be taken as a defiant affirmation of African Americans' humanity and their dire need to be heard in the face of government-sanctioned segregation, Jim Crow laws, and myriad other forms of anti-black racism.

If, indeed, early rhythm & blues sounds harsh to our ears today, then we are only conceding how ingeniously it captured and conveyed African Americans' struggle for human recognition and civil rights between 1945 and 1965. If the "clanging and strumming of the various electrified instruments and the churning rhythm sections" sound slightly off-kilter and conflict with our understanding of what constitutes "good music" (even "good *black music*"), then perhaps that is because early rhythm & blues musicians created their music in the context of an increasingly urban and industrial segregated society, with all of the "clanging" and "churning" such a society entails. Early rhythm & blues represented something raw and real, something working-class and poor black people could feel and know that it was created by one of their own specifically with them in mind. Hence, "somehow the louder the instrumental accompaniment and the more harshly screamed the singing, the more expressive the music was." Indeed, the African Americans who created early rhythm & blues and organized the Civil Rights Movement developed new music and new politics to express themselves—and, that is to say, to express themselves not as the larger society sanctioned and woefully wanted them to, but as they really were, in their full and indignant *ugly beauty* as Thelonious Monk put it on his classic album *Underground* in 1968.

All of this is to say, early rhythm & blues registers as a reclamation of the classic blues aesthetic and the evolution of the anti-racist ethos African Americans' unapologetically embraced during the Reconstruction, post-Reconstruction, Black Women's Club Movement, and New Negro Movement turn of the twentieth century years. Whatever high hopes African Americans held concerning desegregation and integration during World War II soon soured in the years immediately following the fall of Nazi fascism in 1945. Early rhythm & blues expressed the frustrations and ongoing aspirations of a people who had been repeatedly denied and brutally betrayed by their government and fellow citizens. Crying seemed an inadequate response to the double-dealing African Americans had been consistently dealt after 350 years of enslavement and, at the time, close to 100 years of post-enslavement American apartheid. Instead of the sonic cry that was one of the distinguishing characteristics of classic blues, as jump blues evolved into early rhythm & blues the music eventually came to express *a collective sonic scream* or, quite literally, an unmitigated shout. However, as was discussed in detail in the preceding chapter, early rhythm & blues did not have a monopoly on the "shout" aesthetic during the Civil Rights Movement era. Obviously, gospel, with its characteristic "hoarse," "raspy," "gruff," "gravelly," or "throaty" sound and its tendency to "push [. . .] the vocal register to the extreme" indelibly influenced the "shout" aesthetic of early rhythm & blues. Being one of, if not *the* primary point of departure for rock & roll, rhythm & blues bequeathed the "shout" aesthetic and the tendency to "push [. . .] the vocal register to the extreme" to rock & roll, as will be discussed in the next chapter.

Even the early rhythm & blues instrumentalists seemed to "shout" and make their instruments mirror the human voice, saying with blue notes, coded cultural sounds, and pulsating polyrhythms all the things they felt they could not say with their mouths. Early rhythm & blues' *musical shouting* is inextricable from the *spiritual shouting* that takes place in African American churches each and every Sunday morning, and both kinds of shouting are nothing if not cathartic releases, momentarily freeing the shouter from the inferiority complexes, racism, poverty, and other ills that have plagued African America since its inception. Hence, what has been long referred to as "the honking saxophonist" might actually be better explained by turning not simply to musicology but also to sociology and, even more, to *the socio-musicology of early rhythm & blues saxophonists' segregated social world.*

Along with the shouting and screaming so typical of early rhythm & blues singing, equally telling, Baraka contended, are the "uncommonly weird sounds that were made to come out of the instruments. The screaming saxophone is the most characteristic" (172). He importantly continued, "during the heyday of rhythm & blues, blues-oriented instrumentalists, usually saxophone players, would vie to see who could screech, or moan, or shout the loudest and longest on their instruments." In explaining the shouting and screaming in early rhythm & blues Baraka, perhaps, partially explained much about every major form of black popular music that rose in the aftermath of the classic rhythm & blues era between 1945 and 1965:

The point, it seemed, was to spend oneself with as much attention as possible, and also to make the instruments sound as unmusical, or as *non-Western*, as possible. It was almost as if the blues people were reacting against the softness and "legitimacy" that had crept into black instrumental music with the advent of swing. In a way, this is what happened, and for this reason, rhythm & blues sat as completely outside of the mainstream as earlier blues forms, though without that mainstream this form of music might have been impossible. Rhythm & blues also became more of an anathema to the Negro middle-class, perhaps, than the earlier blues forms, which by now they might have forgotten, because it was contemporary and existed as a legitimate expression of a great many Negroes and as a gaudy reminder of the real origins of Negro music. (172, emphasis in original)[22]

It would seem that early rhythm & blues' connections to the Civil Rights Movement could not be more pronounced. For example, notice how early rhythm & blues, to a certain extent, represented working-class and poor black peoples' interface with and integration into modern industry and technology (e.g., amplifying the saxophone and electrifying the lead, rhythm, and bass guitars). Where early rhythm & blues was one of the first forms of music to regularly utilize electric instruments, the Civil Rights Movement was one of the first black popular movements to skillfully and consistently utilize telecommunications, especially radio and television, to bring awareness of African Americans' ongoing search for social justice and democracy.

Paralleling early rhythm & blues saxophonists' screaming, screeching, and honking, as discussed in the previous chapter, gospel and freedom songs' characteristic "hoarse," "raspy," "gruff," "gravelly," or "throaty" sound, and gospel and freedom singers' tendency to "push [. . .] the vocal register to the extreme" were more or less the musical equivalent of the eloquent oratory of Martin Luther King, the raspy radical rhetoric of Malcolm X, and the heavy, visceral vibrato of Fannie Lou Hamer. More specifically, I would like to suggest that just as Martin Luther King, Ella Baker, Malcolm X, Fannie Lou Hamer, Medgar Evers, and Septima Clark's speeches and sermons helped to inspire a long over-due deconstruction and reconstruction of American citizenship and democracy, early rhythm & blues, and the early rhythm & blues honking saxophonists in specific, represented a kind of sonic deconstruction and aural reconstruction of black popular music, simultaneously updating and adapting it to the post-war world of black America in particular, and the United States in general. It is easy to comprehend how the early rhythm & blues honking saxophone sound eventually evolved into the screaming electric guitar sound that became the hallmark of early rock & roll.

Obviously Adolphe Sax, the inventor of the saxophone, did not intend the instrument to be played the way the early rhythm & blues honkers, such as Illinois Jacquet, Arnett Cobb, Earl Bostic, Red Prysock, Big Jay

Neely, Frank "Floorshow" Culley, Willis Jackson, and Jimmy Forrest, did. Just as, we can be certain, George Beauchamp and Paul Barth, the inventors of the electric guitar, never intended their invention to be used the way black guitarists have over the years. Whether we turn to the early gospel, blues, and jazz pioneers and popularizers of the electric guitar, such as Lonnie Johnson, Tampa Red, Sister Rosetta Tharpe, T-Bone Walker, Charlie Christian, and Memphis Minnie, or later black guitar gods, such as Muddy Waters, Howlin' Wolf, B. B. King, Elmore James, Chuck Berry, Bo Diddley, Jimmy Rogers, Hubert Sumlin, Earl Hooker and, of course, Jimi Hendrix, post-war black popular music hinges on African Americans innovative interface with (post)modern technology. Indeed, the point I wish to emphasize here is that one of the major motifs of the Civil Rights Movement and its rhythm & blues soundtrack has much to do with African Americans incredibly intense and rapidly evolving relationship with technology, both musical *and* industrial technology, during the post-war period.

If, via early rhythm & blues, it was "almost as if the blues people were reacting against the softness and 'legitimacy' that had crept into black instrumental music with the advent of swing." Then, in a similar fashion, it could be observed that early rhythm & blues registers as mid-twentieth century blues people's rejection of, and resistance to the "softness and 'legitimacy'" that had increasingly whitewashed and watered-down black popular music, from classic blues to classic jazz, with the infamous emergence of "sweet" music. In other words, early rhythm & blues saxophonists' honks were more than mere "honks" or hoots. Likewise, early rhythm & blues singers' shouts were more than mere "shouts" or whoops. These sounds came from an anguish-filled existential place deep within the souls of these artists and the racially segregated, colored section-quarantined "blues people" they lived among, suffered with, and passionately performed for.

Many may find it ironic that rhythm & blues grew out of a musical style, jump blues, that was initially known for its preoccupation with jive, novelty dances, comedy routines, and "country cuisine," but rhythm & blues' remarkable evolution only appears ironic or erratic if it is divorced from the long history of black popular music and black popular culture. Black popular culture, and especially black popular music, has always expressed aspects of African American social and political thought. Mirroring classic gospel, and to a certain extent freedom songs, early rhythm & blues reflected a distinct form of African American protest, *musical protest*, which is obviously a form of *aesthetic protest* that was handed down from the spirituals and the Abolitionist Movement.

What needs to be understood here is that unlike most forms of political protest, *aesthetic protest* is very rarely a direct call to action, and this is where there is considerable overlap between gospel, rhythm & blues, and rock & roll as forms of musical protest during the Civil Rights Movement.

Even so, critical aesthetic representation of socio-political problems, political aesthetics, and social realism in the context of African American artistic traditions must be comprehended as constituting extremely powerful socio-political ideas and acts. Most musicologists might interpret instances of protest in early rhythm & blues as mere "complaint," but by the very fact that the alleged "complaint" is publicly articulated to such an eloquent extent that even black popular music's most ahistorical, apolitical, and often incredibly uninformed interpreters understand it to be "complaint" illustrates that musical protest, indeed, is a form of contestation of oppressive and exploitive conditions even when it does not directly translate into concrete political organization and public demonstration. This is part of the distinct power of black popular music, if not black popular culture in general. Indirectly responding to black popular music critics' de-politicization of black song and helping to drive my point home about early rhythm & blues as protest even though it may not have translated into "protest" in the conventional Civil Rights Movement-sense of the word, in *Black Culture and Black Consciousness: Afro-American Folk Thought from Slavery to Freedom* (1977), Lawrence Levine offered remarkable insight:

> To state that black song constituted a form of black protest and resistance does not mean that it necessarily led to or even called for any tangible and specific actions, but rather that it served as a mechanism by which Negroes could be relatively candid in a society that rarely accorded them that privilege, could communicate this candor to others whom they would in no other way be able to reach, and, in the face of the sanctions of the white majority, could assert their own individuality, aspirations, and sense of being. Certainly, if nothing else, black song makes it difficult to believe that Negroes internalized their situation so completely, accepted the values of the larger society so totally, or manifested so pervasive an apathy as we have been led to believe. . . . The African tradition of being able to verbalize publicly in song what could not be said to a person's face, not only lived on among Afro-Americans throughout slavery but continued to be a central feature of black expressive culture in freedom. (239–240, 247)

It is Levine's last sentence that directly connects with jump blues and early rhythm & blues shouters' songs. When he reminds us that the "African tradition of being able to verbalize publicly in song what could not be said to a person's face, not only lived on among Afro-Americans throughout slavery but continued to be a central feature of black expressive culture in freedom," he hints at how generation after jostling generation of African American musicians have, literally, utilized music as a medium to constructively critique their enslavers, oppressors, and abusers, both within and without African American communities. From Billie Holiday's "Strange Fruit" and Nina Simone's "Mississippi Goddam" to Oscar Brown Jr.'s "Forty Acres and A Mule" and Sam Cooke's "A

Change Is Gonna Come," much like the music emerging from the black sacred song tradition during the Civil Rights Movement, in the black secular song tradition of the Civil Rights Movement African Americans were able to sing what they could not unambiguously say "in the face of the sanctions of the white majority" (i.e., violent anti-black racism, Jim Crow, Black Codes, segregation, and other aspects of American apartheid more generally speaking).

It is also important for us to keep in mind that the contention that "black song constituted a form of black protest and resistance does not mean that it necessarily led to or even called for any tangible and specific actions." As with gospel and freedom songs, classic rhythm & blues' "protest and resistance" may not have nicely and neatly paralleled the "protest and resistance" emerging from the dominant African American socio-political movement of its epoch (i.e., the Civil Rights Movement). But, make no mistake about it, classic rhythm & blues folk, which is to say, classic rhythm & blues people, as Levine noted, indeed did protest and resist by way of black popular music and black popular culture, among other social, political, and aesthetic avenues.

CLASSIC RHYTHM & BLUES: THE SECULAR SOUNDTRACK OF THE COLORED SECTION AND AMERICAN APARTHEID

As jump blues began to wane a new form of black popular music took center stage: vocal harmony groups, street corner groups, barbershop quartets or, more simply, *doo-wop groups*. Inspired by the stripped down trio sound and smooth singing of Nat King Cole, Johnny Moore's Three Blazers, and Charles Brown, the doo-wop concept actually reached all the way back to pre-World War II vocal groups, such as the Mills Brothers, the Ink Spots, the Delta Rhythm Boys, and the Charioteers. The first two groups, the Mills Brothers and the Ink Spots, had roots in the barbershop quartet, jazz, and pop traditions, frequently performing with the big bands of Duke Ellington, Glenn Miller, and Lucky Millinder. The latter two groups, the Delta Rhythm Boys and the Charioteers, began their careers as jubilee quartets, primarily singing spirituals, folk songs, and pop songs. Four core features characterized pre-World War II vocal group singing, which consisted of a lead vocalist and supporting background singers: first, alternating lead vocals; second, closely harmonized choruses; third, imitation of instrumental tonality; and fourth, extreme contrasts in vocal range and timbre. It would be the post-war singers' innovative imitation of the sound of musical instruments that would provide their version of vocal harmony group singing with its catchy name: *doo-wop*.[23]

Here it is important to emphasize the two dominant streams running through the African American vocal harmony group tradition prior to the emergence of the post-war vocal harmony group tradition (i.e., *the doo-wop tradition*). Obviously the spirituals and African American folk songs provided many of the pre-war vocal harmony groups with their point of departure, while pop, love, and novelty songs offered others their core repertoire. Hence, the same thread of the sacred and the secular, spirituality and sexuality found in 1960s and 1970s rhythm & blues, as well as 1980s-onward rap and neo-soul, can be traced back to post-war black popular music's roots in 1940s and 1950s rhythm & blues. In fact, as I discussed in detail in *The Hip Hop Movement*, contemporary discussions concerning "commercial rap" vs. "conscious rap" are particularly indebted to early rhythm & blues' gospel-sound vs. pop-sound divide.

Taking its name from the incredibly close harmonies and creative scat singing of the background vocalists, "doo-wop" was a common phrase that 1950s vocal harmony groups used in their efforts to imitate musical instruments. Like rap music, doo-wop emerged from the lives and struggles of African American ghetto youth and, as a consequence, it reflected all of the limitations and idiosyncrasies of African American youth life and culture in the immediate post-war period. Although many have made fun of 1950s black ghetto youth singing "nonsense syllables," when these so-called "nonsense syllables" are placed within the wider context of post-war African American history, culture, and struggle, especially the Civil Rights Movement, alternative meanings and messages can be gleaned from doo-wop. As a matter of fact, I would be one of the first to admit that in a strict musicological sense phrases such as "doo-wop-wop, doo-wop-wop," "be-bop, be-bop, be-bop," "dang-dang-diggy-dang," and "shooby-dooby-doo" are nonsensical. However, in a socio-musicological sense, when dropped within the absurd world of post-war America, with its continued commitment to segregation, denial of decent African American education, and routine violation of African American civil rights, the nonsense phrases of doo-wop seem to mirror, if not mimic, the high-sounding but hollow words of 1950s U.S. government and society as a whole with respect to civil rights and social justice. With doo-wop, African American ghetto youth were, yet again, "implicitly singing what they could not explicitly say." [24]

Even doo-wop's most cynical critics have conceded that it has roots in the hallowed harmonies and emotive phrasing of the spirituals and gospel, especially gospel quartets such as the Golden Gate Quartet, Soul Stirrers, Deep River Boys, Fairfield Four, Harmonizing Four, Swan Silvertones, Pilgrim Travelers, and Dixie Hummingbirds. However, frequently these same critics fail to recognize that just as the spirituals and gospel contained double-meanings and masked messages, as discussed at length in the previous chapter, so too did doo-wop. Doo-wop's double entendres and masked messages, whether perceived as romantic or comedic, provided African American ghetto youth in the 1950s with one of the only avenues open to them at the time to express their worldviews and distinct values.

Indeed, most doo-wop songs centered on love, but we should bear in mind that African Americans composing and beautifully singing love songs in a racially segregated post-war world, where less than a century prior it was basically forbidden for African Americans to have families and against the law for African Americans to enter into matrimony, was indeed political, if not decidedly defiant. This may also explain why rhythm & blues, soul, and neo-soul are primarily perceived as *love-centered musics*. In other words, *black love in a white dominated world is always already political and an act of undaunted defiance, because by loving each other African Americans not only acknowledge the humanity and beauty of their special loved ones, but they also defy the centuries of "civilized" and "scientific" discourse that has habitually dehumanized them and told them that they are not really and truly part of the human species—and not really and truly American citizens.*

The 1950s were the peak years for youthful a cappella group harmony sounds. The new music poured out of city parks and school gyms, and it could also be heard on street corners and the stoops of overcrowded low-income apartment buildings in the inner-cities. Similar to rapping today, back then singing was a diversion from the hard lives and harsh conditions most African American youth faced in the ghetto. Although the African American middle-class made small but steady progress in the 1950s, the African American masses, who were primarily poor and working-class folk, experienced very little change in their day to day lives. With this in mind, it is easy to understand why these youths viewed a hit record and a successful career as a singer as a viable way to get out of the ghetto.

Boldly building on the models and innovations of the pioneering inter-war vocal groups, throngs of African American teenagers (initially known as "street corner" groups) developed post-war harmony styles that directly corresponded with their musical tastes, cultural sensibilities, social values, political views, and lives as poor and working-class youth. Tellingly, the songs they sang were, however juvenile to their critics (and parents), sonic expressions of their aspirations and frustrations, their dreams and nightmares. More than any previous group of African American youths, the doo-woppers of the 1950s were able to draw from two parallel but distinct African American singing traditions.

The first tradition, as alluded to above, grew out of the spirituals and gospel, and always seemed to privilege more of a soulful "church sound" regardless of the thematic content of the song. The second tradition, which was also made mention of above, grew out of the blues and its more secular and sensual sounding offspring, such as jazz and jump blues. The more church-sounding music appealed to the masses of African Americans, who had been raised on the gospel vocal aesthetic,

where—when it could be *whitened* and *lightened* and made to crossover—
the more secular and sensual-sounding music appealed to whites, who
eventually began to accept a vanilla version of black popular music within the white popular music marketplace.

Doo-wop was not the first form of black popular music to "crossover"
to white audiences, both the Mills Brothers and the Ink Spots crossed the
color-line in the 1930s and 1940s. However, it was *the first form of black
popular music to spawn widespread white youth imitation of black popular music*, especially as it evolved into rock & roll. In keeping with the *sonic
segregation* of the music industry in mid-twentieth century America,
which obviously mirrored the social segregation of mid-twentieth century America, there were gospel-sounding doo-wop songs for blacks and
usually a separate set of often-placid pop-sounding doo-wop songs for
whites. A distinction between the more rhythm & blues-based doo-wop
and the more or less white pop-sounding doo-wop—and black popular
music in general—began to be embraced by fans and critics. For instance,
in their classic essay, "The Doo-Wah Sound: Black Pop Groups of the
1950s" (1975), music critics Mike Redmond and Marv Goldberg offered
an insightful analysis of the distinct differences between 1950s pop and
rhythm & blues, essentially characterizing pop as:

> the group singing the entire song in unison, or group members singing
> the chorus or phrase lines behind the lead. Or, in a variation, the group
> members singing a smooth, almost subdued blend of harmony without
> distinctive tenor to bass parts. In this format, the group provides a
> showcase for the lead and remains unobtrusively in the background.
> The material is presented in a cool—almost detached manner, and the
> subject matter is usually non-controversial in nature avoiding such top-
> ics as drinking, crime and associated societal problems, and overt sexu-
> ality. (22–23)

When Redmond and Goldberg wrote about 1950s pop artists avoiding
singing about certain illicit or impolite topics, it is important for us to go
back to Levine's emphasis on the extra-musical meanings inherent in
black song "in the face of the sanctions of the white majority." As was
witnessed with gospel and freedom singers, black pop, jump blues, and
rhythm & blues artists during the Civil Rights Movement were in many
ways lyrically muzzled and muted and, therefore, put into play myriad
forms of musical protest that non-verbally or, rather, non-lyrically conveyed dissent and, however subtly, a commitment to civil rights and
social justice. Clearly the pop music of the twenty-first century, including
commercial or pop rap, echoes and continues to embrace much of the
pop music formula of the 1950s, with the one important exception being
that instead of "avoiding such topics as drinking, crime and associated
societal problems, and overt sexuality," everything except social problems regularly turns up in contemporary pop music, especially sexuality.

In other words, even though it has evolved a great deal over the last sixty years to include topics such as drug use, drinking, crime, and sexuality, the raising of serious social and political problems, at least in terms of contemporary black popular music, has been left to conscious, political, message, underground and alternative rappers, neo-soul singers, or spoken-word artists—all of whom, in one way or another, seem to, however incongruously, correspond with Redmond and Goldberg's definition of 1950s rhythm & blues. They insightful explained:

> the R&B style employs a prominent, often intricate, background harmony pattern with distinguishable tenor and bass parts. The material is presented with an emotionally-charged reading reflecting the influence of gospel and blues music. The lyrical content of R&B songs is usually more representative of black cultural patterns of the period. Generally there are more variations in presentation and a greater tendency toward experimentation in R&B music—as opposed to the more stylized pop form. (23–24)

The first thing we might observe is that classic rhythm & blues, in contrast to much of the contemporary music put out under the "rhythm & blues" moniker, had "more variations in presentation and a greater tendency toward experimentation." Obviously when one listens to, and really hears Atlantic, Chess, King, Motown, and Stax rhythm & blues from the 1950s and 1960s, what is really listening to are the sounds of experimentation: the infectious sounds of Ray Charles synthesizing gospel, jazz, jump blues, and country & western; Etta James melding barrelhouse blues, jazz, and pop; James Brown masterminding his distinct mix of gospel, blues, jazz, and jump blues; Smokey Robinson & the Miracles, the Supremes, the Temptations, Martha Reeves & the Vandellas, the Four Tops, Mary Wells, and Marvin Gaye smoothing out the rough edges of early rhythm & blues; and Otis Redding, Carla Thomas, Wilson Pickett, Sam & Dave, Eddie Floyd, William Bell, and Rufus Thomas fusing the grit of gospel, the bad luck tales of the blues, the jive of jump blues, and the earthiness of early rhythm & blues. In the aftermath of the "sweet soul" and disco of the 1970s, with the shift toward the digitization of black popular music in the 1980s rhythm & blues, almost as a rule, suffered from over-production. Its polished and super-slick sound frequently watered the music down (not to mention the messages in the music), making it sound more like mainstream pop, which was going through its own version of the post-disco digital revolution as well.

In *The Hip Hop Movement*, I argued that it was left to rap and neo-soul to present contemporary black popular music "with an emotionally-charged reading reflecting the influence of gospel and blues music," as well as the gutsy gospel aesthetic of classic rhythm & blues. Not only do rap and neo-soul represent a recommitment to the experimentalism that marked the best rhythm & blues, rock & roll, soul, funk, and disco, their respective lyrical content has been consistently "more representative of black cultural patterns of the [contemporary] period." As I often remind my roughly 18 to 25 year-old undergraduate students, to really understand rap and neo-soul, and the wider Hip Hop Movement they sonically represent, it is important to comprehend classic gospel, rhythm & blues, and rock & roll as "representative of black cultural patterns of the period" in African American history, culture, and struggle between 1945 and 1965. Which is also to say, during the immediate post-war years and the Civil Rights Movement era.

The entangled racial and commercial agendas of the recording and radio industries, as well as "mature," middle-class, and mainstream white America's response to the precipitous widespread popularity of African American and African American-derived musics, greatly influenced the evolution of rhythm & blues between 1954 and 1965. Along with that, there were concomitant currents internal to the African American community that were also equally influential on rhythm & blues' evolution between 1954 and 1965. Undoubtedly, the evolution of African American male vocal harmony group singing during the 1950s demonstrated that significant social, cultural, and demographic changes had converged to create unprecedented African American acceptance of a lighter and sweeter style of rhythm & blues (*à la* Nat King Cole, Charles Brown, Billy Eckstine, and the Four Toppers/Five Red Caps) that was more ballad-focused than previous forms of early rhythm & blues. Consequently, long before the recording industry took up a similar strategy in its efforts to reach the wallets of a wider white audience, African Americans' musical tastes favored a softer, slower, ballad-based form of rhythm & blues. In fact, in the late 1940s and early 1950s, these lighter and sweeter lyrical and musical stylings had periodically enabled a couple of the more sentimental sounding African American harmonizers—classic groups such as the Orioles ("It's Too Soon to Know"), the Ravens ("Count Every Star"), the Five Keys ("The Glory of Love"), the Vocaleers ("Be True"), and the Harp-Tones ("Sunday Kind of Love")—to cross the color-line and integrate the white pop charts.

By the middle of the 1950s the same sentimental and relatively safe-sounding characteristics that put African American harmony groups on the pop charts in the late 1940s and early 1950s had paved the way for the wholesale crossover of several sets of upstarts who spearheaded a wave of *sonic desegregation* and *sonic integration* that has continued to this day. Groups such as the Moonglows, Spaniels, Penguins, Charms, Chords, and Crows all had major hits on the pop charts that, for all intents and purposes, put forward idealized and newfangled versions of male-female relationships that challenged the core characteristics of the African American male blues aesthetic, which revolved around sometimes subtle, and sometimes not-so-subtle, expressions of hyper-masculinity and outright misogyny. These changes in African American musical tastes were indicative of broader changes throughout African America in particular, and the U.S. more generally.

After World War II small crowds of well-meaning and mostly liberal white sociologists and cultural anthropologists marched into African America (especially black ghettoes). When they came out and carefully reviewed their "scientific" findings they concluded that African Americans had created their own unique culture with identifiable value systems, codes of conduct, and standards of excellence. As a result of their distinct historical experiences and ongoing racial segregation in U.S. society, the urban African American masses incrementally evolved their own worldview, created their own cultural institutions, and put forward their own popular art forms geared toward expressing and legitimating their views and values. Among the myriad institutions that synthesized and publicized the post-war urban African American experience, few were more effective and effusive than rhythm & blues and its accompanying ethos and aesthetic.

Much like the gospel artists and freedom singer-songwriters treated in the last chapter, there is no denying the profound impact that mainstream and middle-class white America had on the daily existence, material conditions and, ironically, the growing cultural consciousness of urban black America during the immediate post-war era. Similar to other African American performers and artists—indeed, like most African Americans in general at the time—the exponents of rhythm & blues in the 1950s existed in a racially, culturally, psychologically, religiously, and musically segregated world. They existed and operated at the crossroads of a series of intersecting traditions, mostly African American but many European American as well; mainly Southern, unsophisticated, and rural, but also increasingly Northern, Mid-Western, Western, and undeniably urbane.

As touched on in chapter 2, African Americans' efforts to come to terms with their creolized culture and hybridized heritage was exemplified in their social, political, cultural, and religious expressions, and also reflected in their popular culture and, most especially, in their popular music. It was black popular music in the 1950s that increasingly came to sound like a vocalized version of what W. E. B. Du Bois called "double-consciousness" which, as will be recalled from the prior chapter, he famously identified as the core characteristic of the African American experience. In his classic *The Souls of Black Folk* (1903b), Du Bois declared:

> After the Egyptian and Indian, the Greek and Roman, the Teuton and Mongolian, the Negro is a sort of seventh son, born with a veil, and gifted with second-sight in this American world,—a world which yields him no true self-consciousness, but only lets him see himself through the revelation of the other world. It is a peculiar sensation, this double-consciousness, this sense of always looking at one's self through the eyes of others, of measuring one's soul by the tape of a

world that looks on in amused contempt and pity. One ever feels his two-ness,—an American, a Negro; two souls, two thoughts, two unreconciled strivings; two warring ideals in one dark body, whose dogged strength alone keeps it from being torn asunder.

The history of the American Negro is the history of this strife,—this longing to attain self-conscious manhood, to merge his double self into a better and truer self. In this merging he wishes neither of the older selves to be lost. He would not Africanize America, for America has too much to teach the world and Africa. He would not bleach his Negro soul in a flood of white Americanism, for he knows that Negro blood has a message for the world. He simply wishes to make it possible for a man to be both a Negro and an American, without being cursed and spit upon by his fellows, without having the doors of Opportunity closed roughly in his face. (3–4)

Classic rhythm & blues, being the mid-twentieth century culmination of black popular music up to that point, sonically and succinctly captures and conveys "double-consciousness." It represents the psychological, cultural, and musical aftermath of centuries of enslavement, racial colonization, social segregation, and American apartheid. It is what being emancipated and recurringly re-enslaved sounds like. It is the sound of African Americans expressing that "peculiar sensation," that "sense of always looking at one's self through the eyes of others, of measuring one's soul by the tape of a world that looks on in amused contempt and pity."

Classic rhythm & blues excruciatingly encompasses African Americans' feelings of perpetual "two-ness" and dividedness, their quests to see themselves as they actually are, not as others would like for them to be. Classic rhythm & blues, then, is fundamentally about truth, about black folk speaking their special truths to each other and to the world at large. Part of African Americans' distinct truth undeniably involves the struggle to come to terms with their "American[ness]" and their "Negro[ness]" (i.e., their "Africanness"), their "two souls, two thoughts," their "two unreconciled strivings," their "two warring ideals in one dark body, whose dogged strength alone keeps it from being torn asunder." How else can we explain Ray Charles' innovative Atlantic Records years, where he synthesized the pleading, frenzy-filled and shouting sounds of gospel with the often calm cry and musical melancholia of the blues? Or Etta James' jocular gospel, blues and jazz mix during her Chess Records years, where she seemed to combine the styles of countless black pop divas before her and unambiguously provide a sonic palette for seemingly each of the pop divas who would follow after her, from Aretha Franklin and Janis Joplin to Beyoncé and Christina Aguilera?

Classic rhythm & blues is a musical and cultural manifestation of African Americans' "dogged strength." It represents the evolution of the deep double entendres of the spirituals and the blues, gospel and free-dom songs, and—as with all other forms of black popular music—it makes the music mean one thing to those who have not *lived* the music and wholly another to those who have. *Living the music* and having an authentic relationship—or, rather, "keeping it real"—with the culture and community, or the experiences, individuals, and institutions that one is singing or rapping about represents both the *leitmotif* and *sine qua non* of black popular music and black popular culture. In other words, both the artist and the audience have got to *feel* the existential realness of the lyrics and music. If the lyrics and music do not conjure up and sonically capture the African American experience in a highly original and thoroughly individual way they do not register as "real," or "authentic," or—dare I say—"soulful."

It is the mystical and almost magical category of "soul" that has deter-mined the fate more than a few would-be iconic African American artists. In African America, as in Africa, an artist must do more than represent and express themselves. They must also represent their community and culture. They must speak the special truth of their community and cul-ture to the wider world. No matter how technically proficient one may be on their chosen instrument. No matter how much facility one has to sing high or low, or rap fast or slow, without "soul"—that *je ne sais quoi* of both continental and diasporan African ethos and aesthetics—there would be nothing truly distinct or, more to the point, "African" about African American music.[25]

Classic rhythm & blues' expression of double-consciousness captured and communicated mid-twentieth century African American existence at the intersection of its diverse and incessantly overlapping hybrid heri-tages, which represented African Americans' aspirations and frustrations in the two decades following World War II. On the one hand, by the 1950s both African America and European America regularly recognized that there was indeed something called "white" popular music—al-though, from a historical, cultural, and musicological perspective, the Great American Songbook, especially Tin Pan Alley pop, was greatly indebted to African American music, most notably blues, ragtime, and jazz.[26]

On the other hand, there was African American's creolized musical culture and customs, with their own collection of preferred devices and performance practices, most of which were traceable back to Africa, but all of which had been boldly recreated to speak to the special needs of Africans in America in the middle of the twentieth century. Situated somewhere between those slippery and sliding, theoretical, yet conven-tionally understood and embraced, black and white musical poles the African American masses' musical tastes illusively reside. And, it is here, in-between these two musical poles, that we may be able to better under-stand that *black popular music at a specific historical moment provides us with an imperfect but nonetheless evocative index of African American cultural consciousness at the moment in question.*

All of this is to say, urban African American culture was neither monolithic nor completely autonomous or somehow free from European American musical and cultural influences. Religious, gender, and generational differences were just as important in mid-twentieth century African America as they were within the white world, even if widely shared racial and most often class characteristics produced fundamentally homogenous lived-experiences and core values. Surely, then, African American ghetto culture during the post-war period and the Civil Rights Movement years, and especially as found in black popular culture and black popular music in the 1950s and 1960s, was not—as many liberal, and many not-so-liberal, white sociologists have argued—a "pathological" or, even worse, "pathogenic" response to African Americans' prolonged social predicament, racial oppression, and economic exploitation. Moreover, black ghetto culture during the post-war period and the Civil Rights Movement years was more than a fruitless attempt to apishly imitate the middle-class views and values of white America under less favorable conditions and in greatly reduced circumstances. On the contrary, it audaciously represented an unprecedented and wholly innovative act of agency on the part of working-class and poor black folk to construct an accessible and completely viable cultural arena for communal solidarity and individual achievement, while simultaneously recording and releasing the accumulated discontent and defiance in the face of, literally, centuries of domination and discrimination.

Even more importantly, the African American worldview and the distinct culture it created over time, and through which it was able to evolve, was not inert, even as it firmly grounded itself and deepened its roots in the fertile soil of post-war black (and, to a certain extent, white) America. Needless to say, worldviews are transformed as people transform the world or, rather, as they appear to transform the world. As a consequence, the major modes of creation, re-creation, representation, and interpretation of the African American experience have changed with every apparent breakthrough and setback in African American life, culture, and struggle. The evolution and extraordinary popularity of rhythm & blues in the 1950s and 1960s revealed just such a process of re-creation and cultural adaptation to what many African Americans optimistically perceived to be the birth of a new era of "authentic" American democracy coupled with the requisite expanded opportunities.

Understanding jump blues as an early form of rhythm & blues, it is important to acknowledge that rhythm & blues was the first form of black popular music to emerge during the post-World War II period. As such it became the first form of black popular music to be exposed to the unrestrained mass consumerism that defined the latter half of the twentieth century, and which continues to run rampant in the twenty-first century. With the introduction of the transistor radio in 1954, white youth had unbridled access to the new, hot, and often sensual sounds coming out of black America, which they previously had only limited access to as a consequence of their parents' incessant surveillance of their musical and general listening choices. In fact, prior to the introduction of the television into mainstream American culture in the late 1940s and early 1950s, the old cumbersome radio console served as the undisputed centerpiece of suburban intra-familial entertainment.[27]

In many ways rhythm & blues' remarkable popularity in the 1950s was a double-edged sword. On the one hand, no matter what the songs were really about, suburban white youth developed a distinct tendency to embrace rhythm & blues exclusively as dance music (*à la* England's Northern Soul Movement in the late 1960s and early 1970s). In most white youths' minds classic rhythm & blues was the ultimate party and "make-out" music. Even though most of the lyrics revealed innocuous romantic ideas or registered a popular dance craze at the time, *many of the messages in classic rhythm & blues alluded to the same subversive topics put forward in the spirituals during African American enslavement, chief among them commitments to African American freedom and unity, as well as African American spiritual and physical transcendence.* Although less apparent than gospel and freedom songs, classic rhythm & blues carried over many of the core concepts ensconced in the spirituals and, much like classic blues, subtly secularized the ethos and aesthetics of the black sacred song tradition within the world of post-war black popular music (bear in mind that classic rhythm & blues is unambiguously the bedrock of each and every form of black popular music that arose in its aftermath: from rock & roll to soul, funk to disco, and rap to neo-soul).

On the other hand, classic rhythm & blues bore the marks of Du Bois's double-consciousness in light of the fact that its lyrics were impacted by African Americans' precarious position at the low end of the U.S. social, political, cultural, and economic hierarchy. The truth is, in this instance quite similar to gospel and freedom songs during the Civil Rights Movement, the lyrics of classic rhythm & blues, once comprehended as part and parcel of a commodified commercial product, quite simply could not directly comment on the most pressing problems confronting black America at the time. However, with the *Brown v. Board of Education* victory and the beginning of the Civil Rights Movement in 1954, black America began to noticeably change, and as a consequence the content and style of the major forms of black popular music began to change as well, even if only subtly to the untrained eye and untrained ear. That is to say, where there may not have been a noticeable change in *the lyrics of classic rhythm & blues,* there was certainly an evident change in *the sonics of classic rhythm & blues,* and it is this seismic sonic shift that non-verbally encapsulated and enunciated the social, political, and cultural change afoot in African America that culminated with the *Brown v. Board of Education* victory and the beginning of the Civil Rights Movement in 1954.

From 1954 through to the emergence of soul as the major black popular music in the mid-1960s, at its most resonant rhythm & blues not only registered the hardships and frustrations of urban African American life and its core views and values, but it also expressed African America's most cherished post-war achievements and ongoing aspirations. Black popular culture, as with the more mainstream aspects of U.S. popular culture that African Americans embrace, serves a socio-political function when and where it offers an arena where African Americans can create and critique alternative views and values, as well as an arena where they can explore and express traditional African American views and values. In this sense, classic rhythm & blues reflected and increasingly articulated an idealized vision of not only loving and ultra-romantic African American relationships but also a united and harmonious African America which, truth be told, was more a figment of classic rhythm & blues singer-songwriters' imaginations than a reality in the 1950s and 1960s.

However, the classic rhythm & blues singer-songwriters were not alone in imagining a united and harmonious African America, they were merely translating and transmitting, indeed *transfiguring*, the post-war optimism, spirit of determination, and political pulse of the people then running rampant throughout African America into black popular music. In fact, for the first time since jazz simultaneously served as the soundtrack for both the New Negro Movement and the Harlem Renaissance in the 1920s and 1930s, black popular music unambiguously and unapologetically served as the soundtrack for a black socio-political movement. Beginning with gospel, rhythm & blues, and the Civil Rights Movement and continuing through to rap, neo-soul, and the Hip Hop Movement, since the middle of the twentieth century every major form of black popular music has reflected and articulated, however incongruously, the core views and values of the major African American social and political movement of its era. And, even though it has been regularly ridiculed, rap continues to reflect and articulate the cultural maneuvers, micropolitics, and mini-movements of post-Civil Rights Movement and post-Black Power Movement African America.[28]

MOTOWN AND THE CIVIL RIGHTS MOVEMENT: THE SOUND OF SOCIAL SEGREGATION AND SONIC INTEGRATION

At this point it might be safe to say that in terms of rhythm & blues serving as one of the major soundtracks for the Civil Rights Movement nothing drives this point home better than the triangular relationships between the Civil Rights Movement, the rise of Motown Records, and the inroads they both made in integrating black America into white America.

Foreshadowing countless rap and neo-soul artists' biographies, the iconic founder of Motown Records, Berry Gordy, dropped out of a Detroit high school in the eleventh grade with dreams of becoming a professional boxer. His boxing career was short-lived, as he was drafted by the U.S. Army to serve in the Korean War in 1950. It was in the army that Gordy obtained his General Educational Development (GED) certificate.

Out of the army by 1953, Gordy gravitated toward music, especially jazz, regularly frequenting clubs and eventually opening up a record store, the 3-D Record Mart. In the 1950s jazz was becoming more and more an acquired taste, being eclipsed first by jump blues and then ultimately by rhythm & blues. Needless to say, Gordy's "old hat" jazz-centered record store did not last long. However, it did pique his interest in songwriting, music production, and music promotion. Financially devastated by the failure of his record store Gordy was forced to work in the Lincoln-Mercury plant, making cars on the assembly line. It was a pivotal experience for him, and later he would model his record company on Detroit's auto industry, attempting to achieve the same level of ingenuity, productivity and efficiency.[29]

After writing a string of hits for Jackie Wilson (e.g., "Reet Petite," "That Is Why [I Love You So], "I'll Be Satisfied," and "Lonely Teardrops"), Gordy created Anna Records in 1959 along with two of his sisters, Anna and Gwen Gordy, and his friend Billy Davis. In quick succession after Anna Records he established Tamla Records and later Jobete Music Publishing (named after his daughters: Joy, Betty, and Terry). On April 14, 1960, he incorporated his many music business ventures under the name the Motown Record Corporation ("Motown," being a portmanteau of *motor* and *town*, is a well-known African American colloquialism for Detroit). Beginning with an artist roster that boasted classic rhythm & blues luminaries such as Smokey Robinson & the Miracles, Marv Johnson, Barrett Strong, Mable John, Eddie Holland, Mary Wells, and the Marvelettes, Gordy created what has been repeatedly referred to as "clean" or, rather, "polished" rhythm & blues records that increasingly owed as much to white pop as they did black pop. Even though he greatly respected the raunchier and more mature aspects of 1950s rhythm & blues, Motown Records' rhythm & blues would emphasize anodyne youthful singers and songs, in effect deconstructing and reconstructing rhythm & blues to make it more palatable to a wider, whiter, and younger audience.[30]

Motown artists in the 1960s were in many ways the antithesis of 1950s rhythm & blues artists. For instance, the contrasts between Smokey Robinson and Howlin' Wolf, or Mary Wells and Big Maybelle, or Marv Johnson and Muddy Waters are obvious to anyone with eyes to see and ears to hear. But, Motown's music was more than chocolate-covered pop fluff. By synthesizing black and white pop music, by coloring Motown songs with gospel beats and subdued church choir background singing, throbbing jazz-influenced bass lines, and blues-soaked guitar licks, Berry Gordy revolutionized rhythm & blues' sonic palette. Whatever he lacked in terms of technical proficiency at singing or playing a musical instrument, there simply is no denying Gordy's gargantuan sonic vision. In the 1960s Motown produced a wide range of music, all of which seemed to appeal to a broad audience and several different demographics. Ultimately, Motown created an extremely fluid and flexible sound—the much vaunted "Motown sound"—which, in the most unprecedented manner imaginable, allowed its music to have special meaning for, and appeal to mainstream pop music lovers and discerning black music lovers across the contentious regional, racial, cultural, social, political, and generational chasms afflicting America in the 1960s.[31]

According to Nelson George, in *Where Did Our Love Go?: The Rise & Fall of the Motown Sound* (2007), Gordy "preferred jazz musicians for his sessions, believing that they were both more technically assured and more creative than their blues-based counterparts" (37). Most of Motown's session musicians were actually local luminaries from Detroit's jazz scene: pianists Joe Hunter, Richard "Popcorn" Wylie, Earl Van Dyke, and Johnny Griffith; guitarists Dave Hamilton, Joe Messina, Marvin Tarplin, Melvin "Wah-Wah Watson" Raglin, Robert White, Eddie Willis, and Dennis Coffey; bassists James Jamerson, Bob Babbitt, and Michael Henderson; drummers William "Benny" Benjamin, Uriel Jones, Richard "Pistol" Allen, and Frederick Waites; and percussionists Eddie "Bongo" Brown and Jack Ashford. To complement the supper club soul or uptown jazzy soul sound Gordy was going for, as early as 1960 he "hired members of the Detroit Symphony Orchestra to achieve the upscale R&B sounds" made popular by Nat King Cole, Ray Charles, Jackie Wilson, Sam Cooke, and Aretha Franklin during her Columbia Records years (39). The strings had the "whitening and lightening" effect, smoothing out the rough edges of Motown's rhythm & blues and providing it with an identifiable sound virtually at the outset.[32]

From Gordy's point of view, black popular music, much like black people in the U.S. in the 1950s and 1960s, represented the recording industry's "bastard child and mother lode, an aesthetic and economic contradiction that was institutionalized by white record executives" (50). Hence, Motown's music became a metaphor for urban African American life, culture, and struggle in the 1960s. Gordy demonstrated to the American music industry, and eventually to the world, that African American youths were just like the "clean-cut" boy or girl next door, which was one of the major motifs of Motown's music, and especially the classic recordings by Smokey Robinson & the Miracles, the Supremes, the Temptations, Mary Wells, Marvin Gaye, Tammi Terrell, Stevie Wonder, Kim Weston, the Marvelettes, the Four Tops, Gladys Knight & the Pips, and Martha Reeves & the Vandellas.

As George observed, Motown made it clear that beneath "the glistening strings, Broadway show tunes, and relaxed vocal styles was a music of intense feeling" (50). Rhythm & blues, even the most "pop soul" sounding (*à la* Dionne Warwick, Walter Jackson, Barbara Lewis, Chuck Jackson, Maxine Brown, and Freddie Scott), was more than mere background music. It was a tool that could be used to break down barriers: musical, cultural, social, political, and economic barriers. Paralleling the emergence of the Civil Rights Movement, the rise of Motown sent a clear message to the white-dominated music industry: African Americans would no longer tolerate any form of segregation, neither social nor musical segregation. The message Motown sent to black America was equally provocative. Here was a company owned and operated by an African American armed only with a GED who challenged white corporate interests and white America's perception of African Americans, especially African American youths.

There is a certain kind of sick and twisted irony at play when one seriously ponders the parallels between the emergence of the Civil Rights Movement and the rise of classic rhythm & blues, specifically Motown and Motown sound-derived rhythm & blues. In a nutshell, both the Civil Rights Movement and classic rhythm & blues, for all intents and purposes, were *African American youth issues-centered* and *African American youth activism-centered*. In terms of the Civil Rights Movement: the 1954 *Brown vs. the Board of Education* victory obviously focused on African American youth, as it desegregated public schools; the March 1955 arrest of fifteen year-old Claudette Colvin, who was the first person on record to resist bus segregation in Montgomery, Alabama, alerted many African American adults to the adverse impact that segregation was having on African American youth and made many commit to the then inchoate Civil Rights Movement; the August 1955 lynching of fourteen year-old Emmett Till in Money, Mississippi, enraged even the most moderate African American adults, providing yet another reason to rise up against American apartheid; the September 1957 display of courage on the part of the "Little Rock Nine" (Melba Pattillo Beals, Minnijean Brown, Elizabeth Eckford, Ernest Green, Gloria Ray Karlmark, Carlotta Walls LaNier, Thelma Mothershed, Terrence Roberts, and Jefferson Thomas) as they integrated the all-white Central High School in Little Rock, Arkansas, flanked by gun-toting National Guardsmen clearly made even more freedom-loving folk commit to the principles and practices of the Civil Rights Movement; the August 1958 sit-ins spearheaded by Clara Luper and the NAACP Youth Council accented the brimming youth activism in the Civil Rights Movement, as did the 1960 emergence of a full-blown Sit-In Movement led by African American college students (Diane Nash, James Bevel, Bernard Lafayette, and C. T. Vivian); the May 1961 initiation of the Freedom Riders Movement, primarily led by the Congress of Racial Equality (CORE) and the Student Nonviolent Coordinating Committee

(SNCC), ratcheted up youth radicalism during the movement years; the May 1963 Children's Crusade, led by James Bevel, in Birmingham, Alabama, accented even more youth issues and youth activism in the Civil Rights Movement; and certainly the September 1963 bombing of the 16th Street Baptist Church that took the lives of the schoolgirls Addie Mae Collins, Denise McNair, Cynthia Wesley, and Carole Robertson two weeks after the March on Washington sent shock waves through African America and helped to kick the Civil Rights Movement into an even higher gear. Again, African American youth—their lives and struggles— were squarely at the center of the Civil Rights Movement.[33]

During the same turbulent years that witnessed the backlash against African American youth and their valiant struggle for human, civil, and voting rights, Motown was tapping the teenage talent pool of Detroit's Brewster-Douglass housing projects. According to Nelson George (2007), the Brewster-Douglass housing projects were "low-rent yet well-kept public housing that served as home for the children of Detroit's post-World War II migration. For all intents and purposes, it was a ghetto, but for Detroit's blacks it was one with hope" (80). Berry Gordy's first great discovery from Detroit's public housing projects was Smokey Robinson & the Miracles, and soon thereafter a group of guys called the Primes and their companion girl group called the Primettes. The Motown machine quickly polished and rechristened the guy group as "The Temptations" and their sister group as "The Supremes."

Hence, similar to several contemporary rap stars (e.g., Jay-Z, NaS, Marley Marl, Kool G Rap, MC Shan, Roxanne Shanté, Mobb Deep, Trina, Lil' Wayne, Juvenile, Soulja Slim, and Jay Electronica, among countless others), the ghetto, and public housing projects in particular, provided classic rhythm & blues with the raw talent, tall tales, and innovative subaltern aesthetic that fueled much of its success. But, unlike rap, the ghetto origins, or the otherwise humble beginnings, of many classic rhythm & blues stars was masked to make them more appealing to middle-class and mainstream America, especially middle-class and mainstream white America. As is well known, a lot rap is unapologetically ghetto-centered and often celebrates ghetto life and culture. For the most part, classic rhythm & blues production and promotion teams, especially those at Motown in the 1960s, downplayed the humble beginnings of the bulk their stars, preferring to present them decked out in the glitz and glam fashions of the era. Needless to say, rap music and hip hop culture's hyper-materialism and bold bourgeoisisms did not develop in a vacuum, and Motown and Motown-sound derived music and branding has long served as a major point of departure for contemporary black popular music, especially rap and neo-soul.

Even though it was obviously an oppositional operation within the music industry of the 1960s, Motown was nonetheless deeply committed to the *modus operandi* and mechanisms of the U.S. mass market and, it should be strongly stressed, on the U.S. mass market's mostly anti-African American terms. This, of course, resembles most Civil Rights Movement members' open embrace of the "American Dream" without critically calling into question whether "American democracy"—as articulated by the wealthy, white, slaveholding men who are recognized as the "Founding Fathers"—was a viable goal for African Americans (and other non-whites) in the second half of the twentieth century. Consider for a moment, if you will, Martin Luther King's famous "I Have a Dream" speech, with its scattered references to the Constitution and the Declaration of Independence (M. L. King 1986, 217).

King undeniably critiqued "the architects of our republic" (i.e., the wealthy, white, slaveholding men who are recognized as America's "Founding Fathers"), but he also passionately embraced *their* American dream. As a matter of fact, King's dream—to use his own words—was "a dream deeply rooted in the American dream" (219). For several of the unsung soldiers of the Civil Rights Movement, such as Ella Baker, Malcolm X, James Baldwin and Robert F. Williams, King's articulation of the American dream did not sufficiently differentiate between white America and non-white America's conflicting conceptions of the American dream. As Britta Waldschmidt-Nelson's brilliant *Dreams and Nightmares: Martin Luther King, Jr., Malcolm X, and the Struggle for Black Equality in America* (2012) emphasized, the militants of the Civil Rights Movement were not as interested in the American dream as much as they were concerned with ending the "American nightmare"—to employ Malcolm X's infamous phrase—in which black America continued to be ensnared in the 1960s.[34]

In this sense, Berry Gordy's efforts to upset the white male-dominated music industry of the 1960s by drawing from the successful business models of white America was not out of the ordinary and perfectly mirrored the integrationist and middle-class mindset of most of the black bourgeoisie during the Civil Rights Movement years. In the 1960s most African Americans were, as they remain today, largely working-class and working-poor. What Gordy and Motown provided the black masses with were sonic slices of African American life and culture, not necessarily as they actually were at the time but as the black bourgeoisie *and* the black masses wished them to be, and it was these, literally, phantasmagoria or surreal songs that both black and white America danced, romanced, partied and politicked to during the Civil Rights Movement years.

Working-class and working-poor black folk—those humble human beings frequently treated like second-class citizens in segregated 1960s America—knew that Motown's music grew out of their loves, lives, and struggles. In short, they could genuinely relate to Motown music's timeless, clever, often tongue-in-cheek, and passionate stories of love, loss, loneliness, heartbreak, happiness, and community because in no uncertain terms these stories were *their* stories (as in the often heard refrain at

African American dances, clubs, and house parties: "That's *my* song!"). It really did not matter to them how Gordy managed to create one of the most successful businesses in African American history. Simply said, they did not care about the backstory with all of its tales of trials and tribulations. What was new, exciting, and inspiring about Motown in the 1960s was that it consistently presented African Americans in general, and African American youth in specific, in dignified and sophisticated ways that the white male-dominated music industry—indeed, white America in general—had never dreamed of.

It could be said that Gordy challenged the mainstream American business model by deconstructing and reconstructing the received images of, and stereotypes about African Americans in general, and African American ghetto youth in specific. He, literally, refined, repackaged, and re-presented African Americans, and again African American ghetto youth in particular, employing business paradigms and procedures that were as far removed from African America, especially African American ghetto youth, as they were from the music business. Here, then, we have come back to our discussion concerning African American cultural adaptation or, rather, African American cultural appropriation, and the distinct ways in which black folk practice creolization and hybridization.

No matter how far-fetched and mindboggling it might sound, the truth of the matter is that Berry Gordy meticulously modeled his record company on Detroit's auto industry, selling a sumptuous black youthfulness, black hipness, and black sexiness employing one of the quintessential examples of mass production and consumption in America's market-driven economy. The Motown Record Corporation was simultaneously new and familiar to most middle-class and mainstream-minded Americans, both black and white, because it utilized one of corporate America's most revered models. As Gerald Early explained in *One Nation Under a Groove: Motown and American Culture* (2004), Gordy's work on the assembly line at the Ford factory was pivotal:

> His job at the Ford plant, as Nelson George and other critics have pointed out, made him aware of two things: how production can be efficiently organized and automated for the highest quality. At Motown during the sixties, producers could also write songs and songwriters could produce, but artists—either singers or session musicians—were not permitted to do either. With this type of control, Motown put out a highly consistent product. . . . From his auto plant experience, Gordy also became aware that to keep his company going, it was necessary to provide a series of attractive rewards and incentives for hard work, as well as an elaborate system of shaming for laziness. A record company, like an auto company, requires an almost unbearable atmosphere of competition. Gordy believed in competition with the fervor of a fanatic. (This intense sense of contest not only created a celebrity system within the company but became a point of celebration

about the company, a virtual mark of internal and external prestige.) Thus, producers with hit records at Motown were given more studio time, and the others had to fight for what was left. The hottest song-writers were allowed to work with the hottest singers. At company meetings, Gordy bluntly criticized any song or performance he considered inferior, not permitting the song to be released, thereby angering his producers and songwriters, but also spurring them to do better in order to curry his favor and approval. This system produced an unprecedented number of hit records in relation to the number of records released. (53–54)

Here we have a black record company owner utilizing the production techniques of a white car company owner, Henry Ford, to mass-produce a smoother, more or less white folk-friendly form of black popular music. It was not only ingenious, but it was also indicative of the desegregationist and integrationist ethos sweeping across African America in the late 1950s and early 1960s. By recreating and recasting African American ghetto youth in the anodyne and angelic image of mainstream and middle-class white youth, Motown was increasingly given entry into mainstream American popular culture at the exact same time that African Americans were desperately struggling to integrate into mainstream American society. In short, *1960s Motown music was implicitly Civil Rights Movement music without explicitly espousing traditional Civil Rights Movement themes, politics, and slogans.* This is where we come back to the double entendres and cultural codes contained in black popular culture in general, and black popular music in particular. Motown's *implicit politics* mirrored the Civil Rights Movement's *explicit politics* and, what is more, contemporary black popular music's implicit politics continues to mirror contemporary black popular movements' explicit politics. In essence, whether we turn to the rap or neo-soul soundtracks of the Hip Hop Movement, classic rhythm & blues in general, and Motown in particular, continues to serve as a model for black popular music or, rather, *the politics of black popular music.*

It is not my intention to argue that Motown agreed with or supported each and every social struggle, political campaign, and cultural movement afoot in black America in the 1960s. I am well aware of Berry Gordy's infamous reluctance to associate Motown with any organization or movement that could potentially negatively impact his company's commercial success. For instance, somewhat overstating his case I believe, in *Motown: Music, Money, Sex, and Power* (2002), Gerald Posner went so far to say that Berry Gordy "had no interest in politics or history. He did not read newspapers or books and had little sense of social destiny or moral responsibility stemming from his remarkable success" (172).

However, it should be quickly pointed out, Posner's interpretation directly contradicts Brian Ward's brilliant work in *Just My Soul Responding: Rhythm & Blues, Black Consciousness, and Race Relations* (1998), where he revealed that Gordy actually viewed "his own economic success as a form of progressive racial politics" (268). Bearing this in mind, it is not surprising that Gordy "did not wish to jeopardize his position" and the lucrative middle-of-the-road Motown brand by becoming "too closely associated with a still controversial black Movement for civil and voting rights." Hence, Posner's interpretation flies in the face of the facts and is quite simply untenable, if not outright wrongheaded. Like most African Americans at the time, Berry Gordy was not free from "double-consciousness" and seemed to be an expert at *code-switching for capital gain* (including *cultural capital gain*), frequently saying one thing in public, and another thing in private (*à la* most successful black folk in white supremacist societies).

In addition, Posner's analysis negates the simple fact that although Gordy was the chief executive officer of the Motown Record Corporation, it was, indeed, a "corporation" — which is to say, "a company or group of people authorized to act as a single entity (legally a person) and recognized as such in law," as defined by the *Merriam-Webster Dictionary*. Can Posner not comprehend that Gordy often purposely played the role of mysterious point man or chief executive officer, and allowed his surrogates to, even if only implicitly, mouth via Motown's music African American aspirations and frustrations during the Civil Rights Movement era? Can Posner not comprehend that legendary Motown singer-songwriters, producers, and musicians, such as Smokey Robinson, Marvin Gaye, Stevie Wonder, Harvey Fuqua, William "Mickey" Stevenson, Richard "Popcorn" Wylie, Clarence Paul, Johnny Bristol, Norman Whitfield, Holland–Dozier–Holland and, of course, the Funk Brothers were forced to dance with the dialectics of "double-consciousness," and even still felt deeply and often differently about the civil rights struggle than the big boss Berry Gordy? Autobiographical works by, and biographical works about Motown singer-songwriters, producers, and musicians in most instances reveal that Motown was not completely out of touch with or, worse, dispassionate about and divorced from the Civil Rights Movement.[35]

Ward's painstaking research revealed that Gordy and Motown actually contributed to several 1960s civil rights organizations and causes: from the National Association for the Advancement of Colored People (NAACP) and the Congress of Racial Equality (CORE), to the Negro American Labor Council (NALC) and the 1963 March on Washington. In the liner notes to the compilation, *Power To The Motown People!: Civil Rights Anthems and Political Soul, 1968–1975* (2007), Peter Doggett observed that Motown's support of the Civil Rights Movement steadily, even if subtly initially, increased as the Civil Rights Movement 1960s gave way to the Black Power Movement 1970s. He matter-of-factly stated, "Motown never set out to be a political force" (2). In fact, he went on, "it was simply a stable of incredible musical talent, which earned its reputation as Hitsville USA" and "the Sound of Young America." However, Doggett importantly commented further,

> during that time of civil rights marches and ghetto riots, liberation armies and black martyrs, all African Americans were inevitably sucked into the conflict. Motown Records was no exception. Berry Gordy himself was a strong supporter of the prince of the non-violent Civil Rights Movement, Martin Luther King; Motown even issued several albums of his speeches. As the racial heat increased, and Motown's home city of Detroit erupted into blazing riots in the summer of 1967, it became impossible for Gordy and his artists to avoid the call of the times. Over the next six years, Motown not only founded a subsidiary label entirely devoted to the struggle for Black Power (Black Forum Records); it also allowed its artists to comment directly on the situation of black people in contemporary America. For the first time, you could hear the nation changing shape in the sounds that came out of Hitsville USA. (2–3)

What needs to be emphasized here is essentially a point that I made in the last chapter concerning gospel artists in relationship to the Civil Rights Movement, and that is that "all African Americans were inevitably sucked into the conflict" — "the conflict," meaning the struggle for human rights, civil rights, and voting rights during the Civil Rights Movement era — whether they were active members of the movement or not. As Doggett sternly stated, "Motown Records was no exception." As a matter of fact, as the moderate Civil Rights Movement 1960s evolved into the unapologetically militant Black Power Movement 1970s, "it became impossible for Gordy and his artists to avoid the call of the times." To reiterate, during the Civil Rights Movement Motown put into play the very same *"we can implicitly sing what we cannot explicitly say"* aesthetic as the gospel artists discussed in the previous chapter. Perhaps summing up Gordy and Motown's Civil Rights Movement moderatism best, Nelson George (2007, 54) wryly noted:

> Though he never spoke about the issue overtly, Berry's rise in the early 1960s linked him with the Civil Rights Movement. (Dr. Martin Luther King, Jr., once visited Motown briefly, and Berry would release his "I Have A Dream" speech, along with a few other civil rights-related albums throughout the decade.) Naïvely, some saw Motown as the entertainment-business equivalent of the National Association for the Advancement of Colored People, or the Southern Christian Leadership Conference. To them Motown wasn't just a job; it was part of a movement.

This means, then, that I am not alone in conceiving of black popular music, in this instance Motown, as having deeper, implicit political meanings and being connected to the explicit political expressions of a broader social and cultural movement. No matter how "naïve" I may appear to be to those folk who have little or no real relationship with the

history, politics, sociology *and* musicology of black popular movements—besides what they can glean from ultra-conservative critics such
as Bill O'Reilly, Rush Limbaugh, Sarah Palin, Glenn Beck, Sean Hannity,
Laura Ingraham, Michael Savage, and Mark Levin, among many others—
similar to the African American youth of the 1950s and 1960s, I understand black popular music as more than merely music. To paraphrase
George above, among other things, Motown was "part of a movement,"
the Civil Rights Movement and, therefore, *civil rights music*. If, indeed, the
African American youth of the 1950s and 1960s conceived of their popular music as part of a movement, then, to strike while the iron is hot, isn't
it highly hypocritical of them—now that they are parents, grandparents,
and honored elders—to snicker at and chide their children and grand-
children (i.e., the Hip Hop Generation) for conceiving of their most beloved black popular music as part of an extra-musical, social, political,
and cultural movement: *the Hip Hop Movement*?

The truth of the matter is that Motown's music and its entrepreneurial
acumen were culled from urban African American communities that had
longstanding traditions of asserting their "implicit politics" through
black popular culture, black popular music, and successful black busi-
nesses. By eventually becoming one of Detroit and the country's most
successful producers of black popular music and most successful black
businesses in the midst of a racially segregated American society, Motown was indeed perceived as "political," and that is regardless of
whether or not we have consensus on whether Berry Gordy, Motown, or
its individual artists comprehended it as such. As is the case in white
America, black America has its own unique interpretive communities,
customs of cultural appropriation, and political practices, which do not
cater to the whims and wishes of megastars, music industry moguls,
musicologists, sociologists, political analysts, or cultural critics. Speaking
directly and eloquently to this issue in *Dancing in the Street: Motown and
the Cultural Politics of Detroit* (1999), Suzanne Smith offered remarkable
insight:

> Motown's role as a producer of black culture and its ambitions in the
> business world did not coexist without conflict and contradiction. At
> Hitsville, U.S.A., commercial concerns about the marketability of a re-
> cording often stalled and sometimes canceled projects that manage-
> ment deemed too politically controversial. The political climate at Mo-
> town Records was highly variable. Throughout the civil rights era the
> company wavered between willingness and caution when asked to
> produce recordings—musical or spoken-word—that involved overt
> political or racial messages. Sometimes an atmosphere of race con-
> sciousness prevailed, and other times a politically conservative ethos
> dominated.
>
> Motown's internal ambivalence about its relationship to the Civil
> Rights Movement was, however, only one side of the story. On the

other side were popular music audiences, local artists, and national civil rights leaders, who had their own ideas and disagreements about the meanings of Motown's music and commercial success for the movement. At the national level debates about Motown's role in the struggle for racial justice mirrored larger divisions within the movement itself. From 1963 to 1973 . . . the national civil rights campaign shifted from the unified fight for integration—exemplified by the March on Washington—to a more fractious battle for Black Power. Given these transitions, Motown could not avoid becoming a contested symbol of racial progress. Motown's music symbolized the possibility of amicable racial integration through popular culture. But as a company, Motown represented the possibilities of black economic independence, one of the most important tenets of black nationalism. (18)

All of this means that the connections between classic Motown as a metaphor and soundtrack for the Civil Rights Movement and contemporary rap as a metaphor and soundtrack for the Hip Hop Movement are many. First, mention should be made of Smith's emphasis on the conflicts and contradictions surrounding Motown as "a producer of black culture and its ambitions in the business world." Motown's dilemma in the 1960s seems to prefigure the commercial rap vs. conscious rap debates that have been an integral part of the Hip Hop Movement since its inception. Many of the more critical members of the Civil Rights Movement believed that the "Motown sound" was not the soundtrack to the Civil Rights Movement, but the soundtrack to "selling-out," black pop music that more or less encouraged African Americans to abandon the core principles and practices of the Civil Rights Movement. When rap music crossed out of the ghetto and into mainstream America in the mid-1980s it was denounced by old school rap purists. Supposedly "real" rap music could not be understood by wealthy and white America in general, and sheltered white suburban youth in specific.

Similar to Motown's brand of classic rhythm & blues, at its earliest stages rap was increasingly censored and sanitized for a wider and whiter audience. Which is to say, as with Motown in the 1960s, "commercial concerns about the marketability" of many early rap recordings "often stalled and sometimes canceled projects" 1980s music industry executives "deemed too politically controversial," too racially-charged, or too ghetto-centered. Reflecting the panorama of the cultural, social, and political views and values of the post-Civil Rights Movement generation, from the mid-1980s onward rap music's politics have been "highly variable," sometimes culturally conscious, politically progressive and extremely critical of racism, and at other times rap music has been extremely "politically conservative" and supportive of the status quo, especially on issues revolving around women's rights and sexual orientation.

Harking back to the jump blues era, a lot of early rap downplayed the tragedy of black life during the Reagan and Bush presidencies (between

1980 and 1992) in favor of playing up the comedy of black life. Just as dance, comedy, and novelty songs helped to popularize rhythm & blues amongst a wider and whiter audience between 1945 and 1965 (e.g., Louis Jordan, Clarence "Bull Moose" Jackson, Robert "H-Bomb" Ferguson, Screamin' Jay Hawkins, Napoleon "Nappy Brown" Culp, Eddie "Clean-head" Vinson, Little Richard, Chuck Berry and, of course, Chubby Check-er), after old school rap helped to establish the genre and announce that it was more than a novelty between 1979 and 1983, by 1984 the Fat Boys' comedy rap came into vogue, paving the way for comedy rap artists and groups such as the Beastie Boys, Heavy D & the Boyz, Biz Markie, DJ Jazzy Jeff & the Fresh Prince, Kid 'N' Play, Chubb Rock, Sir Mix-A-Lot, and Fu-Schnickens. Before gangsta rap arguably eclipsed all other forms of rap in the 1990s, comedy rap demonstrated that rap was not merely about dancing, romancing, and the hardships of ghetto life, but that it could also be light, tell funny stories, and make listeners laugh. Similar to classic rhythm & blues, the topical and lyrical range of rap music is a lot broader than many of its erstwhile critics realize, which is one of the reasons their criticisms frequently cause fury-filled and vitriolic re-sponses from hip hoppers and their elder allies.

By bringing so many diverse groups together, at least in terms of a shared aural experience, classic Motown music foreshadowed and laid a foundation for every major form of black popular music that followed, including rap. Motown music in the 1960s, to put it poorly, was the rap music of its time. It captured the comedy and tragedy, and sonically signified the dancing and romancing of 1960s segregated black America in the process of desegregating and integrating into mainstream America. Moreover, Motown also symbolized black powerbrokers and black busi-nesses in the process of desegregating and integrating into corporate America. With its increasingly young white clientele, in the 1960s Mo-town was both a metaphor for, and one of the major black popular music soundtracks of the Civil Rights Movement. Its challenge to America's musical segregation mirrored African Americans' social and political challenges to America's racial segregation. Touching on this point in his classic essay "Crossing Over: 1939–1989" (1990), Reebee Garofalo impor-tantly observed:

> In its early stages, the Civil Rights Movement, as embodied by Dr. Martin Luther King, Jr., had two predominant themes: non-violence and integration. As other, more militant tendencies developed in the black community, such a stance would soon appear to be quite moder-ate by comparison. At the time, however, it seemed to many that the primary task facing black people was to become integrated into the mainstream of American life. It was in this context that Motown devel-oped and defined itself. . . . Gordy once commented that any successful Motown hit sold at least 70 percent to white audiences. Working close-ly with Smokey Robinson on the label's early releases, he laid rich

gospel harmonies over extravagant studio work with strong bass lines and came up with the perfect popular formula for the early civil rights era: upbeat black pop, that was acceptable to a white audience, and irresistibly danceable. This was the "Motown sound." (90)

Similar to a lot of commercial or pop rap, in spite of classic Motown's more or less apolitical lyrics, many of its songs contained metaphors and came to have alternative meanings within the cultural, social, and political context of the Civil Rights Movement. Even the most apolitical lyrics can take on new meanings unfathomed by songwriters, singers, musicians, and record companies when the lyrics resonate with the cultural conventions, social sensibilities, and political praxes of a brutally oppressed people determined to rescue and reclaim their human, civil, and voting rights. For instance, a short list of classic Motown's songs that took on special socio-political meanings within the context of the Civil Rights Movement would most certainly include: Martha Reeves & the Vandellas' "Dancing in the Street," "Heat Wave," "Quicksand," and "Nowhere to Run"; Smokey Robinson & the Miracles' "I Gotta Dance To Keep From Crying," "The Tracks of My Tears," "Going to a Go-Go," "Abraham, Martin, and John," "Whose Gonna Take the Blame?," and "Tears of a Clown"; Marvin Gaye's "Can I Get a Witness?," "I'll Be Doggone," "Ain't That Peculiar?," and "I Heard It Through The Grapevine"; the Supremes' "Where Did Our Love Go?," "Stop in the Name of Love," "Love Child," "I'm Livin' in Shame," and "The Young Folks"; the Temptations' "Ain't Too Proud to Beg," "Beauty is Only Skin Deep," and "Ball of Confusion (That's What the World is Today)"; and, finally, the Four Tops "It's the Same Old Song," and "Reach Out I'll Be There."

Given the social and political situation during the early 1960s, Gordy's idea to create crossover "upbeat black pop" that was "irresistibly danceable" was yet another mark of his managerial and musical genius. Motown's predominantly white consumer base eventually made it one of the most influential record companies of the 1960s. When viewed from the "implicit politics" of black popular culture perspective we witness that as it increasingly exerted its influence on mainstream American popular music and popular culture Motown was transformed into a glowing symbol of the unprecedented economic and cultural opportunities available to African Americans during the Civil Rights Movement years. In this sense, Motown stars were understandably appropriated by most members of the Civil Rights Movement, who viewed them as more than musicians but, even more, as strategic cultural, social, and political icons. The fact that megastars such as Diana Ross, Smokey Robinson, Eddie Kendrick, and Mary Wells were all working-class and working-poor black youth raised in the brutal Brewster-Douglass housing projects prior to their Motown fame and fortune made them, for all intents and purposes, *icons of integration.* However, the success stories of the handful of

African American ghetto youth that Motown took from rags to riches were frequently redeployed by white America in its efforts to quell legitimate critiques coming from the Civil Rights Movement concerning the mistreatment that the black masses continued to experience throughout the 1960s.

This means that America's culture wars are not new, and the utilization of black popular music and black popular culture as a political football, as it were, is not new either. Culture wars were a major part of the Civil Rights Movement, and they have been and remain at the heart of the Hip Hop Movement. The initial backlash against rhythm & blues in the 1950s and 1960s foreshadowed almost identical attacks on early rap music and hip hop culture in the 1980s. However, by the time of rap's emergence America was a much more integrated society, and early rappers benefitted from the struggles and gains of both the Civil Rights Movement and classic rhythm & blues.

CONCLUSION: RHYTHM & BLUES, SONIC INTEGRATION, SOCIAL INTEGRATION, AND THEIR AFTERMATH

Rap music in the 1980s reflected the Hip Hop Generation's simultaneous acceptance and rejection of certain aspects of the Civil Rights Movement. On the one hand, early hip hoppers seemed to accept and sometimes openly celebrate the legal and psychological gains of the Civil Rights Movement: *Brown vs. the Board of Education*; the Montgomery Bus Boycott Movement; the March on Washington; Martin Luther King's Nobel Peace Prize; the Civil Rights Act of 1964; the Voting Rights Act of 1965; and the Fair Housing Act of 1968, etc. On the other hand, coming of age in the aftermath of the radical rhetoric and militantism of the Black Power Movement, early hip hoppers also registered the Hip Hop Generation's frustrations with post-Civil Rights Movement racism and classism, among a host of other inimical issues. Particularly frustrating for early hip hoppers was the growing nostalgia concerning the Civil Rights Movement and the 1960s in general, which frequently omitted the insidious elements of desegregation and integration.

Indeed, African Americans struggled for, and were legally granted their civil and voting rights in the 1960s. However, in the 1980s the U.S. remained segregated to a certain extent, and as racially and economically divided as ever. Rap in the 1980s not only unveiled America's increasing decadence, but it also revealed that for many African American youth Martin Luther King's dream was a dream that had little or no bearing on the non-stop nightmare of their daily lives. Hence, a lot of 1980s rap was not so much a rejection of the Civil Rights Movement as much as it was a refutation of wholesale African American (among other non-whites') assimilation under the guise of integration. Rap music's increasingly in-your-face aesthetics was a far cry from the innocuousness and piousness presented in 1960s Motown music. But, no mistake should be made about it, both 1960s Motown music and 1980s rap are linked because they served a similar function for black folk during intense periods of cultural development and social struggle: *they implicitly expressed via black popular music the explicit politics of black popular movements.*

After gospel and rhythm & blues the final major form of black popular music that served as a soundtrack for the Civil Rights Movement was rock & roll. Indeed, the origins and evolution of rock & roll reveal what I am wont to call the "black roots of what ultimately became white rock." With the emergence of rock & roll black popular music did not merely "cross-over" *à la* Motown. It inspired widespread white youth imitation and emulation, and ultimately the desegregation and integration—even more, *the African Americanization*—of white youth, their popular culture and popular music. Consequently, in our efforts to further understand the ways in which the unsung singing civil rights soldiers put into play *the "we can implicitly sing what we cannot explicitly say" aesthetic*, in the next chapter we turn our attention to the genesis and formative phase of rock & roll and its relationship with the Civil Rights Movement.

NOTES

1. For further discussion of Thomas Dorsey's life and legacy, and for the most noteworthy works which influenced my interpretation here, see Boyer (1995), Darden (2004), De Lerma (1973), Heilbut (1997), J.A. Jackson (1995, 2004), I.L. Johnson (2009), Kalil (1993, 2000), Kemp (2011, 2015), G.P. Lee (2008), Marovich (2015), Reagon (1992, 2001), M.C. Reed (2008), and R.L. Taylor (2013).

2. The black ghetto youth-centered or "ghettocentric" nature of black popular culture and black popular music, essentially from the blues to rap, has been expertly explored by Back (2000), M.P. Brown (1994), Dyson (1997, 2002), M. Ellison (1985), L. Ford (1971), Forman (2000), N. Kelley (2002), R.D.G. Kelley (1994, 1997), Maultsby (2001), Maultsby and Burnim (1987), M.A. Neal (1997), and Rosenthal (1988).

3. In *The Hip Hop Generation Fights Back!: Youth, Activism, and Post-Civil Rights Politics* (2012), Andreana Clay contended that "[s]ocial movement representations of youth suggest that young people have always been at the center of political activism and social change. Youth have been characterized as the backbone of the Civil Rights, Feminist, Anti-War, and Gay & Lesbian Liberation Movements" (3). However, "[l]ittle research has been conducted on adolescence as a significant identity from which to frame social justice organizing," even though "[n]ew social movement scholars have long focused on the importance of identity to social movement activism" (3). For further discussion of black ghetto youth's contributions to past and present African American political culture and social movements, and for the most noteworthy works which influenced my interpretation here, see Bynoe (2004), Bynum (2013), Chong (1991), de Schweinitz (2009), S.M. Franklin (2014), Gellman (2012), Ginwright (2006), Ginwright and James (2002), Joseph (2006a, 2006b), Kinchen (2015), E.S. Levine (1993), A.B. Lewis (2009), Morris (1981, 1984), Ogbar (2004, 2007), Ransby (2003), Van Deburg (1992), and Williamson (2003).

4. My interpretation of the ghetto, and more specifically the black ghetto, has been informed by Geschwender (1971), Glasgow (1981), Hannerz (1969), Hilfiker (2002), N. Jones (2010), Kusmer (1976), Lightfoot (1968), McCord (1969), Meister (1972), Osofsky

(1996), Owens (2007), Polikoff (2005), Rainwater (2006), H.M. Rose (1971, 1972), Schulz (1969), Spear (1967), Tabb (1970), Venkatesh (2000, 2006), Vergara (1995), R.L. Warren (2008), and D. Wilson (2007).

5. My interpretation of working-class and poor African Americans' lives and culture has been informed by E. Anderson (1981, 1990, 1999, 2008), Halpern (1997), Halpern and Horowitz (1996), Huntley and Montgomery (2004), Jaynes (1986), B. Kelly (2001), R.D.G. Kelley (1994, 1997), Lewis and Looney (1983), Lewis-Colman (2008), K.L. Phillips (1999), Roll (2010), and W.J. Wilson (1987, 1997, 1999, 2009).

6. My contention that black popular music has consistently served as the bridge between black political culture and black popular culture, as well as a crude kind of social, political, and cultural barometer allowing us to measure the atmospheric pressure in black America, has been indelibly influenced by Abbott and Seroff (2002), Baraka (1963, 1969, 1987, 1994, 2009), Burnim and Maultsby (2006, 2015), R. Ellison (1964, 1995a, 1995b, 2001), Ellison and Murray (2000), A.C. Jones (1993), Jones and Jones (2001), Lornell (2010), A. Murray (1973, 1976, 1996, 1997), M.A. Neal (1998, 2002, 2003), Peretti (2009), Ramey (2008), and C. Small (1998a, 1998b).

7. My interpretation of the origins and early evolution of rhythm & blues has been influenced by Baptista (2000), Broven (1974, 1978), Govenar and Joseph (2004), Otis (1993), A. Shaw (1978), and Wexler (1993).

8. For further discussion of the assertion that at its emergence rhythm & blues represented the wide range and wide reach of post-war African American thought and culture, see George (1988), Osborne and Hamilton (1980), A. Shaw (1986), and Stamz (2010). And, for further discussion of my contention that early rhythm & blues was *a music of motion*, the sound of a people on the move—figuratively, physically, socially, and politically speaking, see Hildebrand (1994), O.A. Jackson (1995), and Ripani (2006).

9. My emphasis on classic rhythm & blues having two meanings, one musical and the other extra-musical, between 1945 and 1965 has been influenced by several early rhythm & blues musicologists, see Caponi-Tabery (1999, 2008), Eastman (1989), Govenar and Joseph (2004), Maultsby (2006, 2015), McCourt (1983), Ripani (2006), and A. Shaw (1978, 1986).

10. For further discussion of the African American migration during the early-to-mid twentieth century that significantly impacted the emergence of the Civil Rights Movement and its rhythm & blues soundtrack, see Arnesen (2002), D.L. Baldwin (2007), Blocker (2008), Groh (1972), Grossman (1991), Hahn (2003), Johnson and Campbell (1981), Lemann (1991), Marks (1989), Wilkerson (2010), Tolnay and Beck (1992), and Trotter (1991).

11. My interpretation of African American migration between 1940 and 1970 has been informed by Askin (1970), Dodson and Diouf (2004), DuBose-Simons (2013), Gill (1975), Gregory (2005), L.L. Harris (2012), and A. Harrison (1991).

12. The emphasis here on the city-centered nature of post-World War II black popular music, from bebop to hip hop, has been influenced by Banfield (2010), DjeDje and Meadows (1998), Forman (2002), Goosman (2005), M.A. Hunter (2010), Kochman (1972), Peretti (1992, 2009), Ramsey (2003), and L. Thomas (2008),

13. My assertion that every major form of modern African American (or African American-derived) music, from rock & roll and soul to funk and disco, has utilized the innovations of early rhythm & blues as sonic paradigms and points of departure has been influenced by Banfield (2010, 2011), Maultsby (2006, 2015), Ramsey (2003), Ripani (2006), and A. Shaw (1986).

14. My assertion that the Civil Rights Movement can be interpreted as a decade-long synthesis and translation of classic rhythm & blues' extra-musical expressions into action, into collective struggle and radical political praxis, has been indelibly influenced by D. Brackett (2005), Carawan and Carawan (2007), D.C. Carter (2009), Dunson (1965), Garofalo (1992), Guralnick (1986), Maultsby (2006, 2015), Sanger (1995), S.E. Smith (1999), Ward (1998, 2001, 2004), and Werner (2004, 2006b).

15. My interpretation of Louis Jordan and his distinct brand of jump blues has been informed by Chilton (1992), Eastman (1989), Koch (2014), and Robertson, Guerinot, Robertson and Levine (2013).

16. For further discussion of jump blues, and for the most noteworthy works that informed my interpretation here, see Cohodas (2000), Coleman (2006), K.H. Miller (2010), and Shaw (1969, 1978, 1986, 1987b, 1998).

17. For further discussion of the "white violence" (or, rather, anti-black racist violence) against African Americans during and immediately after World War II, and for the most noteworthy works that informed my analysis here, see Berry (1994), A.V. Collins (2012), Kruse and Tuck (2012), Kryder (2000), Markovitz (2004), Nevels (2007), O'Brien (1999), Reddy (2011), H. Shapiro (1988), Waldrep (2001, 2002, 2006, 2009), and A.L. Wood (2009).

18. For further discussion of the anti-black racism of, and segregationist policies in the U.S. military during and immediately after World War II, and for the most noteworthy works that informed my analysis here, see Becton (2008), Brandt (1996), R.B. Edgerton (2001), Hervieux (2015), Hope (1979), Kimbrough (2007), McGuire (1983), Mjagkij (2011), B.L. Moore (1996), C.P. Moore (2005), and C.L. Williams (2010).

19. For further discussion of the "Double V" campaign and its transformative impact on the worldviews of African American soldiers and civilians alike during and immediately after World War II, and for the most noteworthy works that informed my analysis here, see Bailey and Farber (1993), R. James (2013), Jefferson (2008), E.L. Perry (2002a, 2002b), McGuire (1983), K.L. Phillips (2012), Scott and Womack (1998), J.E. Taylor (2013), Washburn (1981, 1986), and Wynn (2010).

20. For further discussion of A. Philip Randolph's life, legacy, and 1940s March on Washington Movement, and for the most noteworthy works that informed my analysis here, see J. Anderson (1973), Bynum (2010), D.S. Davis (1972), W.H. Harris (1977), Kersten (2007), Kersten and Lang (2013), Marable (1980), C.C. Miller (2005), Pfeffer (1990), Randolph (2014), C. Taylor (2006), Welky (2013), and S.E. Wright (1990).

21. Lynne Ianniello's *Milestones Along the March: Twelve Historic Civil Rights Documents, from World War II to Selma* (1965) continues to provide one of the best overviews of key civil rights legislation and is highly recommended to those seeking an understanding of the evolution of civil rights legislation between 1945 and 1965.

22. Beyond Baraka's *Blues People*, my interpretation here has greatly benefitted from close readings of Arnold Shaw's classic *Honkers and Shouters: The Golden Years of Rhythm & Blues* (1978) and Doug Miller's "The Moan within the Tone: African Retentions in Rhythm & Blues Saxophone Style in Afro-American Popular Music" (1995).

23. For further discussion of vocal harmony groups, street corner groups, barbershop quartets or, more simply, *doo-wop groups*, and for the most noteworthy works that informed my analysis here, see Friedman and Gribin (2003), Goldberg (1998), Gribin and Schiff (1992, 2000), J.M. Jackson (2015), B. Morrow (2007), Pruter (1996), Rosalsky (2000), Runowicz (2010), and Santiago and Dunham (2006).

24. My interpretation of the cultural, social, and political world doo-wop emerged from and, more or less, mirrored has been informed by L. Abbott (1992), Averill (2010), Baptista (2000), M. Ellison (1989), Goosman (1992, 1997, 2005), J.M. Jackson (2015), Kaplan (1993), Lornell (1995), Naison (2004), Phinney (2005), Ripani (2006), and Stebbins (1996).

25. For further discussion of authenticity, "realness," and "soulfulness" within the world of black popular music and black popular culture, and for the most noteworthy works that informed my analysis here, see Banfield (2010), Bracey (2003), M. Ellison (1989), Goldman (1999), Le Gendre (2012), Jones and Jones (2001), Moten (2003), Nielsen (1997), and R.F. Thompson (1983).

26. For further discussion of black popular music's contributions to, and influence on the Great American Songbook, especially Tin Pan Alley pop, and for the most noteworthy works that informed my analysis here, see Abbott and Seroff (2002), Appell and Hemphill (2006), Bennett, Shank and Toynbee (2005), Harer (2015), Kempton

(2003), J.M. Jackson (2015), Riis (2006), Rubin and Melnick (2001), and Sanjek and Sanjek (1996).

27. A couple of the most noteworthy works that informed my interpretation of American radio and television history and culture here include N. Browne (1994), Castleman and Podrazik (2003), G.R. Edgerton (2007), Mitchell (2010), Magoun (2007), Rudel (2008), J.A. Walker (2001), and Zook (2008).

28. For further discussion of the contention that since the middle of the twentieth century every major form of black popular music has reflected and articulated, however incongruously, the core views and values of the major black popular movement of its era, and for the most noteworthy works that informed my analysis here, see Banfield (2010, 2011), Burnim and Maultsby (2006, 2015), D.C. Carter (2009), Floyd (1995), B.W. Peretti (2009), Ramsey (2003), T.V. Reed (2005), Roach (1973), Rublowsky (1971), Sanger (1995), Schenbeck (2012), Southern (1997), E.L. Stewart (1998), and Tudor and Tudor (1979).

29. For further discussion of Berry Gordy's life and legacy, and for the most noteworthy works that informed my analysis here, see Abbott (2000), George (2007), Gordy (1994), Hirshey (1984), Maraniss (2015), and Singleton (1990).

30. For further discussion of Motown's origins and early evolution, and for the most noteworthy works that informed my analysis here, see Benjaminson (1979, 2008, 2012), Dahl (2001), S. Davis (1988), Early (2004), Flory (2006), George (2007), Jamerson (1989), Maraniss (2015), Morse (1971), Ribowsky (2009, 2010a, 2010b), J. Ryan (2012), S.E. Smith (1999), Waller (1985), and A. White (1985).

31. For further discussion of the much-celebrated "Motown sound," and for the most noteworthy works that informed my analysis here, see K. Abbott (2000), Carasik (1972), Early (2004), Flory (2006), Fuller and Mack (1985), George (2007), E.E. Jones (2008), Lüthe (2010), Maraniss (2015), and Ribowsky (2009, 2010a, 2010b).

32. It is interesting to observe that around the same time that Motown was "whitening and lightening" its rhythm & blues, over in Chicago Leonard and Phil Chess's Chess Records was pushing Etta James, undoubtedly their most famous rhythm & blues/soul singer, in a pop or "cross-over" direction. Recording thirteen albums for Chess between 1960 and 1978, James's first four Chess albums—which is to say, *At Last!* (1960), *The Second Time Around* (1961), *Etta James Sings for Lovers* (1962), and *Etta James Top Ten* (1963)—were each in their own way string-laden, early "pop soul" or "soft soul" records. By the time she recorded and released more soulful and musically mature albums such as *The Queen of Soul* (1965), *Call My Name* (1966), *Tell Mama* (1968), *Etta James Sings Funk* (1970), and *Losers Weepers* (1971), James had reinvented and rebranded herself as one of the undisputed "Queens of Soul" (alongside the likes of Nina Simone, Tina Turner, Carla Thomas, Patti LaBelle, Gladys Knight, Roberta Flack, Millie Jackson and, of course, Aretha Franklin) and indelibly etched her name into the annals of black popular music. For further discussion of Chess Records, see Broven (2009), Cohodas (2000), R. Cohen (2004, 2005), and Collis (1998). And, for further discussion of Etta James's life and music, see Gulla (2008, 147–166), B. Jackson (2005), and E. James (1995).

33. Several youth-centered or, at the least, youth issues-sensitive historical works on the Civil Rights Movement informed my narrative here, among them Blake (2004), Branch (1988, 1998, 2006), Bullard (1993), T.L. Bynum (2013), Carson, Garrow, Gill, Harding and Hine (1997), Dierenfield (2008), de Schweinitz (2009), Holsaert, Noonan and Richardson (2010), Kelley and Lewis (2000), Lawson and Payne (2006), E.S. Levine (1993), A.B. Lewis (2009), Loder-Jackson (2015), Morris (1981, 1984), Weisbrot (1990), and J. Williams (1987).

34. In his famous, or should I say infamous, "The Ballot or the Bullet" speech in *Malcolm X Speaks* (1990), Malcolm X sternly stated: "No, I'm not an American. I'm one of the 22 million black people who are victims of Americanism. One of the 22 million black people who are victims of democracy, nothing but disguised hypocrisy. So, I'm not standing here speaking to you as an American, or a patriot, or a flag-saluter, or a flag-waver—no, not I. I'm speaking as a victim of this American system. And I see

America through the eyes of the victim. I don't see any American dream; I see an American nightmare" (26). For further discussion of Malcolm X's critique of the "American Dream" and Martin Luther King's, as well as other Civil Rights Movement moderates', embrace of the "American Dream," see Branch (1988, 1998, 2006, 2013), Cone (1991), Garrow (2004), Howard-Pitney (2004), M.L. King (1986, 1992, 1998, 2001), Malcolm X (1971, 1990, 1991, 1992a, 1992b, 1992c), Marable (2011), and W.W. Sales (1994).

35. For examples of autobiographical works by, and biographical works about Motown singer-songwriters, producers, and musicians that make, however muted, connections between 1960s Motown and the Civil Rights Movement, and for the most noteworthy works that factored into my interpretation here, see Benjaminson (1979, 2008, 2012), Dahl (2001), S. Davis (2001), Edmonds (2001), Gordy (1994), G. Knight (1997), Perone (2006), Reeves (1994), Ribowsky (2009, 2010a, 2010b), Ritz (1985), S. Robinson (1989), Taraborrelli (2014), S. Turner (1998), O. Williams (1988), M. Wilson (1999), and Whitall (1998).

FIVE

Rock & Roll and the Civil Rights Movement

INTRODUCTION: THE HIDDEN AFRICAN AMERICAN HISTORY OF
RHYTHM & BLUES-CUM-ROCK & ROLL

At this point it could almost go without saying that the Civil Rights
Movement had more than one musical mouthpiece to (most often implicitly) express its politics, social visions, and cultural values. As was witnessed in chapter 2, gospel and its freedom song subgenre represent the
major sacred music soundtrack of the Civil Rights Movement, where
chapter 3 revealed rhythm & blues to be the major black popular music
soundtrack of the Civil Rights Movement. However, a growing body of
groundbreaking research has begun to increasingly reveal that rock &
roll, which basically began as an offshoot of rhythm & blues, also served
as a sonic symbol of the *integrationist ethos* and *integrationist impulse* of the
Civil Rights Movement. Where gospel and rhythm & blues essentially
represent the internal or intra-communal politics of the Civil Rights
Movement, rock & roll could be said to register as the external or extra-
communal politics of the Civil Rights Movement.[1]

During the same epoch that African Americans began to physically
defy social segregation via the Civil Rights Movement, their popular music began to musically defy sonic segregation via rhythm & blues and
later its mostly black music-derived aural offspring: *rock & roll*. The black
roots of what is now almost universally considered "white rock" are
usually explored in the blues tradition, and more specifically in the music
of luminaries like Robert Johnson, Charley Patton, Muddy Waters, Howlin' Wolf, Big Mama Thornton, T-Bone Walker, Big Maybelle, and Elmore
James. However, even as the black roots of rock & roll are acknowledged
via the blues tradition the early African American rock & rollers who not

only electrified and amplified the blues, but who also innovatively synthesized it with gospel, jazz, jump blues, doo-wop, rhythm & blues, and
country & western to birth rock & roll are, at best, marginalized or, at
worst, altogether erased from rock history at the very moment they
should be upfront and at the center of the discussion.

Revisionist histories of rock & roll and its aftermath, "classic rock,"
parallel revisionist histories of the Civil Rights Movement that either
erase or attribute the contributions of local, grassroots civil rights foot
soldiers, mostly female, to noted high-profile, mostly male, national civil
rights leaders. Which is to say, revisionist histories of rock & roll frequently either erase or attribute the contributions of the unsung singing
civil rights soldiers—whether gospel, freedom song, or rhythm & blues
singer-songwriters—to now-famous white male rockabilly-cum-rock &
rollers, such as Bill Haley, Elvis Presley, Johnny Cash, Carl Perkins, Jerry
Lee Lewis, Buddy Holly, Roy Orbison, the Everly Brothers, Ricky Nelson,
Jerry Reed, Scotty Moore, Tommy Sands, Jimmy Bowen, Charlie Gracie,
Johnny Burnette, Paul Burlison, Billy Adams, Ronnie Dawson, Gene
Summers, and Eddie Cochran. There simply is no way to get around the
historical fact that just as racial segregation and economic exploitation
were key issues in the Civil Rights Movement, they were also, however
clandestinely, significant issues in each of the major soundtracks of the
Civil Rights Movement, including the often shrouded origins and early
evolution of rock & roll. In fact, as we begin our discussion of rock & roll
as one of the central soundtracks of the Civil Rights Movement, it is
important to bear in mind, not merely American history (broadly conceived), but more specifically American *musical* history.

The history of popular music in the United States—at least, in the
twentieth century—can be characterized in terms of an incessant pattern
of black invention and white imitation, black innovation and white popu-
larization. Hence, we should be careful here to turn ample attention to *the
black pioneers of rock & roll* before we focus on *the white popularizers of rock
& roll* because *the black pioneers/white popularizers paradigm* speaks volumes about the ways in which the rules and regulations of social segregation ran parallel with, and undeniably dictated the rules and regulations
of sonic segregation. Part of the real genius of the unsung singing soldiers
of the Civil Rights Movement is that they clearly understood that the
movement was aimed at eradicating all forms of segregation in the United States, including sonic segregation and cultural racism. From their
unique point of view, sonic desegregation and aural integration were an
integral part of the Civil Rights Movement's broader desegregation and
integration efforts because they unambiguously understood that black
popular music has always been a barometer of the frustrations and aspirations of black America. In addition, the unsung singing soldiers of the
Civil Rights Movement clearly comprehended that "we can implicitly
sing what we cannot explicitly say," and that white folk and the wider

world has had a historical tendency to simultaneously and schizophreni-cally accept black music and reject black people.

Obviously, a major frustration of black America during the Civil Rights Movement era was segregation, and a major aspiration was deseg-regation and integration (broadly conceived). As we witnessed with our discussion of Motown in the previous chapter, African Americans had aspirations to desegregate and integrate the American music industry and the pop charts just as much as they had aspirations to desegregate and integrate the government, military, schools, public transportation, hotels, theaters, parks, and restaurants. Keeping this in mind, we can come to conceive of rock & roll from the point of view of the unsung singing soldiers of the Civil Rights Movement, not simply from the point of view of early white rock & roll youth, as *black music aimed at desegregat-ing and integrating the American music industry and the pop charts* or, more accurately, *"cross-over" rhythm & blues*—that is to say, rhythm & blues created for the specific purpose of crossing-over to the pop charts, subur-ban white youth, and, thereby, the wider world of white America.

Truth be told, *the black pioneers/white popularizers paradigm* of early rock & roll was essentially built on, not only the obvious ingenuity that classic rhythm & blues artists brought to post-war popular music, but also on the systematic exclusion of African Americans from positions of power in the American music industry—which, once again, is one of the many reasons that Berry Gordy and Motown was such a game-changing ven-ture. American apartheid, what is commonly called "segregation," de-manded that the color-line Du Bois wrote so agonizingly yet eloquently about in *The Souls of Black Folk* be applied to, and upheld in American popular music. In every aspect of American life and culture U.S. govern-ment-sanctioned segregation separated whites from non-whites, especial-ly blacks. But, by the mid-1950s rhythm & blues artists sought to, howev-er subtly and sonically, challenge the American music industry's distinct brand of *musical racism* and *sonic segregation*, which unmistakably relegat-ed black music, including black sacred song (i.e., the spirituals and gos-pel), to a "separate and unequal" status.

Consequently, prior to rhythm & blues-cum-rock & roll, black music very rarely "crossed-over" into the white world on its own terms. As a matter of fact, the peculiar prickly practices and mechanisms that have historically upheld and institutionalized the "separate and unequal" stat-us of black popular music and musicians has, indeed, transmuted since the emergence of rhythm & blues, but yet remains firmly entrenched in the twenty-first century American music industry. In order to critically understand rhythm & blues' evolution into rock & roll we need to seri-ously consider the fact that African American musicians' success or fail-ure has always hinged on more than merely musical talent and a pop chart-friendly, memorable melody. The relative success or failure of any African American artist is simultaneously musical *and* extra-musical, and primarily predicated on a number of variables that range from personal preference and individual taste to black population migrations, the scarcity of bare necessities, incessant underemployment, economic depressions, recurring economic recessions, technological innovations, exclusionary corporate configurations, organizational memberships, and government investigations. In contending with all of these factors, and the ways in which they were heightened in the period immediately after the end of World War II, a branch of rhythm & blues evolved into a pop chart-friendly form of rhythm & blues that came to be called "rock & roll."[2]

The major point I wish to drive home here is that rhythm & blues-cum-rock & roll was influenced by the prevailing socio-economic and political climate at the moment of its emergence in much the same manner that African Americans' enslavement led to the invention of the spirituals and the innumerable betrayals of the Reconstruction era led to the birth of the blues. This means, then, that the origins and early evolution of rock & roll, however surreptitiously, inherited many of the both musical *and* extra-musical elements of rhythm & blues, and no amount of revisionist whitewashing can change this simple fact into fiction. Whether the mostly white male rock historians are willing to concede it or not, it should be stated in the clearest and most unconvoluted terms we can find: *African American music and the African American musicians who collectively created it ingeniously established and innovatively extended an incredibly creative tradition, against seemingly insurmountable odds, that has historically exerted a disproportionate influence on American popular music, including rockabilly, rock & roll, country, bluegrass, Cajun, zydeco, Tejano, and Hawaiian.*

When African Americans' distinct contributions to the origins and evolution of rock & roll are either erased or attributed to white rock & rollers who came later and who, for the most part, copiously copied black rhythm & blues-cum-rock & roll styles, then and there rock history mirrors conventional whitewashed interpretations of U.S. history, culture, politics, and society. Moreover, without unambiguously understanding how deeply early rock & roll was identified with African American music, life, and culture contemporary rock critics and fans cannot possibly fathom how rebellious and outright offensive early white rock & rollers' music was to much of adult white America during rock & roll's golden age (circa 1954 to 1964). Writing directly about the "rock & roll controversy" and all of its racial undercurrents in *The Death of Rhythm & Blues* (1988), Nelson George explained:

> By applying the term "rock & roll" to what he played, a phrase that often appeared in black music as a euphemism for fucking, [legendary white disc jockey Alan] Freed tried, with some initial success, to disguise the blackness of the music. In the 1950s, "rhythm & blues," like "Negro," meant blacks. Calling it rock & roll didn't fool everybody, as Freed would ultimately find out, but it definitely dulled the racial iden-

tification and made the young white consumers of Cold War America feel more comfortable. If rhythm & blues was ghetto music, rock & roll, at least in name, was perceived to be "universal music" (a key term in the history of black music's purchase by whites). That term made it acceptable for whites to play the music removing the aura of inaccess-ibility. . . . This is not to downplay the impact white covers of black material had on white teens and their attitude toward the music, but the term "rock & roll"—perhaps the perfect emblem of white Negro-ism—was in itself powerful enough to create a sensibility of its own. (67)

We need to understand why the real roots of rock & roll needed to be disguised in order for the music to be seen as "universal." Why was it necessary to "disguise the blackness of the music?" How has more than half a century of "disguis[ing] the blackness" of rock & roll ultimately robbed African Americans of yet another one of their major contributions to U.S. history and culture? Also, how has the hidden black history of rock & roll altered our perception of it as one of the major soundtracks of the Civil Rights Movement? Indeed, the politics of black popular music during the Civil Rights Movement are even more intriguing and reveal-ing when we take into consideration its origins in, and evolution from gospel to rhythm & blues, and then rhythm & blues to arguably the most famous and unquestionably the first great rhythm & blues-derived mu-sic: rock & roll.

When and where we are a willing to acknowledge that the Civil Rights Movement actually had multiple major soundtracks (i.e., gospel, rhythm & blues, and rock & roll), then and there it more clearly emerges as an ideal site to explore the multiple messages of the "we can implicitly sing what we cannot explicitly say" aesthetic of the movement. Much like the New Negro Movement or the Harlem Renaissance, the Civil Rights Movement had both an intra-cultural and black America-centered sound-track in rhythm & blues, and what could be seen as a more or less inte-grationist and white folk-friendly soundtrack in rock & roll. Obviously the argument here is not that each and every form of rock & roll (or, later, "classic rock") conforms to rhythm & blues in relationship to the Civil Rights Movement. On the contrary, the main argument here is that there are enough similarities between rhythm & blues and rock & roll, especial-ly early rhythm & blues-based rock & roll, to make a case for critically engaging them as inter-racial arenas where black and white youths, among others, put forward messages and advanced ideals that were not only informed by the Civil Rights Movement, but ultimately influenced most of the major movements of the 1960s: from the Chicano Movement (*El Movimiento*) and Anti-War Movement to the Women's Liberation Movement and Lesbian & Gay Liberation Movement.

An issue of "inaccessibility" continues to keep white fans from fully embracing the sonic experimentalism and social commentary of many forms of contemporary black popular music beyond commercial rap or "radio rap," especially message rap, neo-soul, and spoken-word. Much like rhythm & blues during the Civil Rights Movement era this music is perceived as "ghetto music" or, especially with respect to neo-soul, mocked as "baby-making music." Just as classic rhythm & blues was more than the dances it helped to popularize during the Civil Rights Movement (e.g., the Twist, the Monkey, the Jerk, the Pony, the Watusi, the Mashed Potato, the Duckwalk, the Camel Walk, the Funky Chicken, the Swim, and the Dog), rock & roll was more than merely post-war white youths' fascination with black popular music and black popular culture.

Through embracing rock & roll music and culture, scores of mostly suburban white youth, even if most often unwittingly, challenged their parents and grandparents' "American" family traditions and social conventions predicated on racial segregation. Building on what the pioneers of rhythm & blues put into play, early rock & rollers created a form of musical protest that was cultural coded, making rock & roll music and rock & roll protest mean one thing to white adults and almost wholly another thing to black and white rock & roll youth. Consequently, this chapter will explore early rhythm & blues-based rock & roll as a major soundtrack for the Civil Rights Movement, and especially its, even if only implicit, emphasis on desegregation, integration, and youth activism. The emphasis here will be on the ways in which rock & roll's relationship with the Civil Rights Movement, even if often unwittingly and often unacknowledged, builds on, and in many ways goes beyond gospel and rhythm & blues' relationship with the Civil Rights Movement in the sense that it was able to capture and convey the movement's *integrationist ethos* and *integrationist impulse* in ways that gospel and rhythm & blues did not. But, in order to understand the initial lyrical and musical overlap between rhythm & blues and rock & roll, and certainly rhythm & blues' evolution into rock & roll, we must critically consider the ways in which the blues was foundational for both rhythm & blues and rock & roll.

THE RHYTHMS AND THE BLUES THAT EVOLVED INTO RHYTHM & BLUES AND ULTIMATELY ROCK & ROLL

One of the hallmarks of classical African griots, priests, praise singers, and dirge singers was their ability to express profoundly personal emotions and offer them up in a way that deeply resonated with their respective communities. They possessed an *aesthetic alchemy* that enabled them to translate individual experience—their own and others'—into collective music and communal expressions. Similar to contemporary African singer-songwriters—for example, Miriam Makeba, Fela Kuti, Thomas Mapfumo, Youssou N'Dour, Angélique Kidjo, Ladysmith Black Mambazo, Salif

Keita, Cheikh Lô, Baaba Maal, and Césaria Évora—classical African singers took seemingly simple lyrics and loaded them with intense and animated emotion, cultural codes, multiple metaphors, indigenous figures of speech, folk philosophy, political ideology, and religious references.[3]

The spirituals and the blues built on and went beyond the classical African lyrical tradition by incorporating proverbs, double entendres, and allegories that grew out of the African American experience during enslavement, Reconstruction, and post-Reconstruction. As discussed in chapter 3, during enslavement the spirituals represented African American sacred music, while work songs and field hollers symbolized African American secular music.[4] It is important to observe that each of the aforementioned musics contained improvisational elements that enabled them to be formulated and reformulated according to the spiritual, psychological, and physical needs of the enslaved—much like every major form of African American music that followed in their wake, including gospel, freedom songs, rhythm & blues, and rock & roll.

The deep double entendres of early African American spirituals, field hollers, work songs, and party songs frequently masked the complexity and hidden meanings of the music. Early African American music was usually draped in seemingly "primitive" lyrics and "simple" melodies—that is to say, of course, purportedly "primitive" lyrics and "simple" melodies when compared with European and European American lyrics and melodies, and not traditional African lyrics and melodies. However, when the lyrics, melodies, and rhythms of the enslaved are scrutinized they reveal music of profound spiritual substance and exceptional insight that often escaped the understanding of outsiders—especially anti-African, enslaving, and colonizing "outsiders."

Like all other major African American musical forms, work songs and spirituals mean more to those who have some working-knowledge of the lives and struggles of the people who produced them. Hence, the body of lyrical literature and beautiful "sorrow songs" that have been handed down to us speak volumes about the ingenuity and intelligence of an alleged "illiterate," "unintelligent," and "primitive" people. That these songs continue to be movingly sung (and, at times, seemingly employed in African American Christian-styled séances) to this day, indeed, says something about the humble humanity and innovative artistry of the people who produced them.[5]

The multiple meanings and multiple purposes of African American music was sonically intensified and socially amplified with the emergence of the blues at the end of the nineteenth century. The blues was the first major African American musical form produced in the post-enslavement period. Which is to say, the blues was conceptually conceived and birthed during the Reconstruction and post-Reconstruction years, roughly between 1865 and 1900. Where work songs, field hollers, and the spirituals could be considered primarily communal music that expressed life

lived in the face of the hard labor, harsh realities, and the other innumerable horrors African American enslavement entailed, the blues encapsulated the experiences and emotions of individual African Americans who
were "freed from the bonds of slavery" but still bound by the Black
Codes, the Klu Klux Klan, Jim Crow laws, lynching, the peonage system,
the share-cropping system, and the convict-lease system. In other words,
their lives remained bound by what is currently more commonly called
"American apartheid."[6]

The blues developed into a dynamic musical and cultural aesthetic
form that harbored an ingenious improvisational element that mutated
and translated contingent on the artist, audience, environment, occasion,
and venue. Consequently, blues music and blues musicians have an extremely fluid or, rather, jazz-like rapport that is incessantly altered by
any number of the aforementioned elements (i.e., the artist, audience,
environment, occasion, or venue). It is ironic that the very post-enslavement racism, poverty, and anti-black racist violence that blocked African
Americans from untold educational, economic, and political opportunities ended up providing them with the wherewithal to create a majestic
musical form and cultural aesthetic that continues to reverberate around
the world, especially via rhythm & blues and rock & roll.

Although women have been recurringly erased from the history of the
blues, as with most other major African American musical forms, they
undoubtedly played a pivotal role in its origins and evolution. Most
blues scholars concede that there is no empirical evidence that provides
us with clear-cut proof of *when, where, why,* and *by whom* the blues was
invented, but musical and historical artifacts reveal that women were
deeply involved as both singers and instrumentalists from its inception.
What we do know with some certainty is that African American women
were the first to record and popularize the blues.

As has been recounted in almost every major book about the blues,
Mamie Smith's version of Perry Bradford's "Crazy Blues" in 1920 was the
first identifiable—at least by modern and postmodern sonic sensibilities—blues recording. The song was so popular that it sold more than
75,000 copies within the first month of its release—no small feat in 1920.
The success of "Crazy Blues" sent shock waves through both black and
white America. It represented something new. It announced the emergence of a "New Negro" identity to America and, even more, a new
expression of black womanhood that was free from the conservatism of
the "cult of True womanhood" that plagued both white and black middle-class women in the first quarter of the twentieth century.[7]

We should take care here to note that the blues was given its first
popular expression by African American women. Even though it eventually (and incorrectly) came to be seen as a marker—if not for some folk *a
maker*—of black masculinity, similar to the origins and early evolution of
rhythm & blues and rock & roll, at its heart the blues is a transgender and

transgenerational art form that initially served as a soundtrack for turn of the twentieth century African American socio-political movements and a new epoch in U.S. history and culture. In other words, according to Francis Davis in *The History of the Blues* (1995), the blues "provides a kind of soundtrack to the gradual urbanization of a once largely rural people" (46).

The blues is the music of a people on the move. It is the sound African Americans created to capture their tribulation-filled transition from the nineteenth century to the twentieth century, from the South to the North, from agricultural labor to industrial labor. The blues, therefore, was what it sounded like to live at the crossroads, somewhere between heaven and hell, spirituality and sexuality, life and death, slavery and freedom, Africa and America, and the oldness and the newness of the African American experience.[8]

I am often amazed by the myriad ways the blues resembles rhythm & blues and rock & roll or, rather, I should more accurately say, vice versa. Rhythm & blues and early rock & roll sonically and socially represented African American life and culture during the immediate post-war period, where initially the blues represented African American life and culture at the turn of the twentieth century. The major difference between blues music, the blues aesthetic, and blues culture and rhythm & blues and rock & roll music and culture revolves around the incredible breakthroughs in post-war politics, technology, and telecommunications that took place in the middle of the twentieth century. However, even in light of the aforementioned "breakthroughs," many of the same themes prevalent in turn of the twentieth century blues continued to dominate at the emergence of both rhythm & blues and rock & roll discourse, so much so that any serious scholar or student of black popular music and black popular culture should solemnly question exactly how life was or, perhaps, *was not* in any significant way qualitatively different for working-class and poor black people in the immediate post-war period between 1945 and 1965.

It would seem that working-class and poor black people, the exiles and outcasts of both "mainstream" *and* middle-class white *and* black America, have consistently created the major African American musical forms—again, including gospel, rhythm & blues, and rock & roll. Therefore, the class-based character of African American music should not be overlooked. Art, especially popular music, has long been one of the few avenues open to working-class and underclass African Americans. It has often appeared to be the only medium through which poor black folk could get upper-class and middle-class white and black America to recognize the humble humanity, the tragedy, and the comedy of the life-worlds and life-struggles of the black masses.[9]

Because the blues was the music that initially painted a sonic portrait of turn of the twentieth century minstrel, medicine, tent, and vaudeville shows, as well as both urban and rural black nightlife (including Jim Crowed juke joints, brothels, dancehalls, clubs, and bars), it was shunned by the emerging and extremely uppity African American middle-class. At the turn of the twentieth century the black bourgeoisie preferred the solemn singing of the spirituals or the refined sounds of ragtime over the blues. Even though ragtime began as a form of red-light district dance music, whose origins have been traced back to African Americans in St. Louis and New Orleans circa 1897, it ultimately achieved widespread respectability and popularity among whites when it became available as sheet music for the piano.[10]

In its "purest" form ragtime is not improvised, which not only made it appear to many to be America's equivalent to European classical music, but its general lack of any form of improvisation clearly distinguished it from early jazz. Undoubtedly an influence on the early development of jazz, ragtime was primarily a vehicle for solo pianists, although several banjoists, such as Vess Ossman and Fred Van Eps, made numerous recordings. Among the three most renowned ragtime composers, Scott Joplin, James Scott and Joseph Lamb, two were African American, Joplin and Scott respectively. The African American middle-class, as to be expected, reveled in the fact that Scott Joplin was universally crowned the "King of Ragtime" and, even more, they delighted in the fact that his "piano rags" were repeatedly offered up as the American equivalent of minuets by Mozart, mazurkas by Chopin, or waltzes by Brahms. Great pride was also taken when European classical composers, such as Claude Debussy, Igor Stravinsky and Ferruccio Busoni, acknowledged the influence of ragtime music.[11]

Where the spirituals and ragtime initially sonically represented African American "hyper-religiosity" and African American "hyper-sexuality," respectively, because European Americans became enamored with these black musical forms the black middle-class apishly followed suit. The blues, on the other hand, was supposedly everything that the spirituals and ragtime were not: The spirituals and ragtime were sophisticated. The blues was unsophisticated. The spirituals and ragtime represented African American "high culture." The blues represented African American "low culture." The spirituals and ragtime were performed in prestigious churches and majestic concert halls. The blues was performed in juke joints and brothels—but, the breakaway success of Mamie Smith's "Crazy Blues" in 1920 challenged and eventually changed the national perception and cultural reception of the blues.

After a prolonged period of gestation, the blues had finally arrived on the national scene, sensuously feminine and fully formed, flamboyant and colorful, with flowing robes, satins, and sequins—not in dirty denim overalls, brogan boots, and a snaggle-toothed smile (*à la* a number of classic blues men). The early American music industry clearly comprehended that there was money to be made from this dark and mysterious music that seemed simultaneously ancient *and* futuristic. In many ways the blues harked back and heaved forward all at once: *back* to the "slavery days" and the "failures of Reconstruction and post-Reconstruction," and *forward* to the jazz of the New Negro Movement, the rhythm & blues of the Civil Rights Movement, the soul music of the Black Power Movement, the myriad musics (e.g., soul, funk, and disco) of the Black Women's Liberation Movement and, of course, the rap and neo-soul music of the Hip Hop Movement.

Smith's "Crazy Blues" was a boon to both the blues and the then fledgingly American music industry. The success of "Crazy Blues" demonstrated the *trans-cultural* and *trans-class* characteristics of the blues, if not early black popular music and early black popular culture. In other words, although the blues was created by a particular *race*, black folk, and a specific *class* within the African American community, working-class and underclass black folk, the lyrics, music, and overall aesthetic nonetheless hit a national nerve that transcended race and class as the 1920s progressed. In many ways the blues provided the first major model for what has come to be called "black popular music" and "black popular culture." In addition, and more specifically, the early cross-over success of the blues undoubtedly provided a paradigm for the cross-over success of rhythm & blues disguised as rock & roll.

To this day, African American expressive culture is, however unwittingly, rooted in blues music, the blues aesthetic, and blues culture. What Mamie Smith and other classic blues artists actually popularized were the sights, sounds, and sorrows of an emerging African American post-enslavement and post-Reconstruction worldview.[12] By adding a dance rhythm to the blues, *post-war blues* (i.e., rhythm & blues) revealed itself to be part of the evolution of *pre-war blues* (i.e., classic blues). But, in order for rhythm & blues to "cross-over" and evolve into rock & roll it would have to be *whitened and lightened*.

THE BLACK ROOTS OF WHITE ROCK: FROM RHYTHM & BLUES TO ROCK & ROLL

Similar to rap in the 1980s, as rhythm & blues grew in popularity among white youth in the 1950s it increasingly imbued with their musical and extra-musical meanings. In the segregated social world of 1950s America, almost anything emerging from or unambiguously associated with black America was looked at in a negative light. As a consequence, as with the blues backlash and the jazz controversy in the 1920s and 1930s, there was an uproar over rhythm & blues' influence on white youth in the 1940s and 1950s. Presaging the resistance to rap in the 1980s and 1990s, white adults in the 1940s and 1950s became increasingly concerned about what they perceived to be the complete disregard for traditional American values surrounding authority, sobriety, chastity, and family in rhythm & blues. For most white adults, rhythm & blues promoted violence, delinquency, promiscuity, drugs, and heavy drinking.[13]

Even after legendary white disc jockey Alan Freed's, among others', efforts to whiten and lighten rhythm & blues for the pop music market resistance increased and intensified. Part of the unpleasantness surrounding rhythm & blues and its whitened and lightened offspring, which Freed dubbed "rock & roll," was the simple but long overlooked fact that, as Greil Marcus noted in *Mystery Train: Images of America in Rock & Roll* (1975), most of "the first rock & roll styles were variations on black forms that had taken shape before the white audience moved in" (166). That is to say, although rock & roll, classic rock, and contemporary rock are most often understood to be "white music" within the context of contemporary American popular music and popular culture, like so much within the American social and cultural world, rock's origins and early evolution owes a great deal to African American life and culture.[14]

Those of us living in Obama's America and its immediate aftermath are quite aware of how fashionable it has become to tout how multicultural America historically has been and currently continues to be. Similar to jazz, rock & roll is frequently raised up as a prime example of America's distinct multiculturalism. Indeed, at its inception rock & roll was deeply multicultural. However, any serious analysis of rock & roll's core characteristics should strive to equitably and accurately allocate its various early influences, many of which are undeniably indebted to black popular music. As a matter of fact none other than Charlie Gillett asserted in his classic, *The Sound Of The City: The Rise Of Rock & Roll* (1996): "The roots of rock & roll are mainly to be found in rhythm & blues music, a term which, like the later expression rock & roll, was coined to provide a convenient catch-all description for several distinct musical styles. Some of the styles of rhythm & blues shared musical features" but, he stressed, "all of them were produced for the Negro market" (121).

The origins of rock & roll have been regularly described as a combination of rhythm & blues and country & western. Unquestionably, rhythm & blues and country & western were the primary musical genres that factored into rock & roll's genesis, but rock & roll drew from more than rhythm & blues and country & western. It also borrowed from all of the musics that rhythm & blues and country & western adapted, most importantly gospel, blues, folk, jazz, and jump blues. As Robert Palmer went even further to point out in "The Church of the Sonic Guitar" (1991), rock & roll also appropriated elements of Caribbean and Latin American music:

> The cliché is that rock & roll was a melding of country music and blues, and if you are talking about, say, Chuck Berry or Elvis Presley, the description, though simplistic, does fit. But the black inner-city vocal

group sound [i.e., the doo-wop sound] . . . had little to do with either blues or country in their purer forms. The Bo Diddley beat . . . was Afro-Cuban in derivation. The most durable . . . bass riff in Fifties rock & roll . . . had been pinched . . . from a Cuban *son* record. The scream-ing, athletic saxophone playing . . . was straight out of Forties big band swing. . . . Traditional Mexican rhythms entered the rock & roll arena through Chicano artists. . . . Rock & roll proved an All-American, multi-ethnic hybrid, its sources and developing sub-styles too various to be explained away by "blues plus country" or any other reductionist formula. (652; see also Palmer 1995, 1996)

As important as it is to acknowledge rock & roll's wide range of influ-ences, then, it is equally important to observe that African Americans contributed more musical building blocks to rock's foundation than any other cultural group. Moreover, African American musicians provided the models for the majority of the early rock & rollers (e.g., Big Joe Turn-er, Ruth Brown, the Crows, Ike Turner, LaVern Baker, Jackie Brenston, the Penguins, the Coasters, the Platters, Big Mama Thornton, Hank Bal-lard & the Midnighters, Clyde McPhatter & the Drifters, Fats Domino, Little Richard, Chuck Berry, and Bo Diddley). Hence, going back to the rhythm & blues plus country & western equals rock & roll equation (i.e., R&B + C&W = R&R), in *Rockin' Out: Popular Music in the U.S.A.* (2011) Reebee Garofalo critically asserted that "one might infer the R&B and C&W contributed equally to the new genre" (82). But, "such an inference invariably undervalues the African American contribution." Garofalo continued:

When rock & roll erupted full-blown in the national pop market in 1956, it presented itself as an integrated phenomenon with performers such as Bill Haley and Elvis Presley sharing the stage equally with artists like Fats Domino, Little Richard, and Chuck Berry. Accordingly, Steve Perry painted the early history of rock & roll in racially glowing terms: "From 1955-1958, the roster of popular rock & rollers was more racially equal than at any time before or since. Chuck Berry, Little Richard, the Coasters, the Platters, Fats Domino, Lloyd Price—major stars all, and on a rough par with the likes of Bill Haley, Jerry Lee Lewis, and Buddy Holly." But this only happened after it had begun to expand to disruptive proportions among mainstream fans. (82)

Here we have come back to Greil Marcus's contention that "[m]ost of the first rock & roll styles were variations on black forms that had taken shape before the white audience moved in." Without in any way dispar-aging the seminal contributions of white rock & roll legends such as Bill Haley, Jerry Lee Lewis, Buddy Holly, Carl Perkins, and Elvis Presley, it is important to understand that part of what made them so controversial within the context of 1950s America is the fact that they were white men who played vanilla versions of what sounded to most folk like rhythm & blues by another name. In other words, they were seemingly proponents of *musical integration* in the midst of an African American-led movement aimed at *social integration* (i.e., the Civil Rights Movement). Whether consciously or unconsciously, early white rock & rollers' challenges to musical segregation were taken by many to be challenges to social segregation.[15]

Without acknowledging how profoundly early rock & roll was identified with African American music, particularly rhythm & blues, many contemporary rock critics and fans unwittingly fail to concede what many of the most rabid racists of the Civil Rights Movement era openly acknowledged. It is hard to understand how racists can concede what many self-described white "liberals," white "progressives," and white "allies" fail to take into serious consideration. This is one of the reasons that even as we acknowledge and identify the influences on early rock & roll we should never lose sight of the fact that at its core it is primarily a synthesis of African American music, among other African diasporan musics. In fact, the majority of the musics that make up rock & roll's sonic DNA are either African American (e.g., gospel, blues, jazz, jump blues, doo-wop, and rhythm & blues) or African diasporan (e.g., *rumba, son,* among other Cuban and Caribbean musics).

Again, as much as we are open to acknowledging rock & roll's multicultural origins, it is important to observe the centrality of African Americans during its most formative phase. Without placing African Americans front and center in our discussions concerning the origins and early evolution of rock & roll, then rock history looks like little more than yet another whitewashed version of American history where African American contributions are appropriated and attributed to yet another set of white "founding fathers" (again, for example, folk like Bill Haley, Jerry Lee Lewis, Buddy Holly, Carl Perkins and, of course, Elvis Presley). In this sense, as Garofalo emphasized, "in the well-intentioned and largely accurate celebration of rock & roll's mongrel character, it is important not to lose sight of the fact that most of its formative influences, as well as almost all of its early innovators, were African American. Among the artists who could have been considered rock & roll musicians prior to 1955, there was only one white act that made a national impact—Bill Haley & His Comets" (83).[16]

Before it was whitened and lightened and renamed "rock & roll" by Alan Freed, rhythm & blues articulated how African Americans lived, loved, laughed, cried and died, first and foremost, to each other and, eventually, to the wider world. It was, as Arnold Shaw perceptively put it in *Honkers and Shouters: The Golden Years of Rhythm & Blues* (1978), the sound of a newfound freedom, a "liberated music, which in its pristine form represented a break with white, mainstream pop. Developing from black sources, it embodied the fervor of gospel music, the throbbing vigor of boogie-woogie, the jump beat of swing, and the gutsiness and sexuality of life in the black ghetto" (xvii).

Encapsulating the full range of mid-twentieth century African American emotions and expressions, spirituality and sexuality, and politics and aesthetics, classic rhythm & blues represents a defining musical moment and an audible emblem of how intensely African American culture and politics changed during the first two decades of the post-war period (circa 1945 to 1965). By synthesizing so many different strands of previous black popular musics with white pop and country & western, as it developed classic rhythm & blues boldly demonstrated that African Americans did not, at least sonically speaking, recognize the color-line and ultimately unrepentantly refused to be confined to the crude category of "race records," which was the term that had been used to designate black popular music since the classic blues era of the 1920s. All of which is to say, *in several senses even before the inauguration of rock & roll classic rhythm & blues represented African Americans' rejection of not only pre-World War II musical categories, but also pre-World War II race relations and cultural conventions.*

With its remarkable synthesis of gospels' jubilation, big beats, handclapping, tambourine-banging, and call and response; the blues' hoarse-voiced vulnerableness, impassioned uneasiness, and anguish-filled tales of wickedness and woe; jazz's emphasis on improvisation, syncopation, and elation; and jump blues' electrification, amplification, and unrestrained celebration, rhythm & blues unapologetically announced a new, even more emboldened spirit in black America between 1945 and 1965. To be sure, black America still had the blues between 1945 and 1965, but in the immediate aftermath of World War II blacks believed they had reasons to be optimistic. Hence, their new post-war blues decidedly and defiantly had a dance beat. It was sung in a way that recalled gospel and jazz vocal stylings just as much as the blues vocal tradition. Indeed, rhythm & blues was blues undergirded by the hip new vernacular-inflected rhymes and dynamic double-time rhythms of black America in the post-war period.

If country blues was bad luck music and city blues was the electrified and amplified sound of migration and urbanization, then classic rhythm & blues was the music of momentary freedom and a night full of fun. If country blues was rural song and city blues was urban song, then classic rhythm & blues was unmistakably inner-city song, the swelling and sweaty sound of African American ghettos in every major city in America. If rural blues symbolized individual expression and yearning, and urban blues a longing for rural life and romance, then classic rhythm & blues was the collective sound of a people discovering happiness and newfound joy whenever and wherever possible in their new inhospitable homes-away-from-home. If country blues musicians howled and city blues musicians crooned, then classic rhythm & blues artists shouted, yelled, screamed and cried, in the process deconstructing and reconstructing conventional notions of both "rhythm" *and* "blues."

Prior to the emergence of rhythm & blues, rural blues featured vocals and guitar, with added harmonica on occasion, and urban blues featured vocals backed by guitar, piano, bass, and drums. In contrast, as discussed in the previous chapter, classic rhythm & blues was characterized by impassioned, blues-drenched, vernacular-laden vocals backed by a combo consisting of electrified and amplified instruments, including honking saxophones, wailing guitars, and bubbling basses. The "impassioned, blues-drenched, vernacular-laden vocals," "honking saxophones," and "wailing guitars" blaring over the equally unbridled and often awry rhythm sections of the classic rhythm & blues combos eventually took on many meanings, perhaps none more telling than the one ascribed to the music by eminent musicologist Arnold Shaw. "Psychologically," he asserted, classic rhythm & blues "was an expression of a people enjoying a new sense of freedom, hemmed in though that freedom was by ghettos" (xvi). He went further, "R&B discs helped blacks establish a new identity—the kind that led a little old lady [i.e., Rosa Parks—who was actually only 43 at the time and ultimately lived to reach the ripe old age of 92] to refuse to yield her seat to a white in an Alabama bus; that led to the rise of Martin Luther King, Jr.; and that resulted in the 1954 Supreme Court ruling on school desegregation" (xvi).[17]

Tapping into African Americans' "new sense of freedom" and "new identity" as expressed through rhythm & blues many white youth in the 1950s were inspired to develop their own new identities and reevaluate their relationships with mainstream American music, culture, and values. Whether they made the connection between African Americans' "new sense of freedom" and "new identit[ies]" and the burgeoning Civil Rights Movement or not, many white youth in the 1950s were increasingly attracted to the exhilarating and, from their point of view, unusually exotic and erotic sounds of rhythm & blues. However, as rhythm & blues evolved into rock & roll in the mid-1950s, according to Peter Guralnick in *Feel Like Going Home: Portraits in Blues and Rock & Roll* (1999), "rock & roll represented not only an implicit social commitment but the explicit embrace of a black subculture which had never previously risen to the surface" of white America (22). This means, then, that some white youth indeed did connect rhythm & blues and its rock & roll offshoot with the Civil Rights Movement, and for many of them a commitment to rock & roll surreptitiously signified a commitment to civil rights and social justice.[18]

While bearing in mind the musical origins of rock & roll, it is also important to accent the social, political, and cultural world rock & roll emerged in. It may be difficult for many of my readers to grasp just how deeply conservative the Cold War world was, but a lot of rock & roll's rebelliousness will be lost without understanding the kind of closed-mindedness, hysteria, and undisguised hatred this period engendered.

Anything not sanctioned by the established order was deemed part of the "communist plot" to destroy America.[19]

Hence, first rhythm & blues, and then rock & roll were regularly derided as "un-American noise" created for the sole purpose of brainwashing white youth and bringing America to its knees. It is interesting to reflect on mainstream America's perception of the power of black popular music during the post-war period. While black people have long been viewed as socially, politically, and culturally inconsequential and impotent in the broader sweep of America's master narrative, their music has been consistently conceived of as possessing special, almost *black magical* powers. Similar to rap, the "more attractive R&B became to white youth, the more controversial it became," contended Glenn Altschuler in *All Shook Up: How Rock & Roll Changed America* (2003, 19). "White teenagers were listening," he continued, "but as they did a furor erupted over R&B. Good enough for blacks, apparently, the music seemed downright dangerous as it crossed the color-line" (18).

When it crossed the color-line rhythm & blues was whitened and lightened and ultimately became "rock & roll," and for many in mainstream and "mature" America rock & roll was nothing more than a metaphor for African American desegregation and integration. As a consequence, rock & roll initially elicited unambiguous anti-black racist responses seemingly from all quarters of the country. For example, in the *New York Times* in 1956, noted psychiatrist Francis Braceland asserted that rock & roll was essentially a "cannibalistic and tribalistic" form of music that appealed to white youths' immaturity, social uncertainty, base passions, and brewing spirit of rebelliousness (8). Because white youth were, in the most unprecedented manner imaginable in Cold War America, emulating African Americans' newfound social assertiveness and musical expressiveness, he concluded that rock & roll was basically a "communicable disease" inexplicably infecting white youth with its supposedly vulgar and vice-laden cultural, social, and highly-sexual views and values.

Another critic who was particularly concerned about the African American musical roots of rock & roll, the Right Reverend John Carroll, speaking to the Teachers Institute of the Archdiocese of Boston in 1956 exclaimed that "[r]ock & roll inflames and excites youth like jungle tom-toms. . . . The suggestive lyrics are, of course, a matter for law enforcement" (32). Moreover, in their best-selling book, *U.S.A. Confidential* (1952), journalists Jack Lait and Lee Mortimer also made several unveiled anti-black racist references to rock & roll's African American roots, directly linking the increase in white juvenile delinquency,

> with tom-toms and hot jive and ritualistic orgies of erotic dancing, weed-smoking and mass mania, with African jungle background. Many music shops purvey dope; assignations are made in them. White

girls are recruited for colored lovers. . . . We know that many platter-spinners are hopheads [i.e., drug addicts]. Many others are Reds, left-wingers, or hecklers of social convention. . . . Through disc jockeys, kids get to know colored and other musicians; they frequent places the radio oracles plug, which is done with design . . . to hook juves [i.e., juveniles] and guarantee a new generation subservient to the Mafia. (37–38)

Lait and Mortimer's criticisms reveal that many of the very same vices that are currently hurled at rap music were already in play in the 1950s. Notice here how rock & roll, like rap, was allegedly connected to, and supposedly promoted gibberish ("hot jive"), promiscuity ("ritualistic or-gies" and "assignations"), miscegenation ("[w]hite girls are recruited for colored lovers"), drug abuse ("weed-smoking," "dope," and "hop-heads"), and violence and criminality ("the Mafia"). Unwittingly, Lait and Mortimer give credence to my contention that black popular music has always been and remains more than merely music. As one of the few mediums through which African Americans have had to more or less fully express themselves, it may be the case that they have imbued their music with more energy, ideals, and allegories than most other aspects of African American life and culture. Even though many African Americans and the white youth who are attracted to black popular music have had a longstanding tendency to see it simply as music in a socially, politically, and culturally neutral sense, the protectors of the established order in America have consistently viewed black popular music as a threat and serious challenge to their conventional conservative views and values.

Black popular music, for whatever else it might represent, has been and remains "political" in light of the fact that it has consistently con-veyed African American perspectives—conservative, liberal, radical and, occasionally, revolutionary perspectives—on major social, political, and cultural issues. Although the U.S. has long imperiously claimed that it is the most democratic country in the world, the very fact of African Americans freely and fully expressing themselves has always been and remains extremely controversial. No matter what black popular music might symbolize to others, for African Americans, especially working-class and working-poor black folk, it has long been one of the few me-diums through which to document, dissent, and express their distinct thoughts and views on the most pressing social, political, and cultural problems confronting African America. In this sense, to reiterate, black popular music at any given moment in African American history invari-ably tells us a great deal about African Americans' inner-thoughts and inner-worlds at the specific historical moment in question.

However, when the fact that black popular music, for the most part, has consistently served as the soundtrack for virtually every major event in U.S. history—from the Civil War through to the Civil Rights Move-ment (and beyond)—it can be conceived of as not merely the soundtrack for African American historical events and popular movements, but also the soundtrack for mainstream American culture, politics, and society. This contention is even more pronounced in the decades leading up to the incremental integration of African Americans into mainstream American society. For instance, as with contemporary white hip hoppers, white rock & rollers in the 1950s were hardly the first group of white youth to utilize black popular music and black popular culture as avenues to express their angst and dissent. As I discussed in detail in *Hip Hop's Amnesia*, during the 1920s countless white youth—calling themselves the "Lost Generation"—appropriated jazz and new "Jazz Age" (F. Scott Fitzgerald's term) styles of speaking, dancing, dressing, flirting, smoking, and drinking to define and express themselves in an increasingly indifferent, urban, and industrialized society.

By the 1930s the Jazz Age gave way to the big band and swing era, and along with its new sense of syncopated music, fashion, and socializing, similar to their Jazz Age predecessors, the "swing kids" of the 1930s understood their commitment to swing to be a form of rebellion against the establishment. Like the white rock & rollers and white hip hoppers who would faithfully follow in their footsteps, the swing kids of the 1930s conspicuously appropriated black popular culture-influenced forms of fashion, language, dance, aesthetics, and other African American elements in their efforts to defy the prevailing cultural conventions and socially sanctioned views and values of their epoch.[20]

In the 1940s bebop and jump blues provided a new generation of white youth—most notably the Beat Generation—with a platform to dissent and distance themselves from their parents and the prevailing conservative culture and segregationist social policies of the time.[21] Hence, long before rock & roll in the 1950s, white parents were increasingly exasperated and consistently concerned about how the obviously black music, dance steps, clothes, language, and behavior that their children were enthusiastically embracing was corrupting them and ruining their relationship with the much-vaunted lily-white morals and values of mainstream America. As Peter Guralnick (1999, 18) coyly contended: "If rock & roll had had no other value it would have been enough merely to dent the smug middle-class consciousness of that time and throw into confusion some of the deadening rigidity of that world. For that was what it unmistakably did."

Far from out of the ordinary, then, white rock & rollers in the 1950s tapped into *the tradition of white youth appropriation of black popular music and black popular culture* that had consistently, albeit ironically, found that black popular music and black popular culture offered the most effective vehicles for verbalizing white youths' discontent and estrangement. With all of this in mind, there can be little doubt that white rock & rollers fascination with, first, rhythm & blues and then what ultimately evolved into rock & roll was part and parcel of *the tradition of white youth appropria-*

tion of black popular music and black popular culture. Moreover, their attraction to post-World War II black popular music and black popular culture noticeably encompassed many of the same rebellious tendencies and, truth be told, subtle anti-black racist fantasies that characterized previous white youths' enthusiastic appropriations of black popular music and black popular culture. Candidly writing about he and his friends' youthful fascination with the blues, which he acknowledged as the foundation of both rhythm & blues and rock & roll, Guralnick gushed:

> There are lots of reasons, of course, why blues should attract a white audience of some proportions. There is, to begin with, the question of color. Most of us had never known a Negro. That didn't stop us, however, from constructing a whole elaborate mythology and modeling ourselves in speech and dress and manner along the lines of what we thought a Negro would be. Norman Mailer has expressed this attraction well in "The White Negro." It was, really, the whole hipster pose. . . . Blues offered the perfect vehicle for our romanticism. What's more, it offered boundless opportunities for embroidery due to its exotic nature, the vagueness of its associations, and certain characteristics associated with the music itself. For one thing it was an undeniably personal music; whatever the autobiographical truth of the words, each singer undoubtedly conveyed something of himself in his song. Then, too, the lyrics in addition to being poetically abstract, were often vague and difficult to understand; the singer made a habit of slurring syllables or dropping off the end of a verse, and the quality of the recording, often from a distance of thirty-five years, added to the aura of obscurity. The life of the singer, too, was shrouded in mystery. Blind Lemon Jefferson, Sleepy John Estes, Jaybird Coleman, Funny Paper Smith, and Bogus Blind Ben Covington: bizarre names from a distant past about whom literally no facts were known. We were explorers in an uncharted land. (22–23)

While Guralnick's deep respect for the blues is obvious, he and his friends' subtle anti-black racism is also equally obvious. For instance, notice that he and his friends begin their explorations of African American music, not with a focus on the overall quality and core characteristics of the music, but precisely where almost all Eurocentric engagements of African American life and culture begin—with "the question of color." From the African American point of view, this is odd, indeed.

Completely flying in the face of white liberals' claims to "color-blindness" that would rise to prominence in the "politically correct" last quarter of the twentieth century, Guralnick highlights white America and, even more, liberal white America's preoccupation with race and skin color when and where they come to African Americans and their culture. In other words, from a Eurocentric point of view, whites are *raceless* and blacks are the epitome of race (that is to say, whatever whites decide "race" is at that specific historical, cultural, social, and political moment).

Hence, when it is all said and done, for many, if not most whites, African Americans are always already over-determined by their race, and since "race" is whatever whites say it is at any given moment, African Americans are whoever and, literally, whatever whites say they are at any given moment.

Interestingly, even though Guralnick and his friends "had never known a Negro," that extremely telling fact in the midst of the Civil Rights Movement did not stop them "from constructing a whole elaborate mythology" surrounding "what [they] thought a Negro would be." Acknowledging their romanticization and exotification of African Americans, as well as African American music and culture, Guralnick and his gang—obviously inadvertently, albeit injuriously nonetheless; let's face it: *unconscious racism* is just as wounding and dehumanizing as *conscious racism*—continued the longstanding tradition of white appreciation and white celebration of black music while simultaneously disregarding black humanity—actual real, flesh and blood black folk. The "bizarre[ly] name[d]" blues musicians and their lives "shrouded in mystery" may not have been so "bizarre" or "mysterious" had Guralnick and his crew simply took the time to cross the "color-line" and to learn about and, even more, befriend African Americans during one of the most turbulent periods in their peculiar history.

By the middle of the twentieth century African Americans had produced several highly competent historians who had published watershed work. If Guralnick and his guys sincerely wished to know more about African Americans they could have easily acquired a copy of W.E.B. Du Bois's *The Souls of Black Folk* (1903b), *The Gift of Black Folk* (1924) or *Black Folk, Then and Now* (1939), or Carter G. Woodson's *The Negro in Our History* (1922), or John Hope Franklin's *From Slavery to Freedom: A History of American Negroes* (1947) the same way they eagerly sought out extremely obscure blues, rhythm & blues, and rock & roll records by African American artists. What is at issue here is the simple fact that the long-standing tradition of white youth appropriation of black popular music and black popular culture has regularly involved privileging African American music over African American history, African American art over African American ideals, and African American athleticism over African American intellectualism.

As African Americans moved further and further away from their rural roots, their music seemed to sonically move further and further away from its roots in the blues. And the more black popular music was electrified and amplified, and laced with exciting lyrics about (ostensibly black) life in the city, the more the music seemed to appeal to the unpredictable and often prickly sensibilities of suburban white youth. For the most part, according to David Szatmary in *Rockin' in Time: A Social History of Rock & Roll* (2010), the "white teens who bought R&B records favored a few showmen who delivered the most frenetic, hard-driving version of an already spirited rhythm & blues that became known as rock & roll" (16). However, very similar to rap music, white youth "especially idolized young R&B performers with whom they could identify." Hence, the very same kind of black youthfulness, black hipness, and black sensuousness that would come to characterize Motown's brand of rhythm & blues—if not rhythm & blues in general—in the 1960s was at the heart of white youths' initial attraction to rock & roll in the 1950s.

As Szatmary importantly shared, by 1955 "Muddy Waters had turned forty, Howlin' Wolf was forty-six, Sonny Boy Williamson was fifty-six, John Lee Hooker was thirty-five, B.B. King was thirty, and Elmore James was thirty-seven" (16). Even though each of the aforementioned obviously pioneered and laid the musical foundation for what is now known as "rock & roll," it was a later group of much younger African American performers who actually popularized and further developed the new, more "frenetic" and "hard-driving version" of rhythm & blues that morphed into rock & roll. A short list of the young African American rock & rollers who white youth strongly identified with in the 1950s should surely include: Chuck Berry, Bo Diddley, Peggy Jones (a.k.a., "Lady Bo"), Fats Domino, Little Richard, Lloyd Price, Big Mama Thornton, Ike Turner, Larry Williams, Etta James, Screamin' Jay Hawkins, Ruth Brown, Hank Ballard & the Midnighters, Chubby Checker, LaVern Baker, the Coasters, the Drifters, the Platters, the Chantels, the Chords, the Crystals, the Five Satins, the Flamingos, the Chiffons, the Penguins, the Ronettes, the Shirelles, and Frankie Lymon & The Teenagers.[22]

As rhythm & blues via rock & roll began to increasingly—even if only implicitly—reflect the integrationist impulse of the Civil Rights Movement, white youth moved from mere rock & roll listeners to undeniable rock & roll innovators and icons. Bill Haley, Elvis Presley, Jerry Lee Lewis, Wanda Jackson, Buddy Holly, Carl Perkins, Roy Orbison, Gale Storm, Ricky Nelson, Gene Vincent, the Chordettes, and the Teen Queens were among the white youth who crossed the color-line and helped to musically desegregate the American music industry in the 1950s. Elvis Presley, perhaps the most noted of the first-wave of white rock & rollers, openly exclaimed in a 1956 interview with Kays Gary in the *Charlotte Observer*, "colored folks been singing and playing it [i.e., rock & roll] just like I'm doing now, man, for more years than I know. They played it like that in the shanties and in their juke joints and nobody paid it no mind until I goosed it up. I got it from them."[23]

What Elvis and the other white rock & roll musicians of the 1950s appropriated from black popular music ultimately provided white youth in general with an unprecedented way to express the differences between themselves and their parents, as well as the powerbrokers most of their parents worked for, and unapologetically idolized. It was as if those "mysterious" and "bizarre[ly] named" African American blues, jump blues, and rhythm & blues musicians' distinct differences—racial, cultural, social, political, and spiritual differences—somehow or another provided an unfettered and, for all intents and purposes, perfect vehicle through which white youth could register their differences. Hence, when Elvis admitted that he "got it from them," meaning African Americans, in so many words he was revealing that black popular music and black popular culture had provided white youth with a musical model, vernacular-inflected vocabulary, dynamic dance steps, flamboyant sense of fashion, and possibly even a new political vision. Guralnick (1999, 18), perhaps, captured the change in the air best when he wrote, "[w]hat I think was happening quite clearly was the convergence of two warring cultures." We should be clear here, he did not have in mind African American culture versus mainstream white culture but, more tellingly, black popular culture-informed white youth culture versus conservative (most often segregationist and otherwise anti-black racist) white adult culture.

"Just as James Dean and Marlon Brando came to represent our unarticulated hurt," Guralnick assuredly explained, "just as it was *The Catcher in the Rye* and *The Stranger* that gave us our literary heroes—the existential ciphers that refused to speak when spoken to—rock & roll provided us with a release and a justification that we had never dreamt of" (18). Drawing directly from rhythm & blues and indirectly from the Civil Rights Movement—that is to say, since rhythm & blues sonically captured and reflected, and was the most widely recognized soundtrack of the Civil Rights Movement—white rock & rollers in the 1950s found "a release and a justification that [they] had never dreamt of," not in the much-vaunted mores of middle-class white America, but ironically in the despised popular music, vibrant dance moves, "uncouth" colloquialisms, bold "bad" attitudes, and populist politics of black America. Putting into words white youths' attraction to what was quickly becoming rhythm & blues' surreptitiously civil rights-saturated biracial sonic baby, rock & roll, Guralnick asserted:

> The very outrageousness of its poses, the swaggering sexuality, the violence which the radio of that day laid at its door, its forbidden and corrupting influence—that was the unfailing attractiveness of rock & roll. The hysteria of its terms, the absurdity of its appeal—Fats Domino bumping a piano offstage with his belly; Jerry Lee Lewis' vocal gymnastics and theatrical virtuosity; Elvis' very presence and Carl Perkins' "Get off of my blue suede shoes"; with Chuck Berry all the while merrily warning, "Roll over Beethoven"—how could we deny it entrance into our lives? The ease with which you could offend the adult world, the sanctimoniousness of public figures and the turnabout that came with success . . . above all the clear line of demarcation between *us* and *them* made it impossible for us to turn our backs and ignore this new phenomenon. (18, 20, all emphasis in original)

To reiterate, the white rock & rollers of the 1950s were not the first gener-ation of white youth to embrace and explore their identity, sexuality, and burgeoning politics via black popular music and black popular culture. But, unmistakably, something wholly different happened in the 1950s. Unlike the Lost Generation of the 1920s and the swing kids of the 1930s and 1940s, and more akin to the Beat Generation of the 1950s, the white rock & rollers of the 1950s seemed to implicitly embrace and be in tune with some of the more popular principles and practices of the major African American social and political movement of their era: the Civil Rights Movement. However, in keeping with their audacious *"us* and *them"* attitude—meaning, *"us"* white youth and *"them"* white adults— even as they drew from the spirit of the Civil Rights Movement white youth, for the most part, existentially turned inward to their own "unar-ticulated hurt," angst, and alienation.[24]

Without in any way downplaying white youths' "unarticulated hurt," angst, and alienation in the 1950s, it is important to call into question whether they sufficiently considered African Americans' increasingly highly-articulated and excruciating hurt, angst, alienation and horrifying experiences in light of racial oppression and segregation. By the very fact that they were ingeniously and, in some senses, therapeutically utilizing what in essence began as a form of black popular music to express their "unarticulated hurt," angst, and alienation, it would seem that white youth were deeply indebted to African Americans. However, as white youth increasingly became the voices and faces of rock & roll, African American rock & rollers faded and, in many cases, were deceitfully forced into the background, and rock & roll was in essence *re-segregated* as opposed to genuinely desegregated.

Consequently, hit song after hit song, rock history began to mirror the Eurocentric master narratives of American history, which have consis-tently racially colonized and plainly plagiarized the contributions of African Americans and fraudulently attributed them to white "founding fathers" in specific, and white America more generally. To crossover to the pop charts the gritty, "dirty" blues elements of rhythm & blues had to be suppressed. Blues and rhythm & blues singer-songwriters were gener-ally considered too adult in their concerns to be acceptable for suburban white teens. As a consequence, the unambiguous sexual content of rhythm & blues-cum-rock & roll songs needed to be *desexualized*. Begin-ning with Bill Haley's cover version of Big Joe Turner's 1954 classic "Shake, Rattle, and Roll," music industry moguls began to alter not mere-ly the words but the sound of the rhythm & blues consumed by white youth. The gospel-influenced and blue note-blurring vocals of rhythm & blues were almost completely wiped out, and often very "safe" white versions of previously very "dangerous" black songs saturated the sub-urbs.

Clearly indicating that the song was altered to make it more appealing to white listeners, Bill Haley's version of "Shake, Rattle, and Roll" erased almost all of the blues and sexual mischievousness of Big Joe Turner's original song. As a matter of fact, the resulting record, much like most of Haley's music from that time forward, exhibited an unmistakable anodyne, almost innocent excitement by replacing references to sexuality with references to dancing. Haley's "Shake, Rattle, and Roll" in essence provided the blueprint for placing rhythm & blues on the pop charts as rock & roll. Although it might be hard for many of my readers to conceive of it now, but when we bear in mind the sexual innuendo free-floating through classic blues (for example, see Robert Johnson's 1937 "Travelling Riverside Blues," where he passionately sang: "I want you to squeeze my lemon until the juice runs down my leg") through to jump blues and ultimately rhythm & blues, it is possible to re-read Haley's classic "(We're Gonna) Rock Around the Clock" as a tongue-in-cheek reference to sexual stamina. Even though it was not an outright copy of Big Joe Turner's 1947 "Around the Clock Blues," yet and still Haley's "(We're Gonna) Rock Around the Clock" obviously "borrowed" a great deal from Charley Patton's 1929 "Going to Move to Alabama," Jim Jackson's 1927 "Kansas City Blues," and Count Basie's 1940 "Red Wagon."

Haley's "(We're Gonna) Rock Around the Clock" can also be read as a response to the Dominoes' more recently released "Sixty Minute Man," which was a number one rhythm & blues hit in 1951 that briefly crossed over to the pop charts and, as a consequence, inspired a series of songs that took up sexual stamina as a topic, including Ruth Brown's "5-10-15 Hours," the Ravens' "Rock Me All Night Long" and, of course, Hank Ballard & the Midnighters' "Work with Me, Annie" and "Annie Had a Baby." With regard to Hank Ballard & the Midnighters' colossal "Work with Me, Annie," the 1955 white cover/response record "Dance with Me Henry" by Georgia Gibbs, which itself was a very whitewashed version of Etta James's "The Wallflower," became a number two pop hit by also substituting dance for sex. It cannot be stressed strongly enough, alterations to both rhythm & blues lyrics and music in the early rock & roll era established what is now referred to as the "whitewashing" model that helped to popularize the genre.

The "King of the Cover Version" was undoubtedly Charles Eugene "Pat" Boone (reportedly a direct descendant of American frontiersman Daniel Boone). During the first decade of rock & roll prior to the British Invasion (circa late 1963/early 1964), Boone was the only American performer who rivaled Elvis Presley's pop chart dominance. With his gleaming Dentyne smile, carefully combed hair, quirky (and often comical) dance moves, and signature white buck shoes, Boone was considered the epitome of wholesome American values and an ideal role model for suburban white teens. At the exact moment when the rise of rock & roll was seen as a sign of the crumbling and eventual end of American culture, he thoroughly whitewashed and watered-down the music, making it appear to be safe and non-threatening, in so doing he scored a remarkable 38 Top 40 hits. Although more attention is lavished on Presley now, it is incredibly important to understand that Boone's musical accomplishments in the late 1950s and early 1960s rank right alongside Elvis' achievements. As a matter of fact, for all of Boone's mainstream American wholesomeness, many contemporary rock critics have failed to fully comprehend that both Boone and Presley's respective hit parades were primarily a consequence of their intense musical colonization and economic exploitation of rhythm & blues music and culture.[25]

Where Presley—with his flashy suits, wild hair, swiveling hips, pulsating pelvis, and suggestive leer—was considered *persona non grata* in many corners of the country, in contrast Boone was openly embraced by teens and even acceptable to mainstream, middle-class parents. In essence, his music smoothed out rock & roll's rough edges, transforming subversive and suggestive songs such a Fats Domino's "Ain't It a Shame" and Little Richard's "Tutti Frutti" into tame, incredibly inoffensive family-friendly ditties for suburban white audiences accustomed to hearing the placid pop sounds of a pre-war era that was quickly being eclipsed by not merely a new, post-war black popular music (rhythm & blues), but also a new, post-war black popular movement (the Civil Rights Movement). According to *Billboard*, Boone was second only to Presley as the biggest charting artist of the late 1950s, and he still holds the *Billboard* record for spending 220 consecutive weeks on the charts with one or more songs each week. Like Elvis, Boone's early career was sparked and defined by his covers of rhythm & blues songs for a white pop-oriented audience. His most noted rhythm & blues remakes include the Charms's "Heart of Stone," Ivory Joe Hunter's "I Almost Lost My Mind," Fats Domino's "Ain't It a Shame," Little Richard's "Tutti Frutti" and "Long Tall Sally," Charles Singleton's "Don't Forbid Me," the El Dorados's "At My Front Door (Crazy Little Mama)," and the Flamingos's "I'll Be Home." In virtually every instance, Boone's cover either equaled or outperformed the originals on the pop charts, which brings us right back to *the black pioneers/white popularizers paradigm* broached above.

With the unprecedented success of Bill Haley, Elvis Presley, Pat Boone, Georgia Gibbs, and Connie Francis, it quickly became standard practice in the American music industry to eagerly watch the rhythm & blues charts for hit records and then have a white singer cover them for the more lucrative pop market. Undoubtedly, this practice greatly reduced the crossover potential for the original rhythm & blues songs and artists, who were invariably African American. This is to say, on top of the musical colonization, white rock & roll covers of black rhythm & blues songs almost inherently involved economic exploitation. Rhythm & blues artists were most often paid a piddling flat-fee for recording their hard-won hit songs and were frequently forced to waive any rights to future royalties they were in fact entitled to as whitewashed versions of their songs raced up the pop charts and made already rich white music industry executives even richer. It should be stated sternly here, *one of the central soundtracks of the Civil Rights Movement, rhythm & blues, ultimately became the bedrock and goldmine of the post-war American music industry.* Rhythm & blues defined and then proceeded to redefine American popular music by contributing *new rhythms* and *new blues*, as well as new words, phrases, verse structures, themes, instrumentation, and musical organization. Most of all, rhythm & blues gave rock & roll its unprecedented style, which was nothing more than a synthesis of a wide range of post-war proto-soul black styles.

ROCK & ROLL: SONIC SEGREGATION, MUSICAL COLONIZATION, AND ECONOMIC EXPLOITATION

White music industry executives utilized racial segregation to their advantage in double-dealing rhythm & blues artists, and even though most modern rock critics routinely downplay and diminish the severity of white music industry executives and rock & roll artists' role in economically exploiting rhythm & blues singer-songwriters, at this point it is important for us to see white rock & roll covers of black rhythm & blues songs from the point of view of the black artists and not merely the long line of American music industry apologists. White rock & roll covers of black rhythm & blues songs were more than merely an odd and unfortunate episode in the history of the American music industry. Much more, these covers set the tone for the musical free-for-all predicated on the colonization and exploitation of post-war black popular music seemingly endemic in the American music industry for the remainder of the twentieth century, as rock ultimately became the best-selling musical genre in America and in many parts of the world abroad.

Once again, African American ingenuity was exploited and colonized in the interests of white America and the generation of white wealth in the face of black poverty, and once again whites—this time white music industry executives and musicians—in so many words, blamed blacks for their exploitation and colonization. For instance, in the immediate post-war period most African American musicians were forced to perform on the "Chitlin' Circuit," which meant that they had to travel the rigidly racially segregated highways and byways in order to provide for themselves and their families. Little attention was given to details when dealing with contracts and other record company paperwork because virtually all contracts were incredibly exploitive and ranting and raving about it was seen as a waste of precious time and energy. What was most important for most rhythm & blues singer-songwriters was to get paid either before or immediately after a recording session since they had to get back on the Chitlin' Circuit, and since many of the small, independent, and therefore financially fragile record companies they recorded for frequently folded before they could collect royalties. Consequently, the real beneficiaries of the black musical genius of rhythm & blues-cum-rock & roll during its first decade were the white music industry executives and the white musicians who placed hit cover versions on the pop charts.[26]

Although there is often a lot of hair-splitting and hyperbole about it by most rock historians, it should be clearly stated that most rock & roll cover versions in most instances copied the rhythm & blues songs' original arrangements in great detail to the extent that often the only substantial difference between the original and the cover was that the cover version had a different record label and the singer was white. Brian Ward (1998) went so far to say, "white covers tended to lift entire arrangements from black records, hoping to reproduce their power and passion through acts of artistic theft against which there was little legal protection" for "second-class citizens" such as African Americans at the time (47–48). Providing even more insight, Ward went further:

> What made this situation worse was the fact that many black artists were locked into extraordinarily exploitative contracts which substantially reduced their capacity to profit from even the records they did sell. When lawyer Howell Begle investigated claims by a number of R&B veterans that they had routinely been deprived of proper payment by their record companies, he discovered that in the 1940s and 1950s most had contracts which paid royalties at a meager rate of between 1 and 4 per cent of the retail price of recordings sold, or else provided one-off payments of around $200 in return for performances which sometimes made millions of dollars. Such practices retarded black capital accumulation within the music industry and ultimately had a chilling effect on the extension of black ownership and economic power. (48)

In keeping with the sonic segregation that mirrored the social segregation of the era, white music industry executives and the white musicians who served as their faithful foot soldiers seemed hell-bent on having white rock & roll cover versions replace the black rhythm & blues original versions on the charts, on the radio, in the jukeboxes, and in the records stores. Looking at this situation from the point of view of *the black pioneers of rock & roll* and not the longstanding tendency to view it almost exclusively from the point of view of *the white popularizers of rock & roll*, it is rather apparent that the very same media machine that tended to have a racially biased response to the Civil Rights Movement put into play a similar response with regard to the cover version craze. Pop radio, by definition, is supposed to play the most popular songs at the time. We need mince no words about this. It should be obvious.

However, roughly between 1954 and 1957 the prevalence, persistence, and sheer power of anti-black racist attitudes and assumptions appear to have influenced the economic agendas of white music industry executives, ultimately allowing them to either downplay or completely dismiss the ways in which their business practices translated into the sonic segregation, musical colonization, and economic exploitation of rhythm & blues and black rock & roll singer-songwriters. To put it as plainly as possible, seriously analysis of pop radio during the Civil Rights Movement reveals the ways in which social segregation intersected and overlapped with sonic segregation because the fact of the matter is that pop radio quite simply did not always and in every instance play the most popular songs in the United States if they were by African American artists. Once again, where most rock critics have downplayed or attempted to gloss over the very real, historically documented sonic segregation, musical colonization, and economic exploitation at the heart of the cover version phenomenon, Portia Maultsby (1985) has described it in contrast and more correctly as "the most widespread, systematic rape and uncompensated cultural exploitation the entertainment industry has ever seen" (xi).

Even when rock critics rattle off how a handful of rhythm & blues singer-songwriters in fact turned an incredibly exploitive and oppressive situation such as the cover version controversy into an avenue of personal and professional advancement, they fail to fully acknowledge how absolutely wrong and actually anti-black racist it was for white music industry executives and white musicians to take advantage of brutally segregated and already incessantly exploited black musicians. White music industry executives and white musicians' exploitation of black rhythm & blues singer-songwriters virtually during the peak period of the Civil Rights Movement (circa 1954 to 1965) is incredibly ironic and, to say the least, speaks volumes about why many African Americans eventually came to view rock & roll as a sonic symbol of cultural banditry or, as Ward worded it above, an act of "artistic theft." As a matter of fact, even the great Elvis Presley, the "King of Rock & Roll," directly and undeniably participated in the exploitation of black rhythm & blues singer-songwriters. Take, for example, the fact that he knowingly did nothing when his manager, the cutthroat Colonel Tom Parker, required Otis Blackwell—the composer of bona fide rock & roll classics such as "Don't Be Cruel," "All Shook Up," and "Return to Sender"—to share specious songwriting credits with Presley even though Presley wrote not one single lyric or note of these classic songs. Colonel Parker claimed that by giving Presley songwriting credit it would generate greater interest in the songs and, as a result, additional publishing royalties. In other words, even a musical genius like Otis Blackwell, who also composed Jerry Lee Lewis's classics "Great Balls of Fire" and "Breathless," Little Willie John's "Fever," Gene Pitney's "I'll Find You," Charlie Gracie's "Cool Baby," and Solomon Burke's "Home In Your Heart," was subjected to unambiguous and unadulterated musical colonization and economic exploitation at the hands of the acclaimed "King of Rock & Roll."[27]

There is something very sick and very twisted about this situation that is heightened by the fact that it took place during the peak years of the Civil Rights Movement. How could white music industry executives and white musicians not comprehend that by exploiting black rhythm & blues singer-songwriters they themselves became complicit in the very oppression and exploitation, the very racial segregation and "separate and unequal" treatment that rhythm & blues was innovatively created to exorcise (especially via its honking and shouting formative phase)? Hence, even the most conservative reading of the previous chapter will surely show that rhythm & blues was much more than post-war black dance and party music. Indeed, it was dance and party music, but it was also a lot more. To put it plainly, rhythm & blues was the first post-war black popular music to spiritedly blur the lines between "race records" and "white pop." Much like the Civil Rights Movement challenged social segregation, rhythm & blues and its rock & roll offspring challenged sonic segregation.[28]

Obviously, rock & roll ultimately eclipsed rhythm & blues in the world of mainstream American popular culture. But, we need to critically comprehend how rhythm & blues' blurring of the lines between "race records" and "white pop" was a musical metaphor for the ways in which the Civil Rights Movement was crisscrossing and contradicting the "color-line" and the wider world of American apartheid at the time. This, of course, brings us to a discussion of how and why *Cashbox*, *Billboard*, and *Music Vendor* created music sales charts that not only divided American music into genres, but also made often disparaging distinctions about music consumers, for the most part, based on widely held assumptions (and much misinformation) concerning race and class. Needless to say, *even American music sales charts were segregated along race and class lines prior to, and during the Civil Rights Movement*, and *Cashbox*, *Billboard*, and *Music Vendor*, although typically thought of in neutral terms, each respectively contributed to the sonic segregation, musical colonization, and economic exploitation of rhythm & blues and black rock & roll singer-songwriters. In *What's That Sound?: An Introduction to Rock and Its History* (2012), John Covach and Andrew Flory helped to drive this point home by writing directly about the often clandestine race and class assumptions of the charts during the early days of rock & roll:

> The charts in these industry periodicals were divided according to the professionals' assessment of how consumers could most effectively be separated, so they were driven by purchasing patterns. Thus, pop charts listed records that would likely be marketed to white, middle-class listeners. Rhythm & blues (originally called "race" and then "sepia") charts followed music that was directed to black urban audiences, and country & western (originally called "hillbilly" and then "folk")

charts kept track of music directed at low-income whites. This system
of parallel charts was based on assumptions about markets and audience tastes, not musical style. The arrangement suggests that rhythm &
blues listeners would not enjoy country & western or pop, but all it
really tries to predict is who is most likely to buy records or play them
on the jukebox. . . . Contrary to beliefs about such segregated listening,
anecdotal evidence suggests that many black listeners enjoyed pop and
country & western, and that many country & western listeners enjoyed
pop and rhythm & blues. Young, middle-class white listeners already
knew some country & western from network broadcasts, although
most white adults were apparently not interested in rhythm & blues.
One of the most significant changes to these business practices that
occurred during the early 1950s was when middle-class white teens
discovered rhythm & blues, which led to the softening of the boundaries between chart classifications. (85–86)

Covach and Flory emphasized that it was rhythm & blues, *not* pop, and
not country & western, that "led to the softening of the boundaries between chart classifications." Obviously rhythm & blues was more or less
doing in the immediate post-war American music industry what the Civil Rights Movement was doing in the immediate post-war period in
American society. Moreover, just as black music consumers contradicted
latent "segregated listening" assumptions, members of the Civil Rights
Movement contradicted segregationist social and cultural assumptions.
Indeed, the very same post-war energy, excitement and, this should be
strongly stressed, adroit *inventiveness* captured and conveyed via the major sacred soundtracks of the Civil Rights Movement, which is to say,
gospel and its freedom songs subgenre, lies at the heart of the major
secular soundtracks of the Civil Rights Movement, which is to say,
rhythm & blues *and* rock & roll. It is only when rock & roll's undeniable
black popular music roots are taken into serious consideration that the
integrationist ethos and *integrationist impulse* of the Civil Rights Movement
free-floating through early rock & roll can be adequately understood.

Perhaps it could go without saying that because rhythm & blues
served as a musical metaphor, its rock & roll offspring was also understood to be a musical metaphor for, not simply the "softening of the
boundaries between chart classifications," that is to say, a form of sonic
desegregation and sonic integration, but also a form social desegregation
and social integration. To be clear here, Ward (1998) weighs in, "rock &
roll was not necessarily a dilution of R&B" (52). Sometimes, and almost
invariably at its inception, "what was dubbed rock & roll simply *was*
R&B" (52, Ward's emphasis). At other times, however, especially as it
attracted more and more, not merely white consumption but also white
participation, rock & roll represented "an innovative hybrid which fused
R&B with other influences to make a new subgenre which, like all forms
of popular music, could be good, bad, or indifferent."

Returning to the notion that for many, if not most African Americans during the Civil Rights Movement there was a common belief that black folk could implicitly sing what they were unable to explicitly say, it would seem that the extra-musical elements of rhythm & blues-cum-rock & roll (i.e., the *integrationist ethos* and *integrationist impulse*) were not widely embraced and unambiguously advocated (as they actually could have been in a customer-driven market—*à la* the Montgomery Bus Boycott Movement) by most white musicians and fans during rock & roll's golden age between 1954 and 1964. Sadly, then, during the peak period of the Civil Rights Movement the majority of whites who enthusiastically embraced rhythm & blues via its rock & roll subgenre rejected or, at the very least, turned a blind eye to the alarming plight of African Americans between 1954 and 1964. As Glenn Altschuler (2003, 48–49) regretfully albeit correctly observed, even though "[m]any whites in the music industry recognized that rock & roll was a metaphor for integration," truth be told, it "did not always raise the racial or political consciousness of fans." In fact, he candidly contended, "[s]ome listeners remained blissfully ignorant of the racial connotations of rock & roll," as vanilla version after vanilla version of rhythm & blues hits were copied or, rather, "covered" and began to dominate the radio airwaves.[29]

On the one hand, rhythm & blues and rock & roll can be viewed as the popular secular music soundtracks of the Civil Rights Movement. What began as rhythm & blues and eventually evolved into rock & roll subtly and frequently unwittingly expressed aspects of the social mission and political sentiments of the Civil Rights Movement. However, as rock & roll garnered more and more white fans, and soon the participation of young white musicians, the music, its modes of communication, and the virtually integrated popular culture that quickly sprang up around it progressively challenged American apartheid and the longstanding color-line. The increase in rhythm & blues on radio airwaves that previously adhered to sonic segregation ("white music only") policies that mirrored the social segregation ("white people only") policies of the larger society, as well as integrated rhythm & blues and rock & roll concerts and dances, steadily exposed post-war white youth to positive or, at the least, more realistic representations of African American life and culture.

In a nation where long-held anti-black racist stereotypes and more than a century of blackface minstrelism-informed misconceptions had regularly blocked the development of serious social dialogue and cultural understanding between African Americans and European Americans, the rock & roll phenomenon initially gave many African Americans high hopes that American apartheid, that the stigma of enslavement, that the long and degrading shadow cast by blackface minstrelism and Jim Crowism might finally come to an end. At long last, African American culture, via rock & roll, was being presented to mainstream American society in dignity-endorsing and unambiguously-uplifting ways that ran counter to the anti-black racist assumptions that were previously projected onto African American life, culture, and aesthetics. Bearing all of this in mind, rock & roll indeed did contribute to white youths' (and, perhaps, many white adults') re-evaluation of race relations and the emerging Civil Rights Movement.

On the other hand, however, echoing Altschuler's caveat above, in *Race, Rock, and Elvis* (2000), Michael Bertrand cautions us to keep in mind that "rock & roll was not a panacea that magically cured the South's [and the nation's] racial ills" (55). By the 1950s, America had been suffering with its anti-black racist affliction for several centuries and, as with any serious illness, time, patience, aggressive treatment, and consistent recuperative care were desperately needed. Bertrand adamantly further asserted:

> Shifting tastes in musical preference did not necessarily obliterate racism. It would be naïve to think that the cultural process functioned in such a rapid, thorough, and uniform fashion. One generation could not completely reverse what had taken centuries to develop. Racism in the United States, moreover, has never been simply a history of attitudes and prejudices. It has been, more importantly, the product of an exploitative economic and political system whose institutions favor wealthy white males. The persistent realities of inadequate and subservient employment opportunities, substandard housing, poor healthcare, and inferior public education not only oppressed the black community but also reiterated the second-class nature of its existence. One must use caution, therefore, in alleging that popular music miraculously healed [the nation and] the region's divisions. Rock & roll did not directly influence the existing social structure, and it did not command or seek the power to abolish institutional discrimination and inequality. As forces for substantive and lasting change in the racial realm, commercial music and culture of the period were limited. (55)

There is only so much music can do to impact and, more to the point, *enact* social change. And, no matter how aurally insurgent any form of music might be at its inception, if it is hyper-commodified, if it is increasingly utilized to tout the latest corporate product or teen dance craze, and if by some perplexing turn of events it is distanced and completely disassociated from its social, political, spiritual, cultural, and musical roots in the lives and struggles of a racially oppressed and economically exploited group, then that music becomes, for all intents and purposes, a part of the very system and social conventions it was created to critique and contest. Guralnick (1999, 34), as perceptive as ever, dispiritedly declared that "[r]ock & roll today, to my mind at least, is a middle-class phenomenon almost exclusively." Moreover, it may not be stretching his statement too far to say that it could actually be read as "[r]ock & roll today . . . is a [*white*] middle-class phenomenon almost exclusively." The truth of the matter is that race, racism, and anti-racism were actually intrinsic to rock

& roll at its inception, and the history of its first decade—from the Chords' "Sh-Boom" in 1954 through to the Rolling Stones' acclaimed eponymous debut in 1964—is dotted with either unsuspecting or subtle reflections on, and references to race, racism, and anti-racism during the Civil Rights Movement years.[30]

In contrast to the often-unacknowledged fact that, not only did almost all of the early African American rock & rollers have working-class and poverty-stricken backgrounds but, as Bertrand (2000, 22) importantly observed, "virtually all the [early white rock & roll] artists were from working-class backgrounds" as well. How, then, did "[r]ock & roll today" eventually grow into "a [*white*] middle-class phenomenon almost exclusively?" Indeed, something was lost in translation as rock & roll was distanced and almost completely disassociated from its roots in rhythm & blues and black America and increasingly bleached to make it more appealing to the "us" white youth versus "them" white adults attitude so prevalent in suburban white youth popular music and culture from the late 1950s onward. Offering even more insight into this issue, Charlie Gillett (1996) not only discussed the whitening and lightening of rhythm & blues-cum-rock & roll, but also the ways in which *the black pioneers of rock & roll* were *sonically* and *racially resegregated* in the aftermath of their eclipse by *the white popularizers of rock & roll*:

> Rock & roll narrowed the reference of songs to adolescence and sim-plified the complicated boogie rhythms to a simple 2/4 with the accent on the backbeat. And once these new conventions were established, the rhythm & blues singers were obliged to either adapt to them or resign themselves to obscurity, at best playing for a local audience in some bar, and at worst abandoning music altogether. Wynonie Harris tended bar until he died in 1969, Amos Milburn worked in a Cincinnati hotel, Percy Mayfield became a songwriter, Harvey Fuqua of the Moonglows became a producer at Berry Gordy's Motown Corporation. A few—[Big] Joe Turner, Jimmy Witherspoon—became jazz singers, and sever-al—John Lee Hooker, Muddy Waters, Sonny Boy Williamson—played alternately in local bars and as "folk-blues" singers before white audi-ences in coffee houses and concert halls. A remarkable number died before they were forty, and a handful—Fats Domino, Ray Charles, Sam Cooke—managed to become pop stars.
>
> Meanwhile rock & roll ran its course—inexplicably long to some, and disappointingly brief to others. To those young people in its audi-ence who did know its source, rock & roll seemed like a necessary, and surely eternal, part of urban life. The industry, with typical sleight of hand, killed off the music but kept the name, so that virtually all popu-lar music (with the exception of what came to be called "easy listen-ing") was branded rock & roll. . . . Upon a younger generation than that which had discovered and insisted on the original rock & roll was palmed off a softer substitute which carried nearly the same name. And, finally, a section of this new music was stuff that still went by the

name "rhythm & blues," although much of it had slight connection
with the pre-rock & roll style of the same name. (167–168)

Gillett highlights the consequences of the eclipse of African Americans in
rock & roll music and culture by the end of its first decade of existence
(again, circa 1954 to 1964). Not only did the whitening and lightening of
rock & roll put into play the new, peculiarly post-war form of sonic
segregation, musical colonization, and economic exploitation discussed
above, it also "killed off the music but kept the name." One cannot help
but to wonder aloud how rock & roll would have evolved and what it
would have sounded like today if it was not musically colonized and
thoroughly whitewashed during its first decade? What if African
Americans had not have been sonically segregated and basically barred
from the mainstream of a music they, in fact, invented or, at the very
least, pioneered? What if white music industry executives, white rock &
roll musicians, and white rock & roll fans had have actually embraced the
integrationist ethos and *integrationist impulse* of rhythm & blues-cum-rock
& roll at its inception and throughout its first decade? If, indeed, white
music industry executives, white rock & roll musicians, and white rock &
roll fans had have passionately and politically embraced the *integrationist
ethos* and *integrationist impulse* of rhythm & blues-cum-rock & roll at its
inception and throughout its first decade would rock & roll be the "softer
substitute," the "[*white*] middle-class phenomenon" that it most often
undeniably is today? Also, wouldn't there have been greater white rock
& roll musician and white rock & roll fan contribution to, and serious
participation in the Civil Rights Movement, since rock & roll, in fact,
began as one of the movement's central secular soundtracks, replete with
"racial connotations" and all the rest?

Gillett expertly emphasized that both rock & roll and rhythm & blues
evolved in the aftermath of the whitening and lightening of rhythm &
blues-cum-rock & roll during its first decade, writing not only about the
"softer substitute" that was "palmed off" as rock & roll, but also about
the new music that "went by the name 'rhythm & blues'" but had only a
"slight connection with the pre-rock & roll style of the same name."
Much like the emphasis on desegregation and integration altered African
American social, political, and cultural consciousness during the Civil
Rights Movement, the sonic segregation, musical colonization, and economic exploitation of rhythm & blues-cum-rock & roll singer-songwriters
between 1954 and 1964, for the most part, ultimately led to *the sonic and
racial resegregation of African Americans in American popular music*. Where
many white rock & rollers achieved fame and fortune during rock &
roll's first decade, Gillett stressed that most of the original black rock &
roll artists either had to "adapt" to the whitened and lightened sound
and style of "whitewashed" rock & roll or "resign themselves to obscur-
ity," or, even worse, "abandon [. . .] music altogether." There are no two

ways about it, the musical colonization of rhythm & blues-cum-rock & roll eventually led to the marginalization of black rock & rollers, sonically resegregating them to the realm of rhythm & blues (essentially the sonic ghetto of the American music industry), and from about 1965 forward rock came to be identified almost exclusively with suburban white youths' loves and lives. Hence, even an African American musician as undeniably talented as Jimi Hendrix ended up having to go to London in 1966 in order to secure a record deal and launch his career as a rock artist.[31]

There is something at once extremely disturbing and undeniably depressing when Guralnick (1999, 32), in his characteristic uncontrived prose style, stated: "In the end everything gets absorbed into the cultural mainstream, and rock & roll was no different. . . . They've even gone and changed the name, and what was once a kind of secret metaphor (like 'ball' and 'Miss Ann' and 'brown-eyed handsome man') has become instead just another explicit Anglo-Saxon epithet." I am in complete agreement with Guralnick when he bemoans the fact that rock & roll has been essentially reduced to yet another "explicit Anglo-Saxon epithet," robbed of its fierce soulfulness, indeed, its blackness—which is to say, its distinct *African Americanness*—and the allusive anti-racism and revolutionary integrationism that marked its origins. However, in my mind at least, the question continues to beg: "Does everything really and truly get 'absorbed into the cultural mainstream'?" And, a corollary question creeps in here: "Did *every* (or, rather, *all*) aspects of rock & roll get 'absorbed into the cultural mainstream'?"

Truth be told, for the most part African Americans, even in the aftermath of the Civil Rights Movement, certainly have not been "absorbed [and genuinely accepted as opposed to assimilated] into the cultural mainstream," and this painful fact stands even though each and every major form of black popular music (from the spirituals and the blues through to rap and neo-soul), to a certain extent, has found high levels of acceptance in the American music industry, if not in American popular culture more generally. In other words, "real" rock & roll actually has not been "absorbed into the cultural mainstream," because "real" rock & roll, as Guralnick intimated above, was "a kind of secret metaphor" that clandestinely conveyed as much about black ghetto youths' "unarticulated hurt," angst, and alienation as it did white suburban youths' "unarticulated hurt," angst, and alienation. What actually has been "absorbed into the cultural mainstream" is a "softer substitute," a vanilla version of rock & roll, an often bland and highly bleached form of black popular music that continues the longstanding white American tradition of accepting those aspects of African American life and culture that are highly colonizable and commodifiable, but unrepentantly rejecting those subversive elements of African American life and culture that do not quickly coincide with blackface minstrelesque and assimilation-obsessed anti-black racist misconceptions and misrepresentations of African Americans. In this sense, rock & roll, "real" rock & roll, Guralnick lamented, "was over before it even had a chance to slyly grin and look around," and "[i]n its place came a new all-synthetic product" that is often as inept as it is ahistorical and apolitical (20).

Entangled in the racial and cultural politics of the 1950s, rock & roll was frequently credited with, and vehemently criticized for advocating integration and providing new economic opportunities for African Americans while simultaneously injecting African American culture and values into mainstream America. In light of the African American origins and early evolution of rock & roll, it quickly became one of the most contentious topics in popular discourse. White Southerners, in particular, associated the music with stereotypical anti-black racist ideas about African Americans as either subhuman, at best, or non-human, at worst. They projected and, consequently, heard echoes of "black emotionalism" and "black expressivism" coupled with "black exoticism" and "black eroticism."

In the face of all of this, we should never lose sight of the fact that rock & roll was also big business—very big business—and, consequently, it was susceptible to the whims and wishes of the white youth-dominated American music market. Preoccupied with the unprecedented profits that rock & roll generated, by the late 1950s and early 1960s the mostly white male music industry moguls did everything they could to avoid controversy and commotion. As a result they exploited countless African American rhythm & blues and rock & roll musicians by encouraging white roll & rollers to copy or, rather, "cover" African American rhythm & blues and rock & roll hits. The African American male sex symbols that were catapulted to stardom during the earliest years of rock & roll had to be stopped, and suburban white youth, especially young white women, were steered away from what was understood to be the hypersexuality of Esquerita, Little Richard, Lloyd Price, Larry Williams, Hank Ballard, Chuck Berry, and Bo Diddley, among many others. In the process what began as a black musical expression and eventually evolved into an inter-racial musical expression was ultimately whitewashed into an ultra-inoffensive "[*white*] middle-class phenomenon almost exclusively."[32]

Seeming to permanently Clorox the complexion and soul of rock & roll in the minds' of the American masses, from the early 1960s onward white rock & rollers would be perfunctorily privileged and promoted over black rock & rollers as "real" and the most righteous rock & roll. Only occasionally in the post-1950s history of rock would African Americans register as "authentic" rock musicians (e.g., Jimi Hendrix, Buddy Miles, Ike & Tina Turner, Sly & the Family Stone, Swamp Dogg, Funkadelic, Prince, Bad Brains, Sound Barrier, Fishbone, Terence Trent D'Arby, Tracy Chapman, Living Colour, 24-7 Spyz, Follow For Now, Lenny Kravitz, Seal, Ben Harper, Meshell Ndegeocello, Michael Franti,

Chocolate Genius, Eagle-Eye Cherry, Cree Summer, Amel Larrieux, Van Hunt, Cody ChesnuTT, Brittany Howard, and Gary Clark, Jr.). But, truth be told, as observed in Raymond Gayle's groundbreaking documentary *Electric Purgatory: The Fate of the Black Rocker* (2010), most modern white rock & roll youth have never even heard of half of the aforementioned, let alone seriously listened to their distinct brands of rock. In other words, paralleling the historical experiences of African Americans, rock & roll was racialized and colonized in the interest of whites, and suburban white youth in particular. Like so many other contributions African Americans have made to American culture, rock & roll went from being rejected, to accepted, to ultimately depoliticized and claimed as "white property" and integral to white popular culture. As Altschuler (2003) stated:

> For African Americans, rock & roll was a mixed blessing. At times a force for integration and racial respect, rock & roll was also an act of theft that in supplanting rhythm & blues deprived blacks of appropriate acknowledgement, rhetorical and financial, of their contributions to American culture. Rock & roll deepened the divide between the generations, helped teenagers differentiate themselves from others, transformed popular culture in the United States, and rattled the reticent by pushing sexuality into the public arena. (34)

When rock & roll is viewed from the point of view of the unsung soldiers of the Civil Rights Movement, when we explore the origins and early evolution of rock & roll utilizing the "we can implicitly sing what we cannot explicitly say" aesthetic, then, and perhaps only then, does rock & roll register as one of the central soundtracks of the Civil Rights Movement. Never in the history of the American music industry have so many white musicians imitated and later emulated black singer-songwriters, and black musicians more generally. In initially appreciating and later participating in rock & roll during its first decade, throngs of white youth were, even if most often unwittingly, taking part in "a kind of secret metaphor"—once again, replete with "racial connotations" and a, however subtle, emphasis on integration—before corporate America reduced it to "just another explicit Anglo-Saxon epithet." By embracing what was undeniably understood to be a form of black popular music at its inception, the white youth of rock & roll's first decade, in their own adolescent and often incredibly immature way, were willing to acknowledge the beauty and brilliance of an aspect of African American culture (i.e., black popular music) in ways that many of the most "liberal" and "open-minded" white adults were unwilling to at the time.

In a sense, as rock & roll evolved into the "classic rock" of the late-1960s through to the late-1970s, generation after generation of white youth embraced and often innovatively continued to evolve a form of music that not only has its origins in black popular music, especially classic rhythm & blues, but also in the *integrationist ethos* and *integrationist impulse* of arguably the most renowned black popular movement of the twentieth century: the Civil Rights Movement. However, because rock was so severely colonized, depoliticized, and whitewashed, because it came to be viewed as the almost exclusive "property" of white male "rock gods," rock, however covertly, continues the sonic segregation, musical colonization, and economic exploitation discussed above. Moreover, for the most part, African Americans remain marginalized in rock in much the same manner they remain marginalized, even after the Civil Rights Movement, in mainstream American culture, politics, and society. In the final analysis, then, Guralnick seems to have hit the nail on the head when he asserted above, "what was once a kind of secret metaphor . . . has become instead just another explicit Anglo-Saxon epithet." This conclusion is obviously very sad but, placing our feelings aside, we must concede that it is also very true. However, what is also equally true is the simple fact that right alongside the obviously important work of the most famous figures of the Civil Rights Movement sits the inestimable and invaluable contributions of the unsung singing soldiers of the movement.

From gospel and freedom songs, to rhythm & blues and rock & roll, the unsung singing soldiers of the Civil Rights Movement shared their collective views and values, not merely with black America, but with white America and the wider world. Their contributions to the deconstruction and reconstruction of American democracy and American citizenship—indeed, their deconstruction and reconstruction of the "American dream"—is as meaningful and lasting as anything put forward by the famous figures of the Civil Rights Movement. Moreover, as the previous chapters have demonstrated, much of what the famous figures of the Civil Rights Movement said and did was inspired by the most often anonymous, unsung singing soldiers of the movement. This book is a very humble tribute to them, to their words and deeds, to their ideas and actions, to their songs and powerful singing, to the incredibly innovative ways in which they developed the "we can implicitly sing what we cannot explicitly say" aesthetic in the years leading up to, and certainly during the Civil Rights Movement. Above all else, while researching and writing this book I have been most inspired and most deeply moved by the ways in which the unsung singing soldiers of the Civil Rights Movement, whether consciously or unconsciously, embraced the heartfelt and hallowed words of the African American national anthem, which eternally implores us to "lift every voice and sing," and to continue to do so until earth and heaven ring with liberty and justice for all. Let us now, henceforth, and forever more: *Sing a song full of the faith that the dark past has taught us. Sing a song full of the hope that the present has brought us. Facing the rising sun of our new day begun. Let us march on until victory is won.* . . . Indeed, *lift every voice and sing!*

NOTES

1. For further discussion of the emergence and early evolution of rock & roll as indicative of the external or extra-communal politics of the Civil Rights Movement, especially the *integrationist ethos* and *integrationist impulse* of the Civil Rights Movement, and for the most noteworthy works that informed my interpretation here, see R.I. Bell (2007), Broven (2009), Cateforis (2013), Crazy Horse (2004), Delmont (2012), Helper (1996), Kamin (1975), Lauterbach (2011), Pielke (2012), A. Shaw (1969), and Vazzano (2010).

2. The noteworthy works that influenced my interpretation of the centrality of black popular music—especially blues, jump blues, and rhythm & blues—in the emergence and early evolution of rock & roll include Aron (2015), R.I. Bell (2007), Birnbaum (2013), Crazy Horse (2004), Daley (2003), DeCurtis, Henke and George-Warren (1992), Egendorf (2002), Escott (1999), Friedlander (2006), George-Warren (2009), Guralnick (1989, 1999, 2015), J.A. Jackson (1991, 2007), Lee and Lee (2001), Strausbaugh (2007), Talevski (1998), Talevski and West (2010), Tosches (1996, 1999), and Wald (2009).

3. For further discussion of classical and contemporary African music, and for the most noteworthy works that informed my analysis here, see Agawu (2003), Agordoh (2005), Askew (2002), Bebey (1999), Bender (1991), Chernoff (1979), Chikowero (2015), Ewens (1992), Jaji (2014), Kubik (2010a, 2010b), Kyagambiddwa (1955), Nketia (1974), R.M. Stone (1982, 2005, 2008), Stone and Gillis (1976), and Tenaille (2002). Several (ethno)musicological studies have explored the "African roots" of the blues and made more general connections between continental and diasporan African music, see Charters (1981, 2009), Floyd (1995), Kubik (1999), and Palmer (1982).

4. For further discussion of work songs and field hollers, as well as what has come to be called "slave songs," and for the most noteworthy works that influenced my interpretation of African American secular songs during enslavement, see W.F. Allen (1995), Blades (1921), Charters (2015), Epstein (2003), M.M. Fisher (1998), Katz (1969), Parrish (1992), Ramey (2008), K.D. Thompson (2014), White and White (2005), and Work (1998).

5. For further discussion of early African American music, during and after enslavement, and for the most noteworthy works that informed my analysis here, see Abbott and Seroff (2002), Burnim and Maultsby (2006, 2015), Charters (2015), Epstein (2003), Floyd (1995), Johnson and Johnson (2002), Parrish (1992), Peretti (2009), Ramey (2008), Spencer (1990, 1993, 1995), Southern (1997), and K.D. Thompson (2014).

6. For further discussion of Reconstruction and post-Reconstruction anti-black racism and its impact on post-enslavement African American music and culture, and for the most noteworthy works that informed my analysis here, see Abbott and Seroff (2002), Brundage (2011), Du Bois (1935), Lawson (2010), Lhamon (1998, 2003), E. Lott (1993), K.H. Miller (2010), Sotiropoulos (2006), K.D. Thompson (2014), Wondrich (2003), and Wormser (2003).

7. For further discussion of classic blues women, and for the most noteworthy works that influenced my interpretation here, see A.Y. Davis (1998), F. Davis (1995), Garon and Garon (1992), D.D. Harrison (1988, 2006), B. Jackson (2005), Lordi (2013), and McGinley (2014).

8. For further discussion of the Great Migration and African American labor at the turn and during the first decades of the twentieth century, and for the most noteworthy works that informed my analysis here, see Hahn (2003), A. Harrison (1991), Holley (2000), Lemann (1991), Marks (1989), Reich (2013, 2014), Trotter (1991), and Wilkerson (2010).

9. For further discussion of the contention that black popular music provides one of the only mediums through which poor black folk have historically and continue currently to express their views and values to mainstream America, if not the wider world, see Burnim and Maultsby (2006, 2015), M. Ellison (1989), Ferris (2009), Lordi (2013), Sanger (1995), and J.M. Spencer (1990).

10. For further discussion of the emergence and evolution of ragtime, and for the most noteworthy works that influenced my interpretation here, see Batterson (1998), E.A. Berlin (1980, 2016), Blesh (1971), Driggs and Haddix (2005), Gilbert (2015), Harer (2015), Hasse (1985), Jasen (2007), Jasen and Jones (2000, 2002), Jasen and Tichenor (1978), Milan (2009), Schafer and Riedel (1973), and Waldo (1976).

11. For further discussion of Scott Joplin, James Scott, and Joseph Lamb's respective lives and legacies, and for the most noteworthy works that influenced my interpretation here, see Argyle (2009), E.A. Berlin (2016), Binkowski (2012), Curtis (2004), De-Veaux and Kenney (1992), Gammond (1975), and Haskins (1978).

12. For further discussion of the ways in which classic blues artists (especially classic blues women), in essence, popularized the sights, sounds, and sorrows of an emerging African American post-enslavement and post-Reconstruction worldview (circa the 1890s through to the 1930s), and for the most noteworthy works that influenced my interpretation here, see J. Anderson (1993), Barnet (2004), Batiste (2012), Bourgeois (2004), D.A. Brooks (2006), J. Brown (2008), A.Y. Davis (1998), J.B. Ferguson (2008), Griffin (2013), McGinley (2014), Sharpley-Whiting (2015), S. Vogel (2009), Willis and Williams (2002), and J.F. Wilson (2010).

13. For further discussion of the blues backlash and the jazz controversy in the 1920s and 1930s, see my analysis in "remixes" 2 and 3 in *Hip Hop's Amnesia* (Rabaka 2012, 19–166).

14. My interpretation of the African American origins and early evolution of rock & roll, which eventually came to be called "rock" by the late 1960s, has been informed by Altschuler (2003), R.I. Bell (2007), Birnbaum (2013), Crazy Horse (2004), Gillett (1996), Guralnick (1989, 1999, 2015), Kirby (2009), Lauterbach (2011), Mahon (2000, 2004), Othello (2004), Scrivani-Tidd, Markowitz, Smith, Janosik and Gulla (2006), Strausbaugh (2007), Tosches (1999), and Wald (2009). For further discussion of Alan Freed and his controversial place in the emergence and early evolution of rock & roll, see Belz (1972), Bordowitz (2004), M. Fisher (2007), J.A. Jackson (1991, 2007), Martin and Segrave (1993), Redd (1974), and Shaw (1987b).

15. For further discussion of the ways in which early rock & roll was viewed as an implicit expression of the politics and social justice agenda of the Civil Rights Movement, and how early white rock & rollers' music in specific was seen as a challenge to both the musical segregation *and* social segregation of 1950s and early 1960s America, see Aquila (2000), Altschuler (2003), R.I. Bell (2007), Bertrand (2000), Crazy Horse (2004), Daniel (2000), Delmont (2012), Francese and Sorrell (2001), Friedlander (2006), Knowles (2010), and Runowicz (2010).

16. For further discussion of Bill Haley, including a number of studies that arrogantly and erroneously hail him as either the "founder" or "father" of rock & roll, and for the most noteworthy works that influenced my interpretation here, see Birnbaum (2013), Cohn (1969), Dawson (2005), Fuchs (2011), Haley and Von Hoelle (1991), Swenson (1983), and Tosches (1999).

17. For further discussion of Rosa Parks's life and legacy, and for the most noteworthy works that factored into my commentary here, see, first and foremost, Parks (1992, 1994), as well as major secondary sources such as Branch (1988), Brinkley (2000a, 2000b), Hanson (2011), Houck and Dixon (2009), Kohl (2005), McWhorter (2001), and Theoharis (2013).

18. My interpretation here and throughout this section is based on a number of works that not only view rhythm & blues as the foundation of, and essential inspiration for rock & roll, but that connect the emergence and early development of rock & roll with cultural, social, and political changes as a result of the rising Civil Rights Movement. The most noteworthy among the works I have relied on here include Aron (2015), R.I. Bell (2007), Broven (2009), M. Campbell (2007), Crazy Horse (2004), Daniel (2000), Daley (2003), Delmont (2012), Escott (1991, 1999), M. Fisher (2007), Friedlander (2006), Helper (1996), Kirby (2009), Pielke (2012), Redd (1974), Salem (1999), A. Shaw (1969, 1987b), and Strausbaugh (2007).

19. For further discussion of the social, political, and cultural world rock & roll emerged in, and for the most noteworthy works that influenced my interpretation here, see Aquila (2000), R.I. Bell (2007), Brash and Britten (1998), Brode (2015), Covach and Flory (2012), DeCurtis (1992), Ennis (1992), Friedlander (2006), Frith (1981), Gillett (1996), M.K. Hall (2014), Martin and Segrave (1993), J. Miller (1999), Strain (2016), Strausbaugh (2007), Szatmary (2013), Wald (2009), and T. Waldman (2003).

20. For further discussion of the swing kids of the 1930s, as well as white appropriation and commercialization of jazz and black popular culture more generally speaking in the 1930s, and for the most noteworthy works that influenced my interpretation here, see Dance (2001), Hennessey (1994), Oliphant (2002), Schuller (1989a, 1989b), A. Shaw (1998), Stowe (1994), and Zwerin (2000).

21. For further discussion of the Beat Generation, and for the most noteworthy works that informed my analysis here, see J. Campbell (2001), A. Charters (1983, 1986, 1993, 1994, 2001, 2003), Cook (1971), M. Evans (2015), George-Warren (1999), Johnson and Grace (2002), B. Knight (1998), Lawlor (2005), Maynard (1991), McDarrah and McDarrah (2001), B. Morgan (2010), Myrsiades (2002), Tytell (2006), Waldman (2007), Watson (1995), Weidman (2015), and Zott (2003).

22. Although there has not been a book published to date that specifically focuses on the African American origins and early evolution of rock & roll, several more general rock histories informed my interpretation here, including Aquila (2000), R.I. Bell (2007), Birnbaum (2013), Crazy Horse (2004), Delmont (2012), Escott (1999), Friedlander (2006), Kamin (1975), Kirby (2009), Lauterbach (2011), Palmer (1995, 1996), Redd (1974), and Stuessy and Lipscomb (2012).

23. For further discussion of Elvis Presley's life and legacy, especially in relationship to black popular music, and for the most noteworthy works that influenced my interpretation here, see Bertrand (2000), Guralnick (1994, 2000), Guralnick and Jorgensen (1999), Jorgensen (1998), Keogh (2004), A. Webster (2003), and Williamson (2015).

24. For further discussion of white youths' "unarticulated hurt," angst, and alienation in the 1950s, and for the most noteworthy works that influenced my interpretation here, see Brash and Britten (1998), Delmont (2012), Doherty (2002), Franzosa (1999), J.B. Gilbert (1986), Kallen (2000), and J. Savage (2007).

25. For further discussion of Pat Boone's life and legacy, as well as white rock & roll cover versions of black rhythm & blues songs in the 1950s and 1960s, and for the most noteworthy works that influenced my interpretation here, see Altschuler (2003), P. Davis (2001), D. Greene (2014), M.K. Hall (2014), Leszczak (2013, 2014), Silverman (2014), Strausbaugh (2007), Sweeting (2004), and Uslan and Solomon (1981).

26. For further discussion of the emergence and evolution of the Chitlin' Circuit, and for the most noteworthy works that informed my interpretation here, see Elam and Krasner (2001), Lauterbach (2011), McGinley (2014), M.A. Neal (1998), and Wertheim (2006).

27. For further discussion of Otis Blackwell's often overlooked life and legacy, and for the most noteworthy works that influenced my interpretation here, see Altschuler (2003), Blackwell (2012), Emerson (2005), N. George (1988), and Guralnick (1999).

28. For further discussion of white popular music (i.e., "white pop"), especially the emergence and enormous influence of black rhythm & blues-derived white rock & roll in the late 1950s and early 1960s, and for the most noteworthy works that influenced my interpretation here, see Altschuler (2003), Aquila (2000), Birnbaum (2013), Broven (2009), Daley (2003), Fatherley and McFarland (2014), Frame (2007), M.K. Hall (2014), Hartman (2012), Helander (1998), Kotarba (2013), Kubernik (2014), Loss (1999), R. Palmer (1996), Regev (2013), A. Shaw (1969, 1970, 1978, 1986, 1987b), and Zak (2010).

29. For further discussion of the ways in which black rhythm & blues songs via white rock & roll cover versions, literally, revolutionized American radio, especially pop radio, in the 1950s and 1960s, and for the most noteworthy works that influenced my interpretation here, see Broven (2009), Cantor (2005), Daley (2003), Fatherley and McFarland (2014), M. Fisher (2007), Fong-Torres (1998), Gilson and Travis (2012), J.A.

Jackson (1991, 1997, 2007), Leszczak (2013, 2014), Rochelle (2012), W. Smith (1989), and A. Webster (2003).

30. With regard to the either unsuspecting or subtle reflections on, and references to race, racism, and anti-racism during rock & roll's first decade—from the Chords's "Sh-Boom" in 1954 through to the Rolling Stones's acclaimed eponymous debut in 1964, several works factored into and influenced my interpretation here, the most note-worthy among them, Aron (2015), R.I. Bell (2007), Covach and Flory (2012), Daley (2003), Daniel (2000), Delmont (2012), Gillett (1996), Lawson (2010), R. Palmer (1995, 1996), Petigny (2009), Pielke (2012), Redd (1974), and Vazzano (2010).

31. For further discussion of Jimi Hendrix's remarkable life and legacy, and for the most noteworthy works that influenced my interpretation here, see Cross (2005), D. Henderson (2008), Hendrix (2012, 2013), Lawrence (2006), McDermott (1992), C.S. Murray (1989), J. Perry (2004), Roby (2002), Roby and Schreiber (2010), Shadwick (2003), Shapiro and Glebbeek (1991), and Stubbs (2003).

32. For further discussion of black sexuality in early rhythm & blues-cum-rock & roll songs, and for the most noteworthy works that informed my analysis here, see Altschuler (2003), Aquila (2000), R.I. Bell (2007), Brake (1995), Cottrell (2015), Crazy Horse (2004), Daniel (2000), Escott (1999), Lauterbach (2011), J. Miller (1999), Othello (2004), Palmer (1995, 1996), Redd (1974, 1985), Reynolds and Press (1995), and Tosches (1999).

Bibliography

NOTE ON THE BIBLIOGRAPHY

The simultaneously musicological and sociological, interdisciplinary and intersectional nature of this book necessitated idiosyncratic authorial and bibliographic decisions—decisions that will not make any self-respecting environmentalist shudder. My personal commitment to our fragile ecology and the economic realities of making this volume affordable demanded economy of expression and citation wherever possible. As a consequence, I have eliminated citations that are obvious. For example, popular music and popular film citations in most instances have been omitted. Musicologists and film studies scholars are likely to cringe, but I suspect non-academic intellectuals, artists, and activists will greatly appreciate a more affordable and eco-friendly volume.

Abbington, James. (2001a). *Let Mt. Zion Rejoice!: Music in the African American Church*. Valley Forge, PA: Judson Press.
___. (Ed.). (2001b). *Readings in African American Church Music and Worship* (Volume 1). Chicago: GIA Publications.
___. (2009). *Let the Church Sing On!: Reflections on Black Sacred Music*. Chicago: GIA Publications.
___. (Ed.). (2014). *Readings in African American Church Music and Worship* (Volume 2). Chicago, IL: GIA Publications.
Abbott, Kingsley. (Ed.). (2000). *Calling Out Around the World: A Motown Reader*. London: Helter Skelter.
Abbott, Lynn. (1992). "'Play That Barber Shop Chord': A Case for the African American Origin of Barbershop Harmony." *American Music* 10 (3), 289–325.
Abbott, Lynn, and Seroff, Doug. (2002). *Out of Sight: The Rise of African American Popular Music, 1889–1895*. Jackson: University Press of Mississippi.
Ackerman, Bruce A. (2014). *The Civil Rights Revolution*. Cambridge: Harvard University Press.
Adams, Luther. (2010). *Way Up North in Louisville: African American Migration in the Urban South, 1930–1970*. Chapel Hill: University of North Carolina Press.
Adamson, Walter L. (1980). *Hegemony and Revolution: A Study of Antonio Gramsci's Political and Cultural Theory*. Berkeley: University of California Press.
Adelt, Ulrich. (2007). "Black, White and Blue: Racial Politics of Blues Music in the 1960s." PhD dissertation, University of Iowa, Iowa City.
___. (2010). *Blues Music in the Sixties: A Story in Black and White*. New Brunswick, NJ: Rutgers University Press.
___. (2011). "Black, White and Blue: Racial Politics in B.B. King's Music from the 1960's." *Journal of Popular Culture* 44 (2), 195–216.
Adero, Malaika. (1993). *Up South: Stories, Studies, and Letters of This Century's Black Migrations*. New York: New Press.

Agawu, V. Kofi. (2003). *Representing African Music: Postcolonial Notes, Queries, Positions.* New York: Routledge.

Agordoh, Alexander Akorlie. (2005). *African Music: Traditional And Contemporary.* New York: Nova Science Publishers.

Aldridge, Daniel W. (2011). *Becoming American: The African American Quest for Civil Rights, 1861–1976.* Wheeling, IL: Harlan Davidson.

Alger, Dean. (2014). *The Original Guitar Hero and the Power of Music: The Legendary Lonnie Johnson, Music, and Civil Rights.* Denton: University of North Texas Press.

Allen, Carrie Anne. (2009). "A Mighty Long Way: Community, Continuity, and Black Gospel Music on Television in Augusta, Georgia, 1954–2008." Ph.D. dissertation, Hugh Hodgson School of Music, University of Georgia, Athens, GA.

Allen, James. (2005). *Without Sanctuary: Lynching Photography in America.* Santa Fe: Twin Palms.

Allen, Ray. (1991). *Singing in the Spirit: African-American Sacred Quartets in New York City.* Philadelphia: University of Pennsylvania Press.

Allen, William Francis. (Ed.). (1995). *Slave Songs of the United States.* New York: Dover.

Alston, Vermont R. (2011). "Cosmopolitan Fantasies, Aesthetics, and Bodily Value: W.E.B. Du Bois's Dark Princess and the Trans/Gendering of Kautilya." *Journal of Transnational American Studies* 3 (1). Retrieved from: http://escholarship.org/uc/item/8r74n6wq.

Altschuler, Glenn C. (2003). *All Shook Up: How Rock & Roll Changed America.* Oxford: Oxford University Press.

Anderson, Carol. (2003). *Eyes off the Prize: The United Nations and the African American Struggle for Human Rights, 1944–1955.* Cambridge: Cambridge University Press.

Anderson, Elijah. (1981). *Place on the Corner.* Chicago: University of Chicago Press.

___. (1990). *Streetwise: Race, Class, and Change in an Urban Community.* Chicago: University of Chicago Press.

___. (1999). *Code of the Street: Decency, Violence, and the Moral Life of the Inner-City.* New York: Norton.

___. (Ed.). (2008). *Against the Wall: Poor, Young, Black, and Male.* Philadelphia: University of Pennsylvania Press.

Anderson, Jervis. (1973). *A. Philip Randolph: A Biographical Portrait.* New York: Harcourt Brace Jovanovich.

Anderson, Jervis. (1993). *This Was Harlem: A Cultural Portrait, 1900–1950.* New York: Farrar Straus Giroux.

Anderson, Paul Allen. (2001). *Deep River: Music and Memory in Harlem Renaissance Thought.* Durham: Duke University Press.

Anderson, Paul Allen. (2005). "Ralph Ellison on Lyricism and Swing." *American Literary History* 17 (2), 280–306.

Anderson, Robert, and North, Gail. (Eds.). (1979). *Gospel Music Encyclopedia.* New York: Sterling.

Andrews, Kenneth T. (2004). *Freedom Is a Constant Struggle: The Mississippi Civil Rights Movement and Its Legacy.* Chicago: University of Chicago Press.

Apel, Dora. (2004). *Imagery of Lynching: Black Men, White Women, and the Mob.* New Brunswick, NJ: Rutgers University Press.

Apel, Dora, and Smith, Shawn Michelle. (2007). *Lynching Photographs.* Berkeley: University of California Press.

Appell, Glenn, and Hemphill, David. (2006). *American Popular Music: A Multicultural History.* Belmont, CA: Thomson Wadsworth.

Aptheker, Bettina. (1975). "W.E.B. Du Bois and the Struggle for Women's Rights: 1910–1920." *San Jose Studies* 1 (2), 7–16.

Argyle, Ray. (2009). *Scott Joplin and the Age of Ragtime.* Jefferson, NC: McFarland.

Armstrong, Julie B. (Ed.). (2015). *The Cambridge Companion to American Civil Rights Literature.* Cambridge: Cambridge University Press.

Arnesen, Eric (2002). *Black Protest and the Great Migration: A Brief History with Documents.* Bedford: St. Martin's Press.

Aron, Lewis. (2015). "Race, Roots, and Rhythm: Riffing on Rock & Roll: An Introduction." *Psychoanalytic Dialogues* 25 (2), 153–162.

Aquila, Richard. (2000). *That Old-Time Rock & Roll: A Chronicle of an Era, 1954–1963.* Urbana: University of Illinois Press.

Ashford, Jack. (2003). *Motown: The View from the Bottom* (with Charlene Ashford). New Romney: Bank House Books.

Ashmore, Susan Y. (2008). *Carry It On: The War on Poverty and the Civil Rights Movement in Alabama, 1964–1972.* Athens: University of Georgia Press.

Askew, Kelly M. (2002). *Performing the Nation: Swahili Music and Cultural Politics in Tanzania.* Chicago: University of Chicago Press.

Askin, Allan Bradley. (1970). "An Economic Analysis of Black Migration." Ph.D. dissertation, Massachusetts Institute of Technology, Cambridge, MA.

Athearn, Robert G. (1978). *In Search of Canaan: Black to Kansas, 1879–1880.* Lawrence: Regents Press of Kansas.

Averill, Gage. (2010). *Four Parts, No Waiting: A Social History of American Barbershop Harmony.* Oxford: Oxford University Press.

Awkward, Michael. (2007). *Soul Covers: Rhythm & Blues Remakes and the Struggle for Artistic Identity (Aretha Franklin, Al Green, Phoebe Snow).* Durham: Duke University Press.

Back, Les. (2000). "Voices of Hate, Sounds of Hybridity: Black Music and the Complexities of Racism." *Black Music Research Journal* 20 (2), 127–149.

Bailey, Beth, and Farber, David. (1993). "The 'Double-V' Campaign in World War II Hawaii: African Americans, Racial Ideology, and Federal Power." *Journal of Social History* 26 (4), 817–843.

Baker, Bruce E. (2008). *This Mob Will Surely Take My Life: Lynchings in the Carolinas, 1871–1947.* New York: Continuum.

Baker, Houston A. (1987). *Modernism and the Harlem Renaissance.* Chicago: University of Chicago Press.

Baldwin, Davarian L. (2007). *Chicago's New Negroes: Modernity, the Great Migration & Black Urban Life.* Chapel Hill: University of North Carolina Press.

Baldwin, Lewis V. (2010). *The Voice of Conscience: The Church in the Mind of Martin Luther King, Jr.* Oxford: Oxford University Press.

Balfour, Lawrie. (2005). "Representative Women: Slavery, Citizenship, and Feminist Theory in Du Bois's 'The Damnation of Women.'" *Hypatia* 20 (3), 127–148.

___. (2011). *Democracy's Reconstruction: Thinking Politically with W.E.B. Du Bois.* Oxford: Oxford University Press.

Banfield, William C. (2010). *Cultural Codes: Makings of a Black Music Philosophy—An Interpretive History from Spirituals to Hip Hop.* Lanham, MD: Scarecrow Press.

___. (2011). *Representing Black Music Culture: Then, Now, and When Again?* Lanham, MD: Scarecrow Press.

Baptista, Todd R. (2000). *Group Harmony: Echoes of the Rhythm & Blues Era.* New Bedford, MA: TRB Enterprises.

Baraka, Amiri. (1963). *Blues People: Negro Music in White America.* New York: Morrow.

___. (1969). *Black Magic: Collected Poetry, 1961–1967.* Indianapolis: Bobs-Merrill.

___. (1987). *The Music: Reflections on Jazz and Blues.* New York: Morrow.

___. (1994). *Conversations with Amiri Baraka* (Charlie Reilly, Ed.). Jackson: University Press of Mississippi.

___. (2009). *Digging: The African American Soul of American Classical Music.* Berkeley: University of California Press.

Barnet, Andrea. (2004). *All-Night Party: The Women of Bohemian Greenwich Village and Harlem, 1913–1930.* Chapel Hill, NC: Algonquin Books.

Barrett, Leonard E. (1974). *Soul-Force: African Heritage in Afro-American Religion.* Garden City, NY: Anchor.

Bartley, Numan V. (1969). *Rise of Massive Resistance: Race and Politics in the South During the 1950s.* Baton Rouge: Louisiana State University Press.

Bascom, William R. (1980). *Sixteen Cowries: Yoruba Divination from Africa to the New World*. Bloomington: Indiana University Press.

Baszak, Mark. (2003). *Such Sweet Thunder: Views on Black American Music*. Amherst: University of Massachusetts Press.

Bates, Beth T. (2001). *Pullman Porters and the Rise of Protest Politics in Black America, 1925–1945*. Chapel Hill: University of North Carolina Press.

Bastide, Roger. (1971). *African Civilization in the New World*. New York: Harper & Row.

___. (1978). *The African Religions of Brazil: Toward a Sociology of the Interpretation of Civilization*. Baltimore: Johns Hopkins University Press.

Batiste, Stephanie L. (2012). *Darkening Mirrors: Imperial Representation in Depression-Era African American Performance*. Durham: Duke University Press.

Batterson, Jack A. (1998). *Blind Boone: Missouri's Ragtime Pioneer*. Columbia: University of Missouri Press.

Baumann, Jeffrey Eugene. (2011). "Chords of Discord: Songs of Dissonance, Violence, and Faith in the Civil Rights Movement." M.A. thesis, San Diego State University.

Beacham, Frank. (2010). "This Magic Moment: When the Ku Klux Klan Tried to Kill Rhythm and Blues Music in South Carolina." In Winfred B. Moore and Orville Vernon Burton (Eds.), *Toward the Meeting of the Waters: Currents in the Civil Rights Movement of South Carolina during the Twentieth Century* (119–145). Columbia, SC: University of South Carolina Press.

Becton, Julius. (Ed.). (2008). *The Exclusion of Black Soldiers from the Medal of Honor in World War II: The Study Commissioned by the United States Army to Investigate Racial Bias in the Awarding of the Nation's Highest Military Decoration*. Jefferson, NC: McFarland & Co.

Bell, Kevin. (2003). "The Embrace of Entropy: Ralph Ellison and the Freedom Principle of Jazz Invisible." *boundary 2* 30 (2), 21–45.

Bell, Robert I. (2007). *The Myth of Rock & Roll: The Racial Politics of American Popular Music, 1945–2005*. Philadelphia, PA: Robell Publishing.

Belz, Carl. (1972). *The Story of Rock*. Oxford: Oxford University Press.

Benjaminson, Peter. (1979). *The Story of Motown*. New York: Grove Press.

___. (2008). *The Lost Supreme: The Life of Dreamgirl Florence Ballard*. Chicago: Lawrence Hill Books.

___. (2012). *Mary Wells: The Tumultuous Life of Motown's First Superstar*. Chicago: Chicago Review Press.

Bennett, Andy, Shank, Barry, and Toynbee, Jason. (Eds.). (2005). *The Popular Music Studies Reader*. New York: Routledge.

Berger, Maurice. (2010). *For All the World to See: Visual Culture and the Struggle for Civil Rights*. New Haven: Yale University Press.

Berlin, Edward A. (1980). *Ragtime: A Musical and Cultural History*. Berkeley: University of California Press.

___. (1987). *Reflections and Research on Ragtime*. Brooklyn, NY: City University of New York Press.

___. (2016). *King of Ragtime: Scott Joplin and His Era* (Second Edition). Oxford: Oxford University Press.

Berlin, Ira. (2010). *The Making of African America: The Four Great Migrations*. New York: Viking.

Bernard, Shane K. (1996). *Swamp Pop: Cajun and Creole Rhythm & Blues*. Jackson: University Press of Mississippi.

Berrey, Stephen A. (2015). *The Jim Crow Routine: Everyday Performances of Race, Civil Rights, and Segregation in Mississippi*. Chapel Hill: University of North Carolina Press.

Berry, Mary Frances. (1994). *Black Resistance, White Law: A History of Constitutional Racism in America*. New York: Penguin.

Bertrand, Michael T. (2000). *Race, Rock, and Elvis*. Urbana: University of Illinois Press.

Bebey, Francis. (1999). *African Music: A People's Art*. New York: Lawrence Hill Books.

Bilbija, Marina. (2011). "Democracy's New Song: Black Reconstruction in America, 1860–1880 and the Melodramatic Imagination." *Annals of the American Academy of Political and Social Science* 637 (1), 64–77.

Billingsley, Andrew. (1999). *Mighty Like a River: The Black Church and Social Reform.* Oxford: Oxford University Press.

Bimmler, Lauren. (2008). "The Grassroots Gospel: How Spirituals and Freedom Songs Democratized the Civil Rights Movement." B.A. thesis, Honors College, Florida Atlantic University, Boca Raton, FL.

Binkowski, Carol J. (2012). *Joseph F. Lamb: A Passion for Ragtime.* Jefferson: McFarland Publishers.

Birnbaum, Larry. (2013). *Before Elvis: The Prehistory of Rock & Roll.* Lanham, MD: Scarecrow Press.

Black, Timuel D. (2003). *Bridges of Memory: Chicago's First Wave of Black Migration* (Vol. 1). Evanston: Northwestern University Press.

___. (2008). *Bridges of Memory: Chicago's First Wave of Black Migration* (Vol. 2). Evanston: Northwestern University Press.

Blackmon, Douglas A. (2008). *Slavery by Another Name: The Re-Enslavement of Black Americans from the Civil War to World War II.* New York: Doubleday.

Blackwell, Otis. (Songwriter). (2012). *Handy Man: The Otis Blackwell Songbook.* London: Ace Records.

Blades, William C. (1921). *Negro Poems, Melodies, Plantation Pieces, Camp Meeting Songs, etc.* Boston: R.G. Badger.

Blake, John. (2004). *Children of the Movement.* Chicago: Lawrence Hill Books.

Blesh, Rudi. (1971). *They All Played Ragtime: The True Story of an American Music.* New York: Oak Publications.

Blocker, Jack S. (2008). *A Little More Freedom: African Americans Enter the Urban Midwest, 1860–1930.* Columbus: Ohio State University Press.

Bloom, Jack M. (1987). *Class, Race, and the Civil Rights Movement: The Changing Political Economy of Southern Racism.* Bloomington: Indiana University Press.

Blum, Edward J. (2007). *W.E.B. Du Bois: American Prophet.* Philadelphia, PA: University of Pennsylvania Press.

Blum, Edward J., and Young, Jason R. (Eds.). (2009). *The Souls of W.E.B. Du Bois: New Essays and Reflections.* Macon, GA: Mercer University Press.

Bodroghkyozy, Anika. (2013). *Equal Time: Television and the Civil Rights Movement.* Urbana: University of Illinois Press.

Boehm, Lisa K. (2009). *Making a Way out of No Way: African American Women and the Second Great Migration.* Jackson: University Press of Mississippi.

Boggs, Carl. (1976). *Gramsci's Marxism.* London: Pluto Press.

Bonilla-Silva, Eduardo, and Zuberi, Tukufu. (Eds.). (2008). *White Logic, White Methods: Racism and Methodology.* Lanham, MD: Rowman & Littlefield.

Bordowitz, Hank. (2004). *Turning Points in Rock & Roll: The Key Events that Affected Popular Music in the Latter Half of the 20th Century.* New York: Citadel Press.

Bourgeois, Anna Stong. (2004). *Blueswomen: Profiles of 37 Early Performers, with an Anthology of Lyrics, 1920–1945.* Jefferson, NC: McFarland.

Boyd, Tim S.R. (2012). *Georgia Democrats, the Civil Rights Movement, and the Shaping of the New South.* Gainesville: University Press of Florida.

Boyer, Horace Clarence. (1979). "Contemporary Gospel Music." *Black Perspective in Music* 7 (1), 5–58.

___. (1983). "Charles Albert Tindley: Progenitor of Black-American Gospel Music." *Black Perspective in Music* 11 (2), 103–132.

___. (1985). "A comparative analysis of traditional and contemporary Gospel music." In Irene V. Jackson (Ed.), *More Than Dancing: Essays on Afro-American Music and Musicians* (127–146). Westport, CT: Greenwood.

___. (1988). "Tracking the Tradition: New Orleans Sacred Music. *Black Music Research Journal* 8 (1), 135–147.

___. (1995). *How Sweet the Sound: The Golden Age of Gospel.* Washington, D.C.: Elliott & Clark.

___. (2000). *The Golden Age of Gospel.* Urbana: University of Illinois Press.

___. (2001). "African American Gospel Music." In Vincent L. Wimbush (Ed.), *African Americans and the Bible: Sacred Texts and Social Structures* (464–488). New York: Continuum.

Boyett, Patricia M. (2015). *Right to Revolt: The Crusade for Racial Justice in Mississippi's Central Piney Woods.* Jackson: University Press of Mississippi.

Bracey, Earnest N. (2003). *On Racism: Essays on Black Popular Culture, African American Politics, and the New Black Aesthetics.* Lanham, MD: University Press of America.

Brackett, David. (Ed.). (2005). *The Pop, Rock, and Soul Reader: Histories and Debates.* Oxford: Oxford University Press.

Bracks, Lean'tin L., and Smith, Jessie Carney. (Eds.). (2014). *Black Women of the Harlem Renaissance Era.* Lanham: Rowman & Littlefield.

Brake, Mike. (1995). *The Sociology of Youth Culture and Youth Subcultures: Sex and Drugs and Rock & Roll?* Boston: Routledge & Kegan Paul

Branch, Taylor. (1988). *Parting the Waters: America in the King Years, 1954–1963.* New York: Simon & Schuster.

___. (1998). *Pillar of Fire: America in the King Years, 1963–1965.* New York: Simon & Schuster.

___. (2006). *At Canaan's Edge: America in the King Years, 1965–1968.* New York: Simon & Schuster.

___. (2013). *The King Years: Historic Moments in the Civil Rights Movement.* New York: Simon & Schuster.

Brandt, Nat. (1996). *Harlem at War: The Black Experience in WWII.* Syracuse: Syracuse University Press.

Brar, Dhanveer Singh. (2013). "Blackness, Radicalism, Sound: Black Consciousness and Black Popular Music in the U.S.A (1955–1971)." Ph.D. dissertation, Goldsmiths, University of London.

Brash, Sarah, and Britten, Loretta. (Eds.). (1998). *Rock & Roll Generation: Teen Life in the 50s.* Alexandria, VA: Time-Life Books.

Bridges, Flora W. (2001). *Resurrection Song: African American Spirituality.* Maryknoll, NY: Orbis Books

Brinkley, Douglas. (2000a). *Mine Eyes Have Seen the Glory: The Life of Rosa Parks.* London: Weidenfeld & Nicolson.

___. (2000b). *Rosa Parks: A Life.* New York: Viking.

Brode, Douglas. (2015). *Sex, Drugs & Rock & Roll: The Evolution of an American Youth Culture.* New York: Peter Lang.

Brooks, Daphne A. (2006). *Bodies in Dissent: Spectacular Performances of Race and Freedom, 1850–1910.* Durham: Duke University Press.

Brooks, Tilford. (1984). *America's Black Musical Heritage.* Englewood Cliffs, NJ: Prentice-Hall.

Broughton, Viv. (1985). *Black Gospel: An Illustrated History of the Gospel Sound.* New York: Distributed by Sterling Pub. Co.

___. (1996). *Too Close to Heaven: The Illustrated History of Gospel Music.* London: Midnight Books.

Broven, John. (1974). *Walking to New Orleans: The Story of New Orleans Rhythm & Blues.* Bexhill-on-Sea, East Sussex, UK: Blues Unlimited.

___. (1978). *Rhythm & Blues in New Orleans.* Gretna, LA: Pelican.

___. (1983). *South To Louisiana: The Music of the Cajun Bayous.* Gretna, LA: Pelican.

___. (2009). *Record Makers and Breakers: Voices of the Independent Rock & Roll Pioneers.* Urbana: University of Illinois Press.

Brown, Courtney. (2008). *Politics in Music: Music and Political Transformation from Beethoven to Hip Hop.* Atlanta, GA: Farsight Press.

Brown, Jayna. (2008). *Babylon Girls: Black Women Performers and the Shaping of the Modern.* Durham: Duke University Press.

Brown, Lois. (2008). *Pauline Elizabeth Hopkins: Black Daughter of the Revolution*. Chapel Hill: University of North Carolina Press.

Brown, Matthew P. (1994). "Funk Music as Genre: Black Aesthetic, Apocalyptic Thinking and Urban Protest in Post-1965 African American Pop." *Cultural Studies* 8 (3), 484–508.

Brown, Teresa L.F. (2003). *Weary Throats and New Songs: Black Women Proclaiming God's Word*. Nashville, TN: Abingdon Press.

Brown-Nagin, Tomiko. (2011). *Courage to Dissent: Atlanta and the Long History of the Civil Rights Movement*. Oxford: Oxford University Press.

Browne, Errol Tsekani. (2000). "The Widest Possible Application of Democratic Principles": Gender & Nation in W.E.B. Du Bois's Political Thought. M.A. thesis, University of California, Los Angeles.

Browne, Nick. (Eds.). (1994). *American Television: New Directions in History and Theory*. Langhorne, PA: Harwood Academic.

Brundage, W. Fitzhugh. (1993). *Lynching in the New South: Georgia and Virginia, 1880–1930*. Urbana: University of Illinois Press.

___. (Ed.). (1997). *Under Sentence of Death: Lynching in the South*. Chapel Hill: University of North Carolina Press.

___. (2005). *The Southern Past: A Clash of Race and Memory* . Cambridge: Harvard University Press.

___. (2011). *Beyond Blackface: African Americans and the Creation of American Popular Culture, 1890–1930*. Chapel Hill: University of North Carolina Press.

Bullard, Sara. (1993). *Free at Last: A History of the Civil Rights Movement and Those Who Died in the Struggle*. Oxford: Oxford University Press.

Burnim, Mellonee V. (1980a). "The Black Gospel Music Tradition: Symbol of Ethnicity." Ph.D. dissertation, Indiana University, Bloomington, IN.

___. (1980b). "Gospel Music Research." *Black Music Research Journal* 1, 63–70.

___. (1985a). "The Black Gospel Music Tradition: A Complex of Ideology, Aesthetic and Behavior." In Irene V. Jackson (Ed.), *More Than Dancing: Essays on Afro-American Music and Musicians* (147–167). Westport, CT: Greenwood.

___. (1985b). "Culture Bearer and Tradition Bearer: An Ethnomusicologist's Research on Gospel Music." *Ethnomusicology* 29 (3), 432–447.

___. (1988). "Functional Dimensions of Gospel Music Performance." *Western Journal of Black Studies* 12 (2), 112–121.

___. (2006). "Gospel Women." In Mellonee V. Burnim and Portia K. Maultsby (Eds.), *African American Music: An Introduction* (493–508). New York: Routledge.

___. (2015). "Gospel" In Mellonee V. Burnim and Portia K. Maultsby (Eds.), *African American Music: An Introduction* (2nd Edition) (189–212). New York: Routledge.

Burnim, Mellonee V. and Maultsby, Portia K. (Eds.). (2006). *African American Music: An Introduction*. New York: Routledge.

___. (Eds.). (2015). *African American Music: An Introduction* (2nd Edition). New York: Routledge.

Burns, Gary. (Ed.). (2016). *A Companion to Popular Culture*. Malden: Blackwell.

Burns, Stewart. (1990). *Social Movements of the 1960s: Searching for Democracy*. Boston: Twayne Publishers.

Butler, J. Michael. (2016). *Beyond Integration: The Black Freedom Struggle in Escambia County, Florida, 1960–1980*. Chapel Hill: University of North Carolina Press.

Burton, Frederick. (2003). *Cleveland's Gospel Music*. Charleston, SC: Arcadia.

Bynoe, Yvonne. (2004). *Stand and Deliver: Political Activism, Leadership, and Hip Hop Culture*. Brooklyn, NY: Soft Skull Press.

Bynum, Cornelius L. (2010). *A. Philip Randolph and the Struggle for Civil Rights*. Urbana: University of Illinois Press.

Bynum, Thomas L. (2013). *NAACP Youth and the Fight for Black Freedom*. Knoxville: University of Tennessee Press.

Campbell, James. (2001). *This is the Beat Generation: New York, San Francisco, Paris*. Berkeley: University of California Press.

Campbell, Michael. (2007). *Rock & Roll: An Introduction* (with James Brody). New York: Schirmer.

Cantor, Louis. (2005). *Dewey and Elvis: The Life and Times of a Rock & Roll Deejay.* Urbana: University of Illinois Press.

Caponi-Tabery, Gena. (1999). "Jump for Joy: The Jump Trope in African America, 1937–1941." *Prospects* 24, 521–574.

___. (2008). *Jump for Joy: Jazz, Basketball, and Black Culture in 1930s America.* Amherst: University of Massachusetts Press.

Carasik, Diane Sue. (1972). "Motown Record Corporation and the Revival of Rhythm & Blues Music." M.A. thesis, Boston University, Boston, MA.

Carawan, Guy and Carawan, Candie. (Eds.). (1963). *We Shall Overcome!: Songs of the Southern Freedom Movement.* New York: Oak Publications.

___. (1968). *Freedom is a Constant Struggle: Songs of the Freedom Movement.* New York: Oak Publications.

___. (Eds.). (2007). *Sing for Freedom: The Story of the Civil Rights Movement Through Its Songs.* Montgomery, AL: NewSouth Books.

Carby, Hazel V. (1998). *Race Men.* Cambridge: Harvard University Press.

Carle, Susan D. (2013). *Defining the Struggle: National Organizing for Racial Justice, 1880–1915.* Oxford: Oxford University Press.

Carmichael, Stokely. (2003). *Ready for Revolution!: The Life and Struggles of Stokely Carmichael (Kwame Ture)* (with Ekwueme Michael Thelwell). New York: Scribner.

Carr, Cynthia. (2006). *Our Town: A Heartland Lynching, A Haunted Town, and the Hidden History of White America.* New York: Crown Publishers.

Carrigan, William D. (2004). *The Making of a Lynching Culture: Violence and Vigilantism in Central Texas, 1836–1916.* Urbana: University of Illinois Press.

___. (2008). *Lynching Reconsidered: New Perspectives in the Study of Mob Violence.* New York: Routledge

Carrigan, William D., and Webb, Clive. (2013). *Forgotten Dead: Mob Violence Against Mexicans in the United States, 1848–1928.* Oxford: Oxford University Press.

Carson, Clayborne. (1981). *In Struggle: SNCC and the Black Awakening of the 1960s.* Cambridge: Harvard University Press.

Carson, Clayborne, Garrow, David J., Gill, Gerald, Harding, Vincent, and Hine, Darlene Clark. (Eds.). (1997). *The Eyes on the Prize Civil Rights Reader.* New York: Penguin.

Carter, David C. (2009). *The Music Has Gone Out of the Movement: Civil Rights and the Johnson Administration, 1965–1968.* Chapel Hill: University of North Carolina Press.

Cash, Floris Loretta. (1986). "Womanhood and Protest: The Club Movement Among Black Women, 1892–1922." Ph.D. dissertation, State University of New York, Stony Brook.

___. (2001). *African American Women and Social Action: The Clubwomen and Volunteerism from Jim Crow to the New Deal, 1896–1936.* Westport, CT: Greenwood Press.

Cashman, Sean D. (1991). *African Americans & the Quest for Civil Rights, 1900–1990.* New York: New York University Press.

Castellini, Michael. (2013). "Sit-In, Stand Up and Sing Out!: Black Gospel Music and the Civil Rights Movement." M.A. thesis, Department of History, Georgia State University, Atlanta, GA. http://scholarworks.gsu.edu/history_theses/76.

Cateforis, Theo. (Ed.). (2013). *The Rock History Reader* (2nd Edition.). New York: Routledge.

Castleman, Harry, and Podrazik, Walter J. (2003). *Watching TV: Six Decades of American Television.* Syracuse: Syracuse University Press.

Chadbourn, James Harmon. (1933). *Lynching and the Law.* Chapel Hill: University of North Carolina Press.

Chappell, David L. (1994). *Inside Agitators: White Southerners in the Civil Rights Movement.* Baltimore: Johns Hopkins University Press.

Charters, Ann. (Ed.). (1983). *The Beats, Literary Bohemians in Post-War America* (2 Volumes). Detroit: Gale.

___. (1986). *Beats & Company: A Portrait of a Literary Generation*. Garden City, NY: Doubleday.

___. (Ed.). (1993). *The Penguin Book of the Beats*. New York: Penguin.

___. (1994). *Kerouac: A Biography*. New York: St. Martin's Press.

___. (Ed.). (2001). *Beat Down to Your Soul: What Was the Beat Generation?* New York: Penguin Books.

___. (Ed.). (2003). *The Portable Beat Reader*. New York: Penguin Classics.

Charters, Samuel Barclay. (1963). *The Poetry of the Blues*. New York: Oak Publications.

___. (1975). *The Country Blues*. New York: Da Capo Press.

___. (1977). *The Legacy of the Blues: A Glimpse into the Art and the Lives of Twelve Great Bluesmen*. New York: Da Capo.

___. (1981). *The Roots of the Blues: An African Search*. New York: Putnam.

___. (2005). *Walking a Blues Road: A Selection of Blues Writing, 1956–2004*. New York: Marion Boyars Publishers.

___. (2008). *A Trumpet Around the Corner: The Story of New Orleans Jazz*. Jackson: University Press of Mississippi.

___. (2009). *A Language of Song: Journeys in the Musical World of the African Diaspora*. Durham: Duke University Press.

___. (2015). *Songs of Sorrow: Lucy McKim Garrison and Slave Songs of the United States*. Jackson: University Press of Mississippi.

Chernoff, John Miller. (1979). *African Rhythm and African Sensibility: Aesthetics and Social Action in African Musical Idioms*. Chicago: University of Chicago Press.

Chikowero, Mhoze. (2015). *African Music, Power, and Being in Colonial Zimbabwe*. Indianapolis: Indiana University Press.

Chilisa, Bagele. (2012). *Indigenous Research Methodologies*. Thousand Oaks, CA: Sage.

Chilton, John. (1992). *Let the Good Times Roll: The Story of Louis Jordan and His Music*. Ann Arbor: University of Michigan Press.

Chong, Dennis. (1991). *Collective Action and the Civil Rights Movement*. Chicago: University of Chicago Press.

Classen, Steven D. (2004). *Watching Jim Crow: The Struggles over Mississippi TV, 1955–1969*. Durham: Duke University Press.

Clay, Andreana. (2012). *The Hip Hop Generation Fights Back!: Youth, Activism, and Post-Civil Rights Politics*. New York: New York University Press.

Clayson, William S. (2010). *Freedom Is Not Enough: The War on Poverty and the Civil Rights Movement in Texas*. Austin: University of Texas Press.

Crazy Horse, Kandia. (Ed.). (2004). *Rip It Up!: The Black Experience in Rock & Roll*. New York: Palgrave Macmillan.

Cohen, Rich. (2004). *Machers and Rockers: Chess Records and the Business of Rock & Roll*. New York: Norton.

___. (2005). *The Record Men: The Chess Brothers and the Birth of Rock & Roll*. New York: Norton.

Cohn, Nik. (1969). *Rock from the Beginning*. New York: Stein & Day.

Cohodas, Nadine (2000). *Spinning Blues into Gold: The Chess Brothers and the Legendary Chess Records*. New York: St. Martin's Press.

Coleman, Rick. (2006). *Blue Monday: Fats Domino and the Lost Dawn of Rock & Roll*. Cambridge, MA: Da Capo Press

Colley, Zoe A. (2013). *Ain't Scared of Your Jail: Arrest, Imprisonment, and the Civil Rights Movement*. Gainesville: University Press of Florida.

Collier-Thomas, Bettye, and Franklin, V.P. (Eds.). (2001). *Sisters in the Struggle: African American Women in the Civil Rights-Black Power Movement*. New York: New York University Press.

Collins, Ann V. (2012). *All Hell Broke Loose: American Race Riots from the Progressive Era through World War II*. Santa Barbara, CA: Praeger.

Collis, John. (1998). *The Story of Chess Records*. New York: Bloomsbury Publishing.

Combs, James E. (1984). *Polpop: Politics and Popular Culture in America*. Bowling Green, OH: Bowling Green University Popular Press.

Cone, James H. (1991). *Martin & Malcolm & America: A Dream or A Nightmare*. Maryknoll, NY: Orbis.

Cook, Bruce. (1971). *The Beat Generation: The Tumultuous '50s Movement and Its Impact on Today*. New York: Charles Scribner's Sons.

Costen, Melva W. (2004). *In Spirit and In Truth: The Music of African American Worship*. Louisville: Westminster John Knox Press.

Cottrell, Robert C. (2015). *Sex, Drugs, and Rock & Roll: The Rise of America's 1960s Counterculture*. Lanham: Rowman & Littlefield.

Countryman, Matthew. (2006). *Up South: Civil Rights and Black Power in Philadelphia*. Philadelphia: University of Pennsylvania Press.

Covach, John, and Flory, Andrew. (2012). *What's That Sound?: An Introduction to Rock and Its History* (Third Edition). New York: Norton.

Crawford, Vicki L., Rouse, Jacqueline Anne, and Woods, Barbara. (Eds.). (1990). *Women in the Civil Rights Movement: Trailblazers and Torchbearers, 1941–1965*. Brooklyn, NY: Carlson.

Cripps, Thomas. (1977). *Slow Fade to Black: The Negro in American Film*. Oxford: Oxford University Press.

___. (1993). *Making Movies Black: The Hollywood Message Movie from World War II to the Civil Rights Era*. Oxford: Oxford University Press.

Crosby, Emily. (2011). *Civil Rights History from the Ground Up: Local Struggles, A National Movement*. Athens: University of Georgia Press.

Cross, Charles R. (2005). *Room Full of Mirrors: A Biography of Jimi Hendrix*. New York: Hyperion.

Cruz, Jon David. (1986). "The Politics of Popular Culture: Black Popular Music as Public Sphere." Ph.D. dissertation, University of California, Berkeley.

___. (1999). *Culture on the Margins: The Black Spiritual and the Rise of American Cultural Interpretation*. Princeton: Princeton University Press.

Curtis, Susan. (2004). *Dancing to a Black Man's Tune: a Life of Scott Joplin*. Columbia: University of Missouri Press.

Dahl, Bill. (2001). *Motown: The Golden Years, The Stars and Music That Shaped a Generation*. Iola, WI: Krause.

Daley, Mike. (2003). "'Why Do Whites Sing Black?': The Blues, Whiteness, and Early Histories of Rock." *Popular Music and Society* 26 (2), 161–167.

Dalton, Russell J., and Kuechler, Manfred. (Eds.). (1990). *Challenging the Political Order: New Social and Political Movements in Western Democracies*. New York: Oxford University Press.

Dance, Stanley. (2001). *The World of Swing: An Oral History of Big Band Jazz*. Cambridge, MA: Perseus Books.

Daniel, Pete. (2000). *Lost Revolutions: The South in the 1950s*. Chapel Hill: University of North Carolina Press.

Darden, Bob. (2004). *People Get Ready!: A New History of Black Gospel Music*. New York: Continuum.

___. (2014). *Nothing but Love in God's Water: Black Sacred Music from the Civil War to the Civil Rights Movement*. University Park: Pennsylvania State University Press.

Dargan, William T. (2006). *Lining Out the Word: Dr. Watts Hymn Singing in the Music of Black Americans*. Berkeley: University of California Press.

David, Jonathan C. (2007). *Together Let Us Sweetly Live: The Singing and Praying Bands*. Urbana: University of Illinois Press.

Davies, David R. (Ed.). (2001). *The Press and Race: Mississippi Journalists Confront the Movement*. Jackson: University Press of Mississippi.

Davis, Angela Y. (1998). *Blues Legacies and Black Feminism: Gertrude "Ma" Rainey, Bessie Smith, and Billie Holiday*. New York: Pantheon.

Davis, Daniel S. (1972). *Mr. Black Labor: The Story of A. Philip Randolph, Father of the Civil Rights Movement*. New York: E.P. Dutton.

Davis, Elizabeth L. (1996). *Lifting As They Climb: The National Association of Colored Women*. New York: G.K. Hall.

Davis, Francis. (1995). *The History of the Blues.* New York: Hyperion.

Davis, Jack E. (Ed.). (2001). *The Civil Rights Movement.* Malden, MA: Blackwell.

Davis, Nathan T. (1996). *African American Music: A Philosophical Look at African American Music in Society.* Needham Heights, MA: Simon & Schuster.

Davis, Paul. (2001). *Pat Boone: The Authorized Biography.* New York: HarperCollins.

Davis, Sharon. (1988). *Motown: The History.* Enfield, Middlesex: Guinness Publishing.

___. (2001). *Marvin Gaye: I Heard It Through the Grapevine.* Edinburgh: Mainstream.

Davis, Townsend. (1998). *Weary Feet, Rested Souls: A Guided History of the Civil Rights Movement.* New York: Norton.

Dawson, Jim. (2005). *Rock Around the Clock!: The Record That Started the Rock Revolution.* San Francisco: Backbeat Books.

DeCurtis, Anthony. (Ed.). (1992). *Present Tense: Rock & Roll and Culture.* Durham: Duke University Press.

DeCurtis, Anthony, Henke, James, and George-Warren, Holly Georg. (Eds.). (1992). *The Rolling Stone Illustrated History of Rock & Roll.* New York: Random House.

Deffaa, Chip. (1996). *Blue Rhythm: Six Lives in Rhythm & Blues.* Urbana: University of Illinois Press.

DjeDje, Jacqueline C., and Meadows, Eddie S. (Eds.). (1998). *California Soul: Music of African Americans in the West.* Berkeley: University of California Press.

de Jong, Greta. (2002). *A Different Day: African American Struggles for Justice in Rural Louisiana, 1900–1970.* Chapel Hill: University of North Carolina Press.

De Lerma, Dominique-René. (1973). *Reflections on Afro-American Music.* Kent, OH: Kent State University Press.

Delmont, Matthew F. (2012). *The Nicest Kids in Town: American Bandstand, Rock & Roll, and the Struggle for Civil Rights in 1950s Philadelphia.* Berkeley: University of California Press.

Denisoff, R. Serge. (1970). "The Religious Roots of the American Song of Persuasion." *Western Folklore* 29 (3), 175–184.

Denzin, Norman K., Lincoln, Yvonna S., and Smith, Linda Tuhiwai. (Eds.). (2008). *Handbook of Critical and Indigenous Methodologies.* Los Angeles: Sage.

de Schweinitz, Rebecca. (2009). *If We Could Change the World: Young People and America's Long Struggle for Racial Equality.* Chapel Hill: University of North Carolina Press.

DeVeaux, Scott Knowles, and Kenney, William Howland. (Eds.). (1992). *The Music of James Scott.* Washington, DC: Smithsonian Institution Press.

Dickerson, Vanessa D. (2008). *Dark Victorians.* Urbana: University of Illinois Press.

Dickson, Lynda Faye. (1982). "The Early Club Movement Among Black Women in Denver, 1890–1925." Ph.D. dissertation, University of Colorado at Boulder.

Dierenfield, Bruce J. (2008). *The Civil Rights Movement.* New York: Pearson Longman.

Diggs, Irene. (1974). "Du Bois and Women: A Short Story of Black Women, 1910–1934." *Current Bibliography on African Affairs* 7 (Summer), 260–307.

Dillard, Angela D. (2007). *Faith in the City: Preaching Radical Social Change in Detroit.* Ann Arbor: University of Michigan Press.

Dittmer, John. (1994). *Local People: The Struggle for Civil Rights in Mississippi.* Urbana: University of Illinois Press.

Dixon, Robert, Godrich, John, and Rye, Howard. (Eds.). (1997). *Blues & Gospel Records, 1890–1943.* New York: Oxford University Press.

Dodge, Timothy. (2013). *The School of Arizona Dranes: Gospel Music Pioneer.* Lanham: Lexington Books.

Dodson, Howard, and Diouf, Sylviane A. (2004). *In Motion: The African-American Migration Experience.* Washington, DC: National Geographic.

Doggett, Peter. (Compiler and Annotator). (2007). *Power To The Motown People!: Civil Rights Anthems and Political Soul, 1968–1975* [Compact Disc]. Santa Monica, CA: Motown/Universal Music Group.

Doherty, Thomas P. (2002). *Teenagers and Teenpics: The Juvenilization of American Movies in the 1950s.* Philadelphia: Temple University Press.

Dorrien, Gary J. (2015). *The New Abolition: W. E. B. Du Bois and the Black Social Gospel.* New Haven: Yale University Press.

Driggs, Frank, and Haddix, Chuck. (2005). *Kansas City Jazz: From Ragtime to Bebop—A History.* Oxford: Oxford University Press.

Dublin, Thomas, Arias, Franchesca, and Carreras, Debora. (2003). *What Gender Perspectives Shaped the Emergence of the National Association of Colored Women, 1895–1920?* Alexandria, VA: Alexander Street Press.

DuBose-Simons, Carla J. (2013). "The 'Silent Arrival': The Second-Wave of the Great Migration and its Affects on Black New York, 1940–1950." Ph.D. dissertation, City University of New York.

Dudziak, Mary L. (2011). *Cold War Civil Rights: Race and the Image of American Democracy.* Princeton: Princeton University Press

Draper, Alan. (1994). *Conflict of Interests: Organized Labor and the Civil Rights Movement in the South, 1954–1968.* Ithaca, NY: ILR Press.

Du Bois, W.E.B. (1899). *The Philadelphia Negro: A Social Study.* Philadelphia: University of Pennsylvania Press.

___. (1903a). *The Negro Church* Atlanta University Press.

___. (1903b). *The Souls of Black Folk: Essays and Sketches.* Chicago: A.C. McClurg.

___. (1910). "The Souls of White Folk." *Independent* 69 (August 18), 339–342.

___. (1917). "Of the Culture of White Folk." *Journal of International Relations* 7 (April), 434–447.

___. (1920). *Darkwater: Voices From Within the Veil.* New York: Harcourt, Brace and Howe.

___. (1924). *The Gift of Black Folk: The Negroes in the Making of America.* Boston: Stratford.

___. (1939). *Black Folk Then and Now: An Essay in the History and Sociology of the Negro Race.* New York: Henry Holt.

___. (1935). *Black Reconstruction in America, 1860–1880.* New York: Harcourt, Brace & Co.

___. (1970). *The Gift of Black Folk: The Negro in the Making of America.* New York: Simon & Schuster.

___. (1971). *The Seventh Son: The Thought and Writings of W.E.B. Du Bois,* (Volume 2, Julius Lester, Ed.). New York: Vintage Books.

___. (1978). *W.E.B. Du Bois on Sociology and the Black Community* (Dan S. Green and Edwin D. Driver, Eds.). Chicago: University of Chicago Press.

___. (1980). *Prayers for Dark People* (Herbert Aptheker, Ed.). Amherst: University of Massachusetts Press.

___. (1982). *Writings in Periodicals Edited by Others* (Volume 1, Herbert Aptheker, Ed.). Millwood, NY: Kraus-Thomson.

___. (1985). *Against Racism: Unpublished Essays, Papers, Addresses, 1887–1961* (Herbert Aptheker, Ed.). Amherst, MA: University of Massachusetts Press.

___. (2000). *Du Bois on Religion* (Phil Zuckerman, Ed.). Walnut Creek: Altamira.

Dunaway, David K. (2008). *How Can I Keep from Singing?: The Ballad of Pete Seeger.* New York: Villard.

Dunson, Josh. (1965). *Freedom in the Air: Song Movements of the Sixties.* New York: International Publishers.

Dupont, Carolyn R. (2013). *Mississippi Praying: Southern White Evangelicals and the Civil Rights Movement, 1945–1975.* New York: New York University Press.

Dwyer, Owen J., and Alderman, Derek H. (2008). *Civil Rights Memorials and the Geography of Memory.* Athens: University of Georgia Press.

Dyson, Michael Eric. (1997). *Between God and Gangsta Rap : Bearing Witness to Black Culture.* Oxford: Oxford University Press.

___. (2002). *Holler If You Hear Me : Searching for Tupac Shakur.* New York: Basic Civitas.

Eagles, Charles W. (1986). *The Civil Rights Movement in America: Essays.* Jackson: University Press of Mississippi.

Early, Gerald L. (2004). *One Nation Under a Groove: Motown and American Culture.* Ann Arbor: University of Michigan Press.

Eastman, Ralph. (1989). "Central Avenue Blues: The Making of Los Angeles Rhythm and Blues, 1942–1947." *Black Music Research Journal* 9 (1), 19–33.

Edgerton, Gary R. (2007). *The Columbia History of American Television*. New York: Columbia University Press.

Edgerton, Robert B. (2001). *Hidden Heroism: Black Soldiers in America's Wars*. Boulder, CO: Westview Press.

Edmonds, Ben. (2001). *Marvin Gaye: What's Going On and the Last Days of the Motown Sound*. Edinburgh: Mojo Books.

Edwards, Korie L. (2009). "Race, Religion, and Worship: Are Contemporary African American Worship Practices Distinct?" *Journal for the Scientific Study of Religion* 48 (1), 30–52.

Egendorf, Laura K. (Ed.). (2002). *Rock & Roll*. San Diego, CA: Greenhaven Press.

Egerton, John. (1994). *Speak Now Against the Day: The Generation Before the Civil Rights Movement in the South*. New York: Knopf.

Elam, Harry J., and Krasner, David. (Eds.). (2001). *African American Performance and Theater History: A Critical Reader*. Oxford: Oxford University Press.

Ellis, Sylvia. (2013). *Freedom's Pragmatist: Lyndon Johnson and Civil Rights*. Gainesville: University Press of Florida.

Ellison, Mary. (1985). "Consciousness of Poverty in Black Music." *Popular Music & Society* 10 (2), 17–46.

____. (1989). *Lyrical Protest: Black Music's Struggle Against Discrimination*. New York: Praeger.

Ellison, Ralph. (1964). *Shadow and Act*. New York: Random House.

____. (1995a). *Collected Essays of Ralph Ellison* (John F. Callahan, Ed.). New York: Modern Library.

____. (1995b). *Conversations with Ralph Ellison* (Maryemma Graham and Amritjit Singh, Eds.). Jackson: University Press of Mississippi.

____. (2001). *Living With Music: Ralph Ellison's Jazz Writings* (Robert G. O'Meally, Ed.). New York: Modern Library.

Ellison, Ralph, and Murray, Albert. (2000). *Trading Twelves: The Selected Letters of Ralph Ellison and Albert Murray* (John F. Callahan, Ed.). New York: Modern Library.

Emerson, Ken. (2005). *Always Magic in the Air: The Bomp and Brilliance of the Brill Building Era*. New York: Viking.

Ennis, Philip H. (1992). *The Seventh Stream: The Emergence of Rock & Roll in American Popular Music*. Hanover, NH: University Press of New England.

Epstein, Dena J.P. (2003). *Sinful Tunes and Spirituals: Black Folk Music to the Civil War*. Urbana: University of Illinois Press.

Escott, Colin. (1991). *Good Rockin' Tonight: Sun Records and the Birth of Rock & Roll* (with Martin Hawkins). New York: St. Martin's Press.

____. (Ed.). (1999). *All Roots Lead to Rock: Legends of Early Rock & Roll: A Bear Family Reader*. New York: Schirmer.

Eskew, Glenn T. (1997). *But for Birmingham: The Local and National Movements in the Civil Rights Struggle*. Chapel Hill: University of North Carolina Press.

Estes, Steve. (2005). *I Am a Man!: Race, Manhood, and the Civil Rights Movement*. Chapel Hill: University of North Carolina Press.

____. (2015). *Charleston in Black and White: Race and Power in the South after the Civil Rights Movement*. Chapel Hill: University of North Carolina Press.

Evans, Curtis. (2007). "W.E.B. Du Bois: Interpreting Religion and the Problem of *The Negro Church*." *Journal of the American Academy of Religion* 75 (2), 268–297.

Evans, Mike. (2007). *The Beats: From Kerouac to Kesey—An Illustrated Journey through the Beat Generation*. London: Running Press.

Ewens, Graeme. (1992). *Africa O-Ye!: A Celebration of African Music*. New York: Da Capo.

Eyerman, Ron, and Jamison, Andrew. (1991). *Social Movements: A Cognitive Approach*. University Park: Pennsylvania State University Press.

___. (1995). "Social Movements and Cultural Transformation: Popular Music in the 1960s." *Media Culture Society* 17 (3), 449–486.

___. (1998). *Music and Social Movements: Mobilizing Traditions in the Twentieth Century.* Cambridge: Cambridge University Press.

Ezra, Michael. (2013). *The Economic Civil Rights Movement: African Americans and the Struggle for Economic Power.* New York: Routledge.

Fairclough, Adam. (2008). *Race & Democracy: The Civil Rights Struggle in Louisiana, 1915–1972.* Athens: University of Georgia Press.

Fatherley, Richard W., and McFarland, David T. (2014). *The Birth of Top 40 Radio: The Storz Stations' Revolution of the 1950s and 1960s.* Jefferson, NC: McFarland & Company.

Feintuch, Burt. (1980). "A Noncommercial Black Gospel Group in Context: We Live the Life We Sing About." *Black Music Research Journal* 1, 37–50.

Feldstein, Ruth. (2013). *How It Feels to Be Free: Black Women Entertainers and the Civil Rights Movement.* Oxford: Oxford University Press.

Ferguson, Jeffrey B. (2008). *The Harlem Renaissance: A Brief History with Documents.* Boston: Bedford/St. Martin's.

Ferguson, Karen. (2002). *Black Politics in New Deal Atlanta.* Chapel Hill: University of North Carolina Press.

Ferris, William. (2009). *Give My Poor Heart Ease Voices of the Mississippi Blues.* Chapel Hill: University of North Carolina Press.

Findlay, James F. (1993). *Church People in the Struggle: The National Council of Churches and the Black Freedom Movement, 1950–1970.* Oxford: Oxford University Press.

Finkelman, Paul. (Ed.). (1992). *Lynching, Racial Violence, and Law.* New York: Garland.

Fiori, Giuseppe. (1990). *Antonio Gramsci: Life of a Revolutionary.* New York: Verso.

Fisher, Marc. (2007). *Something in the Air: Radio, Rock, and the Revolution that Shaped a Generation.* New York: Random House.

Fisher, Miles Mark. (Ed.). (1998). *Negro Slave Songs in the United States.* New York: Citadel.

Flamming, Douglas. (2005). *Bound for Freedom: Black Los Angeles in Jim Crow America.* Berkeley: University of California Press.

Fligstein, Neil. (1982). *Going North: Migration of Blacks and Whites from the South, 1900–1950.* New York: Academic Press, Inc.

Flory, Jonathan Andrew. (2006). "I Hear a Symphony: Making Music at Motown, 1959–1979." Ph.D. dissertation, University of North Carolina at Chapel Hill, Chapel Hill, NC.

Floyd, Samuel A. (1995). *The Power of Black Music: Interpreting its History from Africa to the United States.* Oxford: Oxford University Press.

Fong-Torres, Ben. (1998). *The Hits Just Keep On Coming: The History of Top 40 Radio.* San Francisco: Miller Freeman Books.

Ford, Larry. (1971). "Geographic Factors in the Origin, Evolution, and Diffusion of Rock and Roll Music." *Journal of Geography* 70 (8), 455–464.

Forman, Murray (2000). "'Represent': Race, Space and Place in Rap Music." *Popular Music* 19 (1), 65–90.

___. (2002). *The Hood Comes First: Race, Space, and Place in Rap and Hip Hop.* Middletown, CT: Wesleyan University Press.

Forney, Craig Allen. (2002). "W. E. B. Du Bois: The Spirituality of a Weary Traveler." Ph.D. dissertation, University of Chicago, Chicago, IL.

Fosl, Catherine, and K'Meyer, Tracy E. (2009). *Freedom on the Border: An Oral History of the Civil Rights Movement in Kentucky.* Lexington: University Press of Kentucky.

Foucault, Michel. (1971). *The Order of Things: An Archaeology of the Human Sciences.* New York: Pantheon.

___. (1973). *Madness and Civilization: A History of Insanity in the Age of Reason.* New York: Vintage.

___. (1974). *The Archaeology of Knowledge and the Discourse on Language.* New York: Pantheon.

___. (1977). *Language, Counter-Memory, Practice: Selected Essays and Interviews by Michel Foucault* (Donald F. Bouchard, Ed.). Ithaca: Cornell University Press.

___. (1979). *Discipline and Punish: The Birth of the Prison.* New York: Vintage.

___. (1980). *Power/Knowledge: Selected Interviews and Other Writings, 1972–1977* (Colin Gordon, Ed.). New York: Pantheon.

___. (1984). *The Foucault Reader* (Paul Rabinow, Ed.). New York: Pantheon.

___. (1988). *Politics, Philosophy, Culture: Interviews and Other Writings, 1977–1984* (Lawrence D. Kritzman, Ed.). New York: Routledge.

___. (1990a). *The History of Sexuality, Volume 1: The Will to Knowledge.* New York: Vintage.

___. (1990b). *The History of Sexuality, Volume 2: The Use of Pleasure.* New York: Vintage.

___. (1990c). *The History of Sexuality, Volume 3: The Care of the Self.* New York: Vintage.

___. (1994). *The Birth of the Clinic: An Archaeology of Medical Perception.* New York: Vintage.

___. (1996). *Foucault Live: Interviews, 1961–1984* (Sylvère Lotringer, Ed.). New York: Semiotext(e).

___. (2009). *The History of Madness in the Classical Age.* New York: Routledge.

Frame, Peter. (2007). *The Restless Generation: How Rock Music Changed the Face of 1950s Britain.* London: Rogan House.

Francese, Carl, and Sorrell, Richard S. (2001). *From Tupelo to Woodstock: Youth, Race, and Rock & Roll in America, 1954–1969.* Dubuque, IA: Kendall/Hunt.

Francis, Megan Ming. (2014). *Civil Rights and the Making of the Modern American State.* Cambridge: Cambridge University Press.

Franklin, John Hope. (1947). *From Slavery to Freedom: A History of American Negroes.* New York: Knopf.

Franklin, Sekou M. (2014). *After the Rebellion: Black Youth, Social Movement Activism, and the Post-Civil Rights Generation.* New York: New York University Press.

Franzosa, Susan D. (Ed.). (1999). *Ordinary Lessons: Girlhoods of the 1950s.* New York: Peter Lang.

Frederick, Nathaniel. (2009). "Praise God and Do Something: The Role of Black American Gospel Artists as Social Activists, 1945–1960." Ph.D. dissertation, Pennsylvania State University, University Park, State College, PA.

Freeland, Gregory (2009). "'We're a Winner': Popular Music and the Black Power Movement." *Social Movement Studies* 8 (3), 261–288.

Friedland, Michael B. (1998). *Lift Up Your Voice Like a Trumpet: White Clergy and the Civil Rights and Antiwar Movements, 1954–1973.* Chapel Hill: University of North Carolina Press.

Friedlander, Paul. (2006). *Rock & Roll: A Social History.* Boulder, CO: Westview Press.

Friedman, Douglas E., and Gribin, Anthony J. (2003). *Who Sang Our Songs?: The Official Rhythm & Blues and Doo-wop Songography.* West Long Branch, NJ: Harmony Songs Publications.

Frith, Simon. (1981). *Sound Effects: Youth, Leisure and the Politics of Rock & Roll.* New York: Pantheon.

Fuchs, Otto. (2011). *Bill Haley: The Father of Rock & Roll.* Gelnhausen, Germany: Wagner.

Fuller, Graham, and Mack, Lorrie. (Eds.). (1985). *The Motown Story.* London: Orbis.

Gallien, Louis B. (2011). "Crossing Over Jordan: Navigating the Music of Heavenly Bliss and Earthly Desire in the Lives and Careers of Three Twentieth-Century African American Holiness-Pentecostal 'Crossover' Artists." In Amos Yong and Estrelda Alexander (Eds.), *Afro-Pentecostalism: Black Pentecostal and Charismatic Christianity in History and Culture* (117–140). New York: New York University Press.

Gammond, Peter. (1975). *Scott Joplin and the Ragtime Era.* New York: St. Martin's Press.

Garb, Margaret. (2014). *Freedom's Ballot: African American Political Struggles in Chicago from Abolition to the Great Migration.* Chicago: University of Chicago Press.

Garofalo, Reebee. (1990). "Crossing Over: 1939–1989." In Jannette L. Dates and William Barlow (Eds.), *Split Image: African Americans in the Mass Media* (57–130). Washington, D.C.: Howard University Press.

___. (1992). *Rockin' the Boat: Mass Music and Mass Movements.* Boston: South End Press.

___. (2002). "Crossing Over: From Black Rhythm & Blues to White Rock & Roll." In Norman Kelley (Ed.), *R&B, Rhythm and Business: The Political Economy of Black Music* (112–137). New York: Akashic.

___. (2011). *Rockin' Out: Popular Music in the USA.* Upper Saddle River, NJ: Pearson/ Prentice Hall.

Garoian, Charles R., and Gaudelius, Yvonne. (2008). *Spectacle Pedagogy: Art, Politics, and Visual Culture.* Albany: State University of New York Press.

Garon, Paul, and Garon, Beth. (1992). *Woman with Guitar: Memphis Minnie's Blues.* New York: Da Capo Press.

Garrow, David J. (1989). *St. Augustine, Florida, 1963–1964: Mass Protest and Racial Violence.* Brooklyn: Carlson.

___. (2004). *Bearing the Cross: Martin Luther King, Jr., and the Southern Christian Leadership Conference.* New York: Perennial Classics.

Gart, Galen. (1986). *First Pressings: The History of Rhythm & Blues.* Milford, NH: Big Nickel Publications.

Gellman, Erik S. (2012). *Death Blow to Jim Crow: The National Negro Congress and the Rise of Militant Civil Rights.* Chapel Hill: University of North Carolina Press.

George, Nelson. (1985). *Where Did Our Love Go?: The Rise & Fall of the Motown Sound.* New York: St. Martin's Press.

___. (1988). *The Death of Rhythm & Blues.* New York: Pantheon Books.

___. (1989). "Rap's Tenth Birthday." *Village Voice* 24, 40.

___. (Ed.). (1990). *Stop the Violence: Overcoming Self-Destruction.* New York: Pantheon.

___. (1992). *Buppies, B-Boys, Baps & Bohos: Notes on Post-Soul Black Culture.* New York: HarperCollins.

___. (1994). *Blackface: Reflections on African Americans and the Movies.* New York: HarperCollins.

___. (1999). *Hip Hop America.* New York: Viking.

___. (2007). *Where Did Our Love Go?: The Rise and Fall of the Motown Sound.* Urbana: University of Illinois Press.

George-Warren, Holly. (Ed.). (1999). *The Rolling Stone Book of the Beats: The Beat Generation and American Culture.* New York: Hyperion.

George-Warren, Holly. (2009). *The Rock and Roll Hall of Fame: The First 25 Years—The Definitive Chronicle of Rock & Roll as Told by Its Legends.* New York: Collins Design.

Germino, Dante L. (1990). *Antonio Gramsci: Architect of a New Politics.* Baton Rouge: Louisiana State University Press.

Geschwender, James A. (1971). *The Black Revolt: The Civil Rights Movement, Ghetto Uprisings, and Separatism.* Englewood Cliffs, NJ: Prentice-Hall.

Giddings, Paula. (1984). *When and Where I Enter: The Impact of Black Women on Race and Sex in America.* New York: Morrow

Gilbert, David W. (2015). *The Product of Our Souls: Ragtime, Race, and the Birth of the Manhattan Musical Marketplace.* Chapel Hill: University of North Carolina Press.

Gilbert, James B. (1986). *A Cycle of Outrage: America's Reaction to the Juvenile Delinquent in the 1950s.* Oxford: Oxford University Press

Gilkes, Cheryl Townsend. (1996). "The Margin as the Center of a Theory of History: African American Women, Social Change, and the Sociology of W.E.B. Du Bois." In Bernard W. Bell, Emily R. Grosholz, and James B. Stewart (Eds.), *W.E.B. Du Bois: On Race and Culture.* (111–141). New York: Routledge.

___. (2000). *If It Wasn't for the Women: Black Women's Experience and Womanist Culture in Church and Community.* Maryknoll, NY: Orbis

Gill, Flora. (1975). "Economics and the Black Exodus: An Analysis of Negro Emigration from the Southern United States, 1910–1970." Ph.D. dissertation, Department ofEconomics, Stanford University, Stanford, CA.

Gillett, Charlie. (1996). *The Sound of the City: The Rise of Rock & Roll.* London: Souvenir Press.

Gillman, Susan, and Weinbaum, Alys E. (Eds.). (2007). *Next to the Color-Line: Gender, Sexuality, and W.E.B. Du Bois.* Minneapolis: University of Minnesota Press.

Gilmour, Michael J. (2005). *Call Me the Seeker: Listening to Religion in Popular Music.* New York: Bloomsbury Publishing.

Gilson, Chris F., and Travis, Carolyn. (Directors). (2012). *Airplay: The Rise and Fall of Rock Radio.* Renton, WA: Topics Entertainment.

Ginwright, Shawn A. (2006). "Toward a Politics of Relevance: Race, Resistance and African American Youth Activism." *Youth Activism: A Web Forum Organized by the Social Science Research Council.* http://ya.ssrc.org/african/Ginwright/.

Ginwright, Shawn and James, Taj. (2002). "From Assets to Agents of Change: Social Justice, Organizing, and Youth Development." *New Directions for Youth Development* 96 (Winter), 27–46.

Glasgow, Douglas G. (1981). *The Black Underclass: Poverty, Unemployment, and Entrapment of Ghetto Youth.* New York: Vintage Books.

Glasrud, Bruce A., and Pitre, Merline. (Eds.). (2013). *Southern Black Women in the Modern Civil Rights Movement.* College Station: Texas A&M University Press.

Glaude, Eddie S. (2000). *Exodus!: Religion, Race, and Nation in Early Nineteenth-Century Black America.* Chicago: University of Chicago Press.

Goff, James R. (2002). *Close Harmony: A History of Southern Gospel.* Chapel Hill: University of North Carolina Press.

Goldberg, Marv. (1998). *More Than Words Can Say: The Ink Spots and Their Music.* Lanham, MD: Scarecrow Press.

Goldman, Vivien. (1999). *Black Chord: Visions of the Groove—Connections Between Afro-Beats, Rhythm & Blues, Hip Hop, and More* (with photographs by David Corio). New York: Universe.

Goldsby, Jacqueline Denise. (2006). *A Spectacular Secret: Lynching in American Life and Literature.* Chicago: University of Chicago Press.

Gomez, Michael A. (1998). *Exchanging Our Country Marks: The Transformation of African Identities in the Colonial and Antebellum South.* Chapel Hill: University of North Carolina Press.

Gonda, Jeffrey D. (2015). *Unjust Deeds: The Restrictive Covenant Cases and the Making of the Civil Rights Movement.* Chapel Hill: The University of North Carolina Press.

Gonzales-Day, Ken. (2006). *Lynching in the West, 1850–1935.* Durham: Duke University Press.

Goodwin, Jeff, and Jasper, James M. (Eds.). (2003). *Rethinking Social Movements: Structure, Meaning, and Emotion.* Lanham, MD: Rowman & Littlefield.

Goosman, Stuart L. (1992). "The Social and Cultural Organization of Black Group Vocal Harmony in Washington, D.C. and Baltimore, Maryland, 1945–1960." Ph.D. dissertation, University of Washington, Seattle, WA.

___. (1997). "The Black Authentic: Structure, Style, and Values in Group Harmony." *Black Music Research Journal* 17 (1), 81–99.

___. (2005). *Group Harmony: The Black Urban Roots of Rhythm & Blues.* Philadelphia: University of Pennsylvania Press.

Gordy, Berry. (1994). *To be Loved: The Music, the Magic, the Memories of Motown: An Autobiography.* New York: Warner Books.

Gore, Dayo F., Theoharis, Jeanne, and Woodard, Komozi. (Eds.). (2009). *Want to Start a Revolution?: Radical Women in the Black Freedom Struggle.* New York: New York University Press.

Goreau, Laurraine. (1975). *Just Mahalia, Baby!: The Mahalia Jackson Story.* Waco, TX: Word Books.

Gottlieb, Peter. (1987). *Making Their Own Way: Southern Blacks' Migration to Pittsburgh, 1916–1930.* Urbana: University of Illinois Press.

Gourse, Leslie. (Ed.). (1997). *The Billie Holiday Companion: Seven Decades of Commentary.* New York: Schirmer Books.

Govenar, Alan B., and Joseph, Benny. (2004). *The Early Years of Rhythm & Blues*. Houston: Rice University Press.

Gramsci, Antonio. (1971). *Selections from the Prison Notebooks of Antonio Gramsci* (Quintin Hoare and Geoffrey Nowell-Smith, Eds.). New York: International.

___. (1977). *Selections from the Political Writings, 1910–1920* (Quintin Hoare, Ed.). New York: International.

___. (1978). *Selections from the Political Writings, 1921–1926* (Quintin Hoare, Ed.). New York: International.

___. (1985). *Selections from the Cultural Writings*. (David Forgacs and Geoffrey Nowell-

___. (1995). *Antonio Gramsci: Further Selections from the Prison Notebooks* (Derek Boothman, Ed). Minneapolis: University of Minnesota Press.

___. (2000). *The Antonio Gramsci Reader: Selected Writings, 1916–1935* (David Forgacs, Ed.). New York: New York University Press.

Grant, Jacquelyn. (1989). *White Women's Christ and Black Women's Jesus: Feminist Christology and Womanist Response*. Atlanta: Scholars Press.

Gray, Herman. (2005). *Cultural Moves: African Americans and the Politics of Representation*. Berkeley: University of California Press.

Greene, Christina. (2005). *Our Separate Ways: Women and the Black Freedom Movement in Durham, North Carolina*. Chapel Hill: University of North Carolina Press.

Greene, Doyle. (2014). *The Rock Cover Song: Culture, History, Politics*. Jefferson, NC: McFarland.

Gregory, Hugh. (1998). *The Real Rhythm And Blues*. New York: Sterling.

Gregory, James N. (2005). *The Southern Diaspora: How the Great Migrations of Black and White Southerners Transformed America*. Chapel Hill: University of North Carolina Press.

Gribin, Anthony J., and Schiff, Matthew M. (1992). *Doo-Wop: The Forgotten Third of Rock & Roll*. Iola, WI: Krause Publications.

Griffin, Farah Jasmine. (2000). "Black Feminists and W.E.B. Du Bois: Respectability, Protection, and Beyond." *Annals of the American Academy of Politicaland Social Science* 568 (March), 28–40.

___. (2001). *If You Can't Be Free, Be a Mystery: In Search of Billie Holiday*. New York: Free Press.

___. (2013). *Harlem Nocturne: Women Artists and Progressive Politics During World War II*. New York: Basic Civitas.

Groh, George W. (1972). *The Black Migration: The Journey to Urban America.* New York: Weybright & Talley.

Groia, Philip. (1983). *They All Sang on the Corner: A Second Look at New York City's Rhythm & Blues Vocal Groups*. West Hempstead, NY: P. Dee Enterprises.

Grossman, James R. (1991). *Land of Hope: Chicago, Black Southerners, and the Great Migration*. Chicago: University of Chicago Press.

Gulla, Bob. (Ed.). (2008). *Icons of R&B and Soul: An Encyclopedia of the Artists Who Revolutionized Rhythm* (2 Vols.). Westport, CT: Greenwood.

Gunaratnam, Yasmin. (2003). *Researching Race and Ethnicity: Methods, Knowledge, and Power*. Thousand Oaks, CA: Sage.

Guralnick, Peter. (1986). *Sweet Soul Music: Rhythm & Blues and the Southern Dream of Freedom*. New York: Harper & Row.

___. (1989). *Lost Highway: Journeys & Arrivals of American Musicians.* New York: Harper & Row.

___. (1994). *Last Train to Memphis: The Rise of Elvis Presley*. New York: Little, Brown & Company.

___. (1999). *Feel Like Going Home: Portraits in Blues & Rock & Roll*. Boston: Little Brown.

___. (2000). *Careless Love: The Unmaking of Elvis Presley*. New York: Little, Brown & Company.

___. (2015). *Sam Phillips: The Man Who Invented Rock & Roll*. New York: Little, Brown & Company.

Guralnick, Peter, and Jorgensen, Ernst. (1999). *Elvis Day by Day: The Definitive Record of His Life and Music*. New York: Ballantine Books.

Guy-Sheftall, Beverly. (1990). *Daughters of Sorrow: Attitudes Toward Black Women, 1880–1920*. Brooklyn, NY: Carlson.

Hahn, Steven. (2003). *A Nation Under Our Feet: Black Political Struggles in the Rural South, from Slavery to the Great Migration*. Cambridge: Harvard University Press.

Hale, Jon N. (2016). *The Freedom Schools: Student Activists in the Mississippi Civil Rights Movement*. New York: Columbia University Press.

Haley, John W., and Von Hoelle, John J. (1991). *Sound and Glory: The Incredible Story of Bill Haley, the Father of Rock & Roll and the Music That Shook the World*. Wilmington, DE: Dyne-American Publishing.

Hall, Kermit L., and Urofsky, Melvin I. (2011). *New York Times v. Sullivan: Civil Rights, Libel Law, and the Free Press*. Lawrence: University Press of Kansas.

Hall, Mitchell K. (2014). *The Emergence of Rock & Roll: Music and the Rise of American Youth Culture*. New York: Routledge.

Hall, Simon. (2005). *Peace and Freedom: The Civil Rights and Antiwar Movements in the 1960s*. Philadelphia: University of Pennsylvania Press.

Halpern, Rick. (1997). *Down on the Killing Floor: Black and White Workers in Chicago's Packinghouses, 1904–1954*. Urbana: University of Illinois Press.

Halpern, Rick, and Horowitz, Roger. (1996). *Meatpackers: An Oral History of Black Packinghouse Workers and Their Struggle for Racial and Economic Equality*. New York: Twayne Publishers.

Hamlin, Françoise N. (2012). *Crossroads at Clarksdale: The Black Freedom Struggle in the Mississippi Delta after World War II*. Chapel Hill: University of North Carolina Press.

Hampton, Henry, and Fayer, Steve. (2011). *Voices of Freedom: An Oral History of the Civil Rights Movement from the 1950s Through the 1980s*. New York: Bantam.

Hancock, Ange-Marie. (2005). "W.E.B. Du Bois: Intellectual Forefather of Intersectionality?" *Souls* 7 (3–4), 74–84.

Hannerz, Ulf. (1969). *Soulside: Inquiries into Ghetto Culture and Community*. New York: Columbia University Press.

Hannusch, Jeff. (1985). *I Hear You Knockin': The Sound of New Orleans Rhythm & Blues*. Ville Platte, LA: Swallow Publications.

___. (2001). *The Soul of New Orleans: A Legacy of Rhythm & Blues*. Ville Platte, LA: Swallow Publications.

Hanson, Joyce A. (2011). *Rosa Parks: A Biography*. Santa Barbara, CA: Greenwood Press.

Harding, Vincent. (1981). *There Is A River: The Black Struggle for Freedom in America*. New York: Harcourt Brace Jovanovich.

Harer, Ingeborg. (2015). "Ragtime." In Mellonee V. Burnim and Portia K. Maultsby (Eds.), *African American Music: An Introduction* (2nd Edition) (97–118). New York: Routledge.

Harper, Kimberly. (2010). *White Man's Heaven: The Lynching and Expulsion of Blacks in the Southern Ozarks, 1894–1909*. Fayetteville: University of Arkansas Press.

Harris, Fredrick C. (1999). *Something Within: Religion in African-American Political Activism*. Oxford: Oxford University Press.

Harris, Laurie Lanzen. (2012). *The Great Migration North, 1910–1970*. Detroit: Omnigraphics, Inc.

Harris, Michael W. (1992). *The Rise of Gospel Blues: The Music of Thomas Andrew Dorsey in the Urban Church*. New York: Oxford University Press.

Harris, Trudier. (1984). *Exorcising Blackness: Historical and Literary Lynching and Burning Rituals*. Bloomington: Indiana University Press.

Harris, William Hamilton. (1977). *Keeping the Faith: A. Philip Randolph, Milton P. Webster, and the Brotherhood of Sleeping Car Porters, 1925–1937*. Urbana: University of Illinois Press.

Harrison, Alferdteen. (Ed.). (1991). *Black Exodus: The Great Migration from the American South*. Jackson: University Press of Mississippi.

Harrison, Daphne Duval. (1988). *Black Pearls: Blues Queens of the 1920s*. New Brunswick: Rutgers University Press.

___. (2006). "Blues Women." In Mellonee V. Burnim and Portia K. Maultsby (Eds.), *African American Music: An Introduction* (528–540). New York: Routledge.

Hartman, Kent. (2012). *The Wrecking Crew: The Inside Story of Rock & Roll's Best-Kept Secret*. New York: St. Martin's Press.

Harvey, Louis-Charles. (1986). "Black Gospel Music and Black Theology." *Journal of Religious Thought* 43 (2), 19–37.

Haskins, James. (1978). *Scott Joplin: The Man Who Made Ragtime*. New York: Doubleday.

Hasse, John Edward. (1985). *Ragtime: Its History, Composers, and Music*. New York: Schirmer.

Hattery, Angela J., and Smith, Earl. (2005). "William Edward Burghardt Du Bois and the Concepts of Race, Class, and Gender." *Sociation Today* 3 (1). Online at: http://www.ncsociology.org/sociationtoday/v31/smith.htm.

Haynes, Jeffrey. (1997). *Democracy and Civil Society in the Third World: Politics and New Political Movements*. Malden, MA: Blackwell.

Heble, Ajay, and Fischlin, Daniel. (Eds.). (2003). *Rebel Musics: Human Rights, Resistant Sounds, and the Politics of Music-making*. Montréal: Black Rose Books.

Heilbut, Anthony. (1982). "The Secularization of Black Gospel Music." In William Ferris and Mary L. Hart (Eds.), *Folk Music and Modern Sound*. Jackson: University Press of Mississippi.

___. (1997). *The Gospel Sound: Good News and Bad Times*. New York: Limelight.

Helander, Brock. (1998). *The Rockin' '50s: The People Who Made the Music*. New York: Schemer Books.

Helper, Laura. (1996). "Whole Lot of Shakin' Going On!: An Ethnography of Race Relations and Crossover Audiences for Rhythm & Blues and Rock & Roll in 1950s Memphis." Ph.D. dissertation, Rice University, Houston, TX.

Henderson, David. (2008). *'Scuse Me While I Kiss the Sky: Jimi Hendrix: Voodoo Child*. New York: Atria.

Hendricks, Wanda A. (1998). *Gender, Race, and Politics in the Midwest: Black Clubwomen in Illinois*. Bloomington: Indiana University Press.

Hendrix, Jimi. (2012). *Hendrix on Hendrix: Interviews and Encounters with Jimi Hendrix* (Steven Roby, Ed.). Chicago: Chicago Review Press.

___. (2013). *Starting At Zero: His Own Story*. New York: Bloomsbury.

Hennessey, Thomas J. (1994). *From Jazz to Swing: African American Jazz Musicians and Their Music, 1890–1935*. Detroit: Wayne State University Press.

Henri, Florette. (1975). *Black Migration: Movement North, 1900–1920*. Garden City, NY: Anchor Press.

Herbert, Sharnine S. (2000). "Rhythm & Blues, 1968–1972: An African-centered Rhetorical Analysis." Ph.D. dissertation, Howard University, Washington, D.C.

Hervieux, Linda. (2015). *Forgotten: The Untold Story of D-Day's Black Heroes, at Home and at War*. New York: Harper.

Higginbotham, Evelyn B. (1993). *Righteous Discontent: The Women's Movement in the Black Baptist Church, 1880–1920*. Cambridge: Harvard University Press.

Hildebrand, Lee. (1994). *Stars of Soul and Rhythm & Blues: Top Recording Artists and Show-Stopping Performers, from Memphis and Motown to Now*. New York: Billboard Books.

Hilfiker, David. (2002). *Urban Injustice: How Ghettos Happen*. New York: Seven Stories Press.

Hill, Lance E. (2004). *The Deacons for Defense: Armed Resistance and the Civil Rights Movement*. Chapel Hill: University of North Carolina Press.

Hillsman, Joan R. (1983). *The Progress of Gospel Music: From Spirituals to Contemporary Gospel*. New York: Vantage Press.

___. (1990). *Gospel Music: An African American Art Form*. Washington, D.C.: Middle Atlantic Regional Press.

Hine, Darlene Clark. (1997). *Hine Sight: Black Women and the Re-Construction of American History*. Indianapolis: Indiana University Press.

Hine, Darlene Clark, Hine, William C., and Harrold, Stanley. (2010). *The African American Odyssey Combined Volume (5th Edition)*. Boston: Pearson/Prentice Hall

Hine, Darlene Clark, and Thompson, Kathleen. (1998). *A Shining Thread of Hope: The History of Black Women in America*. New York: Broadway Books.

Hinson, Glenn. (2000). *Fire in My Bones: Transcendence and the Holy Spirit in African American Gospel*. Philadelphia: University of Pennsylvania Press.

Hirshey, Gerri. (1984). *Nowhere to Run: The Story of Soul Music*. New York: Times Books.

Hoare, George, and Sperber, Nathan. (2015). *An Introduction to Antonio Gramsci: His Life, Thought, and Legacy*. London: Bloomsbury.

Hogan, Wesley C. (2007). *Many Minds, One Heart: SNCC's Dream for a New America*. Chapel Hill: University of North Carolina Press.

Holley, Donald. (2000). *The Second Great Emancipation: The Mechanical Cotton Picker, Black Migration, and How They Shaped the Modern South*. Fayetteville: University of Arkansas.

Holloway, Joseph E. (Ed.). (1991). *Africanisms in American Culture*. Bloomington: Indiana University Press.

Holsaert, Faith S., Noonan, Martha P. N., and Richardson, Judy. (Eds.). (2010). *Hands on the Freedom Plow: Personal Accounts by Women in SNCC*. Urbana: University of Illinois Press.

Holub, Renate. (1992). *Antonio Gramsci: Beyond Marxism and Postmodernism*. New York: Routledge.

Hope, Richard O. (1979). *Racial Strife in the U.S. Military: Toward the Elimination of Discrimination*. New York: Praeger.

Horsfall, Sara, Meij, Jan-Martijn, and Probstfield, Meghan D. (Eds.). (2013). *Music Sociology: Examining the Role of Music in Social Life*. Boulder, CO: Paradigm Publishers.

Houck, Davis W., and Dixon, David E. (Eds.). (2006). *Rhetoric, Religion, and the Civil Rights Movement, 1954–1965* (Volume 1). Waco, TX: Baylor University Press.

Houck, Davis W., and Dixon, David E. (Eds.). (2009). *Women and the Civil Rights Movement, 1954–1965*. Jackson: University Press of Mississippi.

Houck, Davis W., and Dixon, David E. (Eds.). (2014). *Rhetoric, Religion, and the Civil Rights Movement, 1954–1965* (Volume 2). Waco, TX: Baylor University Press.

Howard-Pitney, David. (2004). *Martin Luther King, Malcolm X, and the Civil Rights Struggle of the 1950s and 1960s: A Brief History with Documents*. Boston: Bedford/St. Martin's.

Hufford, Don. (1997). "The Religious Thought of W.E.B. Du Bois." *Journal of Religious Thought* 53–54 (2-1), 73–94.

Hullet, John, and Carmichael, Stokely. (1966). *The Black Panther Party: Speech by John Hulett, Interview with Stokely Carmichael, Report from Lowndes County*. New York: Merit Publishers.

Hunt, Scott A., and Benford, Robert D. (2004). "Collective Identity, Solidarity, and Commitment." In David A. Snow, Sarah Anne Soule, and Hanspeter Kriesi (Eds.), *The Blackwell Companion to Social Movements* (433–457). Malden, MA: Blackwell.

Hunter, Erika. (2006). *Stokely Carmichael*. Toledo, OH: Great Neck Publishing.

Hunter, Marcus Anthony. (2010). "The Nightly Round: Space, Social Capital, and Urban Black Nightlife." *City and Community* 9 (2), 165–186.

Huntley, Horace, and Montgomery, David. (2004). *Black Workers' Struggle for Equality in Birmingham*. Urbana: University of Illinois Press.

Ianniello, Lynne. (1965). *Milestones Along the March: Twelve Historic Civil Rights Documents, from World War II to Selma*. New York: F.A. Praeger.

Ifill, Sherrilyn A. (2007). *On the Courthouse Lawn: Confronting the Legacy of Lynching in the Twenty-First Century*. Boston: Beacon Press.

Isserman, Maurice and Kazin, Michael. (2015). *America Divided: The Civil War of the 1960s*. Oxford: Oxford University Press.

Jackson, Buzzy. (2005). *A Bad Woman Feeling Good: Blues and the Women Who Sing Them.* New York: Norton.

Jackson, Jerma A. (1995). "Testifying at the Cross: Thomas Andrew Dorsey, Sister Rosetta Tharpe, and the Politics of African American Sacred and Secular Music." Ph.D. dissertation, Rutgers University, New Brunswick, NJ.

___. (2004). *Singing in My Soul: Black Gospel Music in a Secular Age.* Chapel Hill: University of North Carolina Press.

Jackson, John A. (1991). *Big Beat Heat: Alan Freed and the Early Years of Rock & Roll.* New York: Schemer.

___. (1997). *American Bandstand: Dick Clark and the Making of a Rock & Roll Empire.* Oxford: Oxford University Press

___. (2007). *The Alan Freed Story: The Early Years Of Rock & Roll.* New York: Collectables Press.

Jackson, Joyce Marie. (2015). "Quartets: Jubilee to Gospel." In Mellonee V. Burnim and Portia K. Maultsby (Eds.), *African American Music: An Introduction* (2nd Edition) (75–96). New York: Routledge.

Jackson, Mahalia. (1966). *Movin' On Up: The Warmly Personal Story of America's Favorite Gospel Singer* (with Evan McLeod Wylie). New York: Hawthorn Books.

Jackson, Oscar A. (1995). *Bronzeville: A History of Chicago Rhythm & Blues.* Chicago: Heno.

Jaji, Tsitsi E. (2014). *Africa in Stereo: Modernism, Music, and Pan-African Solidarity.* Oxford: Oxford University Press.

Jamerson, James. (1989). *Standing in the Shadows of Motown: The Life and Music of Legendary Bassist James Jameson.* Milwaukee: Hal Leonard Publishing.

James, Etta. (1995). *Rage to Survive: The Etta James story* (with David Ritz). New York: Villard Books.

James, Joy A. (1996). "The Profeminist Politics of W.E.B. Du Bois, with Respects to Anna Julia Cooper and Ida B. Wells Barnett." In Bernard W. Bell, Emily R. Grosholz, and James B. Stewart (Eds.), *W.E.B. Du Bois: On Race and Culture.* (141–161). New York: Routledge.

___. (1997). *Transcending the Talented Tenth: Black Leaders and American Intellectuals.* New York: Routledge.

James, Rawn. (2013). *The Double-V: How Wars, Protest, and Harry Truman Desegregated America's Military.* New York: Bloomsbury Press.

Jasen, David A. (2007). *Ragtime: An Encyclopedia, Discography, and Sheetography.* New York: Routledge.

Jasen, David A., and Jones, Gene. (2000). *That American Rag: The Story of Ragtime from Coast to Coast.* New York: Schirmer Books.

___. (2002). *Black Bottom Stomp: Eight Masters of Ragtime and Early Jazz.* New York: Routledge.

Jasen, David A., and Tichenor, Trebor J. (1978). *Rags and Ragtime: A Musical History.* New York: Seabury Press.

Jaynes, Gerald David. (1986). *Branches Without Roots: Genesis of the Black Working-Class in the American South, 1862–1882.* Oxford: Oxford University Press.

Jefferson, Robert F. (2008). *Fighting for Hope: African American Troops of the 93rd Infantry Division in World War II and Postwar America.* Baltimore: Johns Hopkins University Press.

Jeffries, Hasan Kwame. (2009). *Bloody Lowndes: Civil Rights and Black Power in Alabama's Black Belt.* New York: New York University Press.

Jenkins, Henry, McPherson, Tara, and Shattuc, Jane. (Eds.). (2002). *Hop on Pop: The Politics and Pleasures of Popular Culture.* Durham: Duke University Press.

Jenkins, Maude T. (1984). "The History of the Black Women's Club Movement in America." Ed.D. dissertation, Teachers College, Columbia University, New York, NY.

Johnson, Brain L. (2008). *W.E.B. Du Bois: Toward Agnosticism, 1868–1934.* Lanham, MD: Rowman and Littlefield.

Johnson, Daniel M., and Campbell, Rex R. (1981). *Black Migration in America: A Social Demographic History*. Durham: Duke University Press.

Johnson, Idella Lulamae. (2009). "Development of the African American Gospel Piano Style (1926–1960): A Socio-Musical Analysis of Arizona Dranes and Thomas A. Dorsey." Ph.D. dissertation, University of Pittsburgh, Pittsburgh, PA.

Johnson, Daniel M., and Campbell, Rex R. (1981). *Black Migration in America: A Social Demographic History*. Durham: Duke University Press.

Johnson, James Weldon, and Johnson, J. Rosamond. (Eds.). (2002). *The Books of the American Negro Spirituals*. New York: Da Capo Press.

Johnson, Joan Marie. (2004). *Southern Ladies, New Women: Race, Region, and Clubwomen in South Carolina, 1890–1930*. Gainesville: University Press of Florida.

Johnson, Ronna, and Grace, Nancy. (Eds.). (2002). *Girls Who Wore Black: Women Writing the Beat Generation*. New Brunswick: Rutgers University Press.

Johnson, Sylvester A. (2015). *African American Religions, 1500–2000: Colonialism, Democracy, and Freedom*. Cambridge: Cambridge University Press.

Johnson, Terrence L. (2012). *Tragic Soul-Life: W.E.B. Du Bois and the Moral Crisis Facing American Democracy*. Oxford: Oxford University Press.

Jones, Arthur C. (1993). *Wade in the Water: The Wisdom of the Spirituals*. Maryknoll, NY: Orbis Books.

Jones, Ebony Elizabeth. (2008). "Motown and the Movement." M.A. thesis, University of Toledo, Toledo, OH.

Jones, Ferdinand, and Jones, Arthur C. (2001). *The Triumph of the Soul: Cultural and Psychological Aspects of African American Music*. Westport, CT: Praeger.

Jones, Nikki. (2010). *Between Good and Ghetto: African American Girls and Inner-City Violence*. New Brunswick: Rutgers University Press.

Jones, Stacy L.H. (2007). *Torch Singing: Performing Resistance and Desire from Billie Holiday to Edith Piaf*. Lanham, MD: AltaMira Press.

Jones, Steven J. (2006). *Antonio Gramsci*. New York: Routledge.

Jones, Thomas Frederick. (1973). "A Rhetorical Study of Black Songs: 1860–1930." M.A. thesis, University of Georgia, Athens, GA.

Jones-Branch, Cherisse. (2014). *Crossing the Line: Women's Interracial Activism in South Carolina during and after World War II*. Gainesville: University Press of Florida.

Jorgensen, Ernst. (1998). *Elvis Presley: A Life In Music*. New York: St. Martin's Press.

Joseph, Peniel E. (Ed.). (2006a). *Black Power Movement: Rethinking the Civil Rights-Black Power Era*. New York: Routledge.

___. (2006b). *Waiting 'Til the Midnight Hour: A Narrative History of Black Power in America*. New York: Henry Holt.

___. (2014). *Stokely: A Life*. New York: Basic Civitas.

Kahn, Jonathon S. (2009). *The Divine Discontent: The Religious Imagination of W.E.B. Du Bois*. Oxford: Oxford University Press.

Kalil, Timothy M. (1993). "The Role of the Great Migration of African Americans to Chicago in the Development of Traditional Black Gospel Piano by Thomas A. Dorsey, circa 1930." Ph.D. dissertation, Kent State University, Kent, OH.

___. (2000). "Thomas A. Dorsey and the Development and Diffusion of Traditional Black Gospel Piano." In Michael Saffle (Ed.), *Perspectives on American Music, 1900–1950* (171–191). New York: Garland.

Kallen, Stuart A. (2000). *The 1950s*. San Diego, CA: Greenhaven Press.

Kamin, Jonathan Liff. (1975). "Rhythm & Blues in White America: Rock & Roll as Acculturation and Perceptual Learning." Ph.D. dissertation, Princeton University, Princeton, NJ.

Kaplan, Max. (1993). *Barbershopping: Musical and Social Harmony*. Rutherford, NJ: Fairleigh Dickinson University Press.

Katagiri, Yasuhiro. (2014). *Black Freedom, White Resistance, and Red Menace: Civil Rights and Anticommunism in the Jim Crow South*. Baton Rouge: Louisiana State University Press.

Katz, Bernard. (1969). *The Social Implications of Early Negro Music in the United States.* New York: Arno Press.

Keck, George R., and Martin, Sherrill V. (Eds.). (1988). *Feel the Spirit: Studies in Nineteenth-Century Afro-American Music.* New York: Greenwood Press.

Kelley, Norman. (2002). *R&B, Rhythm and Business: The Political Economy of Black Music.* New York: Akashic.

Kelley, Robin D.G. (1994). *Race Rebels: Culture, Politics, and the Black Working-Class.* New York: Free Press.

___. (1997). *Yo' Mama's Disfunktional!: Fighting the Culture Wars in Urban America.* Boston: Beacon.

Kelley, Robin D.G. and Lewis, Earl. (Eds.). (2000). *To Make Our World Anew: A History of African Americans.* Oxford: Oxford University Press.

Kelly, Brian. (2001). *Race, Class, and Power in the Alabama Coalfields, 1908–1921.* Urbana: University of Illinois Press.

Kelly, Christine A. (2001). *Tangled Up in Red, White, and Blue: New Social Movements in America.* Lanham, MD: Rowman & Littlefield.

Kemp, Kathryn B. (2011). *Make a Joyful Noise!: A Brief History of Gospel Music Ministry in America.* Chicago: Joyful Noise Press.

___. (2015). *Anointed to Sing the Gospel: The Levitical Legacy of Thomas A. Dorsey.* Chicago: Joyful Noise Press.

Kempton, Arthur. (2003). *Boogaloo: The Quintessence of American Popular Music.* New York: Pantheon Books.

Kendi, Ibram X. (2012). *The Black Campus Movement: Black Students and the Racial Reconstitution of Higher Education, 1965–1972.* New York: Palgrave Macmillan.

Keogh, Pamela C. (2004). *Elvis Presley: The Man. The Life. The Legend.* New York: Atria.

Kerkering, Jack. (2001). *"'Of Me and of Mine': The Music of Racial Identity in Whitman and Lanier, Dvorak and Du Bois."* *American Literature* 73 (1), 147–184.

Kersten, Andrew Edmund. (2007). *A. Philip Randolph: A Life in the Vanguard.* Lanham, MD: Rowman & Littlefield.

Kersten, Andrew E., and Lang, Clarence. (Eds.). (2013). *Reframing Randolph: Labor, Black Freedom, and the Legacies of A. Philip Randolph.* New York: New York University Press.

Kimbrough, Natalie. (2007). *Equality or Discrimination?: African Americans in the U.S. Military during the Vietnam War.* Lanham, MD: University Press of America.

Kinchen, Shirletta J. (2015). *Black Power in the Bluff City: African American Youth and Student Activism in Memphis, 1965–1975.* Knoxville: University of Tennessee Press.

King, Martin Luther. (1958). *Stride Toward Freedom: The Montgomery Story.* New York: Harper & Row.

___. (1964). *Why We Can't Wait.* New York: Harper & Row.

___. (1986). *A Testament of Hope: The Essential Writings of Martin Luther King, Jr.* (James Melvin Washington, Ed.). San Francisco: Harper & Row.

___. (1992). *I Have a Dream: Writings and Speeches That Changed the World* (James Melvin Washington, Ed.). San Francisco: Harper.

___. (1998). *The Autobiography of Martin Luther King, Jr.* (Claiborne Carson, Ed.). New York: Warner Books.

___. (2001). *A Call to Conscience: The Landmark Speeches of Dr. Martin Luther King, Jr.* (Clayborne Carson and Kris Shepard, Eds.). New York: Warner Books.

Kirby, David. (2009). *Little Richard: The Birth of Rock & Roll.* New York: Continuum.

Klarman, Michael J. (2007). *Brown v. Board of Education and the Civil Rights Movement.* Oxford: Oxford University Press.

Knight, Brenda. (1998). *Women of the Beat Generation: The Writers, Artists and Muses at the Heart of a Revolution.* Berkeley, CA: Conari Press

Knight, Gladys. (1997). *Between Each Line of Pain and Glory: My Life Story.* New York: Hyperion.

Knowles, Christopher. (2010). *The Secret History of Rock & Roll: The Mysterious Roots of Modern Music.* Berkeley, CA: Viva Editions.

Knupfer, Anne Meis. (1996). *Toward a Tender Humanity and a Nobler Womanhood: African American Women's Clubs in Turn-of-the-Century Chicago.* New York: New York University Press.

___. (2006). *The Chicago Black Renaissance and Women's Activism.* Urbana: University of Illinois Press.

Koch, Stephen. (2014). *Louis Jordan: Son of Arkansas, Father of R&B.* Charleston, SC: History Press.

Kochman, Thomas. (1972). *Rappin' and Stylin' Out: Communication in Urban Black America.* Urbana: University of Illinois Press.

Kohl, Herbert R. (2005). *She Would Not Be Moved: How We Tell the Story of Rosa Parks and the Montgomery Bus Boycott.* New York: New Press.

Kot, Greg. (2014). *I'll Take You There: Mavis Staples, the Staple Singers, and the Music That Shaped the Civil Rights Era.* New York: Scribner.

Kotarba, Joseph A. (2013). *Baby Boomer Rock & Roll Fans: The Music Never Ends.* Lanham, MD: Scarecrow Press.

Kovach, Margaret. (2009). *Indigenous Methodologies: Characteristics, Conversations and Contexts.* Toronto: University of Toronto Press.

Kruse, Kevin M., and Tuck, Stephen G.N. (Eds.). (2012). *Fog of War: The Second World War and the Civil Rights Movement.* Oxford: Oxford University Press.

Kryder, Daniel. (2000). *Divided Arsenal: Race and the American State during World War II.* Cambridge: Cambridge University Press.

Kubernik, Harvey. (2014). *Turn Up the Radio!: Rock, Pop, and Roll in Los Angeles, 1956–1972.* Solana Beach, CA: Santa Monica Press.

Kubik, Gerhard. (1999). *Africa and the Blues.* Jackson: University Press of Mississippi.

___. (2010a). *Theory of African Music,* Volume I. Chicago: University of Chicago Press.

___. (2010b). *Theory of African Music,* Volume II. Chicago: University of Chicago Press.

Kuhn, Thomas S. (1970). *The Structure of Scientific Revolutions* (Second Edition). Chicago: University of Chicago Press.

Kusmer, Kenneth L. (1976). *A Ghetto Takes Shape: Black Cleveland, 1870–1930.* Urbana: University of Illinois Press.

Kyagambiddwa, Joseph. (1955). *African Music From the Source of the Nile.* New York: Praeger.

Lait, Jack, and Mortimer, Lee. (1952). *U.S.A. Confidential.* New York: Crown Publishers.

Laraña, Enrique, Johnston, Hank, and Gusfield, Joseph R. (Eds.). (1994). *New Social Movements: From Ideology to Identity.* Philadelphia: Temple University Press.

Lauterbach, Preston. (2011). *The Chitlin' Circuit: And the Road to Rock & Roll.* New York: W.W. Norton.

Lavelle, Kristen M. (2014). *Whitewashing the South: White Memories of Segregation and Civil Rights.* Lanham: Rowman & Littlefield.

Lawlor, William. (Ed.). (2005). *Beat Culture: Icons, Lifestyles, and Impact.* Santa Barbara, CA: ABC-CLIO.

Lawrence, Sharon. (2006). *Jimi Hendrix: The Intimate Story of a Betrayed Musical Legend.* New York: Harper.

Lawson, R. A. (2010). *Jim Crow's Counterculture: The Blues and Black Southerners, 1890–1945.* Baton Rouge: Louisiana State University Press.

Lawson, Steven F. (2014). *Running for Freedom: Civil Rights and Black Politics in America since 1941.* Hoboken, NJ: Wiley-Blackwell.

Lawson, Steven F., and Payne, Charles M. (2006). *Debating the Civil Rights Movement, 1945–1968.* Lanham, MD: Rowman & Littlefield.

Le Blanc, Paul and Yates, Michael. (2013). *A Freedom Budget for All Americans: Recapturing the Promise of the Civil Rights Movement in the Struggle for Economic Justice Today.* New York: Monthly Review Press

Le Gendre, Kevin. (2012). *Soul Unsung: Reflections on the Band in Black Popular Music.* Bristol, CT: Equinox.

Lee, George Perry. (2008). "Thomas A. Dorsey's Influence on African American Worship." Ph.D. dissertation, Southern Baptist Theological Seminary, Louisville, KY.

Lee, Patti Meyer, and Lee, Gary. (2001). *Don't Bother Knockin' . . . This Town's A Rockin': A History of Traditional Rhythm & Blues and Early Rock & Roll In Buffalo, New York.* Buffalo, NY: Buffalo Sounds Press.

Lee, Sonia Song-Ha. (2014). *Building a Latino Civil Rights Movement: Puerto Ricans, African Americans, and the Pursuit of Racial Justice in New York City.* Chapel Hill: University of North Carolina Press.

Lee, Su H. (2007). *Debating New Social Movements: Culture, Identity, and Social Fragmentation.* Lanham, MD: University Press of America.

Lee, Taeku. (1992). *Mobilizing Public Opinion: Black Insurgency and Racial Attitudes in the Civil Rights Era.* Chicago: University of Chicago Press.

Lefever, Harry G. (2005). *Undaunted by the Fight: Spelman College and the Civil Rights Movement, 1957–1967.* Macon: Mercer University Press.

Leidholdt, Alexander. (1997). *Standing Before the Shouting Mob: Lenoir Chambers and Virginia's Massive Resistance to Public School Integration.* Tuscaloosa: University of Alabama Press.

Lemann, Nicholas (1991). *The Promised Land: The Great Black Migration and How It Changed America.* New York: Knopf.

Lemke-Santangelo, Gretchen. (1996). *Abiding Courage: African American Migrant Women and the East Bay Community.* Chapel Hill: University of North Carolina Press.

Lemons, Gary L. (2001). "'When and Where [We] Enter': In Search of a Feminist Forefather—Reclaiming the Womanist Legacy of W.E.B. Du Bois." In Rudolph P. Byrd and Beverly Guy-Sheftall (Eds.), *Traps: African American Men on Gender and Sexuality* (71–89). Indianapolis: Indiana University Press.

___. (2009). *Womanist Forefathers: Frederick Douglass and W. E. B. Du Bois.* Albany: State University of New York Press.

Leonard, Stephen J. (2002). *Lynching in Colorado, 1859–1919.* Boulder: University Press of Colorado.

Leszczak, Bob. (2013). *Who Did It First? Great Rhythm & Blues Cover Songs and Their Original Artists.* Lanham, MD: Scarecrow Press.

___. (2014). *Who Did It First?: Great Rock & Roll Cover Songs and Their Original Artists.* Lanham, MD: Rowman & Littlefield.

Levine, Ellen S. (1993). *Freedom's Children: Young Civil Rights Activists Tell Their Own Stories.* New York: Putnam.

Levine, Lawrence. (1977). *Black Culture and Black Consciousness: Afro-American Folk Thought from Slavery to Freedom.* New York: Oxford University Press.

Levinson, David. (2006). *Sewing Circles, Dime Suppers, and W. E. B. Du Bois: A History of the A.M.E. Zion Church.* Great Barrington, MA: Berkshire Publishing Group.

Levy, Peter B. (1992). *Let Freedom Ring: A Documentary History of the Modern Civil Rights Movement.* New York: Praeger.

___. (1998). *The Civil Rights Movement.* Westport: Greenwood.

___. (2003). *Civil War on Race Street: The Civil Rights Movement in Cambridge, Maryland.* Gainesville: University Press of Florida.

___. (Ed.). (2015). *The Civil Rights Movement in America: From Black Nationalism to the Women's Political Council.* Santa Barbara, CA: Greenwood.

Lewis, Andrew B. (2009). *The Shadows of Youth: The Remarkable Journey of the Civil Rights Generation.* New York: Hill & Wang.

Lewis, George. (2006). *Massive Resistance: The White Response to the Civil Rights Movement.* London: Hodder Arnold.

Lewis, Jerry M., and Looney, John G. (1983). *The Long Struggle: Well-Functioning Working-Class Black Families.* New York: Brunner/Mazel.

Lewis-Colman, David M. (2008). *Race Against Liberalism: Black Workers and the UAW in Detroit.* Urbana: University of Illinois Press.

Lhamon, W.T. (1998). *Raising Cain: Blackface Performance from Jim Crow to Hip Hop.* Cambridge, MA: Harvard University Press.

___. (Ed.). (2003). *Jump Jim Crow: Lost Plays, Lyrics, and Street Prose of the First Atlantic Popular Culture.* Cambridge, MA: Harvard University Press.

Lightfoot, Claude M. (1968). *Ghetto Rebellion to Black Liberation*. New York: International Publishers.

Lincoln, C. Eric, and Mamiya, Lawrence H. (1990). *The Black Church in the African American Experience*. Durham: Duke University Press.

Ling, Peter J., and Monteith, Sharon. (Eds.). (2004). *Gender and the Civil Rights Movement*. New Brunswick, NJ: Rutgers University Press.

Lipsitz, George. (1990a). "Listening to Learn and Learning to Listen: Popular Culture, Cultural Theory, and American Studies." *American Quarterly* 42 (4), 615–636.

___. (1990b). *Time Passages: Collective Memory and American Popular Culture*. Minneapolis: University of Minnesota Press.

___. (1994). *Dangerous Crossroads: Popular Music, Postmodernism, and the Poetics of Place*. New York: Verso.

___. (1998). *The Possessive Investment in Whiteness: How White People Profit from Identity Politics*. Philadelphia: Temple University Press.

___. (2001). *American Studies in a Moment of Danger*. Minneapolis: University of Minnesota Press.

___. (2007). *Footsteps in the Dark: The Hidden Histories of Popular Culture*. Minneapolis: University of Minnesota Press.

___. (2011). *How Racism Takes Place*. Philadelphia: Temple University Press.

Little, Kimberly K. (2009). *You Must Be from the North: Southern White Women in the Memphis Civil Rights Movement*. Jackson: University Press of Mississippi.

Loder-Jackson, Tondra L. (2015). *Schoolhouse Activists: African American Educators and the Long Birmingham Civil Rights Movement*. Albany: State University of New York Press.

Logan, Rayford W. (1954). *The Negro in American Life and Thought: The Nadir, 1877–1901*. New York: Dial Press.

Logan, Shirley W. (Ed.). (1995). *With Pen and Voice: A Critical Anthology of Nineteenth Century African American Women*. Carbondale: Southern Illinois University Press.

___. (1999). *We Are Coming: The Persuasive Discourse of Nineteenth Century Black Women*. Carbondale: Southern Illinois University Press.

London, Samuel G. (2009). *Seventh-Day Adventists and the Civil Rights Movement*. Jackson: University Press of Mississippi.

Lordi, Emily J. (2013). *Black Resonance: Iconic Women Singers and African American Literature*. New Brunswick: Rutgers University Press.

Lornell, Kip. (1995). *Happy in the Service of the Lord: African American Sacred Vocal Harmony Quartets in Memphis*. Knoxville: University of Tennessee Press.

___. (Ed.). (2010). *From Jubilee to Hip Hop: Readings in African American Music*. Upper Saddle River, NJ: Prentice Hall.

Loss, Archie K. (1999). *Pop Dreams: Music, Movies, and the Media in the American 1960s*. Fort Worth, TX: Harcourt Brace College Publishers.

Lott, Eric. (1993). *Love and Theft: Blackface Minstrelsy and the American Working-Class*. New York: Oxford University Press.

Love, Nancy S. (2006). *Musical Democracy*. Albany: State University of New York Press.

Lovell, John. (1972). *Black Song: The Forge and the Flame—The Story of How the Afro-American Spiritual was Hammered Out*. New York: Macmillan.

Lovett, Bobby L. (2005). *The Civil Rights Movement in Tennessee: A Narrative History*. Knoxville: University of Tennessee Press.

Lucal, Betsy. (1996). "Race, Class, and Gender in the Work of W.E.B. Du Bois: An Exploratory Study." *Research in Race & Ethnic Relations* 9, 191–210.

Lucks, Daniel S. (2014). *Selma to Saigon: The Civil Rights Movement and the Vietnam War*. Lexington: University Press of Kentucky.

Luders, Joseph E. (2010). *The Civil Rights Movement and the Logic of Social Change*. Cambridge: Cambridge University Press.

Lüthe, Martin. (2010). "Color-line and Crossing-over Motown and Performances of Blackness in 1960s American Culture." Ph.D. dissertation, Justus Liebig University, Giessen, Germany.

Lutz, Tom. (1991). "Curing the Blues: W. E. B. Du Bois, Fashionable Diseases, and Degraded Music." *Black Music Research Journal* 11 (2), 137–156.

Lyon, Danny. (1992). *Memories of the Southern Civil Rights Movement.* Chapel Hill: University of North Carolina Press.

Maffly-Kipp, Laurie F., and Lofton, Kathryn. (Eds.). (2010). *Women's Work: An Anthology of African American Women's Historical Writings from Antebellum America to the Harlem Renaissance.* Oxford: Oxford University Press.

Magoun, Alexander B. (2007). *Television: The Life Story of a Technology.* Westport, CT: Greenwood Press.

Mahon, Maureen. (2000). "Black Like This: Race, Generation, and Rock in the Post-Civil Rights Era." *American Ethnologist* 27 (2), 283–311.

___. (2004). *Right to Rock: The Black Rock Coalition and the Cultural Politics of Race.* Durham: Duke University Press.

Malcolm X. (1971). *The End of White World Supremacy: Four Speeches.* Merlin House/Seaver Books.

___. (1990). *Malcolm X Speaks: Selected Speeches and Statements.* New York: Grove-Weidendfeld.

___. (1991). *Malcolm X Speeches at Harvard* (Archie Epps, Ed.). New York: Paragon House.

___. (1992a). *The Autobiography of Malcolm X* (with Alex Haley). New York: Ballantine Books.

___. (1992b). *By Any Means Necessary.* New York: Pathfinder.

___. (1992c). *The Final Speeches, February 1965.* New York: Pathfinder.

Manis, Andrew Michael. (1999). *A Fire You Can't Put Out: The Civil Rights Life of Birmingham's Reverend Fred Shuttlesworth.* Tuscaloosa: University of Alabama Press.

Mann, Robert. (2007). *When Freedom Would Triumph: The Civil Rights Struggle in Congress, 1954–1968.* Baton Rouge: Louisiana State University Press.

Mantler, Gordon K. (2013). *Power to the Poor: Black-Brown Coalition and the Fight for Economic Justice, 1960–1974.* Chapel Hill: University of North Carolina Press.

Marable, Manning. (1980). "A. Philip Randolph and the Foundations of Black American Socialism." *Radical America* 14, 7–29.

___. (2011). *Malcolm X: A Life of Reinvention.* New York: Viking.

Marable, Manning and Mullings, Leith. (Eds.). (2000). *Let Nobody Turn Us Around: Voices of Resistance, Reform, and Renewal—An African American Anthology.* Lanham, MD: Rowman and Littlefield.

Maraniss, David. (2015). *Once in a Great City: A Detroit Story.* New York: Simon & Schuster.

Marcus, Greil. (1975). *Mystery Train: Images of America in Rock & Roll Music.* New York: E.P. Dutton.

Marcuse, Herbert. (1964). *One-Dimensional Man: Studies in the Ideology of Advanced Industrial Society.* Boston: Beacon.

Margolick, David. (2000). *Strange Fruit: Billie Holiday, Cafe Society, and an Early Cry for Civil Rights.* Philadelphia: Running Press.

___. (2001). *Strange Fruit: The Biography of a Song.* New York: Ecco Press.

Markovitz, Jonathan. (2004). *Legacies of Lynching: Racial Violence and Memory.* Minneapolis, MN: University of Minnesota Press.

Marks, Carole. (1989). *Farewell, We're Good and Gone: The Great Black Migration.* Bloomington: Indiana University Press.

Marovich, Robert M. (2015). *A City Called Heaven: Chicago and the Birth of Gospel Music.* Urbana: University of Illinois Press.

Marshall, James P. (2013). *Student Activism and Civil Rights in Mississippi: Protest Politics and the Struggle for Racial Justice, 1960–1965.* Baton Rouge: Louisiana State University Press.

Martin, Linda, and Segrave, Kerry. (1993). *Anti-Rock: The Opposition To Rock & Roll.* New York: Da Capo Press.

Mason, Mack C. (2004). *Saints in the Land of Lincoln: The Urban Development of a Pentecostal Denomination and the Birth of the Gospel Music Industry*. Hazel Crest, IL: Faithday Press.

Mattern, Mark. (1998). *Acting in Concert: Music, Community, and Political Action*. New Brunswick: Rutgers University Press.

Maultsby, Portia K. (1981). *Afro-American Religious Music: A Study in Musical Diversity*. Springfield, Ohio: Hymn Society of America.

___. (1983). "Soul Music: Its Sociological and Political Significance in American Popular Culture." *Journal of Popular Culture* 17 (2), 51–60.

___. (1985). "Beginnings of a Black Music Industry." In Robert E. Rosenthal and Portia Maultsby (Eds.), *Who's Who in Black Music* (i–xxi). New Orleans: Edwards Printing.

___. (1992). "The Impact of Gospel Music on the Secular Music Industry." Bernice Johnson Reagon (Ed.), *We'll Understand It Better By and By: Pioneering African American Gospel Composers* (19–33). Washington, D.C.: Smithsonian Institution Press.

___. (2001). "Funk Music: An Expression of Black Life in Dayton, Ohio and the American Metropolis." In Hans Krabbendam, Marja Roholl and Tity De Vries (Eds.), *The American Metropolis: Image and Inspiration* (197–213). Amsterdam: Vu University Press.

___. (2006). "Rhythm & Blues." In Mellonee V. Burnim and Portia K. Maultsby (Eds.), *African American Music: An Introduction* (245–270). New York: Routledge.

___. (2015). "Rhythm & Blues/R&B." In Mellonee V. Burnim and Portia K. Maultsby (Eds.), *African American Music: An Introduction* (2nd Edition) (239–276). New York: Routledge.

Maultsby, Portia K., and Burnim, Mellonee V. (1987). "From Backwoods to City Streets: The Afro-American Musical Journey." In Geneva Gay and Willie Baber (Eds.), *Expressively Black: The Cultural Basis of Ethnic Identity*. (109–136). New York: Praeger Press.

Maxwell, William J. (2004). "Ralph Ellison and the Constitution of Jazzocracy." *Journal of Popular Music Studies* 16 (1), 40–57.

Maynard, John A. (1991). *Venice West: The Beat Generation in Southern California*. New Brunswick: Rutgers University Press.

McAdam, Doug, McCarthy, John D., Zald, Mayer N. (Eds.). (1996). *Comparative Perspectives on Social Movements: Political Opportunities, Mobilizing Structures, and Cultural Framings*. New York: Cambridge University Press.

McAllister, Anita Bernadette. (1995). "The Musical Legacy of Dorothy Love Coates: African American Female Gospel Singer with Implications for Education and Theater Education." Ed.D. dissertation, Kansas State University, Manhattan, KS.

McCanless, Anne S. (1997). Uniting Voices in Song: The Music of the Civil Rights Movement. M.A. thesis, University of South Florida, Tampa, FL.

McCluskey, Audrey T. (2014). *A Forgotten Sisterhood: Pioneering Black Women Educators and Activists in the Jim Crow South*. Lanham: Rowman & Littlefield.

McCord, William Maxwell. (1969). *Life Styles in the Black Ghetto*. New York: Norton.

McCourt, Tom. (1983). "Bright Lights, Big City + A Brief History of Rhythm & Blues, 1945–1957." *Popular Music & Society* 9 (2), 1–18.

McDaniel, Eric L. (2008). *Politics in the Pews: The Political Mobilization of Black Churches*. Ann Arbor: University of Michigan Press

McDarrah, Fred W., and McDarrah, Gloria S. (2001). *Beat Generation: Glory Days in Greenwich Village*. New York: Schirmer.

McDermott, John. (1992). *Hendrix: Setting the Record Straight* (with Eddie Kramer). New York: Warner Books.

McGinley, Paige A. (2014). *Staging the Blues: From Tent Shows to Tourism*. Durham: Duke University Press.

McGregory, Jerrilyn. (2010). *Downhome Gospel: African American Spiritual Activism in Wiregrass Country*. Jackson: University Press of Mississippi.

McGuire, Phillip. (Ed.). (1983). *Taps For A Jim Crow Army: Letters from Black Soldiers in World War II*. Santa Barbara, CA: ABC-CLIO.

McKay, Nellie Y. (1985). "W.E.B. Du Bois: The Black Woman in His Writings—Selected Fictional and Autobiographical Portraits." In William L. Andrews (Ed.), *Critical Essays on W.E.B. Du Bois* (230–252). Boston: G.K. Hall.

___. (1990). "The Souls of Black Women Folk in the Writings of W.E.B. Du Bois." In Henry Louis Gates, Jr. (Ed.), *Reading Black/Reading Feminist: A Critical Anthology* (227–243). New York: Meridian.

McMickle, Marvin A. (2014). *Pulpit & Politics: Separation of Church & State in the Black Church*. Valley Forge, PA: Judson Press.

McMillen, Neil R. (1971). *The Citizens' Council: Organized Resistance to the Second Reconstruction, 1954–1964*. Urbana: University of Illinois Press.

McNally, Mark. (2015). *Antonio Gramsci*. New York: Palgrave Macmillan.

McWhorter, Diane. (2001). *Carry Me Home: Birmingham, Alabama: The Climactic Battle of the Civil Rights Revolution*. New York: Simon & Schuster.

Meister, Richard J. (1972). *The Black Ghetto: Promised Land or Colony?* Lexington, MA: Heath.

Mendel-Reyes, Meta. (1995). *Reclaiming Democracy: The Sixties in Politics and Memory*. New York: Routledge.

Mertens, Donna M., Cram, Fiona, and Chilisa, Bagele. (Eds.). (2013). *Indigenous Pathways into Social Research: Voices of a New Generation*. Walnut Creek, CA: Left Coast Press.

Meyer, David S., and Tarrow, Sidney G. (Eds.). (1998). *The Social Movement Society: Contentious Politics for a New Century*. Lanham, MD: Rowman & Littlefield.

Milan, Jon. (2009). *Detroit Ragtime And The Jazz Age*. Charleston, SC: Arcadia Publishing.

Miles, Kevin Thomas. (2000). "Haunting Music in The Souls of Black Folk." *boundary 2* 27 (3), 199–214.

Miles, Timothy Lee. (1994). "African American Rhythm & Blues Music as a Cultural Expression of the African American Experience: A Comparative Analysis of Two Number One Hit Songs which Mirror the Civil Rights and Black Power Movements: 1964, Respect by Aretha Franklin; 1968, Say It Loud, I'm Black and I'm Proud by James Brown." M.A. thesis, University of North Carolina at Chapel Hill, Chapel Hill, NC.

Miller, Calvin Craig. (2005). *A. Philip Randolph and the African American Labor Movement*. Greensboro, NC: Morgan Reynolds Publishing.

Miller, Calvin Craig. (2012). *Backlash: Race Riots in the Jim Crow Era*. Greensboro, NC: Morgan Reynolds.

Miller, Doug. (1995). "The Moan within the Tone: African Retentions in Rhythm & Blues Saxophone Style in Afro-American Popular Music." *Popular Music* 14 (2), 155–174.

Miller, Jim. (1999). *Flowers in the Dustbin: The Rise of Rock & Roll, 1947–1977*. New York: Simon & Schuster.

Miller, Karl Hagstrom. (2010). *Segregating Sound: Inventing Folk and Pop Music in the Age of Jim Crow*. Durham: Duke University Press.

Mills, C. Wright. (1959). *The Sociological Imagination*. Oxford: Oxford University Press.

Millward, Steve. (2012). *Changing Times : Music and Politics in 1964*. Leicester: Troubador.

Mitchell, Jason. (2010). *Television and American Culture*. Oxford: Oxford University Press.

Mjagkij, Nina. (2011). *Loyalty in Time of Trial: The African American Experience During World War I*. Lanham: Rowman & Littlefield Publishers.

Moore, Brenda L. (1996). *To Serve My Country, To Serve My Race: The Story of the Only African American WACS Stationed Overseas during World War II*. New York: New York University Press.

Moore, Christopher P. (2005). *Fighting for America: Black Soldiers—The Unsung Heroes of World War II*. New York: One World.

Moore, Winfred B. and Burton, Orville Vernon. (Eds.). (2008). *Toward the Meeting of the Waters: Currents in the Civil Rights Movement of South Carolina during the Twentieth Century*. Columbia: University of South Carolina Press.

Morgan, Bill. (2010). *The Typewriter is Holy: The Complete, Uncensored History of the Beat Generation*. New York: Free Press.

Morgan, Iwan W., and Davies, Philip. (Eds.). (2012). *From Sit-Ins to SNCC: The Student Civil Rights Movement in the 1960s*. Gainesville: University Press of Florida.

Morris, Aldon. (1981). "Black Southern Student Sit-In Movement: An Analysis of Internal Organization." *American Sociological Review* 46 (6), 744–767.

___. (1984). *The Origins of the Civil Rights Movement: Black Communities Organizing for Change*. New York: Free Press.

Morris, Aldon D., and Mueller, Carol M. (Eds.). (1992). *Frontiers in Social Movement Theory*. New Haven: Yale University Press.

Morrow, Bruce (2007). *Doo-Wop: The Music, the Times, the Era* (with Rich Maloof). New York: Sterling.

Morse, David. (1971). *Motown and the Arrival of Black Music*. New York: Macmillan.

Moten, Fred. (2003). *In the Break: The Aesthetics of the Black Radical Tradition*. Minneapolis: University of Minnesota Press.

Mullings, Leith. (Ed.). (2009). *New Social Movements in the African Diaspora: Challenging Global Apartheid*. New York: Palgrave Macmillan.

Murphy, Joseph M. (1994). *Working the Spirit: Ceremonies of the African Diaspora*. Boston: Beacon.

Murray, Albert. (1976). *Stomping the Blues*. New York: McGraw-Hill.

___. (1996). *The Blue Devils of Nada: A Contemporary American Approach to Aesthetic Statement*. New York: Pantheon Books.

___. (1973). *The Hero and the Blues*. Columbia: University of Missouri Press.

___. (1997). *Conversations with Albert Murray* (Roberta S. Maguire, Ed.). Jackson: University Press of Mississippi.

Murray, Charles Shaar. (1989). *Crosstown Traffic: Jimi Hendrix and the Post-War Rock & Roll Revolution*. New York: St. Martin's Press.

Murray, Peter C. (2004). Methodists and the Crucible of Race, 1930–1975. Columbia: University of Missouri Press.

Muyumba, Walton M. (2009). *The Shadow and the Act: Black Intellectual Practice, Jazz Improvisation, and Philosophical Pragmatism*. Chicago: University of Chicago Press.

Myers, Marc. (2013). *Why Jazz Happened*. Berkeley: University of California Press.

Myrsiades, Kostas. (Ed.). (2002). *The Beat Generation: Critical Essays*. New York: Peter Lang.

Naison, Mark. (2004). "From Doo-Wop to Hip Hop: The Bittersweet Odyssey of African Americans in the South Bronx." *Socialism & Democracy* 18 (2), 37–49.

Neal, Mark Anthony. (1997). "Sold Out on Soul: The Corporate Annexation of Black Popular Music." *Popular Music and Society* 21 (3), 117–135.

___. (1998). *What the Music Said: Black Popular Music and Black Public Culture*. New York: Routledge.

___. (2002). *Soul Babies: Black Popular Culture and the Post-Soul Aesthetic*. New York: Routledge.

___. (2002). "Soul for Sale: The Marketing of Black Musical Expression." In Norman Kelley (Ed.), *R&B, Rhythm and Business: The Political Economy of Black Music* (158–175). New York: Akashic.

___. (2003). *Songs in the Key of Black Life: A Rhythm and Blues Nation*. New York: Routledge.

___. (2005a). *New Black Man: Rethinking Black Masculinity*. New York: Routledge.

___. (2005b). "Rhythm and Bullshit: The Slow Decline of R&B (Rhythm & Blues)." ALTERNET.ORG. www.alternet.org/story/23384/rhythm_and_bullshit_the_slow_decline_of_r%26b.

Nevels, Cynthia S. (2007). *Lynching to Belong: Claiming Whiteness Through Racial Violence*. College Station: Texas A&M University Press.

Newman, Mark. (2004a). *Divine Agitators: The Delta Ministry and Civil Rights in Mississippi*. Athens: University of Georgia Press.

___. (2004b). *The Civil Rights Movement*. Westport: Praeger.

Newman, Richard. (1998). *Go Down, Moses: Celebrating the African American Spiritual*. New York: Clarkson Potter.

Nielsen, Aldon Lynn. (1997). *Black Chant: Languages of African American Postmodernism*. Cambridge: Cambridge University Press.

Nketia, J.H. Kwabena. (1974). *The Music of Africa*. New York: W.W. Norton.

Norrell, Robert J. (1998). *Reaping the Whirlwind: The Civil Rights Movement in Tuskegee*. Chapel Hill: University of North Carolina Press.

O'Brien, Gail Williams. (1999). *The Color of the Law: Race, Violence, and Justice in the Post-World War II South*. Chapel Hill: University of North Carolina Press.

O'Foran, Shelly. (2006). *Little Zion: A Church Baptized by Fire*. Chapel Hill: University of North Carolina Press.

Ogbar, Jeffrey O.G. (2004). *Black Power: Radical Politics and African American Identity*. Baltimore: Johns Hopkins University Press.

___. (2007). *The Hip Hop Revolution: The Culture and Politics of Rap*. Lawrence: University of Kansas Press.

Oliphant, Dave. (2002). *The Early Swing Era, 1930 to 1941*. Westport, CT: Greenwood Press.

Oliver, Paul. (2006). *Broadcasting the Blues: Black Blues in the Segregation Era*. New York: Routledge.

Olson, Lynne. (2001). *Freedom's Daughters: The Unsung Heroines of the Civil Rights Movement from 1830 to 1970*. New York: Scribner.

O'Meally, Robert G. (2001). "'Trying to Blow All Life Through a Brass Trombone': Ralph Ellison Preaches the Blues." *Journal of Religion and Health* 40 (1), 15–40.

Ongiri, Amy Abugo. (2010). *Spectacular Blackness: The Cultural Politics of the Black Power Movement and the Search for a Black Aesthetic*. Charlottesville: University of Virginia Press.

Ortizano, Giacomo L. (1993). "On Your Radio!: A Descriptive History of Rhythm & Blues Radio during the 1950s." Ph.D. dissertation, Ohio University, Athens, OH.

Osborne, Jerry, and Hamilton, Bruce. (1980). *Blues, Rhythm & Blues, Soul*. Phoenix: O'Sullivan Woodside.

Osofsky, Gilbert. (1996). *Harlem, The Making of a Ghetto: Negro New York, 1890–1930*. Chicago: Ivan R. Dee.

Othello, Jeffrey. (2004). *The Soul of Rock & Roll: A History of African Americans in Rock Music*. Oakland, CA: Regent Press.

Otis, Johnny. (1993). *Upside Your Head!: Rhythm & Blues on Central Avenue*. Hanover, NH: University Press of New England.

Owens, Michael Leo. (2007). *God and Government in the Ghetto: The Politics of Church-State Collaboration in Black America*. Chicago: University of Chicago Press.

Ownby, Ted. (Ed.). (2002). *The Role of Ideas in the Civil Rights South*. Jackson: University Press of Mississippi.

___. (Ed.). (2008). *The Civil Rights Movement in Mississippi*. Jackson: University Press of Mississippi.

Painter, Nell Irvin. (1976). *Exodusters: Black Migration to Kansas After Reconstruction*. New York: Knopf.

Palmer, Robert. (1982). *Deep Blues: A Musical and Cultural History of the Mississippi Delta*. New York: Penguin.

___. (1991). "The Church of the Sonic Guitar." *South Atlantic Quarterly* 90 (4), 649–673.

___. (1995). *Rock & Roll: An Unruly History*. New York: Harmony Books.

___. (1996). *Dancing in the Street: A Rock & Roll History*. London: BBC Books.

Paris, Peter J. (1991). *Black Religious Leaders: Conflict in Unity*. Louisville, KY: Westminster/John Knox Press.

Parks, Rosa. (1992). *Rosa Parks: My Story* (with James Haskins). New York: Puffin Books.

___. (1994). *Quiet Strength: The Faith, the Hope, and the Heart of a Woman Who Changed a Nation* (with Gregory J. Reed). Grand Rapids, MI: Zondervan Publishing.

Parrish, Lydia. (1992). *Slave Songs of the Georgia Sea Islands*. Athens: University of Georgia Press.

Patterson, James T. (2002). *Brown v. Board of Education: A Civil Rights Milestone and Its Troubled Legacy*. Oxford: Oxford University Press.

Pauley, Garth E. (2000). "W.E.B. Du Bois on Woman Suffrage: A Critical Analysis of His Crisis Writings." *Journal of Black Studies* 30 (3), 383–410.

Payne, Charles. (2011). *I've Got the Light of Freedom: The Organizing Tradition and the Mississippi Freedom Struggle*. Berkeley: University of California Press.

Payne, Charles M., and Green, Adam. (Eds.). (2003). *Time Loner Than Rope: A Century of African American Activism, 1850–1950*. New York: New York University Press.

Pecknold, Diane. (Ed.). (2013). *Hidden in the Mix: The African American Presence in Country Music*. Durham: Duke University Press.

Peddie, Ian. (Ed.). (2006). *The Resisting Muse: Popular Music and Social Protest*. Aldershot, England: Ashgate.

Perone, James E. (2006). *The Sound of Stevie Wonder*. Westport, CT: Praeger.

Peretti, Burton W. (1992). *The Creation of Jazz: Music, Race, and Culture in Urban America* Urbana: University of Illinois Press.

___. (2009). *Lift Every Voice: The History of African American Music*. Lanham: Rowman & Littlefield Publishers.

Perry, Earnest L. (2002a). "A Common Purpose: The Negro Newspaper Publishers Association's Fight for Equality During World War II." *American Journalism* 19 (2), 34–37.

___. (2002b). "It's Time to Force a Change: The African American Press' Campaign for a True Democracy during World War II." *Journalism History* 28 (2), 85–95.

Perry, John. (2004). *Jimi Hendrix's Electric Ladyland*. New York: Continuum.

Peters, Erskine. (Ed.). (1993). *Lyrics of the Afro-American Spiritual: A Documentary Collection*. Westport, CT: Greenwood Press.

Petigny, Alan C. (2009). *The Permissive Society: America, 1941–1965*. New York: Cambridge University Press.

Petras, James F. (2003). *The New Development Politics: The Age of Empire Building and New Social Movements*. Aldershot, England: Ashgate.

Pfaff, Eugene E. (2011). *Keep on Walkin', Keep on Talkin': An Oral History of the Greensboro Civil Rights Movement*. Greensboro: Tudor Publishers

Pfeffer, Paula F. (1990). *A. Philip Randolph: Pioneer of the Civil Rights Movement*. Baton Rouge: Louisiana State University Press.

Pfeifer, Michael J. (2004). *Rough Justice: Lynching and American Society, 1874–1947*. Urbana: University of Illinois Press.

Phillips, Kimberley L. (1999). *AlabamaNorth: African American Migrants, Community, and Working-Class Activism in Cleveland, 1915–1945*. Urbana: University of Illinois Press.

___. (2012). *War!, What is it Good For?: Black Freedom Struggles and the U.S. Military from World War II to Iraq*. Chapel Hill: University of North Carolina Press.

Phillips, Romeo Eldridge. (1982). "Some Perceptions of Gospel Music." *Black Perspective in Music* 10 (2), 167–178.

Phinney, Kevin. (2005). *Souled American: How Black Music Transformed White Culture*. New York: Billboard Books.

Pickens, William. (1921). *Lynching and Debt-Slavery*. New York: American Civil Liberties Union.

Pielke, Robert G. (2012). *Rock Music in American Culture: The Sounds of Revolution*, (2nd Edition). Jefferson, NC: McFarland.

Pitts, Walter F. (1993). *Old Ship of Zion: The Afro-Baptist Ritual in the African Diaspora*. Oxford: Oxford University Press.

Pleck, Elizabeth H. (1979). *Black Migration and Poverty in Boston, 1865–1900*. New York: Academic Press.

Polikoff, Alexander. (2005). *Waiting for Gautreaux: A Story of Segregation, Housing, and the Black Ghetto*. Evanston: Northwestern University Press.

Pollard, Deborah Smith. (2008). *When the Church Becomes Your Party: Contemporary Gospel Music*. Detroit: Wayne State University Press.

Polletta, Francesca, and Jasper, James M. (2001). "Collective Identity in Social Movements." *Annual Review of Sociology* 27, 283–305.

Polsgrove, Carol. (2001). *Divided Minds: Intellectuals and the Civil Rights Movement*. New York: Norton.

Porta, Donatella Della, and Diani, Mario. (2006). *Social Movements: An Introduction*. Malden, MA: Blackwell.

Porter, Horace A. (2001). *Jazz Country: Ralph Ellison in America*. Iowa City: University of Iowa Press.

Posner, Gerald L. (2002). *Motown: Music, Money, Sex, and Power*. New York: Random House.

Posnock, Ross. (Ed.). (2005). *The Cambridge companion to Ralph Ellison*. Cambridge: Cambridge University Press.

Pratt, Ray. (1994). *Rhythm and Resistance: The Political Uses of American Popular Music*. Washington, D.C.: Smithsonian Institution Press.

Pruitt, Bernadette. (2013). *The Other Great Migration: The Movement of Rural African Americans to Houston, 1900–1941*. College Station: Texas A&M University Press.

Pruter, Robert. (1996). *Doo-Wop: The Chicago Scene*. Urbana: University of Illinois Press.

Rabaka, Reiland. (2007). *W.E.B. Du Bois and the Problems of the Twenty-First Century: An Essay on Africana Critical Theory*. Lanham: Lexington Books.

___. (2008). *Du Bois's Dialectics: Black Radical Politics and the Reconstruction of Critical Social Theory*. Lanham: Lexington Books.

___. (2009). *Africana Critical Theory: Reconstructing the Black Radical Tradition, from W.E.B. Du Bois and C.L.R. James to Frantz Fanon and Amilcar Cabral*. Lanham: Lexington Books.

___. (2010a). *Against Epistemic Apartheid: W.E.B. Du Bois and the Disciplinary Decadence of Sociology*. Lanham: Lexington Books.

___. (2010b). *Forms of Fanonism: Frantz Fanon's Critical Theory and the Dialectics of Decolonization*. Lanham: Lexington Books.

___. (Ed.). (2010c). *W.E.B. Du Bois: A Critical Reader*. Surrey, UK: Ashgate Publishing.

___. (2011). *Hip Hop's Inheritance: From the Harlem Renaissance to the Hip Hop Feminist Movement*. Lanham: Lexington Books.

___. (2012). *Hip Hop's Amnesia: From Blues and the Black Women's Club Movement to Rap and the Hip Hop Movement*. Lanham: Lexington Books.

___. (2013). *The Hip Hop Movement: From R&B and the Civil Rights Movement to Rap and the Hip Hop Generation*. Lanham: Lexington Books.

___. (2014). *Concepts of Cabralism: Amilcar Cabral and Africana Critical Theory*. Lanham: Lexington Books.

___. (2015). *The Negritude Movement: W.E.B. Du Bois, Leon Damas, Aime Cesaire, Leopold Senghor, Frantz Fanon, and the Evolution of an Insurgent Idea*. Lanham, MD: Lexington Books.

Raboteau, Albert. (1978). *Slave Religion: The "Invisible Institution" in the Antebellum South*. Oxford: Oxford University Press.

Radano, Ronald M. (1995). "Soul Texts and the Blackness of Folk." *Modernism/Modernity* 2 (1), 71–95.

Radford, Andrew. (2003). "The Invisible Music of Ralph Ellison." *Raritan* 23 (1), 39–62.

Raines, Howell. (1977). *My Soul is Rested: Movement Days in the Deep South Remembered*. New York: Putnam.

Rainwater, Lee. (2006). *Behind Ghetto Walls: Black Families in a Federal Slum*. New Brunswick, NJ: Transaction Publishers.

Ralph, James R. (1993). *Northern Protest: Martin Luther King, Jr., Chicago, and the Civil Rights Movement*. Cambridge: Harvard University Press, 1993.

Ramey, Lauri. (2008). *Slave Songs and the Birth of African American Poetry*. New York: Palgrave Macmillan.

Ramsey, Guthrie P. (2003). *Race Music: Black Cultures from Be-Bop to Hip Hop*. Berkeley: University of California Press.

Randall, Annie Janeiro. (Ed.). (2005). *Music, Power, and Politics*. New York: Routledge.

Randolph, A. Philip. (2014.). *For Jobs and Freedom: Selected Speeches and Writings of A. Philip Randolph Andrew* (Edmund Kersten and David Lucander, Eds.). Amherst: University of Massachusetts Press.

Ransby, Barbara. (2003). *Ella Baker and the Black Freedom Movement: A Radical Democratic Vision*. Chapel Hill: University of North Carolina Press.

Raper, Arthur Franklin. (1969). *The Tragedy of Lynching*. New York: Negro Universities Press.

Reagon, Bernice Johnson. (1975). "Songs of the Civil Rights Movement, 1955–1965: A Study in Culture History." Ph.D. dissertation, Department of History, Howard University, Washington, D.C.

___. (1992). *We'll Understand It Better By and By: Pioneering African American Gospel Composers*. Washington, D.C.: Smithsonian Institution Press.

___. (1993). "Women as Culture Carriers in the Civil Rights Movement: Fannie Lou Hamer." In Vicki L. Crawford, Jacqueline Anne Rouse and Barbara Woods (Eds.), *Women in the Civil Rights Movement: Trailblazers and Torchbearers, 1941–1965* (203–217). Indianapolis: Indiana University Press.

___. (2000). "Civil Rights and Black Protest Music." In Jonathon Birnbaum and Clarence Taylor (Eds.), *Civil Rights Since 1787: A Reader on the Black Struggle* (24–28). New York: New York University Press.

___. (2001). *If You Don't Go, Don't Hinder Me: The African American Sacred Song Tradition*. Lincoln: University of Nebraska Press.

Redd, Lawrence N. (1974). *Rock is Rhythm & Blues: The Impact of Mass Media*. East Lansing: Michigan State University Press.

___. (1985). "Rock!: It's Still Rhythm and Blues." *The Black Perspective in Music* 13 (1), 31–47.

Reddy, Chandan. (2011). *Freedom with Violence: Race, Sexuality, and the US State*. Durham: Duke University Press.

Redmond, Mike, and Goldberg, Marv. (1975). "The Doo-Wah Sound: Black Pop Groups of the 1950s." *Yesterday's Memories* 1 (1), 22–26.

Redmond, Shana L. (2014). *Anthem: Social Movements and the Sound of Solidarity in the African Diaspora*. New York: New York University Press.

Reed, Christopher Robert. (2014). *Knock at the Door of Opportunity: Black Migration to Chicago, 1900–1919*. Carbondale: Southern Illinois University Press.

Reed, Monica C. (2008). "'The Lord Has Led Me, and He Will Lead You': The Role of Gospel Music in the Formation of Early Twentieth Century Chicago Culture." M.A. thesis, Florida State University, Tallahassee, FL.

Reed, Teresa L. (2003). *The Holy Profane: Religion in Black Popular Music*. Lexington: University Press of Kentucky.

Reed, T.V. (2005). *The Art of Protest: Culture and Activism from the Civil Rights Movement to the Streets of Seattle*. Minneapolis: University of Minnesota Press.

Reeves, Martha. (1994). *Dancing in the Street: Confessions of a Motown Diva* (with Mark Bego). New York: Hyperion.

Regev, Motti. (2013). *Pop-Rock Music: Aesthetic Cosmopolitanism in Late Modernity*. Cambridge: Polity.

Reich, Steven A. (2013). *A Working People: A History of African American Workers since Emancipation*. Lanham: Rowman & Littlefield Publishers.

___. (Ed.). (2014). *The Great Black Migration: A Historical Encyclopedia of the American Mosaic*. Santa Barbara, CA: Greenwood.

Reynolds, Simon, and Press, Joy. (1995). *The Sex Revolts: Gender, Rebellion, and Rock & Roll*. Cambridge: Harvard University Press.

Ribowsky, Mark. (2009). *The Supremes: A Saga of Motown Dreams, Success, and Betrayal*. Cambridge, MA: Da Capo Press.

___. (2010a). *Ain't Too Proud to Beg: The Troubled Lives and Enduring Soul of the Temptations*. Hoboken, NJ: John Wiley & Sons.

___. (2010b). *Signed, Sealed, and Delivered: The Soulful Journey of Stevie Wonder*. Hoboken, NJ: John Wiley & Sons.

Ricks, George R. (1977). *Some Aspects of the Religious Music of the United States Negro: An Ethnomusicological Study with Special Emphasis on the Gospel Tradition*. New York: Arno Press.

Riis, Thomas L. (2006). "Musical Theater." In Mellonee V. Burnim and Portia K. Maultsby (Eds.), *African American Music: An Introduction* (185–210). New York: Routledge.

Ripani, Richard J. (2006). *The New Blue Music: Changes in Rhythm & Blues, 1950–1999*. Jackson: University Press of Mississippi.

Ritz, David. (1985). *Divided Soul: The Life Of Marvin Gaye*. New York: McGraw-Hill.

Roach, Hildred. (1973). *Black American Music: Past and Present*. Boston: Crescendo Publishing Co.

Robertson, Robbie, Guerinot, Jim, Robertson, Sebastian, and Levine, Jared. (2013). *Legends, Icons & Rebels: Music That Changed the World*. Toronto: Tundra Books.

Robinson, Cedric J. (1997). *Black Movements in America*. New York: Routledge.

Robinson, Smokey. (1989). *Smokey Inside Life*. New York: McGraw-Hill.

Robnett, Belinda. (1997). *How Long? How Long?: African-American Women in the Struggle for Civil Rights*. Oxford: Oxford University Press.

Roby, Steven. (2002). *Black Gold: The Lost Archives of Jimi Hendrix*. New York: Billboard Books.

Roby, Steven, and Schreiber, Brad. (2010). *Becoming Jimi Hendrix: From Southern Crossroads to Psychedelic London, The Untold Story of a Musical Genius*. Philadelphia: Da Capo Press.

Rochelle, LinDee. (2012). *Blast From Your Past!—Rock & Roll Radio DJs: The First Five Years, 1954–1959*. West Conshohocken, PA: Infinity Publishing.

Rogers, Kim Lacy. (1993). *Righteous Lives: Narratives of the New Orleans Civil Rights Movement*. New York: New York University Press.

Roll, Jarod. (2010). *Spirit of Rebellion: Labor and Religion in the New Cotton South*. Urbana: University of Illinois Press.

Romano, Renee Christine. (2014). *Racial Reckoning: Prosecuting America's Civil Rights Murders*. Cambridge: Harvard University Press.

Romano, Renee Christine, and Raiford, Leigh (Eds.). (2006). *Civil Rights Movement in American Memory*. Athens: University of Georgia Press.

Rosalsky, Mitch. (Ed.). (2000). *Encyclopedia of Rhythm & Blues and Doo-Wop Vocal Groups*. Lanham, MD: Scarecrow Press.

Rose, Harold M. (1971). *The Black Ghetto: A Spatial Behavioral Perspective*. New York: McGraw-Hill.

___. (Ed.). (1972). *Geography of the Ghetto: Perceptions, Problems, and Alternatives*. DeKalb: Northern Illinois University Press.

Rose, Tricia. (1994). *Black Noise: Rap Music and Black Culture in Contemporary America*. Middletown, CT: Wesleyan University Press.

Rosenberg, Jonathan. (2006). *How Far the Promised Land?: World Affairs and the American Civil Rights Movement from the First World War to Vietnam*. Princeton: Princeton University Press.

Rosengarten, Frank. (2014). *The Revolutionary Marxism of Antonio Gramsci*. Leiden: Brill.

Rosenthal, David H. (1988). "Jazz in the Ghetto: 1950–70." *Popular Music* 7 (1), 51–56.

Rosenthal, Rob, and Flacks, Richard. (2015). *Playing for Change: Music and Musicians in the Service of Social Movements*. New York: Routledge.

Roy, William G. (2010). *Reds, Whites, and Blues: Social Movements, Folk Music, and Race in the United States*. Princeton: Princeton University Press.

Royster, Jacqueline J. (2000). *Traces Of A Stream: Literacy and Social Change Among African American Women*. Pittsburgh: University of Pittsburgh Press.

Rubin, Rachel, and Melnick, Jeffrey Paul. (Eds.). (2001). *American Popular Music: New Approaches to the Twentieth Century*. Amherst: University of Massachusetts Press.

Rublowsky, John. (1971). *Black Music in America*. New York: Basic Books.

Rudel, Anthony J. (2008). *Hello, Everybody!: The Dawn of American Radio*. Orlando: Harcourt.

Runowicz, John Michael. (2010). *Forever Doo-Wop: Race, Nostalgia, and Vocal Harmony*. Amherst: University of Massachusetts Press.

Ryan, Jack. (2012). *Recollections The Detroit Years: The Motown Sound By The People Who Made It*. Whitmore Lake, MI: Glendower Media.

Ryan, Jennifer. (2008). "'Can I Get A Witness?': Soul and Salvation in Memphis Music." Ph.D. dissertation, Department of Ethnomusicology, University of Pennsylvania, Philadelphia, PA.

Salem, James M. (1999). *The Late, Great Johnny Ace, and the Transition from R&B to Rock & Roll*. Urbana: University of Illinois Press.

Sales, William W. (1994). *From Civil Rights to Black Liberation: Malcolm X and the Organization of Afro-American Unity*. Boston: South End Press.

Salmond, John A. (1997). *My Mind Set on Freedom: A History of the Civil Rights Movement, 1954–1968*. Chicago: Ivan R. Dee.

Salvatore, Nick. (2006). *Singing in a Strange Land: C.L. Franklin, the Black Church, and the Transformation of America*. Urbana: University of Illinois Press.

Sandoval, Chela. (2000). *Methodology of the Oppressed*. Minneapolis: University of Minnesota Press.

Sanger, Kerran L. (1995). *"When the Spirit Says Sing!": The Role of Freedom Songs in the Civil Rights Movement*. New York: Garland.

Sanjek, Russell, and Sanjek, David. (1996). *Pennies from Heaven: The American Popular Music Business in the Twentieth Century*. New York: Da Capo Press.

Santiago, Abraham J., and Dunham, Steven J. (2006). *Acappella Street Corner Vocal Groups: A Brief History and Discography of 1960s Singing Groups*. Glencoe: Mellow Sound Press.

Savage, Barbara D. (1999). *Broadcasting Freedom: Radio, War, and the Politics of Race, 1938–1948*. Chapel Hill: University of North Carolina Press.

___. (2000). "W.E.B. Du Bois and 'The Negro Church'." *Annals of the American Academy of Political and Social Science* 568, 253–249.

___. (2012). *Your Spirits Walk Beside Us: The Politics of Black Religion*. Cambridge: Belknap Press of Harvard University Press.

Savage, Jon. (2007). *Teenage: The Creation of Youth Culture*. New York: Viking.

Savage, Robert L., and Nimmo, Dan D. (1990). *Politics in Familiar Contexts: Projecting Politics through Popular Media*. Norwood, NJ: Ablex Publishing.

Schafer, William J., and Riedel, Johannes. (1973). *The Art of Ragtime: Form and Meaning of an Original Black American Art*. Baton Rouge: Louisiana State University Press.

Schenbeck, Lawrence. (2012). *Racial Uplift and American Music, 1878–1943*. Jackson: University Press of Mississippi.

Schuller, Gunther. (1989a). *The History of Jazz*. Oxford: Oxford University Press.

___. (1989b). *The Swing Era: The Development of Jazz, 1930–1945*. New York: Oxford University Press.

Schwerin, Jules Victor. (1992). *Got To Tell It!: Mahalia Jackson, Queen of Gospel*. New York: Oxford University Press.

Schulz, David A. (1969). *Coming Up Black: Patterns of Ghetto Socialization*. Englewood Cliffs, NJ: Prentice-Hall.

Scott, Alan. (1990). *Ideology and the New Social Movements*. London: Unwin Hyman.

Scott, Lawrence P., and Womack, William M. (1998). *Double-V: The Civil Rights Struggle of the Tuskegee Airmen*. East Lansing: Michigan State University Press.

Scrivani-Tidd, Lisa M., Markowitz, Rhonda, Smith, Chris, Janosik, MaryAnn, and Gulla, Bob. (Eds.). *The Greenwood Encyclopedia of Rock History*. (6 vols.). Westport, CT: Greenwood.

Seeger, Pete, and Reiser, Bob. (1989). *Everybody Says Freedom: A History of the Civil Rights Movement in Songs and Pictures*. New York: W. W. Norton.

Sernett, Milton C. (1997). *Bound For the Promised Land: African American Religion and the Great Migration*. Durham: Duke University Press.

Sernett, Milton C. (Ed). (1999). *African American Religious History: A Documentary Witness* . Durham: Duke University Press.

Seroff, Doug. (1985). "On the Battlefield: Gospel Quartets in Jefferson County, Alabama." In Geoffrey Haydon and Dennis Marks (Eds.), *Repercussions: A Celebration of African American Music* (30–53). London: Century.

Shadwick, Keith. (2003). *Jimi Hendrix: The Musician*. San Francisco: Backbeat Books.

Shapiro, Harry, and Glebbeek, Caesar. (1991). *Jimi Hendrix: Electric Gypsy*. New York: St. Martin's Press.

Shapiro, Herbert. (1988). *White Violence and Black Response: From Reconstruction to Montgomery*. Amherst: University of Massachusetts Press.

Sharpley-Whiting, T. Denean. (2015). *Bricktop's Paris: African American Women in Paris Between the Two World Wars*. Albany: State University of New York Press.

Shaw, Arnold. (1969). *The Rock Revolution*. New York: Crowell-Collier Press.

___. (1970). *The World of Soul: Black America's Contributions to the Pop Music Scene*. New York: Cowles Book Co.

___. (1977). *52nd Street: The Street of Jazz*. New York: Da Capo.

___. (1978). *Honkers and Shouters: The Golden Years of Rhythm & Blues*. New York: Macmillan.

___. (1986). *Black Popular Music in America: From the Spirituals, Minstrels, and Ragtime to Soul, Disco, and Hip Hop*. New York: Schirmer Books.

___. (1987a). *The Jazz Age: Popular Music in the 1920s*. Oxford: Oxford University Press.

___. (1987b). *The Rockin' '50s: The Decade that Transformed the Pop Music Scene*. New York: Da Capo Press.

___. (1998). *Let's Dance: Popular Music in the 1930s* (Bill Willard, Ed.). Oxford: Oxford University Press.

Shaw, Stephanie J. (1991). "Black Club Women and the Creation of the National Association of Colored Women." *Journal of Women's History* 3 (2), 1–25.

___. (2013). *W. E. B. Du Bois and The Souls of Black Folk*. Chapel Hill: University of North Carolina Press.

Shumway, David R. (2014). *Rock Star: The Making of Musical Icons from Elvis to Springsteen*. Baltimore: Johns Hopkins University Press.

Silverman, Sue William. (2014). *The Pat Boone Fan Club: My Life as a White Anglo-Saxon Jew*. Lincoln: University of Nebraska Press.

Simien, Evelyn M. (2011). *Gender and Lynching: The Politics of Memory*. New York: Palgrave Macmillan.

Simpson, George E. (1978). *Black Religions in the New World*. New York: Columbia University Press.

Singh, Nikhil Pal. (2004). *Black Is A Country: Race and the Unfinished Struggle for Democracy*. Cambridge: Harvard University Press.

Sinitiere, Phillip Luke. (2012). "Of Faith and Fiction: Teaching W. E. B. Du Bois and Religion." *History Teacher* 45 (3), 421–436.

Singleton, Raynoma Gordy. (1990). *Berry, Me, and Motown: The Untold Story* (with Bryan Brown and Mim Eichler). Chicago: Contemporary Books.

Sitkoff, Harvard. (2008). *The Struggle for Black Equality*. New York: Hill & Wang.

Small, Christopher. (1998a). *Music of the Common Tongue: Survival and Celebration in African American Music*. Hanover, NH: University Press of New England.

___. (1998b). *Musicking: The Meanings of Performing and Listening*. Hanover, NH: Wesleyan University Press.

Smith, C. Fraser. (2008). *Here Lies Jim Crow: Civil Rights in Maryland*. Baltimore: Johns Hopkins University Press.

Smith, Linda Tuhiwai. (1999). *Decolonizing Methodologies: Research and Indigenous Peoples*. Dunedin: University of Otago Press.

Smith, R. Drew. (Ed.). (2003). *New Day Begun: African American Churches and Civic Culture in Post-Civil Rights America*. Durham: Duke University Press.

___. (Ed.). (2004). *Long March Ahead: African American Churches and Public Policy in Post-Civil Rights America*. Durham: Duke University Press.

___. (Ed.). (2013). *From Every Mountainside: Black Churches and the Broad Terrain of Civil Rights*. Albany: State University of New York Press.

Smith, R. Drew, and Harris, Fredrick C. (Eds.). (2005). *Black Churches and Local Politics: Clergy Influence, Organizational Partnerships, and Civic Empowerment*. Lanham: Rowman & Littlefield

Smith, Susan Lynn. "The Black Women's Club Movement: Self-Improvement and Sisterhood, 1890–1915." Master's thesis, University of Wisconsin, Madison.

Smith, Suzanne E. (1999). *Dancing in the Street: Motown and the Cultural Politics of Detroit*. Cambridge: Harvard University Press.

Smith, Thérèse. (2004). *Let the Church Sing!: Music and Worship in a Black Mississippi Community*. Rochester: University of Rochester Press.

Smith, Wes. (1989). *The Pied Pipers of Rock & Roll: Radio Deejays of the 50s and 60s*. Marietta, GA: Longstreet Press.

Snow, David A., Soule, Sarah Anne, and Kriesi, Hanspeter. (Eds.). (2004). *The Blackwell Companion to Social Movements*. Malden, MA: Blackwell.

Sokol, Jason. (2006). *There Goes My Everything: White Southerners in the Age of Civil Rights, 1945–1975*. New York: Knopf.

Sotiropoulos, Karen. (2006). *Staging Race: Black Performance in Turn of the Century America*. Cambridge: Harvard University Press.

Southern, Eileen. (1997). *Music of Black Americans: A History*. New York: Norton.

Spaulding, A. Timothy. (2004). "Embracing Chaos in Narrative Form: The Bebop Aesthetic and Ralph Ellison's Invisible Man." *Callaloo* 27 (2), 481–501.

Spear, Allan H. (1967). *Black Chicago: The Making of a Negro Ghetto, 1890–1920*. Chicago: University of Chicago Press.

Spencer, Jon Michael. (1988). *Sacred Symphony: The Chanted Sermon of the Black Preacher*. New York: Greenwood Press.

___. (Ed.). (1989). *Theology of American Popular Music: Black Sacred Music*. Durham: Duke University Press.

___. (1990). *Protest & Praise: The Sacred Music of Black Religion*. Minneapolis: Fortress Press.

___. (1993). *Blues & Evil*. Knoxville: University of Tennessee Press.

___. (Ed.). (1994). *Theomusicology: A Special Issue of Black Sacred Music: A Journal of Theomusicology*. Durham: Duke University Press.

___. (1995). *The Rhythms of Black Folk: Race, Religion, and Pan-Africanism*. Trenton, NJ: Africa World Press.

___. (1996). *Re-searching Black Music*. Knoxville: University of Tennessee Press.

___. (1997). *The New Negroes and Their Music: The Success of the Harlem Renaissance*. Knoxville: University of Tennessee Press.

Stack, Carol B. (1996). *Call To Home: African Americans Reclaim The Rural South*. New York: BasicBooks.

Stamz, Richard. (2010). *Give 'Em Soul, Richard!: Race, Radio, and Rhythm & Blues in Chicago* (with Patrick A Roberts). Urbana: University of Illinois Press.

Staton, Sandra Louise. (2001). "They Have Girded Themselves for Work: The Emergence of the Feminist Argument in the Novels of William Edward Burghardt Du Bois." Ph.D. dissertation, Howard University, Washington, D.C.

Stebbins, Robert A. (1996). *The Barbershop Singer: Inside the Social World of a Musical Hobby*. Toronto: University of Toronto Press.

Stewart, Carole L. (2008). "Civil Religion, Civil Society, and the Performative Life and Work of W. E. B. Du Bois." *Journal of Religion* 88 (3), 307–330.

___. (2010). *Strange Jeremiahs: Civil Religion and the Literary Imaginations of Jonathan Edwards, Herman Melville, and W. E. B. Du Bois.* Albuquerque: University of New Mexico Press.

Stewart, Earl L. (1998). *African American Music: An Introduction.* New York: Schirmer.

Stewart, James B. (2005). "Message in the Music: Political Commentary in Black Popular Music from Rhythm and Blues to Early Hip Hop." *Journal of African American History* 90 (3), 196–225.

Stone, Robert L. (2010). *Sacred Steel: Inside an African American Steel Guitar Tradition.* Urbana: University of Illinois Press.

Stone, Ruth M. (1982). *Let the Inside Be Sweet: The Interpretation of Music Event among the Kpelle of Liberia.* Indianapolis: Indiana University Press.

___. (2005). *Music in West Africa: Experiencing Music, Expressing Culture.* Oxford: Oxford University Press.

___. (Ed.). (2008). *The Garland Handbook of African Music.* New York: Garland.

Stone, Ruth M., and Gillis, Frank J. (Eds.). (1976). *African Music—Oral Data: A Catalog of Field Recordings, 1902–1975.* Indianapolis: Indiana University Press.

Stowe, David W. (1994). *Swing Changes: Big Band Jazz in New Deal America.* Cambridge: Harvard University Press.

Strain, Christopher. (2016). *The Long Sixties: America, 1954–1974.* Malden: Blackwell.

Strausbaugh, John. (2007). *Black Like You: Blackface, Whiteface, Insult & Imitation in American Popular Culture.* New York: Penguin.

Street, Joe. (2007). *The Culture War in the Civil Rights Movement.* Gainesville: University Press of Florida.

Street, John. (1986). *Rebel Rock: The Politics of Popular Music.* New York: Blackwell.

___. (1997). *Politics and Popular Culture.* Philadelphia: Temple University Press.

___. (2012). *Music and Politics.* Cambridge: Polity Press.

Stubbs, David. (2003). *Jimi Hendrix: Voodoo Child: The Stories Behind Every Song.* New York: Thunder's Mouth Press.

Stuckey, Sterling. (1987). *Slave Culture: Nationalist Theory and the Foundations of Black America.* Oxford: Oxford University Press.

Stuessy, Joe, and Lipscomb, Scott. (2012). *Rock & Roll: Its History and Stylistic Development* (7th Edition). Englewood Cliffs, NJ: Prentice Hall.

Sturkey, William, and Hale, Jon N. (Eds.). (2015). *To Write in the Light of Freedom: The Newspapers of the 1964 Mississippi Freedom Schools.* Jackson: University Press of Mississippi.

Sugrue, Thomas J. (2008). *Sweet Land of Liberty: The Forgotten Struggle for Civil Rights in the North.* New York: Random House.

Sullivan, Patricia. (2009). *Lift Every Voice: The NAACP and the Making of the Civil Rights Movement.* New York: New Press.

Sutton, Philip W. (2000). *Explaining Environmentalism: In Search of a New Social Movement.* Aldershot, Enlgand: Ashgate.

Sweeting, Adam W. (2004). *Cover Versions: Singing Other People's Songs.* London: Pimlico.

Swenson, John. (1983). *Bill Haley: The Daddy of Rock & Roll.* New York: Stein & Day.

Szatmary, David P. (2010). *Rockin' in Time: A Social History of Rock & Roll* (7th Edition). Upper Saddle River, NJ: Prentice Hall.

___. (2013). *Rockin' in Time: A Social History of Rock & Roll* (8th Edition). Boston: Pearson.

Tabb, William K. (1970). *The Political Economy of the Black Ghetto.* New York: Norton.

Talevski, Nick. (1998). *The Unofficial Encyclopedia of the Rock & Roll Hall of Fame.* Westport, CT: Greenwood Press.

Talevski, Nick, and West, Robert D. (2010). *The Origins and Early History of Rock & Roll.* Green, OH: Guardian Express Media.

Taraborrelli, J. Randy. (2014). *Diana Ross: A Biography*. New York: Citadel Press/Kensington Publishing.

Tasker, Yvonne, and Negra, Diane. (Eds.). (2007). *Interrogating Post-Feminism: Gender and the Politics of Popular Culture*. Durham: Duke University Press.

Taylor, Clarence. (2002). *Black Religious Intellectuals: The Fight for Equality from Jim Crow to the 21st Century*. New York: Routledge.

___. (2011). *Civil Rights in New York City: From World War II to the Giuliani Era*. New York: Fordham University Press.

Taylor, Cynthia. (2006). *A. Philip Randolph: The Religious Journey of an African American Labor Leader*. New York: New York University Press.

Taylor, Jon E. (2013). *Freedom to Serve: Truman, Civil Rights, and Executive Order 9981*. New York: Routledge.

Taylor, Robert L. (2013). *Thomas A. Dorsey Father of Black Gospel Music an Interview: Genesis of Black Gospel Music*. Bloomington, IN: Trafford Publishing.

Tenaille, Frank. (2002). *Music is the Weapon of the Future: Fifty Years of African Popular Music*. Chicago: Lawrence Hill.

Terborg-Penn, Rosalyn. (1998). *African American Women in the Struggle for the Vote, 1850–1920*. Bloomington: Indiana University Press.

Theoharis, Jeanne. (2013). *The Rebellious Life of Mrs. Rosa Parks*. Boston: Beacon.

Theoharis, Jeanne, and Woodard, Komozi. (Eds.). (2005). *Groundwork: Local Black Freedom Movements in America*. New York: New York University.

Thomas, Lorenzo. (2008). *Don't Deny My Name: Words and Music and the Black Intellectual Tradition* (Aldon Lynn Nielsen, Ed.). Ann Arbor: University of Michigan Press.

Thompson, Katrina D. (2014). *Ring Shout, Wheel About: The Racial Politics of Music and Dance in North American Slavery*. Urbana: University of Illinois Press.

Thompson, Robert Farris. (1983). *Flash of the Spirit: African and Afro-American Art and Philosophy*. New York: Random House.

Thuesen, Sarah C. (2013). *Greater than Equal: African American Struggles for Schools and Citizenship in North Carolina, 1919–1965*. Chapel Hill: University of North Carolina Press.

Tilly, Charles. (2004). *Social Movements, 1768–2004*. Boulder: Paradigm Publishers.

Tolnay, Stewart E. and Beck, E.M. (1992). "Racial Violence and Black Migration in the American South, 1910 to 1930." *American Sociological Review* 57 (1), 103–116.

Torres, Sasha. (2003). *Black, White, and in Color: Television and Black Civil Rights*. Princeton: Princeton University Press.

Tosches, Nick. (1996). *Country: The Twisted Roots Of Rock & Roll*. New York: Da Capo Press.

___. (1999). *Unsung Heroes of Rock & Roll: The Birth of Rock in the Wild Years Before Elvis*. New York: Da Capo Press.

Trost, Theodore Louis. (Ed.). (2007). *African Diaspora and the Study of Religion*. New York: Palgrave-Macmillan.

Trotter, Joe William, Jr. (Ed.). (1991). *The Great Migration in Historical Perspective: New Dimensions of Race, Class, and Gender*. Bloomington: Indiana University Press.

Tsesis, Alexander. (2008). *We Shall Overcome: A History of Civil Rights and the Law*. New Haven: Yale University Press.

Tudor, Dean, and Tudor, Nancy. (1979). *Black Music*. Littleton, CO: Libraries Unlimited.

Turner, Steve. (1998). *Trouble Man: The Life and Death of Marvin Gaye*. New York: Ecco Press.

Turner, Steve. (2010). *An Illustrated History of Gospel*. Oxford: Lion Hudson.

Tytell, John. (2006). *Naked Angels: The Lives and Literature of the Beat Generation*. Landhom: Ivan R. Dee Publishing.

Umoja, Akinyele Omowale. (2013). *We Will Shoot Back: Armed Resistance in the Mississippi Freedom Movement*. New York: New York University Press.

Uslan, Michael, and Solomon, Bruce. (1981). *Dick Clark's First Twenty-Five Years of Rock & Roll*. New York: Dell.

Valk, Anne M., and Brown, Leslie. (2010). *Living with Jim Crow: African American Women and Memories of the Segregated South*. New York: Palgrave Macmillan.

Van Deburg, William L. (1992). *New Day in Babylon: The Black Power Movement and American Culture, 1965–1975*. Chicago: University of Chicago Press.

van Rijn, Guido. (1997). *Roosevelt's Blues: African American Blues and Gospel Songs on FDR*. Jackson: University Press of Mississippi.

___. (2001). "'Climbing the Mountain Top': African American Blues and Gospel Songs from the Civil Rights Years." In Brian Ward (Ed.), *Media, Culture, and the Modern African-American Freedom Struggle* (122–144). Gainesville: University Press of Florida.

___. (2004). *The Truman and Eisenhower Blues: African American Blues and Gospel Songs, 1945–1960*. New York: Continuum.

___. (2007). *Kennedy's Blues: African American Blues and Gospel Songs on JFK*. Jackson: University Press of Mississippi.

___. (2009). *President Johnson's Blues: African American Blues and Gospel Songs on LBJ, Martin Luther King, Robert Kennedy and Vietnam, 1963–1968*. Overveen, The Netherlands: Agram Blues Books.

___. (2011). *The Nixon and Ford Blues: African American Blues and Gospel Songs on Vietnam, Watergate, Civil Rights and Inflation, 1969–1976*. Overveen, The Netherlands: Agram Blues Books.

___. (2012). *The Carter, Reagan, Bush Sr., Clinton, Bush Jr. & Obama Blues: African American Blues and Gospel songs, 1976–2012*. Overveen, The Netherlands: Agram Blues Books.

Vazzano, Frank. (2010). *From Slavery to the Sixties: The Roots and Cultural Foundation of Rock Music*. Dubuque, IA: Kendall/Hunt.

Venkatesh, Sudhir Alladi. (2000). *American Project: The Rise and Fall of a Modern Ghetto*. Cambridge: Harvard University Press.

___. (2006). *Off the Books: The Underground Economy of the Urban Poor*. Cambridge: Harvard University Press.

Vergara, Camilo J. (1995). *The New American Ghetto*. New Brunswick: Rutgers University Press.

Vogel, Shane. (2009). *The Scene of Harlem Cabaret: Race, Sexuality, Performance*. Chicago: University of Chicago Press.

Wagnleitner, Reinhold, and May, Elaine T. (Eds.). (2000). *Here, There, and Everywhere: The Foreign Politics of American Popular Culture*. Hanover, NH: University Press of New England.

Wald, Elijah. (2009). *How the Beatles Destroyed Rock & Roll: An Alternative History of American Popular Music*. Oxford: Oxford University Press.

Waldman, Anne. (Ed.). (2007). *The Beat Book: Writings from the Beat Generation*. Boston: Shambhala.

Waldman, Tom. (2003). *We All Want to Change the World: Rock and Politics from Elvis to Eminem*. Lanham, MD: Taylor Trade.

Waldo, Terry. (1976). *This Is Ragtime*. New York: Hawthorn Books.

Waldrep, Christopher. (Ed.). (2001). *Racial Violence on Trial: A Handbook with Cases, Laws, and Documents*. Santa Barbara, CA: ABC-CLIO.

___. (2002). *Many Faces of Judge Lynch: Extralegal Violence and Punishment in America*. New York: Palgrave-Macmillan.

___. (Ed.). (2006). *Lynching in America: A History in Documents*. New York: New York University Press.

___. (2009). *African Americans Confront Lynching: Strategies of Resistance from the Civil War to the Civil Rights Era*. Lanham, MD: Rowman & Littlefield.

Waldschmidt-Nelson, Britta. (2012). *Dreams and Nightmares: Martin Luther King, Jr., Malcolm X, and the Struggle for Black Equality in America*. Gainesville: University Press of Florida.

Walker, John Albert. (2001). *Art in the Age of Mass Media*. London: Pluto.

Walker, Wyatt Tee. (1979). *"Somebody's Calling My Name": Black Sacred Music and Social Change*. Valley Forge, PA: Judson Press.

Wall, Wendy. (2008). *Inventing the "American Way": The Politics of Consensus from the New Deal to the Civil Rights Movement*. Oxford: Oxford University Press.

Wallenstein, Peter. (2008). *Higher Education and the Civil Rights Movement: White Supremacy, Black Southerners, and College Campuses*. Gainesville: University Press of Florida.

Waller, Don. (1985). *The Motown Story*. New York: Scribner.

Walters, Ronald W. (1993). *Pan-Africanism in the African Diaspora: An Analysis of Modern Afrocentric Political Movement*. Detroit: Wayne State University Press.

Ward, Brian. (1998). *Just My Soul Responding: Rhythm & Blues, Black Consciousness, and Race Relations*. Berkeley: University of California Press.

___. (Ed.). (2001). *Media, Culture, and the Modern African American Freedom Struggle*. Gainesville: University Press of Florida.

___. (2002). "'All for One, and One for All': Black Enterprise, Racial Politics and the Business of Soul." In Norman Kelley (Ed.), *R&B, Rhythm and Business: The Political Economy of Black Music* (138–157). New York: Akashic.

___. (2004). *Radio and the Struggle for Civil Rights in the South*. Gainesville: University Press of Florida.

___. (2012). " 'People Get Ready': Music and the Civil Rights Movement of the 1950s and 1960s." http://www.gilderlehrman.org/history-by-era/civil-rights-movement/essays/"people-get-ready"-music-and-civil-rights-movement-1950s.

Ward, Jason M. (2011). *Defending White Democracy: The Making of a Segregationist Movement and the Remaking of Racial Politics, 1936–1965*. Chapel Hill: University of North Carolina Press.

Warren, Roland L. (Ed.). (2008). *Politics and African American Ghettos*. New Brunswick, NJ: Aldine Transaction.

Washburn, Patrick S. (1981). "The 'Pittsburgh Courier's Double V Campaign in 1942." Paper presented at the Annual Meeting of the Association for Education in Journalism (64th, East Lansing, MI, August 8–11, 1981).

___. (1986). "The Pittsburgh Courier's Double V Campaign in 1942." *American Journalism* 3 (2), 73–86.

Washington, Joseph R. (1964). *Black Religion: The Negro and Christianity in the United States*. Boston: Beacon.

Waters, Kristin and Conaway, Carol B. (Eds.). (2007). *Black Women's Intellectual Traditions: Speaking Their Minds*. Burlington, VT: University of Vermont Press.

Watson, Steven. (1995). *The Birth of the Beat Generation: Visionaries, Rebels, and Hipsters, 1944–1960*. New York: Pantheon Books.

Watters, Pat. (1971). *Down To Now: Reflections on the Southern Civil Rights Movement*. New York: Pantheon.

Webb, Clive. (2005). *Massive Resistance: Southern Opposition to the Second Reconstruction*. Oxford: Oxford University Press.

Weber, Deanna Frith. (2010). "The Freedom Singers: Their History and Legacy for Music Education." D.M.A. dissertation, Boston University, Boston, MA.

Webster, Aaron. (2003). *Elvis, the New Rage: A Radio History from 1945 to 1955*. Plano, TX: Republic of Texas Press.

Webster, Dwight. (2011). "Gospel Music in the United States of America 1960s–1980s: A Study of the Themes of 'Survival,' 'Elevation,' and 'Liberation' in a Popular Urban Contemporary Black Folk Sacred Mass Music." Graduate Theological Union, University of California, Berkeley, CA.

Weidman, Richard. (2015). *The Beat Generation FAQ: All That's Left to Know About the Angelheaded Hipsters*. Montclair, NJ: Backbeat Books.

Weinbaum, Alys Eve. (2001). "Reproducing Racial Globality: W.E.B. Du Bois and the Sexual Politics of Black Internationalism." *Social Text* 19 (2), 15–41.

Weinbaum, Alys Eve. (2013). "Gendering the General Strike: W. E. B. Du Bois's Black Reconstruction and Black Feminism's 'Propaganda of History'." *South Atlantic Quarterly* 112 (3), 437–464.

Weisbrot, Robert. (1990). *Freedom Bound: A History of America's Civil Rights Movement.* New York: Norton.

Weissman, Dick. (2005). *Which Side Are You On?: An Inside History of the Folk Music Revival in America.* New York: Continuum.

Welky, David. (2013). *Marching Across the Color-Line: A. Philip Randolph and Civil Rights in the World War II Era.* Oxford: Oxford University Press.

Werner, Craig H. (2004). *Higher Ground: Stevie Wonder, Aretha Franklin, Curtis Mayfield, and the Rise and Fall of American Soul.* New York: Crown Publishers.

___. (2006a). "Black music and black possibility: from be-bop to hip-hop." In Robert L. Harris and Rosalyn Terborg-Penn (Eds.), *The Columbia Guide to African American History since 1939* (172–193). New York: Columbia University Press.

___. (2006b). *Change is Gonna Come: Music, Race & the Soul of America.* Ann Arbor: University of Michigan Press.

Wertheim, Arthur F. (2006). *Vaudeville Wars: How Keith-Albee and Orpheum Circuits Controlled the Big-Time and Its Performers.* New York: Palgrave Macmillan

Wesley, Charles H. (1984). *The History of the National Association of Colored Women's Clubs: A Legacy of Service.* Washington, D.C.: National Association of Colored Women.

Wexler, Jerry. (1993). *Rhythm And The Blues: A Life in American Music* (with David Ritz). New York: Knopf.

Whitall, Susan. (1998). *Women of Motown: An Oral History.* New York: Avon Books.

White, Adam. (1985). *The Motown Story.* Boston: Bedford Press.

White, Marjorie L., and Manis, Andrew Michael. (Eds.). (2000). *Birmingham Revolutionaries: The Reverend Fred Shuttlesworth and the Alabama Christian Movement for Human Rights.* Macon: Mercer University Press.

White, Shane, and White, Graham J. (2005). *The Sounds of Slavery: Discovering African American History through Songs, Sermons, and Speech.* Boston: Beacon Press.

Wilder, Craig S. (2001). *In the Company of Black Men: The African Influence on African American Culture in New York City.* New York: New York University.

Wilkerson, Isabel. (2010). *The Warmth of Other Suns: The Epic Story of America's Great Migration.* New York: Random House.

Wilkerson, William S., and Paris, Jeffrey. (Eds.). (2001). *New Critical Theory: Essays on Liberation.* Lanham, MD: Rowman & Littlefield.

Williams, Chad Louis. (2010). *Torchbearers of Democracy: African American Soldiers in the World War I Era.* Chapel Hill: University of North Carolina Press.

Williams, Johnny E. (2002). "Linking Beliefs to Collective Action: Politicized Religious Beliefs and the Civil Rights Movement." *Sociological Forum* 17 (2), 203–22.

Williams, Johnny E. (2003). *African American Religion and the Civil Rights Movement in Arkansas.* Jackson : University Press of Mississippi.

Williams, Juan. (1987). *Eyes on the Prize: America's Civil Rights Years, 1954–1965.* New York: Viking.

Williams, Otis. (1988). *Temptations* (with Patricia Romanowski Bashe). New York: Putnam.

Williams, Rhys H. (2004). "The Cultural Contexts of Collective Action: Constraints, Opportunities, and the Symbolic Life of Social Movements." In David A. Snow, Sarah Anne Soule, and Hanspeter Kriesi (Eds.), *The Blackwell Companion to Social Movements* (91–115). Malden, MA: Blackwell.

Williams, Yohuru R. (2015). *Rethinking the Black Freedom Movement.* New York: Routledge.

Williams-Jones, Pearl. (1975). "Afro-American Gospel Music: A Crystallization of the Black Aesthetic." *Ethnomusicology* 19 (3), 373–85.

Williamson, Joel. (1984). *South Since Emancipation.* Oxford: Oxford University Press.

___. (1986). *A Rage for Order: Black/White Relations in the American South Since Emancipation.* Oxford: Oxford University Press.

___. (2015). *Elvis Presley: A Southern Life.* Oxford: Oxford University Press.

Willis, Deborah, and Williams, Carla. (2002). *The Black Female Body: A Photographic History.* Philadelphia: Temple University Press.

Wilmore, Gayraud S. (1998). *Black Religion and Black Radicalism: An Interpretation of the Religious History of Afro-American People.* Maryknoll, NY: Orbis.

Wilson, David. (2007). *Cities and Race: America's New Black Ghetto.* New York: Routledge.

Wilson, James F. (2010). *Bulldaggers, Pansies, and Chocolate Babies: Performance, Race, and Sexuality in the Harlem Renaissance.* Ann Arbor: University of Michigan Press.

Wilson, Mary. (1999). *Dreamgirl and Supreme Faith: My Life as a Supreme.* New York: Cooper Square.

Wilson, Shawn. (2008). *Research Is Ceremony: Indigenous Research Methods.* Black Point: Fernwood.

Wilson, William J. (1987). *The Truly Disadvantaged: The Inner-City, the Underclass, and Public Policy.* Chicago: University of Chicago Press.

___. (1997). *When Work Disappears: The World of the New Urban Poor.* New York: Knopf/Random House.

___. (1999). *The Bridge Over the Racial Divide: Rising Inequality and Coalition Politics.* Berkeley: University of California Press.

___. (2009). *More Than Just Race: Being Black and Poor in the Inner-City.* New York: Norton.

Winters, Paul A. (Ed.). (2000). *The Civil Rights Movement.* San Diego: Greenhaven.

Wolcott, Victoria W. (2012). *Race, Riots, and Roller Coasters: The Struggle over Segregated Recreation in America.* Philadelphia: University of Pennsylvania Press.

Wolff, Daniel J. (1995). *You Send Me: The Life and Times of Sam Cooke.* New York: Morrow.

Wondrich, David. (2003). *Stomp and Swerve: American Music Gets Hot, 1843–1924.* Chicago: Chicago Review Press.

Wood, Amy Louise. (2009). *Lynching and Spectacle: Witnessing Racial Violence in America, 1890–1940.* Chapel Hill: University of North Carolina Press.

Woodson, Carter G. (1922). *The Negro in Our History.* Washington, D.C.: Associated Publishers.

___. (1969). *A Century of Negro Migration.* New York: Russell & Russell.

Work, John W. (Ed.). (1998). *American Negro Songs: 230 Folk Songs and Spirituals, Religious and Secular.* Mineola, NY: Dover.

Wormser, Richard. (Producer). (2002). *The Rise and Fall of Jim Crow: A Century of Segregation* (4 Episodes). San Francisco, CA: California Newsreel.

Wortham, Robert A. (2005a). "Du Bois and the Sociology of Religion: Rediscovering a Founding Figure." *Sociological Inquiry* 75 (4), 433–452.

___. (2005b). "Du Bois and the Sociology of Religion: Rediscovering a Founding Figure." *Sociological Inquiry* 75 (4), 433–452.

___. (2009). "W.E.B. Du Bois, the Black Church, and the Sociological Study of Religion." *Sociological Spectrum* 29 (2), 144–172.

Wright, Gavin. (2013). *Sharing the Prize: The Economics of the Civil Rights Revolution in the American South.* Cambridge: Harvard University Press.

Wright, Sarah E. (1990). *A. Philip Randolph: Integration in the Workplace.* Englewood Cliffs, NJ: Silver Burdett Press.

Wynn, Neil A. (2010). *The African American Experience during World War II.* Lanham, MD: Rowman & Littlefield Publishers.

Yancey, Eddie. (2007). "Rhythm & Blues Protest Songs: Voices of Resistance." Ph.D. dissertation, Department of African American Studies, Clark Atlanta University, Atlanta, GA.

Yellin, Jean Fagan. (1973). "Du Bois's Crisis and Woman's Suffrage." *Massachusetts Review* 14 (2), 365–375.

Young, Alan. (1997). *Woke Me Up This Morning: Black Gospel Singers and the Gospel Life*. Jackson: University Press of Mississippi.

___. (2001). *The Pilgrim Jubilees*. Jackson: University Press of Mississippi.

Young, Richard P. (1970). *Roots of Rebellion: The Evolution of Black Politics and Protest Since World War II*. New York: Harper & Row.

Zak, Albin. (2010). *I Don't Sound Like Nobody: Remaking Music in 1950s America*. Ann Arbor: University of Michigan Press.

Zangrando, Robert L. (1980). *The NAACP Crusade Against Lynching, 1909–1950*. Philadelphia: Temple University Press.

Zinn, Howard. (1965). *SNCC: The New Abolitionists*. Boston: Beacon.

Zolten, Jerry. (2003). *Great God A'Mighty! The Dixie Hummingbirds: Celebrating the Rise of Soul Gospel Music*. Oxford: Oxford University Press, 2003.

Zook, Kristal B. (2008). *I See Black People: The Rise and Fall of African American-Owned Television and Radio*. New York: Nation Books.

Zott, Lynn M. (Ed.). (2003). *The Beat Generation: A Gale Critical Companion*. Detroit: Gale.

Zuckerman, Phil. (2002). "The Sociology of Religion of W.E.B. Du Bois." *Sociology of Religion* 63 (2), 239–253.

___. (2009). "The Irreligiosity of W.E.B. Du Bois." In Edward J. Blum and Jason R. Young (Eds.), *The Souls of W.E.B. Du Bois: New Essays and Reflections* (pp. 3–17). Macon: Mercer University Press.

Zwerin, Michael. (2000). *Swing Under the Nazis: Jazz as a Metaphor for Freedom*. New York: Cooper Square Press.

Index

24-7 Spyz, 195

Adams, Billy, 160
Africana critical theory, 45–46, 52n15, 52n16
Abolitionist Movement, 1, 2, 13, 41, 42, 73, 86, 125
Aguilera, Christina, 134
Albany Movement, 105
Allen, Richard "Pistol", 140
Altschuler, Glenn, 175, 190, 191, 196
American Independent Party, 96
Anderson, Tanisha, 3
Armstrong, Louis, 8, 105
Ashford, Jack, 140
Atlantic Records, 5, 131, 134

Babbitt, Bob, 140
Bad Brains, 195
Baker, Ella, 3, 6, 12, 124, 143
Baker, Houston, 41
Baker, LaVern, 1, 5, 7, 116, 171, 180
Baldwin, James, 8, 10, 39, 143
Ballard, Hank, & the Midnighters, 171, 180, 183, 195
Banfield, William, 24
Baraka, Amiri, 120–121, 121, 123–124
Barth, Paul, 124
Basie, Count, 183
Beals, Melba Pattillo, 141
Beastie Boys, 149
Beat Generation, 177, 182, 200n21
Beauchamp, George, 124
Beck, Glen, 147
Belafonte, Harry, 39
Bell, William, 131
Begle, Howell, 186
Benford, Robert, 30
Benjamin, William "Benny", 140

Berry, Chuck, 5, 124, 149, 170–171, 180, 181, 195
Bertrand, Michael, 191–192
Bevel, James, 141
Beyoncé, 134
Blackwell, Otis, 187, 200n27
Black Women's Club Movement, 13, 50, 65, 75–76, 100n13, 105, 107, 108–109, 110, 122
Bland, Sandra, 3
Blind Boys of Alabama, 5, 91
Blind Boys of Mississippi, 5, 91
Block, Sam, 61, 99n5
blues, 64–65, 70, 104, 110, 111–115, 119–120, 121, 123–124, 129, 131, 164–169
Boone, Daniel, 183
Boone, Pat, 183–184, 200n25
Bostic, Earl, 124
Bowen, Jimmy, 160
Boyd, Rekia, 3
Braceland, Francis, 175
Bradford, Perry, 166
Brahms, Johannes, 168
Brando, Marlon, 181
Brenston, Jackie, 171
Bright Light Quartet, 91
Bristol, Johnny, 146
Brooks, Gwendolyn, 39
Brown, Charles, 127, 132
Brown, Courtney, 24
Brown, Eddie "Bongo", 140
Brown, James, 131
Brown, John, 76
Brown, Maxine, 141
Brown, Michael, 3
Brown, Minnijean, 141
Brown, Oscar, Jr., 126
Brown, Roy, 116
Brown, Ruth, 1, 5, 41, 116, 171, 180, 183

Burke, Solomon, 187
Burlison, Paul, 160
Burnette, Johnny, 160
Burnim, Mellonee, 24, 65, 87–88, 93
Busoni, Ferruccio, 168

Carroll, Reverend John, 175
Cash, Johnny, 160
Carby, Hazel, 100n14
Carmichael, Stokely, 55–56, 58, 99n4
CBS Trumpeteers, 91
Chantels, 180
Chapman, Tracy, 195
Charioteers, 127
Charles, Ray, 39, 131, 134, 140, 192
Charms, 132, 184
Checker, Chubby, 149, 180
Cherry, Eagle-Eye, 195
ChesnuTT, Cody, 195
Chess, Leonard, 156n32
Chess, Phil, 156n32
Chess Records, 5, 131, 134, 156n32
Chiffons, 180
Children's Crusade, 141
Chitlin' Circuit, 185, 200n26
Chocolate Genius, 195
Chopin, Frédéric François, 168
Chordettes, 180
Chords, 132, 180, 191, 201n30
Chosen Gospel Singers, 91
Christian, Charlie, 124
Civil Rights Act of 1964, 66, 152
Clark, Gary, Jr., 195
Clark, Septima, 3, 124
Clay, Andreana, 153n3
Clefs of Calvary, 91
Coasters, 171, 180
Coates, Dorothy Love, 1, 5, 39
Cobb, Arnett, 124
Cochran, Eddie, 160
Coffey, Dennis, 140
Cole, Nat King, 39, 127, 132, 140
Coleman, Jaybird, 178
Collins, Addie Mae, 141–142
Colvin, Claudette, 141
Congress of Racial Equality (CORE),
    141, 146
Connor, Bull (Theophilus Eugene
    Connor), 57

Cooke, Sam, 1, 7, 39, 126, 140, 192
Covach, John, 188–189
Covington, Bogus Blind Ben, 178
Crawford III, John, 3
Crows, 132, 171
Crummell, Alexander, 77
Crystals, 180
Culley, Frank "Floorshow", 124
Culp, Napoleon "Nappy Brown", 149

D'Arby, Terence Trent, 195
Darden, Bob, 40, 64
Davis, Angela, 10, 114
Davis, Billy, 139
Davis, Francis, 166
Davis, Nathan, 24
Davis, Ossie, 39
Davis, Sammy, Jr., 39
Dawson, Ronnie, 160
Dean, James, 181
Debussy, Claude, 168
Dee, Ruby, 39
Deep River Boys, 128
Delta Rhythm Boys, 127
Diddley, Bo, 5, 124, 170–171, 180, 195
Dillard, Varetta, 116
Dixie Hummingbirds, 91, 128
DJ Jazzy Jeff & the Fresh Prince, 149
Doggett, Peter, 146–147
Domino, Fats, 5, 171, 180, 181, 183, 184,
    192
Dominoes, 183
doo-wop, 64, 81, 127–138, 155n23,
    155n24, 159, 170, 172
Dorsey, Thomas, 66–67, 103–105, 153n1
"Double V" campaign, 118, 155n19
Douglass, Frederick, 77
Drifters, 171, 180
Du Bois, W.E.B., 1, 7–12, 19n4, 53, 63,
    65, 71–83, 95, 96, 100n14, 133–135,
    137, 161
DuBose, Samuel, 3

Early, Gerald, 144–145
Eckford, Elizabeth, 141
Eckstine, Billy, 132
Edwin Hawkins Singers, 64
El Dorados, 184
Electronica, Jay, 142

Ellington, Duke, 8, 105, 127
Ellison, Ralph, 1, 18n1
Esquerita, 116, 195
Estes, Sleepy John, 178
Everly Brothers, 160
Evers, Medgar, 3, 124
Évora, Césaria, 164
Eyerman, Ron, 13–14, 16, 24, 30–31, 44,
    46–47, 48–49

Fairfield Four, 91, 128
Fair Housing Act of 1968, 152
Fat Boys, 149
Feintuch, Burt, 88
Feldstein, Ruth, 24, 40
Ferguson, Kate, 77
Ferguson, Robert "H-Bomb", 149
field hollers, 165, 198n4
Fishbone, 195
Fisk Jubilee Singers, 63
Fitzgerald, F. Scott, 177
Five Keys, 132
Five Satins, 180
Flack, Roberta, 156n32
Flamingos, 180, 184
Flory, Andrew, 188–189
Floyd, Eddie, 131
Floyd, Samuel, 63
Follow For Now, 195
Ford, Ezell, 3
Ford, Henry, 145
Forrest, Jimmy, 124
Foucault, Michel, 14–16, 19n6
Four Toppers/Five Red Caps, 132
Four Tops, 1, 131, 140, 151
Francis, Connie, 184
Francis, Shereese, 3
Franklin, Aretha, 134, 140, 156n32
Franklin, John Hope, 179
Franti, Michael, 195
Freedom Riders Movement, 53, 55, 93,
    96, 105, 114, 141
Freed, Alan, 162, 170, 172, 199n14
freedom songs, 2, 12, 13, 17, 24–25,
    47–48, 48–50, 53–62, 64, 69, 70, 73,
    75, 79, 81, 87, 97, 99n3, 103, 124, 125,
    127, 134, 137, 165, 189, 197
Fuqua, Harvey, 146, 192
Funkadelic, 195

Funk Brothers, 146
Fu-Schnickens, 150

Garner, Eric, 3
Garofalo, Reebee, 150–151, 171–172
Garvey, Marcus, 118
Gary, Kays, 180
Gaye, Marvin, 131, 140, 146, 151
Gayle, Raymond, 195
George, Nelson, 140–141, 142, 144, 147,
    162–163
Gibbs, Georgia, 183, 184
Gillett, Charlie, 170, 192–193
Golden Gate Quartet, 91, 128
gospel, 53–98
"gospel highway", 66–68, 86
Goldberg, Marv, 130–131
Gordy, Anna, 139
Gordy, Berry, 138–152, 156n29, 161, 192
Gordy, Betty, 139
Gordy, Gwen, 139
Gordy, Joy, 139
Gordy, Terry, 139
Gourse, Leslie, 114–115
Gracie, Charlie, 160, 187
Gramsci, Antonio, 26–27, 51n5
Grant, Jacquelyn, 72
Grant, Oscar, 3
Gray, Freddie, 3
Green, Ernest, 141
Gregory, Dick, 39
Griffin, Farah Jasmine, 114
Griffith, Johnny, 140
Guralnick, Peter, 174, 177–179,
    180–182, 191, 194, 196

Haley, Bill, 160, 171–172, 180, 182–184,
    199n16
Hamer, Fannie Lou, 3, 6, 7, 12, 124
Hamilton, Dave, 140
Hannity, Sean, 147
Hansberry, Lorraine, 39
Harlem Renaissance, 13, 41, 50, 65, 105,
    110, 118, 138, 163
Harmonizing Four, 91, 128
Harper, Ben, 195
Harp-Tones, 132
Harris, Michael, 66, 103, 104
Harris, Wynonie, 116, 192

Havens, Richie, 1, 7, 39
Hawkins, Screamin' Jay, 149, 180
Heavy D & the Boyz, 149
Heilbut, Anthony, 54, 69–70, 84, 85–86
Helper, Laura, 40
Henderson, Michael, 140
Hendrix, Jimi, 124, 193, 195, 201n31
Holiday, Billie, 114, 126
Holland, Eddie, 139
Holland–Dozier–Holland (Brain
     Holland, Lamont Dozier, and Eddie
     Holland), 146
Holly, Buddy, 160, 171–172, 180
Hooker, Earl, 124
Hooker, John Lee, 180, 192
Horne, Lena, 39
Howard, Brittany, 195
Hunt, Scott, 30
Hunt, Van, 195
Hunter, Ivory Joe, 184
Hunter, Joe, 140

Ianniello, Lynne, 155n21
Ingraham, Laura, 147
Ink Spots, 127, 130

Jackson, Chuck, 141
Jackson, Clarence "Bull Moose", 149
Jackson, Jim, 183
Jackson, Mahalia, 1, 5, 8, 39, 41, 48, 53,
     66, 105
Jackson, Millie, 156n32
Jackson, Walter, 141
Jackson, Wanda, 180
Jackson, Willis, 124
Jacquet, Illinois, 124
Jamerson, James, 140
James, Elmore, 124, 159, 180
James, Etta, 5, 131, 134, 156n32, 180, 183
Jamison, Andrew, 13–14, 16, 24, 30–31,
     44, 46–47, 48–49
Jasper, James, 29
Jay-Z, 142
jazz, 41, 63–64, 65, 66–67, 68, 105,
     109–110, 111, 112–113, 115–116, 121,
     124–125, 127, 129, 131, 134, 135, 138,
     139, 139–140, 166, 168, 169, 170, 173,
     176–177, 192
Jefferson, Blind Lemon, 178

John, Little Willie, 187
John, Mable, 139
Johnson, Lonnie, 125
Johnson, Marv, 139
Johnson, Robert, 159, 183
Johnny Moore's Three Blazers. *See*
     Moore, Johnny
Jones, LeRoi, 39
Jones, Peggy (a.k.a., "Lady Bo"), 180
Jones, Stacy, 114
Jones, Uriel, 140
Joplin, Janis, 134
Joplin, Scott, 105, 168, 199n11
Jordan, Louis, 114–115, 149, 155n15
jump blues, 114–116, 121, 122, 125, 126,
     127, 129, 130, 131, 136, 139, 149,
     155n15, 155n16, 159, 173, 177, 180,
     183, 198n2
Juvenile (rapper), 142

Kamin, Jonathan, 40
Karlmark, Gloria Ray, 141
Keita, Salif, 164
Kendrick, Eddie, 151
Kidjo, Angélique, 164
Kid 'N' Play, 149
King, B.B., 124, 180
King, Martin Luther, 3, 6–7, 8, 12, 53,
     56, 58, 59, 89, 124, 142–143, 147, 150,
     152, 156n34, 174
King Records, 131
Knight, Gladys, 140, 156n32
Knight, Gladys, & the Pips. *See* Knight,
     Gladys
Kool G Rap, 142
Kot, Greg, 66
Kravitz, Lenny, 195
Ku Klux Klan, 96, 97
Kuhn, Thomas, 46–47
Kuti, Fela, 164

LaBelle, Patti, 156n32
Ladysmith Black Mambazo, 164
Lafayette, Bernard, 141
Lait, Jack, 175–176
Lamb, Joseph, 168, 199n11
LaNier, Carlotta Walls, 141
Larrieux, Amel, 195
Lemons, Gary, 100n14

Leonard, Freddy, 55
Levin, Mark, 147
Levine, Lawrence, 125–127, 130
Lewis, Barbara, 141
Lewis, Jerry Lee, 160, 171, 172, 180, 181, 187
Lil' Wayne, 142
Limbaugh, Rush, 147
Lipsitz, George, 47
"Little Rock Nine", 141
Living Colour, 195
Lô, Cheikh, 164
Logan, Rayford, 102n16
Lost Generation, 176, 182
Luper, Clara, 141
Lymon, Frankie, & The Teenagers, 180

Maal, Baaba, 164
Mailer, Norman, 178
Makeba, Miriam, 164
Mapfumo, Thomas, 164
March on Washington (1963), 105, 141, 146, 148, 152
March on Washington Movement, 105, 118, 120–121, 155n20
Marcus, Greil, 170, 171
Margolick, David, 114
Markie, Biz, 149
Marl, Marley, 142
Martin, Trayvon, 4
Marvelettes, 139, 140
Mattern, Mark, 25
Maultsby, Portia, 24, 86–87, 186
May, Brother Joe, 1, 5
Maybelle, Big, 116, 139, 159
Mayfield, Percy, 192
McCanless, Anne, 40
McNair, Denise, 141
McKay, Nellie, 100n14
McKenna, Natasha, 3
McPhatter, Clyde, & the Drifters, 171
MC Shan, 142
Messina, Joe, 140
Mighty Clouds of Joy, 90, 91
Milburn, Amos, 192
Miles, Buddy, 195
Miller, Doug, 155n22
Miller, Glen, 127
Miller, Karl, 109

Millinder, Lucky, 127
Mills, C. Wright, 35
Mills Brothers, 127, 130
Minnie, Memphis, 125
Mobb Deep, 142
Monk, Thelonious, 122
Montgomery Bus Boycott, 53, 56, 105, 152, 190
Montgomery Improvement Association, 53
Moonglows, 132, 192
Moore, Johnny, 127
Moore, Scotty, 160
Mortimer, Lee, 175–176
Mothershed, Thelma, 141
Motown Records, 5, 48, 63, 109, 131, 138–152, 152–153, 156n29, 156n31, 157n35, 179, 192
Mozart, Wolfgang Amadeus, 168

NaS, 142
Nash, Diane, 141
National Association for the Advancement of Colored People (NAACP), 9, 76, 141, 146, 147
National Association of Colored Women (NACW), 75–76
Ndegeocello, Meshell, 195
N'Dour, Youssou, 164
Neely, Big Jay, 124
Negro American Labor Council (NALC), 146
Nelson, Ricky, 160, 180
New Negro Movement, 13, 50, 65, 105, 107, 108, 110, 118, 122, 138, 163, 168

Odetta, 1, 7, 39
Oliver, Paul, 109
Orbison, Roy, 160, 180
O'Reilly, Bill, 147
Orioles, 132
Ossman, Vess, 168

Palin, Sarah, 147
Palmer, Robert, 170–171
Parker, Colonel Tom, 187
Parks, Rosa, 8, 174, 199n17
Patton, Charley, 159, 183
Paul, Clarence, 146

Peddie, Ian, 24
Pecknold, Diane, 109
Penguins, 132, 171, 180
Perkins, Carl, 160, 171–172, 180, 181
Perry, Steve, 171
Pickett, Wilson, 131
Pilgrim Jubilees. *See* Pilgrim Jubilee
    Singers
Pilgrim Jubilee Singers, 90, 91
Pilgrim Travelers, 91, 128
Pitney, Gene, 187
Platters, 171, 180
Poitier, Sidney, 39
Polletta, Francesca, 29
Posner, Gerald, 145–146
Presley, Elvis, 160, 170, 171, 172, 180,
    183–184, 187, 200n23
Price, Lloyd, 171, 180, 195
Prince, 195
Prysock, Red, 124

Raboteau, Albert, 71–72, 78
Raglin, Melvin "Wah-Wah Watson",
    140
ragtime, 64, 81, 85, 105, 109, 110, 112,
    116, 135, 167–168, 199n10
Rainey, Ma, 104
Randolph, A. Philip, 3, 118, 155n20
Ravens, 132, 183
Reagon, Bernice Johnson, 24, 40
Red, Tampa, 124
Redding, Otis, 131
Redmond, Mike, 130–131
Redmond, Shana, 40
Reed, Jerry, 160
Reeves, Martha & The Vandellas, 1,
    131, 140, 151
Reiser, Bob, 40
rhythm & blues, 103–153, 159–197
Rice, Tamar, 3
Richard, Little, 1, 5, 7, 41, 48, 116, 149,
    171, 180, 184, 195
Roberts, Terrence, 141
Robertson, Carole, 141
Robinson, Smokey, 1, 41, 131, 139, 140,
    142, 146, 150–151
Robinson, Smokey, & The Miracles. *See*
    Robinson, Smokey
Rock, Chubb, 149

rock & roll, 159–197
Rogers, Jimmy, 124
Rolling Stones, 191, 201n30
Ronettes, 180
Roosevelt, Franklin Delano, 69,
    118–119
Rose, Tricia, 83
Ross, Diana, 151
Roy, William, 24
Rustin, Bayard, 6, 12

Salvatore, Nick, 66
Sam & Dave, 131
Sands, Tommy, 160
Sanger, Kerran, 25, 40
Savage, Michael, 147
Sax, Adolphe, 124
Scott, Freddie, 141
Scott, James, 168, 199n11
Scott, Walter, 3
Seal, 195
Seeger, Pete, 40
Selma to Montgomery Marches, 62
Sensational Nightingales, 91
Shanté, Roxanne, 142
Shaw, Arnold, 116, 119, 155n22, 172,
    174
Shirelles, 180
Simien, Evelyn, 114
Simone, Nina, 1, 7, 39, 41, 48, 126,
    156n32
Singleton, Charles, 184
Sir Mix-A-Lot, 149
Sit-In Movement, 105, 141
slave songs, 198n4
Sly & the Family Stone. *See* Stone, Sly
Smith, Bessie, 8, 104
Smith, Funny Paper, 178
Smith, Mamie, 166, 168, 169
Smith, Suzanne, 148–149
Smith, Yvette, 3
sorrow songs, 50, 53, 56–57, 63, 66, 68,
    71, 82, 165
Soulja Slim, 142
Soul Stirrers, 1, 5, 91, 128
Sound Barrier, 195
Southern Christian Leadership
    Conference (SCLC), 147
Spaniels, 132

Specialty Records, 5
Spencer, Jon Michael, 24, 54–55, 59
Spirit of Memphis, 91
spirituals, 53–59, 61, 63, 64, 70, 71, 73,
    81, 82–84, 85, 98, 104, 109, 110, 111,
    112, 119, 120, 125, 127, 128, 129, 134,
    137, 161, 162, 165, 168, 194
Stanley-Jones, Aiyana, 3
Staple Singers, 1, 63, 66
Stax Records, 5, 131
Stevenson, William "Mickey", 146
Still, Mary, 76
Stone, Sly, 195
Storm, Gale, 180
Stravinsky, Igor, 168
Strong, Barrett, 139
Stuckey, Sterling, 81
Student Nonviolent Coordinating
    Committee (SNCC), 141
Sumlin, Hubert, 124
Summer, Cree, 195
Summers, Gene, 160
Supremes, 1, 131, 140, 142, 151
Swamp Dogg, 195
Swanee Quintet, 91
Swan Silvertones, 91, 128
swing kids (of the 1930s), 177, 182,
    200n20
Szatmary, David, 179–180

Tarplin, Marvin, 140
Teen Queens, 180
Temptations, 1, 131, 140, 142, 151
Terrell, Mary Church, 76
Terrell, Tammi, 140
Tharpe, Sister Rosetta, 5, 124
Thomas, Carla, 131, 156n32
Thomas, Hank, 55
Thomas, Jefferson, 141
Thomas, Rufus, 131
Thornton, Big Mama, 116, 159, 171, 180
Till, Emmett, 141
Tilly, Charles, 26
Trina, 142
Truth, Sojourner, 75, 77
Tubman, Harriet, 75, 76
Turner, Big Joe, 116, 171, 182–183, 192
Turner, Ike, 171, 180
Turner, Tina, 5, 156n32, 195

Van Dyke, Earl, 140
Van Eps, Fred, 168
van Rijn, Guido, 91–94
Vee-Jay Records, 5
Vincent, Gene, 180
Vinson, Eddie "Cleanhead", 149
Vivian, C.T., 141
Vocaleers, 132
Voter Registration Movement, 105
Voting Rights Act of 1965, 4, 19n3, 31,
    152

Waites, Frederick, 140
Waldschmidt-Nelson, Britta, 143
Walker, T-Bone, 124, 159
Walker, Wyatt, 60–61
Ward, Brian, 145–146, 186–187, 189
Ward, Clara, 5
Warwick, Dionne, 141
Washington, Joseph, 58
Waters, Muddy, 124, 139, 159, 180, 192
Wells, Ida B., 76
Wells, Mary, 131, 139, 140, 151
Wesley, Cynthia, 141
Weston, Kim, 140
White, Robert, 140
White Citizens' Council, 96–97
Whitfield, Norman, 146
Williams, Larry, 180, 195
Williams, Rhys, 28
Williams, Robert F., 143
Williamson, Sonny Boy, 180, 192
Willis, Eddie, 140
Wilson, Jackie, 139, 140
Wilson, Tarika, 3
Witherspoon, Jimmy, 192
Wolf, Howlin', 124, 139, 159, 180
Wonder, Stevie, 140, 146
Woodson, Carter G., 179
work songs, 110, 165, 198n4
Wortham, Robert, 74
Wylie, Richard "Popcorn", 140, 146

Young, Alan, 90–91

Zinn, Howard, 55–56
Zion Travelers, 91

About the Author

Reiland Rabaka is Professor of African, African American, and Caribbean Studies in the Department of Ethnic Studies at the University of Colorado at Boulder, where he also has affiliations with the Women & Gender Studies Program, Humanities Program, Graduate Program in Critical Theory, School of Education, College of Media, Communication & Information, and College of Music. He is the author of more than fifty scholarly articles and book chapters, as well as twelve books including: *Du Bois's Dialectics*; *Africana Critical Theory*; *Against Epistemic Apartheid: W.E.B. Du Bois and the Disciplinary Decadence of Sociology*; *Forms of Fanonism: Frantz Fanon's Critical Theory and the Dialectics of Decolonization*; *Concepts of Cabralism: Amilcar Cabral and Africana Critical Theory*; *The Negritude Movement*; *Hip Hop's Inheritance*; *Hip Hop's Amnesia*; and *The Hip Hop Movement*. Rabaka's research has been recognized with several awards, including funding from the National Endowment for the Humanities, the National Endowment for the Arts, the National Science Foundation, the National Museum of African American History & Culture, the National Museum of American History, the Smithsonian Institution, the Eugene M. Kayden Book Award, the Cheikh Anta Diop Book Award, and the National Council for Black Studies' W.E.B. Du Bois-Anna Julia Cooper Career Award. He has conducted archival research and lectured extensively both nationally and internationally, and has been the recipient of numerous community service citations, distinguished teaching awards, and research fellowships. Rabaka's cultural criticism, social commentary, and political analysis has been featured in print, radio, television, and online media venues such as NPR, PBS, BBC, CNN, ABC, NBC, CBS, MTV, BET, VH1, *The Huffington Post*, *The Denver Post*, *The Dallas Morning News*, *The Houston Chronicle*, and *USA Today*, among others. He is also a published poet, spoken-word artist, and musician.